A BIOGRAPHICAL DICTIONARY OF EARLY AMERICAN JEWS

A BIOGRAPHICAL DICTIONARY OF EARLY AMERICAN JEWS

Colonial Times through 1800

by

Joseph R. Rosenbloom

UNIVERSITY OF KENTUCKY PRESS

Copyright © 1960 by the University of Kentucky Press.

Library of Congress catalog card no. 60-8517.
  The publication of this book has been aided by a grant from the Margaret Voorhies Haggin Trust, established in memory of her husband, James Ben Ali Haggin.

PREFACE

A Biographical Dictionary of Early American Jews: Colonial Times through 1800 is an attempt to provide a reference work for historians, a source for sociological and cultural analysis, and a basic tool for the study of American Jewish history. In it are named most Jews who lived in America during the late seventeenth, the eighteenth, and the early nineteenth centuries. The reader is cautioned, however, that although every effort has been made to examine the available published literature as well as manuscript materials, omissions are inevitable. The information on which the present volume has been based was derived from extant records; some individuals, of course, never found their way into the records, and others may have been mentioned only in records that have not survived. It may be estimated that at least some 20 percent of America's Jewish population during this period remains totally obscure and unknown, but it is doubtful that their number would significantly alter the tendencies indicated by the material collected in these pages.

Every person identifiable as a Jew in America before 1800 is included in this dictionary. Incorporated also are Jewish converts to Christianity, and in a number of cases their children, when some contact with events involving other Jews has been noted. In many instances, persons with Jewish names and/or Jewish associations found their way into the lists of "Jews" compiled in previously published works. Often the Jewish identity of such individuals is doubtful. The frequent appearance of an obviously gentile Cohen, Myers, Levy, Franks, Isaacs, and the like, makes it impossible to identify persons as Jews on the basis of their names alone. The present volume takes special notice of such cases, as it does also with respect to persons gleaned from previously unstudied documents. In the analysis of the United States censuses of 1790 and 1800, a few persons could not be positively identified as Jews from contemporary synagogal records and from other sources; they are nevertheless included in this work.

One of the noteworthy facts, then, to emerge from the present volume is the extremely small percentage of Jews in America during the nearly two centuries covered by this dictionary. Without allowance for deaths and emigrations during the years in question, the data suggest that, during the entire period, no more than some 4,000 Jews, 1,500 of whom were born in America, are to be identified, and not all of these positively. In 1783 the population of the United States was estimated at 2,776,000. Viewed against this figure, America's eighteenth-century Jewish population appears to be infinitesimal. It is the compiler's hope that this dictionary will make it possible to test anew previous hypotheses as to the number of Jews in America during the colonial and early national period, their national origins, their occupations, their involvement in the Revolutionary struggle, the places in which they settled, and other features of early American Jewish life.

Since variant spellings abound for many of the surnames included in this dictionary—Isaacs, Nunez, Polock, and Rivera, to cite a few instances—the compiler has generally found it advisable to reduce the variants to a uniform listing. There are, however, numerous instances where certain individuals elude positive identification, and cross references have been included in such cases of presumptive duplication.

A few terms peculiar to the organization of Jewish communal life have been included: *bodek*, a certified official charged with examining an animal or fowl before ritual slaughter; *hazzan*, a cantor or reader presiding over the synagogue's worship services; *mohel*, a person authorized to perform the rite of circumcision according to Jewish law; *shammas*, a synagogal beadle or sexton; and, finally, *shohet*, a Jewish ritual slaughterer.

The work was initially undertaken in 1951 as a rabbinical thesis for the Hebrew Union College—Jewish Institute of Religion. After its completion in 1954, the thesis was temporarily set aside while the writer completed his doctoral studies. Subsequently returning to it, he has added information from newly uncovered manuscripts as well as recent publications. Included also are Canadian materials up to the year 1783, when the national character of the erstwhile thirteen colonies changed from that of their northern neighbor.

Though the compiler himself assumes responsibility for the manuscript in its entirety, there are numerous debts to be acknowledged. From the very inception of this work, Professor Jacob R. Marcus, the compiler's teacher and friend, selflessly made both himself and his excellent and extensive Americana collection available. In deepest personal appreciation, this dictionary is dedicated to the memory of Dr. Marcus' beloved wife, Antoinette Brody Marcus.

Many others have given of themselves and their resources to make the publication of this volume possible. Dr. Malcolm H. Stern, genealogist of the American Jewish Archives, has made his own materials available. The debt to him is readily apparent from the many references to his personal collection and his manuscript, soon to be published, *Americans of Jewish Descent*. The staff of the American Jewish Archives, including Rabbi Stanley F. Chyet, Miss Sarah Grossman, and Miss Jeanette Weiss, has been most useful through the years. The University of Kentucky Research Fund placed at the compiler's disposal two grants: one for travel to places where documents could be studied, and one for the final preparation of the manuscript. Mrs. Pat Hazel has been most valuable and resourceful in her preparation of the final transcript.

And, finally, the compiler acknowledges the patience and efforts of his wife Cordelia, through whose understanding and love this dictionary was enabled to enter its final phases and to achieve its completion.

SYMBOLS

AJA—American Jewish Archives, Cincinnati: Manuscript Collection.
AJAM—*American Jewish Archives*. Vols. I-XI. Cincinnati, 1948-1959.
ALDINE—Aldine Book Company. Catalogue of Americana-Judaica & Hebraica. Brooklyn, undated.
Alexander—Alexander, Henry Aaron. *Notes on the Alexander Family of South Carolina and Georgia and Connections.* Atlanta, 1954.
Arts & Crafts—*The Arts and Crafts in New York, 1726-1776.* Compiled by Rita Susswein Gottesman. New York, 1938.
Beekmans—White, Philip L. *The Beekmans of New York.* New York, 1956.
Blum—Blum, Isidore. *The Jews of Baltimore.* Baltimore, 1910.
Byars—Byars, William Vincent. *B. & M. Gratz, Merchants in Philadelphia, 1754-1798.* Jefferson City, Missouri, 1916.
Carigal—Friedman, Lee M. *Rabbi Haim Isaac Carigal.* Boston, 1940.
Census 1774—*Census of the Inhabitants of the Colony of Rhode Island and Providence Plantations, 1774.* Providence, 1858.
Census A—*The Census of 1790. Heads of Families at the First Census of the United States taken in the Year 1790.* Washington, 1907-1952.
Census B—*The Census of 1800 of the United States.* (A microfilm copy in the American Jewish Archives, Cincinnati.)
Cohen—Cohen, Mary M. *An Old Philadelphia Cemetery. The Resting Place of Rebecca Gratz.* Philadelphia, 1920.
Coldoc—Marcus, Jacob R. *American Jewry: Documents, Eighteenth Century.* Cincinnati, 1959.
Coulter—Coulter, E. Merton and Albert B. Saye. *A List of the Early Settlers of Georgia.* Athens, 1949.
CPG—Rossiter, W. S. *A Century of Population Growth.* Washington, 1909.
CPR—Larabee, Leonard Woods, editor. *The Public Records of the State of Connecticut.* Hartford, 1948.
CRG—Candler, Allen D., editor. *The Colonial Records of the State of Georgia.* Vols. II, IV, X, XVIII. Atlanta, 1904-1910.
CRI—*Commerce of Rhode Island.* Vol. I. Boston, 1914.
DAB—Johnson, Allen, editor. *Dictionary of American Biography.* 22 volumes. New York, 1946.
Douville—Douville, Raymond. *Aaron Hart, Recit historique.* Les Trois Rivieres, 1938.
EHCBE—Elzas, Barnett A. *History of Congregation Beth Elohim of Charleston, S.C., 1800-1818.* Charleston, 1902.
EJM—Elzas, Barnett A. *Jewish Merchants in Charleston.* Charleston, undated.
EJMC—Elzas, Barnett A. *Jewish Marriage Notices of Charleston.* New York, 1917.
EJR—Elzas, Barnett A. *Jews in the Revolution.* Charleston, 1903.
EJRF—Fish, Sidney M. *Early Jewish Religious Functionaries in Philadelphia, 1742-1790.* (Presented to the annual meeting of the American Jewish Historical Society on February 11, 1951.)
EJSC—Elzas, Barnett A. *The Jews of South Carolina.* Philadelphia, 1905.
EJSCA—Elzas, Barnett A. *Jews of South Carolina, through 1750.* Charleston, 1903.
EJSCB—Elzas, Barnett A. *Jews of South Carolina, 1750-1783.* Charleston, 1903.
ELHS—Elzas, Barnett A. *Leaves from My Historical Scrapbook.* Charleston, 1907.
ELJR—Ezekiel, Herbert T. and Gaston Lichtenstein. *The History of the Jews of Richmond from 1769 to 1917.* Richmond, 1917.
ELODN—Elzas, Barnett A. *A List of Death Notices Compiled from Charleston Newspapers.* (From the original in the New York Historical Society.)
Emanuel—Emanuel, Isaac S. *Precious Stones of the Jews of Curaçao.* New York, 1957.
ENAJA—Elzas, Barnett A. *Notes.* (A manuscript in the American Jewish Archives, Cincinnati.)
EOJCC—Elzas, Barnett A. *Old Jewish Cemeteries at Charleston.* Charleston, 1903.
Essays—*Essays in American Jewish History.* Cincinnati, 1958.

SYMBOLS

EVJC—Elzas, Barnett A. *Various Jewish Cemeteries of South Carolina*. Charleston, 1910.

Exponent—*Jewish Exponent*. Vol. 124, no. 27. Philadelphia, July 30, 1954.

FEAJ—Friedman, Lee M. *Early American Jews*. Cambridge, 1934.

Feldman—Feldman, Jacob S. *The Early Migration and Settlement of Jews in Pittsburgh*. Pittsburgh, 1959.

Fish—Fish, Sidney M. *Aaron Levy, Founder of Aaronsburg*. New York, 1951.

FPNL—Friedman, Lee M. *Pilgrims in a New Land*. Philadelphia, 1948.

Freund—Freund, Miriam. *Jewish Merchants in Colonial America*. New York, 1939.

GAV—Schindler, Bruno, editor. *Gaster Anniversary Volume, Occident and Orient*. London, 1936.

GBMIP—Goodman, Leopold D. *Record of the Spruce Street Cemetery of Congregation Mikveh Israel, Philadelphia*. (A collection of handwritten notes, a photostatic copy of which is in the American Jewish Archives, Cincinnati.)

Ginsberg—Ginsberg, Louis. *History of the Jews of Petersburg*. Petersburg, Virginia, 1954.

GLT—Gutstein, Morris A. *Aaron Lopez and Judah Touro*. New York, 1939.

Goldberg—Goldberg, Isaac. *Major Noah: American Jewish Pioneer*. Philadelphia, 1936.

Grollman—Grollman, Earl A. *A History of the Jews of the North American Colonies in the Seventeenth Century, Based Upon a Complete Corpus of Regests*. Cincinnati, 1950. (Typescript in Library of the Hebrew Union College.)

Gutstein—Gutstein, Morris A. *The Story of the Jews of Newport: Two and a Half Centuries of Judaism, 1658-1908*. New York, 1936.

HAB—Hunter, Dr. William. *Account Book*. (In the American Jewish Archives, Cincinnati.)

HDB—Hays, David. *A Daybook of Business at his General Store, Bedford Village, N.Y., 1770-1785*. (A microfilm copy in the American Jewish Archives, Cincinnati.)

HSIM—*History of the Corporation of Spanish and Portuguese Jews "Shearith Israel" of Montreal, Canada*. Montreal, 1918.

Hugsoc—*Publications of the Huguenot Society of London*. Vol. XXIV. Manchester, 1921.

Hyamson—Hyamson, Albert H. *The Sephardim of England*. London, 1951.

ILI—Levy, Isaac. *An Itinerary*. (A photostatic copy in the American Jewish Archives, Cincinnati.)

ITAH—Bridenbough, Carl, editor. *Gentleman's Progress, Itinerary of Alexander Hamilton*. Chapel Hill, 1948.

Jacobus—Jacobus, D. L., editor. *History and Genealogy of the Families of Old Fairfield*. Vol. II. New Haven, 1932.

JCES—Elmaleh, L. H. and J. Bunford Samuel. *The Jewish Cemetery, Ninth and Spruce Streets, Philadelphia*. Philadelphia, 1906.

JE—*The Jewish Encyclopedia*. 12 volumes. New York, 1901-06.

Jefferson—Boyd, Julian P., editor. *The Papers of Thomas Jefferson*. Princeton, 1950-.

JNEA—Broches, S. *Jews in New England*, I. New York City, 1942.

JNEB—Broches, S. *Jews in New England*, II. New York City, 1942.

Johnson—Hamilton, Milton W., editor. *The Papers of Sir William Johnson*. Vol. X. Albany, 1951.

JPP—Friedman, Lee M. *Jewish Pioneers and Patriots*. Philadelphia, 1942.

JRMP—Marcus, Jacob R. Personal Collection.

Katz—Katz, Irving. *The Beth El Story*. Detroit, 1955.

Klein—Klein, Frederic S. *A History of the Jews of Lancaster*. Lancaster, Pennsylvania, 1955.

Kohut—Kohut, George Alexander. *Ezra Stiles and the Jews*. New York, 1902.

LCHS—*Lancaster County Historical Society*. Vol. V. Lancaster, 1901.

LIL—*Life in Letters. American Autograph Journal*. Vol. 7, October, 1941, No. 1.

Link—Link, Eugene P. *Democratic-Republican Societies*. New York, 1942.

Malchelosse—Malchelosse, Gerald. "Les Juifs dans l'histoire canadienne." *Les Cahiers des Dix*. No. 4. Montreal, 1939.

Markens—Markens, Isaac. *The Hebrews in America.* New York, 1888.
MCCCNY—*Minutes of the Common Council of the City of New York.* Vols. II-VII. New York, 1905.
MEAJA—Marcus, Jacob R. *Early American Jewry,* I. Philadelphia, 1951.
MEAJB—Marcus, Jacob R. *Early American Jewry,* II. Philadelphia, 1953.
Memoirs I—Marcus, Jacob R. *Memoirs of American Jews, 1775-1865,* I. Philadelphia, 1955.
Memoirs II—Marcus, Jacob R. *Memoirs of American Jews, 1775-1865,* II. Philadelphia, 1955.
Memoirs III—Marcus, Jacob R. *Memoirs of American Jews, 1775-1865,* III. Philadelphia, 1956.
MHM—Baroway, Aaron. "The Cohens of Maryland." *Maryland Historical Magazine.* Volumes XVIII, XIX, 1923-1924.
MIPR—*Mikveh Israel Adjunta Minutes, Philadelphia (and other miscellaneous records of the congregation).* (Photostatic copies in the American Jewish Archives, Cincinnati.)
MISR—*Mikveh Israel Congregation Records, Savannah.* (Photostatic copies in the American Jewish Archives, Cincinnati.)
Moïse—Moïse, L. C. *Biography of Isaac Harby.* (Sumter, S. C.?, 1931?)
Morais—Morais, Henry Samuel. *The Jews of Philadelphia.* Philadelphia, 1894.
MSGC—Stern, Malcolm H. *A Compendium of American Jewish Genealogy.* (A manuscript copy in the American Jewish Archives, Cincinnati.)
MSP—Stern, Malcolm H. Materials from the personal collection of Dr. Stern.
MTAR—*Archives of Maryland.* Vol. XVIII. (Muster Rolls and other Records of Service of Maryland Troops in the American Revolution, 1775-1783.) Baltimore, 1900.

NHM—*Newport Historical Magazine. (Rhode Island Historical Magazine).* Vols. II and III. Newport, 1882-1883.
NJP—*National Jewish Post.* (A weekly newspaper published in Indianapolis.)
NYHSW—*Collections of the New York Historical Society, Abstracts of Wills on File in the Surrogates Office, City of New York, 1665-1800.* 17 volumes. New York, 1893-1909.

Occident—*The Occident and American Jewish Advocate.* Philadelphia, 1843-1869.
OMMC—*Original Minutes of the Mayor's Court of New York City.* Volume dated dated May 6, 1718, to June 14, 1720.

PA—Linn, J. B. and W. H. Egle, editors. *Pennsylvania Archives, (second series).* Vol. II. Harrisburg, 1876.
PAJHS—*Publications of the American Jewish Historical Society.* Vols. I-XLVIII. 1893-1959.
POFNW—Pool, David and Tamar de Sola. *An Old Faith in the New World.* New York, 1955.
Pool—Pool, David de Sola. *Portraits Etched In Stone.* New York, 1952.

Reznikoff—Reznikoff, Charles and Uriah Z. Engelman. *The Jews of Charleston.* Philadelphia, 1950.
RIHM—*Rhode Island Historical Magazine.* Vol. VI. Newport, 1886.
Rosenbach—Rosenbach, Hyman Polock. *The Jews of Philadelphia prior to 1800.* Philadelphia, 1883.
Rosenbaum—Rosenbaum, Jeanette W. *Myer Myers, Goldsmith, 1723-1795.* Philadelphia, 1954.
Roth—Roth, Cecil. *The Great Synagogue, London, 1690-1940.* London, 1950.
RPJ—Roth, Cecil. *The Rise of Provincial Jewry.* London, 1950.

Sack—Sack, Benjamin G. *History of the Jews in Canada.* Montreal, 1945.
Schappes—Schappes, Morris U. *A Documentary History of the Jews in the United States, 1654-1875.* New York, 1950.
SCHGM—*South Carolina Historical and Genealogical Magazine.* Charleston.
SCMCNY—Morris, Richard B., editor. *Select Cases of the Mayor's Court of New York City, 1674—1784,* Washington, 1935.
Shilstone—Shilstone, E. M. *Monumental Inscriptions in the Burial Ground of the Jewish Synagogue at Bridgetown, Barbados.* New York, 1956.
Shpall—Shpall, Leo. *The Jews of Louisiana.* New Orleans, 1936.
SIMR—*Shearith Israel Congregational Papers, Montreal.* (Photostatic copies in the American Jewish Archives, Cincinnati.)

SYMBOLS

SIR—*Shearith Isreal Trustee Minutes and Other Records of the Congregation, New York.* (Microfilm and photostatic copies in the American Jewish Archives, Cincinnati.)

SRB—*Sheftall Record Book.* (In the Keith Read Manuscript Collection of the University of Georgia Library.)

St. Charles—Kraus, Walter Max. *The Saint Charles.* Vol. I. New York, 1935.

SZ—Szajkowski, Zosa. "Jewish Immigration from Bordeaux During the Eighteenth and Nineteenth Centuries." *Jewish Social Studies.* Vol. XVIII. April, 1956.

Trachtenberg—Trachtenberg, Joshua. *Consider the Years: the Story of the Jewish Community of Easton, 1752-1942.* Easton, 1944.

UJE—*Universal Jewish Encyclopedia.* 10 volumes. New York City, 1939-1943.

VACRI—Towle, Dorothy S., editor. *Records of the Vice-Admiralty Court of Rhode Island, 1716-1752.* Washington, 1936.

WAJA—*Wills Collection.* (In the American Jewish Archives, Cincinnati.)

White—White, Philip L., editor. *The Beekman Mercantile Papers, 1746-1799.* Vol. II. New York, 1956.

Wills—Stern, Malcolm H. *Abstracts of Wills of Early American Jews.* (A manuscript copy kindly made available for this work by Dr. Stern.)

WW—Wolf, Edwin, 2nd, and Maxwell Whiteman. *The History of the Jews of Philadelphia.* Philadelphia, 1957.

A

AARON, Benjamin. In Amherst County, Virginia, in 1783. It is highly doubtful that he was Jewish. (*PAJHS*, XX, 100)

AARON, Hart. Died January 29, 1777, New York City. A Long Island merchant after 1760; a shohet in New York City after 1769. On November 20, 1774, he was married to Richa Simson. (*MEAJA*, 209f; *PAJHS*, XXI, 106, 108, 138, 213; XXVII, 387; *Pool*, 503; *SIR*)

AARON(S), Henry. In New York City from 1791 to 1793; in Philadelphia in 1796. (*MIPR*; *PAJHS*, XXVII, 51; *SIR*)

AARON, Haob. A loyalist in New York City in 1776. (*Schappes*, 52)

AARON, Isaac. A resident of North Carolina, he was active in furnishing supplies to the Revolutionary army. It is highly doubtful that he was Jewish. (*UJE*, VIII, 237)

AARON, Jonas. In Philadelphia in 1703. He is said to have been the first Jew in Philadelphia. (*PAJHS*, V, 198)

AARON, Joseph. In Stockbridge, Massachusetts, in 1790. It is highly doubtful that he was Jewish. (*Census A, Massachusetts*)

AARON, Solomon.[1] In Philadelphia from 1777 to 1785. He was a shopkeeper who enrolled in the Philadelphia homeguard during the Revolution. In 1785 he was about to leave for Europe. (*MIPR*; *PAJHS*, 1, 61; VI, 51, 57f; *WW*, 95)

AARON, Solomon.[2] A merchant in Charleston in 1780. (*EJSC*, 91, *et passim*)

AARON, Solomon, Jr. In Charleston sometime between 1783 and 1800. (*EJSC*, 279)

AARON, William. This name appears in documents of Georgia during the Revolutionary period. He served as a captain in the army. It is highly doubtful that he was Jewish. (*UJE*, IV, 537)

AARONS, Esther.[1] Died July 26, 1772, New York City. Daughter of Jacob Aarons.[1] (*Pool*, 502; *SIR*)

AARONS, Esther.[2] Born November 8, 1772, New York City. Daughter of Jacob Aarons.[1] (*SIR*)

AARONS, Golah (Elizabeth). November, 1786—May 22, 1857, Charleston. Daughter of Levi Aarons, she was married to Simon Levy in Charleston in April, 1805. (*Alexander*, 43, 49; *MSGC*)

AARONS, Hannah. 1789, Philadelphia—May 31, 1865, Augusta, Georgia. Daughter of Levi Aarons, she was married to Abraham Alexander, Jr., on August 26, 1801. (*Alexander*, 43f; *MSGC*)

AARONS, Hartog. Son of Levi Aarons. (*Alexander*, 49)

AARONS, Jacob.[1] In New York City in 1772. He came from Cape François, Guadeloupe. Cf. below. (*SIR*)

AARONS, Jacob.[2] In Charleston sometime between 1783 and 1800. Cf. above. (*EJSC*, 279)

AARONS, Mrs. Jacob.[1] In New York City in 1772. Wife of Jacob Aarons.[2] Cf. below. (*SIR*)

AARONS, Mrs. Jacob.[2] Wife of Jacob Aarons.[2] Cf. above. (*EJSC*, 279)

AARONS (Van Blitz), Levi. Born Holland, died December 2, 1792, Black Mingo, South Carolina. Son of Aaron Emanuel Van Blitz. (*Alexander*, 43, *et passim*; *MSGC*)

AARONS, Mariana. Daughter of Levi Aarons, she was married to Lazarus Joel. (*Alexander*, 49; *MSGC*)

AARONS, Moses. 1778, New York City—August, 1842, Charleston. (*MSGC*)

AARONS, Rachel. 1767—April 19, 1828, Charleston. Daughter of Jacob Aarons, she was married to Joseph Tobias on November 3, 1785, in Charleston. (*EJMC*, 6; *MSGC*)

AARONS, Reuben Simon. Born Philadelphia, died Holland. Son of Levi Aarons, he went to Holland at an early age, where he changed his surname to Krijn. (*Alexander*, 50f)

AARONSON, Woolf. In Charleston in 1800. (*EHCBE*, 6)

ABANDANA, Raphael. In Boston in 1695; in New York City in 1694. He may have been a Jew. (*AJAM*, III, 3; *POFNW*, 468)

ABBO, Jacob. In 1788 he was a money-raiser in New York City. (*POFNW*, 344)

ABENDANA, David. In New York City in 1681. (*POFNW*, 468)

ABENDANA, Mordecai. Died March 31, 1690, New York. (*MSGC*)

ABENDANONE, Abigail. Born December 22, 1738, Savannah. Daughter of Haim Abendanone. (Members of this family are variously listed as Abendoon, Aberdaum, Abernaum, Bendenoone.) (*SRB*)

ABENDANONE, David. In Charleston in 1800. (*EJSC*, 132)

ABENDANONE, Mrs. Grace. 1783, Virginia—December 22, 1857, New York City. Wife of Haim Abendanone. (*MSGC*)

ABENDANONE, Haim. In Georgia in 1733. In 1740 he was seeking funds to leave New York City. He was married to Abigail Cohen on May 2, 1736. (*Coulter*, 61; *PAJHS*, XXI, 43; *SRB*)

ABENDANONE, Joseph. In Philadelphia in 1742 and 1782; in Charleston in 1800. (*EJSC*, 132; *MIPR*; *PAJHS*, I, 24; XXVII, 462)

ABENDANONE, Simon. In Georgia in 1733. He was married to Grace Cohen on July 5, 1736. (*Coulter*, 61; *SRB*)

ABENDANONE, Solomon. Born June 28, 1737, Savannah. Son of Haim Abendanone. (*Coulter*, 61; *SRB*)

ABO, Jacob. In 1788 he applied for assistance from the Jewish community of New York City. (*SIR*)

ABOAF (ABOAB), Moses. A trader in New York City in 1684. (*AJAM*, III, 3; *POFNW*, 468)

ABONDANA, Mrs. Sarah. In business in New York City in 1700. (*PAJHS*, XXXIV, 270f)

ABRAHAM, Ephraim. An Indian trader in Pennsylvania in 1774. (*WW*, 70)

ABRAHAM, Isaac. In 1760 he owned a plantation near Philadelphia. (*WW*, 51)

ABRAHAM, Moses. An Indian trader in Pennsylvania in 1765. (*Feldman*, 3)

ABRAHAM, Noah. In the Cumberland County, Pennsylvania militia, in 1777. It is highly doubtful that he was Jewish. (*Morais*, 458; *UJE*, VIII, 428)

ABRAHAM, Philip. In Charlestown in 1767. (*EJSC*, 45, 277)

ABRAHAM, Rebecca. Wife of Solomon Lyons of Philadelphia, she was in Philadelphia before 1800. (*Wills*, 17)

ABRAHAMS, Abraham.[1] In New York City in 1746. Cf. Abraham Isaac Abrahams. (*PAJHS*, XXI, 51, *et passim*)

ABRAHAMS, Abraham.[2] Son of Abraham Isaac Abrahams. Cf. below. (*MSGC*)

ABRAHAMS, Abraham.[3] In Philadelphia in 1786. Cf. above and below. (*MIPR*)

ABRAHAMS, Abraham.[4] In Charleston sometime between 1783 and 1800. (*EJSC*, 279)

ABRAHAMS, Abraham.[5] In 1798 he was a lieutenant in the militia of Chatham County, Georgia. Cf. Abraham de Lyon Abrahams. (*JRMP*)

ABRAHAMS, Abraham.[6] 1798—January 15, 1819. Son of Isaac Abrahams. (*Pool*, 396)

ABRAHAMS, Abraham Isaac. 1720—August 10, 1796, New York City. This son of Isaac Abrahams was of Lithuanian descent. In 1753 he was a constable in New York City. He was a tobacconist, distiller, and merchant. He traveled widely in the colonies as a mohel, and was also a Hebrew teacher, referred to as "Rabby" and "Ribbi." From 1762 to 1775 he taught for Congregation Shearith Israel in New York City. He was married to Elkaly Esther Lousada. (*MCCCNY*, V, 419; *MEAJA*, 79, *et passim*; *MSGC*; *Pool*, 504)

ABRAHAMS, Abraham de Lyon. August 16, 1772, New York City—April 16, 1844. This son of Joseph Abrahams[4] was in

Savannah in 1791 and in 1795. (*MISR*; *SIR*; *SRB*)

ABRAHAMS, Alexander. In 1776 he was a shopkeeper in Philadelphia. He was also a clerk of the Gratzes. (*Byars*, 154; 159f; *MEAJB*, 46; *WW*, 83)

ABRAHAMS, Alice. 1789—June 14, 1839. Married to Solomon Solomon in August, 1805, in Charleston. (*MSGC*)

ABRAHAMS, Bella. June 13, 1760, New York City—February 10, 1854. Daughter of Abraham Isaac Abrahams. (*Pool*, 484; *SIR*)

ABRAHAMS, Betty. On July 8, 1781, she was married to Cauffman Cohen in New York City. (*SIR*)

ABRAHAMS, Chapman. Died 1783. He came from England, and went from Albany to Canada, where he became one of the first Jewish merchants in Montreal. He was probably the first Jew in the Detroit area in 1762. During the Pontiac uprising he was captured by Indians. He was married to Elizabeth Judah. He may have been baptized. Cf. Nathan Chapman. (*Coldoc*, 109, *et passim*; *Katz*, 12, *et passim*; *MEAJA*, 225, *et passim*; *MSGC*)

ABRAHAMS, Charlotte. June 4, 1779, New York City—August 9, 1839. Daughter of Abraham Isaac Abrahams. (*Pool*, 484; *SIR*)

ABRAHAMS, David. In 1749 he was in New York City, seeking funds for passage to Barbados. (*PAJHS*, XXI, 60)

ABRAHAMS, Deborah. Died February 18, 1830. Daughter of Abraham Isaac Abrahams, she was married to David Simons on August 26, 1795. (*MSGC*)

ABRAHAMS, Elias. 1787, England—August 26, 1851. Son of Emanuel Mordecai,[3] he was married to Catherine Cohen in Charleston on January 18, 1815. (*MSGC*)

ABRAHAMS, Emanuel.[1] In Charleston before 1800. Cf. below. (*Wills*, 35)

ABRAHAMS, Emanuel.[2] About 1718, London—1802, Charleston. He was a tobacconist and a distiller in New York City, where he was a freeman. From 1766 until his death he lived in Charlestown. He served in the Revolutionary army. In 1779 he was married to Judith Mordecai. Cf. Emanuel Abrams. (*EJSC*, 44, *et passim*; *MSGC*; *PAJHS*, VI, 102)

ABRAHAMS, Emanuel.[3] July 25, 1776, New York City—February 23, 1839, New York City. Son of Abraham Isaac Abrahams. (*Pool*, 484; *SIR*)

ABRAHAMS, Mrs. Emanuel. Wife of Emanuel Abrahams,[1] she was buried in Charleston on March 7, 1794. (*MSP*)

ABRAHAMS, Mrs. Esther. Died August 29, 1766, New York City. Wife of Isaac Abrahams.[1] (*Pool*, 502; *SIR*)

ABRAHAMS, Esther. Born December 16, 1779, New York City. Daughter of Isaac Abrahams,[3] she was married to Mr. Leon. (*Pool*, 288)

ABRAHAMS, Feglah. March 30, 1771, New York City—September 9, 1771, New York City. Daughter of Abraham Isaac Abrahams, she was also known as Eglah. (*Pool*, 502; *SIR*)

ABRAHAMS, Hannah.[1] About 1796 she came to America from London. She was married to Samuel Levy in Charleston in June, 1796. (*EJMC*, 6)

ABRAHAMS, Hannah.[2] 1774—July 11, 1838. Daughter of Abraham Isaac Abrahams. (*MSGC*; *Pool*, 484)

ABRAHAMS, Hyman. January 24, 1767—January 28, 1802, Charleston. Son of Abraham Isaac Abrahams, he was in New York City in 1800. (*EOJCC*, 77; *MSGC*; *SIR*)

ABRAHAMS, Isaac.[1] Died about 1760. It is probable that he came to America by 1720, and lived in New York City. He was known as Isaac Brisker. His wife was Esther. (*JNES*, 6; *JRMP*; *MSGC*)

ABRAHAMS, Isaac.[2] In Baltimore in 1782. (*MIPR*; *PAJHS*, I, 18)

ABRAHAMS, Dr. Isaac.[3] June 17, 1756, New York City—1832. This son of Abraham Isaac Abrahams was the first Jewish graduate of King's College in 1774, and became a physician. On November 4, 1778, he was married to Rachel Nathan in Philadelphia. (*PAJHS*, XXII, 161f; XXVII, 150; *Pool*, 288)

ABRAHAMS, Isaac.[4] 1767, Charlestown—November 17, 1849, Savannah. Also known as Isaac Jacob Abrahams, he was a son of Joseph Abrahams.[4] (*MISR; SRB*)

ABRAHAMS, Isaac.[5] Born April 13, 1774, New York City. Son of Joseph Abrahams.[4] (*SIR*)

ABRAHAM(S), Isaac.[6] In Montreal in 1783. (*Katz, 32*)

ABRAHAMS, Isaac A. June 17, 1756, New York City—July, 1813, New York City. Son of Abraham Isaac Abrahams, he was married to Catherine Pollock. He was a tobacconist. (*PAJHS, XXVII, 150; Pool, 335f; SIR*)

ABRAHAMS, Isaac Brisco. In Charlestown sometime between 1770 and 1782. (*EJSCB, 18*)

ABRAHAMS, Israel. A merchant in Newport, he served as the Spanish and Dutch interpreter in the court of the vice-admiralty in Newport in 1746. He was the first husband of Nellie Solomons. (*JNEB, 8; MSP; VACRI, 347, 425*).

ABRAHAMS, Jacob.[1] In 1742 he was elected an assessor in New York City. It is highly doubtful that he was Jewish. (*MCCCNY, V, 62*)

ABRAHAMS, Jacob.[2] In New York City in 1750. (*PAJHS, XXI, 63*)

ABRAHAMS, Jacob.[3] In Charleston in 1800. (*EJSC, 133*)

ABRAHAMS, Jacob.[4] In 1786 he was married to Sally Wellman in Boston. It is highly doubtful that he was Jewish. Cf. above and below. (*FEAJ, 17*)

ABRAHAMS, Jacob.[5] In Philadelphia in 1786. (*MIPR*)

ABRAHAMS, Jacob.[6] In New York City in 1790. (*SIR*)

ABRAHAMS, Jacob.[7] Born September 15, 1781, Philadelphia. (*MSGC; Pool, 288*)

ABRAHAMS, Jacob Levy. Died 1829. Son of Mordecai Abrahams, he was married to Theodotia Armitage, and lived in Virginia. (*MSGC*)

ABRAHAMS, Joseph.[1] In New York City in 1748. (*PAJHS, XXI, 58*)

ABRAHAMS, Joseph.[2] A merchant in Charleston before 1800. (*EJSC, 103*)

ABRAHAMS, Joseph.[3] Born October 29, 1768, New York City. Son of Abraham Isaac Abrahams, he changed his name to Joseph Andrews. Cf. Joseph Andrews.[2] (*SIR*)

ABRAHAMS, Joseph.[4] 1749—February 5, 1795, Savannah. On May 10, 1785, he arrived in Savannah. He was married to Mrs. Moses Cohen nee Judith de Lyon, a widow, in January, 1791. Cf. Joseph Abrahams.[2] (*MISR; SRB*)

ABRAHAMS, Joseph.[5] Born April 25, 1786, Baltimore. Son of Isaac Abrahams.[3] (*Pool, 288*)

ABRAHAMS, Joseph, Jr. In Boston in 1800. (*JRMP*)

ABRAHAMS, Mrs. Joseph. Died November 26, 1788, Savannah. (*SRB*)

ABRAHAMS, Judah.[1] In the Charlestown militia in 1780. (*EJSC, 91*)

ABRAHAMS, Judah.[2] In New York City in 1788. (*SIR*)

ABRAHAMS, Leah. December 14, 1765, New York City—July 30, 1828. Daughter of Abraham Isaac Abrahams. (*Pool, 484; SIR*)

ABRAHAMS, Levy.[1] In Charlestown sometime between 1750 and 1783. Cf. below. (*EJSC, 277*)

ABRAHAMS, Levy.[2] Died December 29, 1809, Savannah. In 1791 he was a merchant in Savannah. In 1786 he was secretary of Congregation Mikveh Israel. Cf. above. (*JRMP; MISR; SRB*)

ABRAHAMS, M. In New York City in 1746. (*PAJHS, XXI, 51*)

ABRAHAMS, Menachem Israel. Born August 2, 1776. Son of Abraham Isaac Abrahams. (*MSGC*)

ABRAHAMS, Mordecai.[1] Born Europe, died 1800, King William County, Virginia. He was married to Sarah Levy. (*MSGC*)

ABRAHAMS, Mordecai.² Son of Mordecai Abrahams,¹ he was married to Rebecca Tucker in 1817, and lived in Virginia. (MSGC)

ABRAHAMS, Moses. July 3, 1762, New York City—October 24, 1816, New York City. Son of Abraham Isaac Abrahams. (Pool, 375)

ABRAHAMS, Fineas. In Philadelphia in 1782. (MIPR; PAJHS, XXVII, 462)

ABRAHAMS, Rachel.¹ In 1788 she received charity from the city of Boston. It is highly doubtful that she was Jewish. (FEAJ, 17)

ABRAHAMS, Rachel.² 1756, New York City—October 19, 1837, New York City. Daughter of Abraham Isaac Abrahams, she was married to Alexander Zuntz on May 4, 1779. (Pool, 399f; 484)

ABRAHAMS, Rachel.³ About 1792—about 1847, Charleston. Daughter of Emanuel Abrahams.² (EOJCC, 40)

ABRAHAMS, Rachel.⁴ Born November 23, 1794, Savannah. Daughter of Joseph Abrahams.⁴ (SRB)

ABRAHAMS, Ralph. In Boston in 1790. It is highly doubtful that he was Jewish. (PAJHS, XXIII, 87)

ABRAHAMS, Reinah. September 5, 1784, probably in Charleston—July 21, 1853, Charleston. Daughter of Emanuel Abrahams,² she was married to David Mordecai. (EOJCC, 40)

ABRAHAMS, Samuel.¹ In New York City in 1792. (PAJHS, XXVII, 51)

ABRAHAMS, Samuel.² In Savannah in 1790. (MISR)

ABRAHAMS, Samuel.³ January 16, 1775, New York City—September 16, 1848, New York City. Son of Abraham Isaac Abrahams. (MSGC; SIR)

ABRAHAMS, Samuel.⁴ Born February 3, 1784, Baltimore. Son of Isaac Abrahams.³ (Pool, 288)

ABRAHAMS, Sarah. A convert to Judaism, she changed her name to Abrahams after her conversion. She was married to Moses Nathan on May 16, 1794, in Philadelphia. Cf. Betty Hart. (MIPR; WW, 234)

ABRAHAMS, Saul. In New York City, and in Newport as a merchant, in 1747. (JNEB, 8; PAJHS, XXI, 55)

ABRAHAMS, Solomon. Son of Mordecai Abrahams,¹ he lived in Virginia. (MSGC)

ABRAHAMS, Solomon Moses. A merchant in New York City in 1746. (JRMP)

ABRAHAMS, William. In Boston in 1790. It is highly doubtful that he was Jewish. (PAJHS, XXIII, 87)

ABRAHAMSON, Abraham. In Bedford, Connecticut, in 1770. It is highly doubtful that he was Jewish. (HDB)

ABRAM, Benjamin. A European entertainer, he advertised his balancing act in New York City in 1773. (Arts & Crafts, 289f)

ABRAMS, Emanuel. In the tobacco and snuff trade. He was involved in a business dispute, which was related in the Boston Weekly Gazette during the months of October and November, 1754. Cf. Emanuel Abrahams.² (FEAJ, 11f; UJE, VII, 403)

ABRAMS, Ephraim. In 1779 he was killed fighting during the American Revolution in Beaufort, South Carolina. It is highly doubtful that he was Jewish. (PAJHS, XIX, 152)

ABRAMS, Hyam. In New York City in 1795, listed as "bar Joseph." (SIR)

ABRAMS, Isaac. A soapboiler in New York City in 1787. (PAJHS, XXVII, 51; POFNW, 471)

ABRAMS, Isaac A. In New York City in 1795. Cf. Isaac A. Abrahams. (SIR)

ABRAMS, Israel. In New York City in 1745. Cf. Israel Abrahams. (PAJHS, XXI, 48)

ABRAMS, Manuel. In New York City in 1792. (PAJHS, XXVII, 51)

ABRAMS, Moïse. 1737, Strasburgh, Germany—May 8, 1809, Charleston. He came to Charleston with his wife and nine children about 1793. He was also in St.

Domingo. (*Census B, South Carolina; EJSC,* 133; *MSGC; SCHGM,* XXXIII, 71f)

ABRAMS, Ralph. A tailor in Boston in 1720. It is highly doubtful that he was Jewish. (*JNEA,* 24)

ABRAMS, Samuel. In 1793 he is recorded as a child in Shearith Israel school in New York City. (*PAJHS,* XXVII, 55)

ABRAMS, Susman. About 1753—1830. A tanner, he came from Hamburg, Germany, to Maine, where he remained during the Revolution. He married a Christian woman and regularly attended the Christian church in his community. (*PAJHS,* XI, 95f)

ABRAMS, William. A tailor in Boston in 1720. It is highly doubtful that he was Jewish. (*JNEA,* 24)

ABRAMSE, Abraham J. In New York City in 1776. He was a loyalist. Cf. Abraham Isaac Abrahams. (*Schappes,* 52)

ADLER, Simon. In New York City in 1795. Cf. Simon Odler Cohen and Simon Odler. (*Coldoc,* 198; *SIR*)

ADOLPH, Peter. In New York City in 1695. It is highly doubtful that he was Jewish. (*AJAM,* III, 3f)

ADOLPHUS, Miss. Daughter of Benjamin Adolphus, she was married to Mr. Israel. (*MSP*)

ADOLPHUS, Hetty. Died September, 1783. Daughter of Benjamin Adolphus, she was married to Jacob Hays.[1] She operated a kosher boarding house. (*MEAJB,* 459f; *MSGC; UJE,* V, 255)

ADOLPHUS, Isaac. About 1725, Bonn, Germany—September 7, 1774, New York City. This son of Ephraim Reine came to America about 1750. He was the uncle and business partner of Benjamin Etting. He was married to Charity Hays.[1] (*Coldoc,* 91f; *PAJHS,* II, 66; *Pool,* 243f; *SIR*)

ADOLPHUS, Philip. Brother of Isaac Adolphus, he was in New York City in 1774. (*NYHSW,* VIII, 197; *Rosenbaum,* 55)

ADOLPHUS, Ritzel Hannah. Died August 5, 1761, New York City. Daughter of Benjamin Adolphus, she was married to Asher Etting and to Ralph de Paz. (*Pool,* 501; *SIR*)

AGUILAR, Emanuel. In Newport between 1783 and 1790. (*PAJHS,* XXVII, 185)

AGUILAR, Judah de Moseh. About 1760 he was taken captive at sea, and lost all his possessions. Thereafter he may have been in New York City, seeking passage to Jamaica, B.W.I. (*PAJHS,* XXVII, 18)

AGUILAR, Moses. About 1759 he came from Jamaica, B.W.I., to New York City, where he remained a short time. Cf. above. (*Pool,* 308)

AGUILAR, Sarah d'. On October 2, 1800, she was married to Abraham Tores in Charleston. He was from Bordeaux, and she from Bayonne, and their marriage may have been an elopement. (*EJMC,* 7; *MSP; Pool,* 308)

AGUILLARO, Joseph d'. Died 1807, New York City. He is also listed as d'Aguilar. In Philadelphia in 1795. (*MIPR; Pool,* 183)

ALBERGO, Judah. In Charleston in 1800. (*EJSC,* 133)

ALEAS, I. In 1793 he was in New York City with his family of three, seeking aid for passage to St. Thomas. (*SIR*)

ALEXANDER, Abraham. In New York City in 1736. (*PAJHS,* XXI, 35)

ALEXANDER, Abraham, Sr. About 1743, London—February 21, 1816, Charleston. This son of Joseph Raphael Alexander was the minister or hazzan of Congregation Beth Elohim in Charlestown from about 1765 through 1784. He was a scribe and auditor for the Charleston Custom House, and was a prominent Mason. He served as a lieutenant in the Revolutionary army. His second wife was Ann Sarah Hugenin Irby, a convert to Judaism. (*Alexander,* 7-15; *EJSC,* 43, *et passim; EOJCC,* 40; *MSGC*)

ALEXANDER, Abraham, Jr. 1771, London—December 19, 1844, Charleston. This son of Abraham Alexander, Sr., came to Charleston from London, and became a hardware merchant. He was married to Hannah Aarons on August 26, 1801. (*Alexander,* 18f; *EJSC,* 133; *EOJCC,* 40; *MSGC; PAJHS,* XIX, 82)

ALEXANDER, Joseph. A resident of Wadmalow Island, South Carolina, his will is dated in 1786. It is highly doubtful that he was Jewish. (WAJA)

ALEXANDER, Judah. June, 1743, London—January 2, 1804, Charleston. Son of Joseph Raphael Alexander, he was in Charleston in 1800. (*Alexander*, 7; EJSC, 133; EOJCC, 79; MSP)

ALEXANDER, Moses. About 1755, England—November 25/26, 1808, Charleston. (EOJCC, 47; PAJHS, XIX, 87; SCHGM, XXXIII, 248)

ALEXANDER, Nathan. In New York City in 1752. (PAJHS, XXI, 68)

ALEXANDER, Mrs. Rebecca. Wife of Joseph Alexander. It is highly doubtful that she was Jewish. (WAJA)

ALEXANDER, Samuel. In Philadelphia in 1785. He was one of the founders of Congregation Beth Shalome in Richmond in 1791. (MIPR; PAJHS, IV, 21)

ALEXANDER, William. Born 1776, Charleston. He lived in Charleston in 1802. It is highly doubtful that he was Jewish. (PAJHS, XIX, 80)

ALFERINO, Phineas. Naturalized in Maryland about 1742. It is highly doubtful that he was Jewish. (PAJHS, V, 116)

ALI, Abraham Adams ben. In New York City in 1795. (PAJHS, XXVII, 58)

ALMEYDA, Jacob. In New York City sometime between 1737 and 1744. (PAJHS, XXI, 45)

ALVARES (Z), Aaron. In Philadelphia in 1792. (MIPR)

ALVARES, Solomon Jessurun. A distiller in New York City in 1703. (Pool, 221)

ALVAREZ, Moses. 1729—October 19, 1766, Newport. He came from Jamaica, B.W.I., and was a merchant in Boston in 1766. (*Gutstein*, 312; PAJHS, XXIII, 85; XXVII, 198)

ALVAREZ, Moses Mendes. In New York City in 1729. (PAJHS, XXI, 20)

ALVAREZ, Rodriguez. In Newport in 1760. Ezra Stiles probably mistook this man for the one he listed as Levarez. (PAJHS, X, 8)

ALVAREZ, Sarah Jessurun. Died July, 1755. She was married to Jacob Mendes da Costa in 1717. She may have been in America. (MSGC)

AMAZIA, Mr. In New York City in 1795. (SIR)

AMBROSIUS, Moses. In 1654 he arrived in New Amsterdam on the *St. Charles*. (AJAM, III, 4)

ANDRADE, Salvador d'. In New Amsterdam by 1655. (POFNW, 468)

ANDREWS, Abraham. On July 2, 1761, he was married to Nellie Solomons in New York City. (SIR)

ANDREWS, Catherine. Daughter of Abraham Andrews, she was married to Samuel Mordecai in December, 1776, in Charlestown. (EJMC, 5)

ANDREWS, Cayle. Born May 26, 1762, New York City. Daughter of Abraham Andrews. (SIR)

ANDREWS, Deborah. Born January 8, 1800. Daughter of Joseph Andrews,[1] she was married to Jonas Horowitz in December, 1817, in Philadelphia. (MSGC; WW, 456)

ANDREWS, Eve. May 20, 1798, New York City—April, 1884, Philadelphia. Daughter of Joseph Andrews,[1] she was married to Abraham Elkin on July 10, 1816. (MSGC; WW, 456)

ANDREWS, Joseph.[1] About 1753, Strasburgh, Germany—October 31/November 1, 1824, Philadelphia. A teacher and a merchant, he was married to Sallie Salomon on August 9, 1794. (JCES; MIPR; MSGC; PAJHS, VI, 110; WW, 456)

ANDREWS, Joseph.[2] Born October 29, 1768, New York City. Son of Abraham Isaac Abrahams, he changed his name from Joseph Abrahams. Cf. Joseph Abrahams.[3] (SIR)

ANDREWS, Miriam. About 1772, America—July 14, 1847. Wife of Reuben Levy. (MSGC)

ANDREWS, Rachel. February 22, 1753, Boston—October 3, 1835, Charleston. She was married first to Myer Moses,[1] about 1772, and then to Solomon Woolf, about 1788. (*EOJCC*, 19; *St. Charles*, 84f; *Wills*, 58)

ARBEC. When he was a young man, he left Jamaica, B.W.I., and arrived in Savannah on February 28, 1784. He left soon for Charleston. (*SRB*)

ARIAS, Dias. About 1760 he was a slave-trader in Louisiana. (*AJA*; *Shpall*, 5f)

ARNOLD, Mayer. December 1, 1785, Ebenhausen, Germany—November 24/25, 1868, Philadelphia. He came to America at the age of thirteen. He was a trader in Kutztown, Pennsylvania, and in Philadelphia, where he was a leader in Jewish activities. On May 9, 1822, he was married to Fanny Wolf. (*Morais*, 245f)

ARNOLD, Myer. In Philadelphia in 1783. (*MIPR*)

ASH, Samuel. Fought in the Revolutionary militia in Charlestown, and was captured by the British in 1781. It is highly doubtful that he was Jewish. (*PAJHS*, XII, 55)

ASHER, Isaack. In New York City in 1683. (*AJAM*, III, 4)

ASHER, Michael. This son of Asher Michaels (Asher Michells de Paul) was a New York merchant trading with the West Indies in 1711. He also served as Boston agent for several New York merchants. In 1716 he operated a snuff mill in Boston. In 1733 he purchased a plot for a Jewish cemetery in Boston. During this period he maintained membership in Congregation Shearith Israel in New York City. (*JNEA*, 17; *MEAJA*, 110, 115; *PAJHS*, XXIII, 82; *SCMCNY*, 189; *UJE*, VII, 402)

ASHER, Rachel. About 1692—October 22, 1732, New York City. Daughter of Asher Michaels, she was married first to Samuel Zanvill Levy, and then to a man named Cotten. (*PAJHS*, XXXIV, 62f; *Pool*, 459f)

ASHER, Rycha. Died September 29, 1716, New York City. Daughter of Asher Michaels, she was the first wife of Moses Levy.[1] (*MSGC;* *PAJHS*, XXXIII, 200; *Pool*, 226)

ASHERS, Chepman. In 1774 he was in New York City. He had arrived from Germany. He was a smelter and refiner of gold and other metals. (*Arts & Crafts*, 314)

ASHUR, Joseph. In 1730 he went from Jersey to Boston. (*JNEA*, 20)

ASHUR, Joshua. In 1730 he went from Jersey to Boston. (*JNEA*, 24)

ASSIAS, Abraham. In New York City in 1795. (*PAJHS*, XXVII, 58)

ATHIAS, Isaac. In Philadelphia in 1754. He wished to flee to Amsterdam. (*JRMP*)

ATIAS, Jacob. In New York City with his family of five in 1793. (*Pool*, 332)

ATTIAS, Mr. Died September, 1793, Savannah. Son of Isaac Attias. Though he had been circumcised, he was not permitted to be buried as a Jew because of his gentile mother. (*MISR*)

ATTIAS, Isaac. A shammas in Congregation Mikveh Israel in Savannah in 1792. (*MISR*)

ATTIAS, Mrs. Isaac. Probably a convert to Judaism. (*MISR*)

AUGILLARE, Abraham d'. In Philadelphia in 1796. (*MIPR*)

AVERA, Isaac. Mentioned in the Revolutionary documents of Georgia. It is highly doubtful that he was Jewish. (*UJE*, IV, 537)

AVILA, Abraham. A merchant in South Carolina, he was naturalized on August 3, 1698. (*AJAM*, III, 4)

AZEVEDO, Miss d'. Probably the daughter of Isaac d'Azevedo, she was in Charleston in 1800. (*Census B, South Carolina*)

AZEVEDO, Isaac Cohen d'. 1759—January 5, 1805, Charleston. The former "head priest" of the Hebrew Congregation of London, he lived briefly in Newport in 1786. He was married to Rachel Woolf. (*EOJCC*, 82; *PAJHS*, XXVII, 349)

AZEVEDO, Moses d'. October 9, 1786, Newport—July 7, 1787, Newport. Son of Isaac Cohen d'Azevedo. (*PAJHS*, XXVII, 349)

AZUBY, Miss. Daughter of Abraham Azuby, she was in Charleston in 1800. (*Census B, South Carolina*)

AZUBY, Abraham. About 1738, Amsterdam—February 10, 1805, Charleston. He came to America in 1764, and served as minister of Congregation Beth Elohim in Charleston until 1805. In 1789 he sent a note to Congregation Mikveh Israel of Philadelphia, seeking funds for his congregation. He signed his name as Abraham de Ely Azuby. He was married to Esther. (*EJSC*, 133, *et passim*; *MIPR*; *MSP*; *SCHGM*, XXVIII, 205)

AZUBY, Mrs. Esther. Died May 30, 1805, Charleston. Wife of Abraham Azuby. (*SCHGM*, XXVIII, 244)

B

BAILEY, Mr. Noted as a lawyer in Lancaster in 1771. He was probably an adventurer. (*MEAJB*, 46f; *PAJHS*, XXXIV, 101)

BARDOS, Moses Mendes. In New York City sometime during the years 1737 to 1744. (*PAJHS*, XXI, 45)

BARENT, Alexander. In New York City in 1754. (*PAJHS*, XXVII, 8)

BARES, Solomon. Naturalized in New York City about 1740. Cf. Solomon Nare. (*PAJHS*, V, 116)

BARET, Solomon. In Charleston in 1795. Cf. Solomon Barrett. (*WAJA*)

BARNARD, Lazarus. In Philadlephia in 1784. Cf. Lazarus Barnet(t). (*MIPR*)

BARNET, Judah. In New York City in 1763. Cf. Judah Barred. (*SIR*)

BARNET(T), Lazarus. In Philadelphia in 1785. He was a merchant recently from Amsterdam. Cf. Lazarus Barnard. (*MIPR*; *WW*, 171)

BARNET, Sara. August 25, 1763, New York City—January 25, 1764, New York City. Daughter of Judah Barnet, she is also listed as Barres, Barred, and Barned. (*Pool*, 501; *SIR*)

BARNETT, Miss. Born 1771. Daughter of Nathan Barnett. (*MSP*)

BARNETT, Mr. Born April 30, 1768. Son of Nathan Barnett. (*MSP*)

BARNETT, Mrs. Anna. In Philadelphia in 1794. She was a shopkeeper who sought permission from Congregation Mikveh Israel to become a Jewess. Cf. Sarah Abrahams. (*MIPR*; *WW*, 352)

BARNETT, Brinah. Born April 30, 1761. Daughter of Nathan Barnett. (*MSP*)

BARNETT, Mrs. Elizabeth (Sheprah). 1767—December 31, 1831, Philadelphia. She was married first to Nathan Barnett, and then to Naphtaly Hart[2] on February 21, 1799, in Easton. (*SIR*)

BARNETT, Isaac. Born November 5, 1763. Son of Nathan Barnett. (*MSP*)

BARNETT, Jonah. Born July 21, 1794, Philadelphia. Son of Nathan Barnett. (*MIPR*)

BARNETT, Jonas. July 29, 1784—August 31, 1847, Allentown, Pennsylvania. This son of Nathan Barnett served as a paymaster in the U.S. Navy. He was married to Maria (Miriam) Marks on March 20, 1816. (*MSGC*; *PAJHS*, VIII, 133)

BARNETT, Joshua. Mentioned in the Georgia Revolutionary documents. It is highly doubtful that he was Jewish. (*PAJHS*, XVII, 99)

BARNETT, Louisa. August 31, 1792—December 24, 1814. Daughter of Nathan Barnett, she was married to Abraham Luria Hart on October 11, 1813. (*PAJHS*, VIII, 133)

BARNETT, Love. Born September 14, 1762. Daughter of Nathan Barnett. (*MSP*)

BARNETT, Nathan. Died July, 1797, Philadelphia. Listed also as Nathan bar Issacher Hacohen. In the records of Congregation Mikveh Israel of Philadelphia in 1792 are listed N. Barnett from Holland and Nathan Barnett from London. These references are probably to the same man who was returning to Philadelphia from a business trip in Europe. His wife was Elizabeth. (*MIPR*; *MSGC*)

BARNETT, Rebecca. Born November 20, 1766. Daughter of Nathan Barnett. (*MSP*)

BARNETT, Sarah. Born January 9, 1765. Daughter of Nathan Barnett. (*MSP*)

BARNSLEY, Woolf. May have been in Philadelphia in 1772. He was in business with Michael Gratz and Myer Myers. Cf. Barnet Woolf. (*Byars*, 121)

BARRED, Fa(-)etje. Born January 14, 1761, New York City. Daughter of Judah Barred (Barnet). (*SIR*)

BARRED, Judah. On November 7, 1759, he was married to Paijero Moses in New York City. Cf. Judah Barnet. (SIR)

BARRETT, Samuel. In Boston in 1796. It is highly doubtful that he was Jewish. (PAJHS, XXXVIII, 150)

BARRETT, Solomon. In Charleston sometime between 1783 and 1800. Cf. Solomon Baret. (EJSC, 279)

BARRETT, Mrs. Starr. 1699—January 9, 1820, Charleston. Her first name is sometimes given as Esther. After having lived in London thirty to forty years, she came to America in 1780. In opposition to the dates of birth and death recorded for her, she is reported to have died at the age of one hundred. (EOJCC, 30; PAJHS, XXVII, 487)

BARRIAS, Abraham. In Philadelphia in 1782. (MIPR; Morais, 15)

BARSIMSON, Jacob. Probably the first Jew to arrive in New Amsterdam in 1654, he had come from Holland. He may have left in 1659. (AJAM, III, 4; PAJHS, XVIII, 3)

BARZELAY, Simon. Also listed as Brasilla. He was a merchant and was in Boston in 1728. Cf. Samuel Brasilla. (JNEA, 18; PAJHS, XXI, 23)

BAZELLAS, Simon. In Boston in 1730. Cf. above and Samuel Brasilla. (FEAJ, 8)

BECKER, Sophi. In New York City in 1798. (SIR)

BENECHUS, Mr. A schoolmaster, he taught Michael Hart's children in Easton in 1786. Cf. Elias Pincus. (Trachtenberg, 28)

BENEDIX, Isaac. Born Holland, died May 31, 1804, Savannah. In Charleston sometime between 1783 and 1800. In 1798 he was a merchant and postmaster in Savannah. (EJSC, 279; SCHGM, XXVII, 224; WAJA)

BENEDIX, Samuel. In Savannah in 1795. (MISR)

BENEDIX, Mrs. Samuel. In Savannah in 1795. (MISR)

BENIDIN, Isaac. In 1792 he petitioned Congregation Mikveh Israel in Savannah to become a member, but his petition was denied. Cf. Isaac Benedix. (MISR)

BENJAMIN, Benjamin.[1] Born December 13, 1758, Philipse's Manor (Westchester County, New York). Son of Myer Benjamin. (PAJHS, XXVII, 151)

BENJAMIN, Benjamin.[2] Born March 18, 1767, New York City. Son of Torres Benjamin. (SIR)

BENJAMIN, David. In Exeter, Rhode Island, in 1781. It is highly doubtful that he was Jewish. (PAJHS, XXVII, 338)

BENJAMIN, Elias. In New York City in 1787. (PAJHS, XXVII, 43)

BENJAMIN, Isaak. In 1772 he came from Germany and went to Philadelphia as an indentured servant. (WW, 57)

BENJAMIN, Jacob. In 1778 he was a merchant in Trenton, New Jersey. If he was a Jew he was not an observant one since he advertised sales every Saturday. He was a Mason there until 1806. (PAJHS, XIX, 41)

BENJAMIN, Joe. In 1721 he arrived in Boston. It is highly doubtful that he was Jewish. Cf. below. (JNEA, 24)

BENJAMIN, Joseph.[1] In 1722 he came to Boston from Barbados. It is highly doubtful that he was Jewish. (JNEA, 24)

BENJAMIN, Joseph.[2] On June 21, 1786, he was married to Perlah Hyman in Philadelphia. (MIPR)

BENJAMIN, Joshua. In 1721 he came to Boston from Barbados. (PAJHS, X, 166)

BENJAMIN, Leah. March 21, 1765, Jamaica, Long Island—July, 1780. Daughter of Torres Benjamin, she was married on January 20, 1779, to David Nunez Cardoza, his first wife. She was also known as Leah Toras. (MEAJB, 362; MSGC; SIR; Wills, 36)

BENJAMIN(S), Myer. About 1733—November 20, 1776, Newport. A poor Hungarian, he lived in Newport, earning his living as a translator. (PAJHS, XXVII, 198, 350; XXXI, 239)

BENJAMIN, Mrs. Myer. In Newport in 1759. (PAJHS, XXVII, 151)

BENJAMIN, Richa (Rachel). August 21/-25, 1762, New York City—November 6, 1847, Charleston. Daughter of Torres Benjamin, she was married to Marks Lazarus on December 11, 1776. (SIR)

BENJAMIN, Samuel. A resident of Massachusetts, he served in the Revolutionary army. It is highly doubtful that he was Jewish. (PAJHS, XII, 104)

BENJAMIN, Simon. In Philadelphia in 1792. (MIPR)

BENJAMIN, Torres (Doras, Todros). In Charleston in 1787. He was married to Ritzel (Rachel) de Torres in 1760 in New York City. (Pool, 476; SIR)

BENNAL, Aaron. Son of Abraham Bennal, he was in Georgia in 1733. (Coulter, 64)

BENNAL, Abraham. In Georgia in 1733. His wife was Sarah. (Coulter, 64)

BENNAL, Benjamin. Son of Abraham Bennal, he was in Georgia in 1733. (Coulter, 64)

BENNAL, David. Son of Abraham Bennal, he was in Georgia in 1733. (Coulter, 64)

BENNAL, Jacob. Son of Abraham Bennal, he was in Georgia in 1733. Cf. Bernal. (Coulter, 64)

BENNAL, Moses. Son of Abraham Bennal, he was in Georgia in 1733. (Coulter, 64)

BENNAL, Rachel. Daughter of Abraham Bennal, she was in Georgia in 1733. Cf. Mrs. Rachel Montsonte. (Coulter, 64)

BENNAL, Sarah.[1] Wife of Abraham Bennal, she was in Georgia in 1733. (Coulter, 64)

BENNAL, Sarah.[2] Daughter of Abraham Bennal, she was in Georgia in 1733. (Coulter, 64)

BENSON, Direck. In New York City in 1695. It is doubtful that he was Jewish. (AJAM, III, 4)

BENZAKEN, Abraham. Born March 8, 1766, New York City. Son of Eleazer Benzaken. (PAJHS, XXVII, 152; SIR)

BENZAKEN, Mrs. Ann. Wife of Isaac Benzaken, she was in Philadelphia in 1799. (Wills, 17)

BENZAKEN, Eleazer. Died about 1787, New York City. A merchant, he was married to Esther in Philadelphia before 1763. (MSGC; NYHSW, XIV, 176, 352)

BENZAKEN, Mrs. Esther. Died about 1790. Wife of Eleazer Benzaken, she was in New York City in 1790. (NYHSW, XIV, 176; SIR)

BENZAKEN, Isaac. June 15, 1764, New York City—about 1799, Philadelphia. Son of Eleazer Benzaken, he was married to Ann. (NYHSW, XIV, 176; SIR; Wills, 17)

BENZAKEN, Jacob.[1] February 28, 1770, New York City—August 23, 1771, New York City. Son of Eleazer Benzaken. (Pool, 502; SIR)

BENZAKEN, Jacob.[2] March 20, 1772, New York City—August 8, 1773, New York City. Son of Eleazer Benzaken. (Pool, 502; SIR)

BENZAKEN, Joseph. January 20, 1763, New York City—April 17, 1779, New York City. Son of Eleazer Benzaken. (Pool, 503; SIR)

BENZAKEN, Princeda. December 5, 1774—July 26, 1775, New York City. Daughter of Eleazer Benzaken. (Pool, 503; SIR)

BENZAKEN, Rachel. Daughter of Eleazer Benzaken. (NYHSW, XIV, 176)

BENZAKEN, Simha. Born January 15, 1769, New York City. Daughter of Eleazer Benzaken. (SIR)

BENZAKIN, Joseph. In Charleston sometime between 1783 and 1800. (EJSC, 279)

BERNAL. Cf. Bennal.

BERNAL, Rafael. In Georgia in 1735. Cf. Raphael Bornal and Bernal Rafael Montsonte. (Coulter, 64)

BICKER, Hart N. In New York City in 1798. (SIR)

BINDONA, Joseph. In 1768 he was a shopkeeper in Montreal. He married Ann Wagins in a Montreal church. (Malchellosse, 171; PAJHS, I, 117)

BINGLEY, Dr. Probably in America before 1800. He was married to Esther Nathan, and was a convert to Judaism. (*MSP*)

BLOCK, Simon. In Baltimore in 1797; in New York City in 1800. (*MSGC; PAJHS, XIX, 57; SIR*)

BLOG, Abraham Solomons. In 1774 he was given money by the Jewish community of New York City to enable him to leave. (*PAJHS, XXI, 121*)

BLOG, Solomon. In America in 1745. (*ILI*)

BLOOM, Daniel. In New York City in 1750. It is doubtful that he was Jewish. (*PAJHS, XXIII, 153*)

BOAZ, Mr. In Philadelphia in 1783. (*MIPR*)

BOGRAGH, Mr. May have been known as Bachrach. He was in Connecticut before 1800. (*JRMP*)

BONAN, Amon. In New York about 1703. It is doubtful that he was Jewish. (*CPG, 172*)

BONAN, Mr. A teenage member of Amon Bonan's family, he was in New York City about 1703. It is doubtful that he was Jewish. (*CPG, 172*)

BONAN, Miss. A member of Simon Bonan's family, she was in New York City about 1703. It is doubtful that she was Jewish. (*CPG, 172*)

BONAN (BONAVE, BONANE), Simon. In some records he is referred to as Simon the Jew. On April 21, 1687, he became a freeman of New York City. In 1720 he was still in New York City. He may have been a slave importer. (*AJAM, III, 4; PAJHS, II, 84; VI, 101*)

BORNAL, Benjamin. Born June 13, 1737, Savannah. Son of Raphael Bornal. (*SRB*)

BORNAL, Raphael. In Georgia about 1733. Cf. Rafael Bernal. (*PAJHS, X, 73*)

BORNAL, Mrs. Raphael. In Georgia about 1733. (*PAJHS, X, 73*)

BOSQUALO, Aaron. In 1774 he was given money for passage to Curaçao by Congregation Shearith Israel of New York City. (*PAJHS, XXI, 117*)

BOSQUILA, Rabbi. Born 1713. He was from Smyrna, and was in Newport in 1774. He also lived in London. He was probably an itinerant money collector. Cf. above. (*PAJHS, X, 18, 21*)

BRAND, B. In Richmond in 1788. It is highly doubtful that he was Jewish. (*PAJHS, XX, 102*)

BRANDEAU, Esther. Daughter of David. On her way to visit relatives in Amsterdam, she was lost at sea. She remained at sea for five years, disguised as a boy. After a short stay in Montreal, about 1738, she was sent back to her home in Bayonne, France. She used the pseudonym Jacques LaFarge. Attempts were made to convert her to Christianity. (*MEAJA, 200; Sack, 22-25*)

BRANDON, Benjamin. An author, he was in Boston in 1756. It is highly doubtful that he was Jewish. (*PAJHS, XI, 82*)

BRANDON, David. In Savannah in 1793. (*MISR*)

BRANDON, Jacob Rodrigues. Given passage by Congregation Shearith Israel, he left New York City for London in 1774. (*PAJHS, XXI, 121*)

BRASILLA, Samuel. In Boston in 1728. He was an agent for Isaac Gomez. Cf. Simon Barzelay and Simon Bazellas. (*PAJHS, XXIII, 81*)

BROCHEZ, Alexander. In New York City in 1793. It is highly doubtful that he was Jewish. (*PAJHS, XIX, 31*)

BROMAL, Mr. The exact spelling of this name is uncertain. In Philadelphia in 1783. Cf. below. (*MIPR*)

BROMAT, Mr. In Philadelphia in 1783. Cf. above. (*MIPR*)

BROWN, Abigail. Died November 20, 1742, Curaçao. Daughter of Saul Pardo Brown, she was in New York City, but returned to Curaçao in 1708. (*Emanuel, 199, 338f*)

BROWN, David. A merchant, he was in New York City in 1704, and in Newport in

1677. (PAJHS, VI, 66, 104; XXIII, 148; Pool, 447)

BROWN, Mrs. Esther. Died 1708, New York City. Wife of Saul Pardo Brown. (Pool, 444)

BROWN, Hannah. Daughter of Saul Pardo Brown, she was in New York City in 1708. (Pool, 444)

BROWN, Joseph.[1] Died April 8, 1690, New York City. Son of Saul Brown. (GAV, 71; Pool, 444)

BROWN, Joseph.[2] Died 1704, New York City. In 1686 he was naturalized in New York City. (PAJHS, XXIII, 148; Pool, 444)

BROWN, Josiah. September 22, 1694, New York City—May 22, 1755, Curaçao. This son of Saul Pardo Brown was a building inspector in New York City in 1708. In 1731 he was married to Esther de Jacob Monsanto. (Emanuel, 327f; Pool, 446)

BROWN, Sarah. Died May 29, 1690, New York City. Daughter of Saul Brown. (GAV, 71; Pool, 444)

BROWN, Sarah Haim. Died July 27, 1723. Daughter of Saul Pardo Brown, she was in New York City, but returned to Curaçao in 1708. (Emanuel, 199, 239f; Pool, 446)

BROWN, Saul Pardo. Died April 17, 1702, Curaçao. The name "Brown" is the English equivalent of the Spanish "pardo." He was probably the son of Josiah Pardo. In 1677 he was a merchant in Newport, and in 1685 he went to New York City as a merchant. He came from a family of rabbis and hazzanim, and was one of the earliest hazzanim of Congregation Shearith Israel in New York City in 1695. (POFNW, 159f; Pool, 443f; Schappes, 569)

BROWN, Simha. Died January 5, 1768. Daughter of Saul Pardo Brown, she was in New York City, but returned to Curaçao in 1708. About 1717 she was married to Samuel Idanha de Casseres in Curaçao. (Emanuel, 199, 325f; Pool, 446)

BUENO, Esther. Died by 1708. She was also known as Esther Bueno de Mesquita. She came to America by 1662, and in 1683 she was licensed to trade in New York City. She was married to Isaac Gabay. Cf. Esther Bueno de Mesquita. (FEAJ, 66; NYHSW, II, 13)

BUENO, Joseph. Died 1708, New York City. Also known as Joseph Bueno de Mesquita. He was a merchant who was engaged in extensive trade with the West Indies. In 1681 or 1682 he purchased a cemetery for Jewish people. He was married to Rachel Dervall. Cf. Joseph Bueno de Mesquita. (AJAM, III, 4; PAJHS, XXIII, 149; UJE, VIII, 177)

BUN, Hiam. Also listed as Hiam Bon. He was the shohet of Congregation Shearith Israel in New York City in 1736. (PAJHS, II, 48; XXI, 58)

BUNN, Rose. About 1727—May 3, 1796. Daughter of Solomon Bunn, she was married to Joseph Simon.[1] (PAJHS, XXIII, 152; Morais, 270)

BUNN, Solomon. In New York City in 1741. He was naturalized in Philadelphia on September 20, 1752. He is listed also as Bone, Boon, Bun, and Solomon Haim Bonn. Cf. Hiam Bun. (PAJHS, V, 117; XXI, 44, et passim)

BURGER, David. In New York City in 1800. It is highly doubtful that he was Jewish. (SIR)

BURGOS, Abraham.[1] Died October 19, 1722, or October 26, 1732, New York City. In 1679 he arrived from Barbados. In 1685 he was one of the early settlers of Rhode Island, where he became a merchant. He was said to have been over one hundred years old at the time of his death. (AJAM, III, 4; Gutstein, 341; Pool, 207f)

BURGOS, Captain Abraham.[2] In New York City in 1744. (PAJHS, XXVII, 245)

BURGOS, Mordecai.[1] About 1680—July 18, 1736, New York City. He was in New York City on a trip from Barbados. (PAJHS, XVIII, 121; Pool, 211f)

BURGOS, Mordecai.[2] In Philadelphia in 1780. (MIPR)

BURRES, Isaac. In Lynchburg, Virginia, in 1800. It is highly doubtful that he was Jewish. (PAJHS, XIX, 60)

BUSH, Abraham. Born October 24, 1768/9, Philadelphia. Son of Mathias Bush. (*MIPR; MSGC*)

BUSH, Catherine. Born March 1, 1761, Philadelphia. She was also known as Caty and Hyah. Daughter of Mathias Bush, she was married to Myer S. Solomons on December 23, 1778. (*MSGC; MSP; PAJHS, XXXIII, 210*)

BUSH, David. March 25, 1762, Philadelphia—April 29, 1823. Also listed as David Bash. Son of Mathias Bush. (*Morais, 16; MSGC; PAJHS, XXXIII, 210*)

BUSH, Elkali. June 7, 1772, Chestnut Hill, Pennsylvania—January 27, 1830, Savannah. Also known as Eleanor Bush. Daughter of Mathias Bush, she was married to Moses Sheftall on March 1/21, 1792, in Philadelphia. (*GBMIP; MIPR; Wills, 79*)

BUSH, Ezekiel. In Philadelphia in 1785. (*MIPR*)

BUSH, Hannah. Born March 9, 1760, Philadelphia. Daughter of Mathias Bush. (*MSGC*)

BUSH, Isaiah. March 28, 1763, Philadelphia—June 10, 1806, Burke County, Georgia. This son of Mathias Bush intended to leave Philadelphia for Charleston in 1785. (*MIPR; MSGC; PAJHS, XIX, 47*)

BUSH, Dr. J. Probably in Philadelphia in 1790. It is doubtful that he was Jewish. (*Schappes, 76*)

BUSH, Jonas. A member of the Masons, he was from Pennsylvania, and served in the Revolutionary army. It is highly doubtful that he was Jewish. (*Morais, 458; PAJHS, XIX, 31*)

BUSH, Joseph. Born October 3, 1776, Chestnut Hill, Pennsylvania. Son of Mathias Bush. (*MSGC*)

BUSH, Margaret. Died December 5, 1799, Savannah. Daughter of Mathias Bush. (*GBMIP; JRMP*)

BUSH, Mathias. May 10, 1722, Prague—March 29, 1790, Philadelphia. A merchant and shipowner, he was in New York City as early as 1748. In 1782 and 1783 he served as tax collector for Germantown, Pennsylvania, and had business relations with the Gratzes. He was a leader of the Philadelphia Jewish community. He was married to Rebecca Myers Cohen and to Tabitha Mears. (*Morais, 22; MSGC; PAJHS, XXI, 58; XXVII, 21; Trachtenberg, 31; UJE, II, 607; WW, 30, et passim*)

BUSH, Nathan. Born April 18, 1756, Philadelphia. Also listed as Nathaniel. Son of Mathias Bush, he was in Philadelphia in 1776, and in Easton in 1778. (*Byars, 160f; MSGC; PAJHS, XXXIII, 210; Trachtenberg, 29*)

BUSH, Peggy (Pier). October 27, 1770, Philadelphia—December 5/November 11, 1799, Savannah. Daughter of Mathias Bush. Cf. Margaret Bush. (*MSGC*)

BUSH, Rachel. Born November 5, 1758, Philadelphia. Daughter of Mathias Bush. (*MSGC*)

BUSH, Richea. December 10, 1765, Philadelphia—February 4, 1844, Philadelphia. Daughter of Mathias Bush. (*GBMIP; MSGC*)

BUSH, Samuel. December 3, 1754, Philadelphia—February 16, 1826. Son of Mathias Bush. (*MSGC*)

BUSH, Sarah. Born May 9, 1774, Chestnut Hill, Pennsylvania. Daughter of Mathias Bush. (*MSGC*)

BUSH, Solomon. Born October 13, 1753, Philadelphia. This son of Mathias Bush was appointed deputy adjutant general for the state militia of Pennsylvania in 1777. He then entered the Revolutionary army, where he was wounded, and was retired with the rank of lieutenant colonel. A fervent patriot, he was the first Philadelphia Jew to take part in civic functions in the new government after the Revolution. Unsuccessfully he sought public office. An abolitionist, he protested the English press gangs. He became assimilated, and was grand master of the Masons of Pennsylvania in 1787 and 1788. He was married to Nancy Marshall, who was of a prominent family. He was buried in Friends Burial Ground. (*MEAJB, 73, et passim; MIPR; MSGC; MSP; UJE, II, 608; WW, 83, et passim*)

C

CADET, Mendes fils. In 1777 he was a shipowner and shipmaster in Portsmouth, New Hampshire. It is doubtful that he was Jewish. (*PAJHS*, XXIII, 171)

CAIGNETT, Mr. In Philadelphia in 1795. (*MIPR*)

CALMER, Solomon. In Philadelphia in 1786. (*MIPR; WW*, 418)

CALONEMOS, Moses. In New York City in 1770; in Newport in 1773. (*JNEB*, 39; *PAJHS*, XXI, 106)

CAMPANAL, Asher. Died 1753, New York City. From 1739 to 1743 he was shammas for Congregation Shearith Israel in New York City, and again from 1744 to 1753. (*PAJHS*, XXI, 41; *POFNW*, 286; *Pool*, 188)

CAMPANAL, David.[1] In Rhode Island in 1685; in New York City in 1700. (*AJAM*, III, 4; *POFNW*, 469)

CAMPANAL, David.[2] Died about 1732, Ipswich, Massachusetts. He was baptized there on May 1, 1728. In 1711 he was married to Marie Wilson. (*FEAJ*, 10; *JNEA*, 25)

CAMPANALL, David. In 1734 he was married to Hannah Newmarch. He served as a soldier in the Revolutionary army. He was warned to leave Boston. He was baptized. (*FEAJ*, 9f)

CAMPANALL, Hannah. Daughter of David Campanall, she was baptized in 1735. (*FEAJ*, 10)

CAMPANALL, Sarah. A resident of Ipswich, Massachusetts, she was unmarried when she was baptized in February, 1726. She may have been related to David Campanal.[2] (*JNEA*, 25)

CAMPANALL, Valentina. In 1728 he served as shammas for Congregation Shearith Israel in New York City. (*PAJHS*, XXI, 4; *SIR*)

CAMPANALL, William. This son of David Campanall was a weaver. He served in the French and Indian War, and in the Revolutionary war. He was baptized in 1739. (*FEAJ*, 10; *UJE*, VII, 403)

CAMPANEL, Rachel. Died September 26, 1770, New York City. In New York City as early as 1753. (*PAJHS*, XXI, 69; *SIR*)

CAMPANNAL, Abraham. A merchant in Rhode Island in 1685, he became a freeman in 1688. (*AJAM*, III, 4)

CAMPANNAL, Daniel. A merchant in Rhode Island in 1685. (*AJAM*, III, 4)

CAMPANNAL, Mordecai. In 1658 he probably arrived in Newport from Holland, and became a merchant. He is noted as the most prominent Jew in Rhode Island. (*AJAM*, III, 5)

CAMPOS, Mr. In Philadelphia in 1795. (*MIPR*)

CAMPOS, Abraham. In New York City about 1740. (*PAJHS*, XXI, 45)

CAMPOS, Esther Rachel. March, 1695—September 29, 1736, New York City. She came from Jamaica, B.W.I., and was married to Mordecai Gomez.[1] (*Pool*, 213)

CAMPOS, Jacob de. About 1740 he was preparing to leave New York City with his family. (*PAJHS*, XXI, 43)

CANTER, Abraham. Born 1776. In 1787 he was brought to Savannah and was there in 1792. (*MISR; SRB*)

CANTER, Charlotte. Sister of Joshua Canter, she was married to Abraham Sasportas in January, 1803, in Charleston. (*Wills*, 55)

CANTER, David. Died November, 1829, New York City. In Charleston in 1800. (*EJSC*, 133; *ELODN*, 15)

CANTER, Emanuel. In Charleston in 1800. Cf. below. (*EJSC*, 133)

CANTER, Emil. In 1798 he was visiting Washington, D.C., from Charleston. (*PAJHS*, XIX, 87)

CANTER, Isaac. In 1798 he was visiting Washington, D.C. from Charleston. He was in Charleston again in 1800. (EJSC, 133; PAJHS, XIX, 87)

CANTER, Jacob. In 1798 he was a merchant in Charleston. He was probably the husband of Mrs. Rebecca Canter. (EJSC, 133; EOJCC, 29; WAJA)

CANTER, John. 1782, St. Croix—January 14, 1823, Charleston. Son of Jacob Canter, he was a painter. (ELODN, 15; EOJCC, 29)

CANTER, Jonathan. In Charleston in 1800. Cf. Jonathan Cantor. (EJSC, 133)

CANTER, Joshua. Died October 28, 1826, New York City. In 1792 he arrived in Charleston from Denmark. He was an artist and taught drawing and painting in Charleston. (EJSC, 140; Wills, 36)

CANTER, Rachel. Died in New York City. Sister of Joshua Canter, she had lived previously in Charleston. (Wills, 36)

CANTER, Mrs. Rebecca. Married to Jacob Canter. (EOJCC, 29)

CANTON, Jacob. In 1798 he was a Charleston merchant. Cf. Jacob Canter, (Wills, 82)

CANTOR, David. In Charleston in 1800. Cf. David Canter. (EJSC, 133)

CANTOR, Jacob, Jr. In Charleston sometime between 1783 and 1800. (EJSC, 279)

CANTOR, Jonathon. In Savannah in 1795. Cf. Jonathan Canter. (MISR)

CANTOR, Judith. 1771—August 27, 1827, Charleston. She was married to Emanuel de la Motta, in Charleston, in December 1787. (EOJCC, 55; JRMP)

CANTOR, Sarah. On June 7, 1797, she was married to Isaac Cantor de la Motta in Charleston. (JRMP)

CAPELLA, Joseph. In 1786 he was a Mason in Pennsylvania. It is doubtful that he was Jewish. Cf. below and Joseph Carpelles. (PAJHS, XIX, 51)

CAPELLE, Joseph. From 1769 to 1784 he was a Mason in Delaware, and again from 1789 to 1795. It is doubtful that he was Jewish. Cf. above and Joseph Carpelles. (PAJHS, XIX, 55)

CARDOZA, Aaron. In New York City in 1750. Cf. Aaron N. Cardozo. (PAJHS, XXI, 61)

CARDOZA, Jacob. In New York City in 1744. (PAJHS, XXI, 47)

CARDOZO, Aaron N. Died July 20, 1800. A London merchant, he came to New York City in 1752. He was in Richmond in 1790. In August, 1739, he was married to Sarah Navarro in London. Cf. Aaron Cardoza. (MSGC; PAJHS, XX, 104; UJE, III, 39)

CARDOZO, Abraham Nunez.[1] Died November 17, 1762, Charlestown. In Charlestown in 1750. His wife was Hannah. (EJSC, 39; PAJHS, XII, 44)

CARDOZO, Abraham Nunez.[2] November 22, 1758, New York City—April 9, 1816, Richmond. Son of Aaron Nunez Cardozo. (MSGC)

CARDOZO, Abraham Nunez.[3] Born 1792, Powhatan City, Virginia. Son of Moses Nunez Cardozo.[1] (MSGC)

CARDOZO, Benjamin. In New Amsterdam in 1656. (POFNW, 468)

CARDOZO, Daniel W. A resident of Charleston, he fought in the Revolutionary army. (PAJHS, IV, 96)

CARDOZO, David Nunez.[1] August 29, 1753, New York City—July 13, 1835, Charleston. This son of Aaron Nunez Cardozo fought in the Revolutionary army. He was married to Leah Benjamin on January 20, 1779; and to Sarah Cohen[3] on March 9, 1785, in Charleston. (EJSC, 84; MSGC; SRB; UJE, III, 43)

CARDOZO, David Nunez.[2] Probably before 1800—1825. This son of Moses Nunez Cardozo[1] was married to Mary Atkinson in 1819. (MSGC)

CARDOZO, Elias. Born April 5, 1758, New York City. Son of Aaron Nunez Cardozo. (PAJHS, XXVII, 151)

CARDOZO, Frances. February 21, 1788—October 4, 1849. Daughter of David Nunez Cardozo.[1] (MSGC)

CARDOZO, Mrs. Hannah. Died before 1793. In Charlestown in 1762. She was the wife of Abraham Nunez Cardozo.[1] (*EJSC*, 39; *MISR*)

CARDOZO, Isaac. In 1655 he was a merchant in New Amsterdam. (*AJAM*, III, 5)

CARDOZO, Isaac N.[1] May 25, 1751, London—July 22, 1832, New York City. This son of Aaron Nunez Cardozo fought in the Revolutionary army in defense of Charlestown harbor. A merchant, he was in Easton from 1799 to 1817. He was married to Sally Hart, in Philadelphia, on January 10, 1798. (*MIPR*; *MSGC*; *UJE*, III, 43; *Trachtenberg*, 29)

CARDOZO, Isaac N.[2] Born about 1788. This son of Moses Nunez Cardozo[1] fought in the War of 1812. He was married to Mahalia Baugh. (*MSGC*)

CARDOZO, Isaac N.[3] 1792—August 18, 1855, Charleston. Son of David Nunez Cardozo,[1] he was employed as a weigher in the Charleston custom house. He was prominent in the Reformed Society of Israelites in Charleston. (*MSGC*; *UJE*, III, 43)

CARDOZO, Jacob Newton. June 17, 1786, Savannah—August 30, 1873, Savannah. This son of David Nunez Cardozo[1] was a journalist and editor who became one of the outstanding newspapermen of the South. From 1817 to 1845 he was editor and later owner of the *Southern Patriot*, a free trade organ. He wrote essays and books such as *Notes on Political Economy* and *Reminiscences of Charleston*. He also founded the *Evening News*. He was an active leader in the Chamber of Commerce. (*DAB*, III, 486f; *UJE*, III, 43)

CARDOZO, Judith Nunez.[1] Born December 27, 1747. Daughter of Aaron Nunez Cardozo, she was probably in America. (*MSGC*)

CARDOZO, Judith N.[2] August 3, 1790—February 25, 1854, Charleston. Daughter of David Nunez Cardozo.[1] (*MSGC*)

CARDOZO, Judith N.[3] Probably born before 1800. Daughter of Moses Nunez Cardozo.[1] (*MSGC*)

CARDOZO, Michael H. November 7/14, 1800, Easton—October 5, 1865, New York City. Son of Isaac Nunez Cardozo,[1] he was married to Ellen Hart on October 22, 1819, in Richmond. (*MIPR*; *MSGC*)

CARDOZO, Moses. A merchant from the West Indies, he was mentioned in the Newport court records in 1747. (*JNEB*, 11)

CARDOZO, Moses Nunez.[1] February 22, 1755, New York City—January 1, 1818, Richmond. This son of Aaron Nunez Cardozo was married to Gitleh Moses on January 11, 1784, in Philadelphia. (*MIPR*; *MSGC*)

CARDOZO, Moses Nunez.[2] Probably born before 1800. Son of Moses Nunez Cardozo.[1] (*MSGC*)

CARDOZO, Rachel Nunez.[1] Born April 26, 1743, London. Daughter of Aaron Nunez Cardozo, she probably came to America. (*MSGC*)

CARDOZO, Rachel Nunez.[2] June 16, 1795, Charleston—February 14, 1860, Savannah. Daughter of David Nunez Cardozo,[1] she was married to Abraham Seixas[3] on April 11, 1821. (*EOJCC*, 20; *MSGC*)

CARDOZO, Rachel Nunez.[3] February 8, 1799—November 28, 1887, New York City. Daughter of Isaac Nunez Cardozo,[1] she was married to Simon Cauffman on May 16, 1816, and to Joseph Phillips on December 10, 1839, in New York. (*MSGC*)

CARDOZO, Rachel Nunez.[4] Probably born before 1800. Daughter of Moses Nunez Cardozo,[1] she was married to Benjamin C. Mosby. (*MSGC*)

CARDOZO, Rebecca. Died May 27, 1766, New York City. Daughter of of Isaac Nunez Cardoza, she was married to Isaac N. Navaro, in London, in 1714. (*MSGC*; *Pool*, 502)

CARDOZO, S. A member of the Revolutionary army, he was living in South Carolina in 1835. His wife was Sarah. Cf. below. (*PAJHS*, XII, 57)

CARDOZO, Sally Nunez. Probably born before 1800. Daughter of Moses Nunez Cardozo.[1] (*MSGC*)

CARDOZO, Samuel Nunez.[1] In Charlestown in 1767. (*EJSC*, 45)

CARDOZO, Samuel Nunez.[2] Probably born before 1800. Son of Moses Nunez Cardozo.[1] (*MSGC*)

CARDOZO, Mrs. Sarah. Wife of S. Cardozo, in 1838 she was a widow, living in South Carolina. (*PAJHS*, XII, 57)

CARDOZO, Mrs. Sarah Nunez.[1] July 25, 1722—May 23, 1761, New York City. Wife of Aaron Nunez Cardozo. (*MSGC; Pool*, 501; *SIR*)

CARDOZO, Sarah Nunez.[2] January 12, 1780, Savannah—October 9, 1837. Daughter of David Nunez Cardozo,[1] she was married to Lyon Levy on May 1, 1801. She died in a shipwreck off the coast of Ocracoka, North Carolina. (*EOJCC*, 14, et passim; *MSGC; Wills*, 46)

CARDOZO, Solomon. Probably born before 1800. Son of David Nunez Cardozo[1] by his second wife. (*MSGC*)

CARIGAL (CARREGAL, KARIGAL), Haim Isaac. October 15, 1733, Hebron, Palestine—1777, Barbados. He came from Hebron, Palestine, and was known to have been in Curaçao in 1761, where he served as rabbi for two years. He was probably an itinerant money collector as well as a rabbi. A learned man who spoke several languages, he traveled widely in Europe and the Near East. He delivered the first Jewish sermon to be published in America. While he was in Newport in 1773, he developed a warm friendship with Ezra Stiles. Through Stiles and the Jewish community, led by Aaron Lopez and Jacob R. Rivera, it was arranged that a portarit of Carigal be presented to Yale College. In July, 1773, he left America, and in 1774, he went from Surinam to Barbados, where he served as rabbi until his death. Just before he died he changed his name to Raphael. (*AJAM*, V, 1, 18; *Carigal; Gutstein*, 149f; *Kohut*, 16, et passim; *MEAJA*, 194; *PAJHS*, XXXI, 242; *Shilstone*, 100; *UJE*, VI, 320f; VIII, 214; X, 65)

CAROES, Aaron. In New York City in 1789. (*SIR*)

CARPLES, Benjamin. In Philadelphia in 1785. (*MIPR*)

CARPELLES (CARPELLESS, CARPLIS, KARPELES), Joseph. This son of Wolf Carpelles of Prague was in Philadelphia by 1782. An innkeeper, he was nevertheless one of the most learned men in Jewish lore in America. Cf. Joseph Capella and Joseph Capelle. (*MIPR; Morais*, 16; *MSP; PAJHS*, XIX, 51, 55; *WW*, 130f, 184)

CARVALHO, David Dias. 1739—April 19, 1775, Savannah. (*SRB*)

CARVALLO, Mr. A merchant in Charlestown in 1735. (*EJSC*, 27; *PAJHS*, XII, 43)

CASSAREZ, Abraham de. In 1718 he was a freeman in New York City. A tallow chandler, he was reputed to have been a descendant of Benedict Spinoza. (*OMMC*, 28)

CASERES, Sarah Gomes de. In New York City in 1735. (*PAJHS*, XXI, 34)

CASSEL, Abraham. In 1776 he was a yeoman in Philadelphia County, where he died. He was probably a convert to Christianity since he asked to be buried in a "Christian-like manner." Husband of Feigal, he had a son, Jacob, and at least two more children, who are not listed. (*WAJA*)

CASSEL, Mrs. Feigal. Wife of Abraham Cassel. (*WAJA*)

CASSEL, Henry. Brother of Abraham Cassel, he was probably in Philadelphia in 1776. (*WAJA*)

CASSEL, Jacob. Son of Abraham Cassel, he was a minor in 1761. (*WAJA*)

CASSERES, Benjamin de. In New York City in 1689. (*POFNW*, 468)

CASSERES, Esther de. In New York City in 1689. (*POFNW*, 468)

CASTELLO, Elias Nunez. In New York City in 1792. (*PAJHS*, XXVII, 51; *SIR*)

CASTELLO, Moses N. In New York City in 1792; in Philadelphia in 1796. (*MIPR; PAJHS*, XXVII, 51)

CASTER, Isaac de. In New York City in 1782. (*JRMP*)

CASTRO, Abraham Mendes. In New York City in 1745. (*PAJHS*, XXI, 48)

CASTRO, Benjamin. A resident of Cape François, he was in Philadelphia in 1792, and in New York City in 1795. (*MIPR*; *SIR*)

CASTRO, Daniel de. In New York City in 1747. (*PAJHS*, XXI, 55)

CASTRO, Isaac Mendes. In New York City in 1745. (*PAJHS*, XXI, 48)

CASTRO, Jacob de. In New York City in 1747. (*PAJHS*, XXI, 55)

CASTRO, Moses Henriques. In Philadelphia in 1784. (*MIPR*)

CAUFFMAN, Joseph. 1720—February 10, 1807, Philadelphia. In 1800 he was in Philadelphia with his family. He was the landlord of a Cherry Street house, where Congregation Mikveh Israel met. It is doubtful that he was Jewish. (*Census B, Pennsylvania*; *MSGC*; *WW*, 116, 121)

CAUFFMAN, Simon. This son of Joseph Cauffman was married to Rachel N. Cardoza on May 16, 1816. (*MSGC*)

CHACON, Abraham. In Philadelphia in 1792. Cf. below. (*MIPR*)

CHAGUN, Mr. In New York City in 1795. Cf. above. (*SIR*)

CHAPMAN, Nathan. A trader in the Detroit area, he was captured there by Indians in 1763, and was still there as late as 1796. Cf. Chapman Abrahams. (*PAJHS*, XXIII, 31f; *UJE*, III, 545; VII, 534)

CHAUVES, I. In New York City in 1792. (*PAJHS*, XXVII, 51)

CHAVAS, Abraham. In 1772 he was a shohet for Congregation Shearith Israel in New York City. Cf. Abraham Lopez Chavez. (*PAJHS*, XXI, 114f)

CHAVES, Charles. In 1798 he came to America from Bordeaux. (*SZ*, 121)

CHAVES, Daniel. In New York City as a child about 1793. (*PAJHS*, XXVII, 55)

CHAVEZ, Abraham Lopez. In Philadelphia in 1792. Cf. Abraham Chavas. (*MIPR*)

CHRISTE, John Gotfred. In Georgia about 1735. A tailor and laborer, he was a Saltsburger who came from Augsburg, Germany. He was converted to Christianity in Germany, where his name had been Salomon Levi. (*Coulter*, 9; *PAJHS*, X, 77)

CLARA. In 1761 she was mentioned in a letter from Mordecai Moses to Barnard Gratz. She was on her way to Philadelphia from New York. (*JRMP*)

CLAVA, Benjamin Moses. Died March 16, 1785, Philadelphia. On September 12, 1762, he was naturalized at Lancaster. He was employed by David Franks and was a partner of Barnard Gratz. He was married to a Christian. Cf. below. (*Hugsoc*, XXIV, 82; *MIPR*; *MSP*; *WW*, 129f)

CLEVA, Moses. May have been in Philadelphia about 1763. Cf. above. (*PAJHS*, XXXIV, 87)

CLORA, Mr. In New York City in 1797. (*SIR*)

COAN, Elias. Listed in the North Carolina census of 1790. It is highly doubtful that he was Jewish. (*UJE*, VIII, 237)

COEN, Daniel. In 1792 he was a silversmith in New York City. His wife was Deborah Ogilvie. It is doubtful that he was Jewish. (*NYHSW*, XV, 151f)

COHAN, Isaiah. In 1774 he was an Indian trader in Pennsylvania. Cf. below and Jacob I. Cohen.[1] (*PA*, II, 627)

COHAN, Jacob Isaiah. In 1773 he was an Indian trader in Pennsylvania. Cf. Jacob Cohen.[1] (*PA*, II, 626)

COHEN, Abigail. On May 2, 1736, she was married to Hyman Abendenoone. (*SRB*)

COHEN, Abraham.[1] On July 23, 1772, he was married to Mary Garman in Pennsylvania. (*PA*, II, 62)

COHEN, Abraham.[2] 1739, London—December 10, 1800, Georgetown, South Carolina. This son of Moses Cohen[2] was in business in Georgetown by 1762. From 1790/1797 to 1800 he was postmaster there. (*EJSC*, 34, et passim; *EVJC*; *MSGC*; *PAJHS*, XII, 53, 164)

COHEN, Abraham.[3] May have been the son of Jacob Cohen. In Philadelphia in 1792. (*MIPR*)

COHEN, Abraham.[4] This son of Solomon Myers Cohen was a bail commissioner. (PAJHS, XX, 108)

COHEN, Abraham.[5] In 1794 he was a trunkmaker in Philadelphia. (WW, 184, 434)

COHEN, Abraham.[6] About 1792 he was in New York City as a child. (PAJHS, XXVII, 55)

COHEN, Abraham.[7] October 25, 1791—March 22, 1793. Son of Solomon Cohen,[1] he was buried in Georgetown, South Carolina. (EVJC)

COHEN, Abraham Eleazer. Died February, 1793, Philadelphia. A schoolmaster, he was shammas for Congregation Mikveh Israel in 1783. His wife was Barbara. (MIPR; Morais, 45; Wills, 17; WW, 124, 141, 421)

COHEN, Abraham Hyam. Died February, 1841, Richmond. This son of Jacob Raphael Cohen was credited with having invented seltzer water and having popularized the use of sodas. He was also a bottler of mineral water. From 1811 until 1815 he acted as a reader for Congregation Mikveh Israel in Philadelphia. In 1828 he was the hazzan for Congregation Beth Shalome. On May 28, 1806, he was married to Miss Pickens, a gentile, who converted to Judaism, in Philadelphia. (ELJR, 219f, 289; Morais, 43; WW, 142, et passim)

COHEN, Abraham Myers.[1] This son of Emanuel Myers Cohen was a New York City shopkeeper who became a freeman of that city about 1737. He was naturalized there about 1741. His wife may have been named Sarah. (PAJHS, V, 116; VI, 102; XXI, 29; XXXIII, 210)

COHEN, Abraham Myers.[2] 1787—February 18, 1859. Son of Solomon Myers Cohen.[1] (MIPR; MSGC)

COHEN, Abraham Sarzedas. Son of Gershom Cohen, he lived in Charleston before 1800. (WAJA)

COHEN, Asher. In Richmond in 1788. (ELJR, 33)

COHEN, Mrs. Asher. In Richmond in 1788. (ELJR, 33)

COHEN, Mrs. Barbara. Wife of Abraham Eleazer Cohen. (Wills, 17)

COHEN, Barnard. In Charleston in 1800. (EJSC, 133)

COHEN, Barnett A. 1770, Bristol, England —March 23, 1839, King Creek, South Carolina. Probably in Charleston before 1800. His wife was Bella. (MSP; RPJ, 41)

COHEN, Benjamin I. September 17, 1797, Richmond—September 20, 1845, Baltimore. This son of Israel I. Cohen was a banker who was socially prominent in Baltimore. From 1825 to 1845 he was an officer of the German Society of Maryland, probably the oldest benevolent organization in Maryland. He is reputed to have been a violinist, a botanist, and a horticulturist. He served in the Maryland militia, and was active in passing the "Jew Bill" in Maryland. On December 15, 1819, he was married to Kitty Etting. (MHM, XIX, 56f)

COHEN, Bilhah.[1] This daughter of Emanuel M. Cohen was married to Joseph Solomon in London, in 1738. She probably came to America. (MSGC; PAJHS, XXIII, 152)

COHEN, Bilhah.[2] Born August 24, 1785, Savannah. Daughter of Moses Cohen.[8] (SRB)

COHEN, Catherine. August 6, 1781, Charlestown—May 30, 1862, Philadelphia. Daughter of Gershom Cohen, she was married to Samson Mears Isaacs[1] on March 25, 1807. (MSGC)

COHEN, Cauffman. On July 18, 1781, he was married to Betty Abrahams in Philadelphia. (MIPR)

COHEN, Charity. Died 1813, New York City. In New York City as early as 1791. (Pool, 183; SIR)

COHEN, Cornelia. On December 19, 1799, she was married to Thomas McIntyre in a Charleston church. (SCHGM, XXXIII, 38)

COHEN, Daniel. A shohet for Congregation Shearith Israel in New York City in 1736. (PAJHS, II, 48)

COHEN, David.[1] In Savannah in 1733. (Coulter, 68)

COHEN, David.[2] Died about 1784, Charleston. A shopkeeper. (*WAJA*)

COHEN, David I. April 30, 1800, Richmond—July 4, 1847, Baltimore. This son of Israel I. Cohen was a financier who aided in the founding of the Baltimore Stock Exchange. He was married to Harriet Rahmah in 1830. (*MSGC; UJE*, III, 236)

COHEN, Deborah. 1776—August 29, 1848, St. Joseph, Florida. Daughter of Jacob Raphael Cohen, she was married to Israel Moses[2] on December 5, 1810. (*MSGC; WAJA*)

COHEN, Dinah (Divinah). April 21, 1787, Georgetown, South Carolina—February 17, 1874, Savannah. Daughter of Solomon Cohen,[1] she was married to Isaac Minis at Georgetown on December 4, 1803. (*MSGC*)

COHEN, Mrs. Eleanor. About 1776, Hamburg, Germany—December 7, 1849, Charleston. Wife of Solomon I. Cohen. (*EOJCC*, 36)

COHEN, Eleazar.[1] Died about 1786, Philadelphia. (*MIPR*)

COHEN, Eleazar.[2] Son of Solomon M. Cohen, he was a search clerk in a court in Philadelphia. (*PAJHS*, XX, 108)

COHEN, Eliza. Died October, 1811, Charleston, age eleven. Daughter of Mordecai Cohen. (*ELODN*, 19)

COHEN, Elkaleh.[1] 1735—August 8, 1765, New York City. Daughter of Samuel M. Cohen,[1] she was the first wife of Myer Myers.[1] (*Pool*, 300f; *SIR*)

COHEN, Elkaleh.[2] 1749—October 30, 1785, New York City. Daughter of Abraham Myers Cohen,[1] she was the first wife of Gershom M. Seixas on September 6, 1775. (*Pool*, 249f)

COHEN, Elkaleh.[3] 1785—1875. Daughter of Solomon M. Cohen. (*MSGC*)

COHEN, Emanuel Myers. In New York City in 1741. (*NYHSW*, III, 405; *PAJHS*, XXI, 45)

COHEN, Ellis. In Philadelphia in 1785. (*MIPR*)

COHEN, Esther.[1] Daughter of Emanuel M. Cohen. (*NYHSW*, III, 405)

COHEN, Esther.[2] 1748—December 8, 1826, Georgetown, South Carolina. Daughter of Moses Cohen,[2] she was married to Mordecai Myers.[1] (*MSGC*)

COHEN, Esther.[3] 1769, England—May 2, 1855. This daughter of Jacob Raphael Cohen became the second wife of Michael Hart,[1] in Philadelphia, on February 7, 1787. (*MIPR; Morais*, 30; *MSGC; PAJHS*, VIII, 132)

COHEN, Esther.[4] 1784—November 21, 1816, Wilmington, North Carolina. This daughter of Gershom Cohen was married to Aaron Lazarus on May 10, 1803. (*MSGC*)

COHEN, Fanny. Daughter of Isaac Cohen,[3] she was married to Solomon Nathan of England. (*WAJA*)

COHEN, Francis. In Charlestown in 1767. (*EJSC*, 45)

COHEN, Frumet (Fanny). Died May 14, 1795, New York City. Daughter of Isaac A. Cohen, and wife of Sampson Lazarus. (*MSP; Pool*, 503)

COHEN, Gershom. 1748—January 24, 1802, Charleston. He came to America in 1772, was engaged as a merchant, and fought in the Revolution. He worked for close relations with Christians. On August 27, 1779 he was married to Rebecca Sarzedas in Charlestown. They had nine children. (*Coldoc*, 181f; *EJSC*, 91, *et passim; MSGC; PAJHS*, XII, 53; XIX, 79)

COHEN, Gitlah. Born June 27, 1769. Daughter of Jacob Cohen.[2] (*MSGC*)

COHEN, Goody (Goodhaur). 1767—May 1, 1848, Philadelphia. Daughter of Jacob Raphael Cohen, she was married to Henry Phillips on October 8, 1794. (*MSGC; Wills*, 15)

COHEN, Grace. Wife of Simon Abendenoone on July 5, 1736. (*SRB*)

COHEN, Henrietta. February 28, 1799—June 19, 1886. This daughter of Solomon Cohen[1] was married to Mordecai Myers[3] about 1820. She was also known as Sarah Henrietta. (*JRMP; MSGC*)

COHEN, Henry. In Charleston in 1800. (*EJSC*, 133)

COHEN, Hettie. Daughter of Jacob Cohen.² (*MSGC*)

COHEN, Hetty. In Bedford, Connecticut, in 1790. (*HDB*)

COHEN, Hiah Myers. Daughter of Samuel Myers Cohen,¹ she was in New York City in 1741. (*NYHSW*, III, 294f; *PAJHS*, XXIII, 152)

COHEN, Hyam. 1789—August, 1850. This son of Gershom Cohen served in the War of 1812. From 1838 to 1850 he was a city assessor of Charleston. He was married to Hetty Moses Moïse. (*EJSC*, 133, *et passim; MSGC; WAJA*)

COHEN, I. Abraham. In Philadelphia in 1792. (*MIPR*)

COHEN, I. H. In Philadelphia in 1796. (*PAJHS*, XXVII, 62)

COHEN, I. Myers. In New York City in 1739. (*SIR*)

COHEN, Isaac.¹ During the years 1750 through 1783 he was active in Charlestown. He was probably the husband of Joel Pimenta. (*EJSC*, 278; *Wills*, 54)

COHEN, Isaac.² Came to America from Hamburg, Germany. In 1747 he was in Lancaster. He is thought to have been the first Jewish physician in Pennsylvania. (*PAJHS*, IX, 30; *UJE*, VIII, 426f)

COHEN, Isaac.³ Died sometime between 1787 and 1797, Charleston. A merchant, he was the son of Moses Cohen,² and the husband of Judith Lyon. (*EJMC*, 7; *MSGC; WAJA*)

COHEN, Isaac.⁴ June 27, 1772, Nobletown, Pennsylvania—probably before 1810. Son of Jacob Raphael Cohen. (*MSGC; SIR*)

COHEN, Isaac.⁵ June 26, 1793, Charleston —September 6, 1871, Savannah. This son of Moses Cohen⁵ was married to Rebecca Sheftall on November 20, 1816, in Savannah. (*Wills*, 79)

COHEN, Isaac.⁶ January 18, 1794—September 22, 1800. Son of Solomon Cohen,¹ he was buried in Georgetown, South Carolina. (*EVJC*)

COHEN, Isaac A. About 1798, Charleston —September 29, 1819, Williamsburg, South Carolina. (*EOJCC*, 29)

COHEN, Israel I. April 8, 1751, Oberdorf, Germany—July 29, 1803, Richmond. This son of Joshua Cohen was a constable in Richmond, and one of the founders of Congregation Beth Shalome. The Cohens of Baltimore are his descendants. On December 21, 1787, he was married to Judith Solomon, in England. (*MHM*, XVIII, 362f; *UJE*, II, 53; III, 234, 236)

COHEN, Jacob.¹ A prominent trader, he was in New Amsterdam in 1655. (*AJAM*, III, 3)

COHEN, Jacob.² In 1759 he was a merchant in Long Island. On September 3, 1760, he was married to Charity Hays,² in New York City. (*MEAJA*, 209; *PAJHS*, XXVII, 387; *Pool*, 331; *SIR*)

COHEN, Jacob.³ Son of Moses Cohen, he lived in Charleston. He was taken prisoner by the English during the Revolutionary War. Cf. Jacob Cohen.⁶ (*EJSC*, 91, *et passim; MHM*, XVIII, 360; *PAJHS*, XX, 96f)

COHEN, Jacob.⁴ His Revolutionary activities, begun as early as 1776, included his commandeering a company of cavalry in Cumberland County, Virginia. He was a silversmith. He was married to Margaret, who was probably a Christian. (*PAJHS*, XX, 96f; *WAJA*)

COHEN, Jacob.⁵ Died June, 1800, Charleston. (*Wills*, 37)

COHEN, Jacob.⁶ About 1740, probably in England—December 16, 1808, Charleston. Son of Moses Cohen,² he was a vendue master. Cf. Jacob Cohen.³ (*MSGC; SCHGM*, XXXII, 249f)

COHEN, Jacob.⁷ November 5, 1796, Georgetown, South Carolina—June 13, 1871, Charleston. Son of Solomon Cohen,¹ he was married to Rachel Lopez² on February 19, 1816, and then to Sarah Barrett. (*EOJCC*, 81; *MSGC*)

COHEN, Jacob A. Died about 1800, Charleston. A shopkeeper in Charleston sometime between 1783 and 1800. (*EJSC*, 279; *WAJA*)

COHEN, Jacob I.[1] January 2, 1744, Oberdorf, Germany—October 9, 1823, Philadelphia. This son of Joshua Cohen resided first in Lancaster and then in Charleston for a short time. He lived in Richmond intermittently from 1781 through 1799. He settled finally in Philadelphia, where he served as president of Congregation Mikveh Israel in 1810 and 1811. A prominent Mason, he owned a fine library. As a merchant and banker he speculated in land. He was in a business partnership with Isaiah Isaacs of Richmond, and he also had business dealings with Daniel Boone of Kentucky. Cohen fought in the Revolution. His first wife was Elizabeth Whitlock Mordecai; his second wife was Rachel Jacobs.[1] Cf. Isaiah Cohan and Jacob Isaiah Cohan. (*Coldoc*, 115, *et passim*; *ELJR*, 15f; *MHM*, XVIII, 359f; *UJE*, III, 233f; V, 598; *WW*, 70, *et passim*)

COHEN, Jacob I.[2] September 16, 1784, Charleston—October 16, 1849, New York City. Son of Gershom Cohen, he was married to Grace Seixas on April 5, 1814. (*MSGC*)

COHEN, Jacob I., Jr.[3] September 30, 1789, Richmond—April 6, 1869, Baltimore. This son of Israel I. Cohen was a banker who was prominent in public affairs. He fought to eliminate civil and political disabilities of the Jews in Maryland. In 1826 he was elected to the Baltimore city council, and served as its president from 1845 through 1851. He aided in the organization of the Philadelphia, Wilmington, and Baltimore Railroad. (*MHM*, XVIII, 364f; *UJE*, III, 234)

COHEN, Jacob Philip. In 1786 he came to Savannah. (*SRB*)

COHEN, Jacob Raphael. About 1738, perhaps in the Barbery states—September 9, 1811, Philadelphia. In 1778 he was in Montreal. Later in Philadelphia, he became hazzan of Congregation Mikveh Israel, and he was also hazzan, mohel, and shohet for Congregation Shearith Israel in Montreal and in New York City. (*Coldoc*, 55, *et passim*; *MIPR*; *MSGC*; *PAJHS*, XXI, 142, *et passim*; XXVII, 34, *et passim*; *Sack*, 62; *SIMR*; *WW*, 121, *et passim*)

COHEN, Jacob Solomon. In Philadelphia in 1782. (*PAJHS*, XXVII, 462)

COHEN, Johannes. In America in 1745. (*ILI*)

COHEN, Joseph. About 1745, Elberfeld, Westphalia—August 1, 1822, London. In 1766 and 1768 he was in Philadelphia. He fought in the Revolutionary War. In 1798 he served as shohet for Congregation Shearith Israel in New York City; he later served Congregation Beth Elohim in Charleston. He was a clerk for the Gratz brothers. Although he visited briefly in America, he returned to England to live. He was married in England, first to Rose Barnet and then to Hannah Moses. (*Memoirs* I, 27, 29-31; *MSGC*; *PAJHS*, IX, 36; *WW*, 51)

COHEN, Joseph M. In Philadelphia in 1783. (*MIPR*)

COHEN, Joseph Simon. 1791—February 3, 1858, Philadelphia. This son of Solomon Myers Cohen was a graduate of the University of Pennsylvania. An attorney, he was admitted to the bar in 1813. From 1840 until 1853 he was prothonotary of the Supreme Court of Pennsylvania. (*Morais*, 412, 432; *MSGC*; *PAJHS*, IX, 35; *WW*, 202, *et passim*)

COHEN, Joseph Solomon. In 1772 he was an Indian trader in Pennsylvania. (*WW*, 70)

COHEN, Joshua.[1] June 28, 1788—September 12, 1788. Son of Israel I. Cohen. (*MHM*, XVIII, 362, 364)

COHEN, Joshua.[2] Born 1788, Richmond. Son of Asher Cohen. (*ELJR*, 33)

COHEN, Joshua J. In Philadelphia in 1784. (*MIPR*)

COHEN, Judah. Also listed as Judah Joseph Cohen. He may have been a son of Isaac A. Cohen. In 1779 he was a merchant in Philadelphia. (*MIPR*; *MSP*; *PAJHS*, III, 149)

COHEN, Mrs. Judith. In Savannah in 1785. She may have been the wife of Moses Cohen.[8] (SRB)

COHEN, Levi. In Charleston sometime between 1783 and 1800. (EJSC, 279)

COHEN, Levi A. In 1747 he came to New York City from Germany. (MSP)

COHEN, Levy.[1] Died April, 1784, Corlear Hook, New York. Son of Isaac A. Cohen. (MSP; Pool, 503)

COHEN, Levy.[2] In New York City in 1785. (PAJHS, XXI, 148; XXVII, 43)

COHEN, Lewis (Levy) J. (I). July 23, 1800, Lancaster—April 14, 1868, Maida Vale, Middlesex, England. Son of Joseph Cohen, he was married to Sophia Andrade. (MSGC; PAJHS, IX, 36)

COHEN, Mrs. Margaret. Wife of Jacob Cohen[3] whom she married before 1798. She lived in Charleston. It is doubtful that she was Jewish. (WAJA)

COHEN, Maria I. September 30, 1794, Richmond—January 23, 1834, Baltimore. Daughter of Israel I. Cohen, she was also known as Miriam. (MHM, XVIII, 364, 370)

COHEN, Mayer M. In Philadelphia in 1782. Cf. Myer M. Cohen. (Morais, 15)

COHEN, Mendes I. May 25, 1796, Richmond—May 7, 1879, Baltimore. This son of Israel I. Cohen was a prominent banker and public servant who served a term in the Maryland House of Delegates in 1847. He fought in the War of 1812. After his retirement he traveled abroad extensively. He donated a sum of money to Johns Hopkins University. (ELJR, 30f; MSGC; UJE, III, 234)

COHEN, Meyer. In New York City in 1736. Cf. Myer Cohen. (PAJHS, XXIII, 151)

COHEN, Mordecai. About 1763; Zamosc, Poland—July 8, 1848, Charleston. A planter, he was one of the wealthiest and most philanthropic men of South Carolina. From 1826 until 1832 he was commissioner of markets for Charleston. In 1795 he was married to Leah Lazarus in Charleston. (EJSC, 134, et passim; EOJCC, 32; UJE, III, 116, 252; Wills, 37)

COHEN, Moses.[1] In New York City in 1734. (PAJHS, XXI, 33)

COHEN, Moses.[2] 1709, England—April 19, 1762, Charlestown. A shopkeeper, he came to Charlestown by 1750. He was the first "rabbi"—probably a volunteer hazzan—of Congregation Beth Elohim there. He was married to Dinah Comigle. (EJSC, 30, et passim; MSGC; Wills, 37)

COHEN, Moses.[3] Born 1754, Charlestown. He fought in the Revolution. (JRMP)

COHEN, Moses.[4] Born September 13, 1761, "Sckenekouty," New York. Son of Jacob Cohen.[2] (SIR)

COHEN, Moses.[5] 1768—October 15, 1829, Savannah. This son of Isaac Cohen[3] was in Charlestown in 1779. In June, 1791, he was married to Rachel Moses.[1] (MSGC; PAJHS, XIX, 152)

COHEN, Moses.[6] Son of Isaac Cohen,[3] he was probably in Charleston before 1800. (MSGC)

COHEN, Moses.[7] In Philadelphia in 1782. He opened an intelligence office there in 1782. (PAJHS, VI, 50; Schappes, 581)

COHEN, Moses.[8] About 1747—1790, Savannah. This son of Liepman Cohen came to Charlestown from England about 1772. He went to Savannah in 1774, where he married Judith de Lyon. He fought in the Revolutionary army. (SRB; Wills, 75)

COHEN, Moses.[9] May 1, 1790—September 4, 1790. Son of Solomon Cohen,[1] he was buried in Georgetown, South Carolina. (EVJC)

COHEN, Moses.[10] In Philadelphia in 1795. A poor Jew, he may have come from Hamburg, Germany, and probably left immediately. (MIPR)

COHEN, Myer. A shohet for Congregation Shearith Israel in 1728. (Pool, 229)

COHEN, Myer M. Died 1799, Richmond. A watchmaker, he was in Philadelphia in 1782, and in Richmond in 1790. A Whig, he took refuge in Philadelphia during the Revolution, but served in the Philadelphia militia. He later lived in New York City. (*MEAJB*, 216; *MIPR*; *PAJHS*, XIX, 66f; XX, 104; *WW*, 96)

COHEN, Phila. October 10, 1787—June 5, 1805. Daughter of Gershom Cohen, she was married to Aaron Moïse in April, 1805. She lived in Charleston. (*MSGC*)

COHEN, Philip I. April 17, 1793, Richmond—September 30, 1852, Norfolk. This son of Israel I. Cohen served in the War of 1812. He was postmaster of Norfolk. On January 25, 1826, he was married to Augusta Myers. (*ELJR*, 30; *MHM*, XVIII, 370)

COHEN, Philip Jacob.[1] Died September 22, 1790, Savannah. This son of Liepman Cohen was a German who came to America by way of England. In 1772 he was a merchant in Charlestown. He fought in the Revolution. (*EJSC*, 91f; *ENAJA*; *SRB*; *Wills*, 75)

COHEN, Philip Jacob.[2] About 1781—May 20, 1866, Charleston. In June, 1799, he was married to Eleanor Moses. (*EOJCC*, 61; *MSGC*)

COHEN, Rachel.[1] Daughter of Emanuel Myers Cohen, she was married to Solomon Bunn. (*PAJHS*, XXIII, 152; XXXIII, 210)

COHEN, Rachel.[2] Daughter of Samuel Myers Cohen.[1] (*PAJHS*, XXXIII, 210)

COHEN, Rachel.[3] 1777—August 18, 1838, Columbia, South Carolina. Daughter of Jacob Raphael Cohen, she lived in Columbia, South Carolina. On May 22, 1803, she was married to Isaac Lyons. (*MIPR*; *MSGC*; *Wills*, 15)

COHEN, Rachel.[4] Daughter of Joseph Cohen. (*MSGC*)

COHEN, Rachel.[5] Daughter of Moses Cohen,[2] she was married to Nathans. (*MSGC*)

COHEN, Rebecca.[1] In Philadelphia in 1764. Daughter of Samuel Myers Cohen,[1] she was married to Mathias Bush. (*PAJHS*, XXXIII, 202, 210)

COHEN, Rebecca.[2] Before 1796—July 5, 1840. Daughter of Solomon M. Cohen. (*MSGC*)

COHEN, Rebecca.[3] November 2, 1797, Charleston—March 3, 1876, Nyack, New Jersey. Daughter of Moses Cohen,[5] she was married to Abraham Isaacs.[3] (*MSGC*)

COHEN, Rebecca.[4] May 5, 1800—April 16, 1884. Daughter of Philip Jacob Cohen,[2] she was married to Jacob Moïse. (*MSGC*)

COHEN, Richea.[1] 1731—1801. Daughter of Samuel M. Cohen,[1] she was married to Barnard Gratz on December 10, 1760. (*MSGC*; *PAJHS*, XXXIII, 210)

COHEN, Richea.[2] Daughter of Jacob Raphael Cohen, she was married to Abraham Forst sometime after 1811. (*MIPR*)

COHEN, Rina. In Savannah in 1785. Daughter of Moses Cohen,[8] she was married to David Mordecai. (*MSGC*; *SRB*)

COHEN, Robert. This son of Jacob Cohen[4] lived in Alexandria, Virginia. He probably did not profess Judaism. (*WAJA*)

COHEN, Sally. 1776, Philadelphia—September 29, 1849, New York. Daughter of Jacob Cohen,[2] she was married to Eleazar Leon in 1807. (*MSGC*; *PAJHS*, XXVII, 55; *Pool*, 331f)

COHEN, Samson. Son of Samuel Myers Cohen.[1] (*PAJHS*, XXXIII, 210)

COHEN, Samuel. He came to America from Jerusalem as an itinerant preacher and money collector. He was known as "rabbi" to Ezra Stiles in Newport in 1775. While he was in Newport, he preached in the synagogue. (*Coldoc*, 100f; *PAJHS*, X, 18, 21f; 27, 184)

COHEN, Samuel Myers.[1] February, 1703—September 21, 1743, New York City. This son of Emanuel Myers Cohen served as shohet and bodek at Congregation Shearith Israel in New York City. A merchant, he was elected constable in New York City in 1730. He was married to Rachel Levy.[1] (*MCCCNY*, IV, 27; *MSGC*; *PAJHS*, XVIII, 121; *Pool*, 228f)

COHEN, Samuel Myers.[2] About 1744—February 15, 1796, New York City. This son of Abraham Myers Cohen[1] was a prominent merchant who served in the Revolutionary army. In 1773 he was president of Congregation Shearith Israel in

New York City. He was married to Belle Simon. (*Pool*, 262f)

COHEN, Samuel Myers.[3] Died 1863. Son of Solomon Myers Cohen. (*MSGC*)

COHEN, Mrs. Sarah.[1] Wife of Abraham Myers Cohen.[1] (*PAJHS*, XXXIII, 210)

COHEN, Mrs. Sarah.[2] 1737—June 7, 1784, Philadelphia. Widow of Henry Marks. (*MSGC; MSP; PAJHS*, VI, 108)

COHEN, Sarah.[3] June 12, 1766—October 25, 1853, Charleston. This daughter of Isaac Cohen[3] was the second wife of David Nunez Cardozo[1] in 1785. (*EOJCC*, 12; *MSGC; WAJA*)

COHEN, Sarah.[4] 1791—March 1, 1828. Daughter of Gershom Cohen, she was married to Aaron Moïse on December 2, 1807. (*MSGC*)

COHEN, Sarah M. Died November 19, 1850. Daughter of Solomon M. Cohen. (*MSGC*)

COHEN, Simon Odler. In New York City about 1788. Cf. Simon Adler and Simon Odler. (*PAJHS*, XXVII, 43)

COHEN, Solomon.[1] October 13, 1757—May 23, 1835, Georgetown, South Carolina. This son of Moses Cohen[2] was a postmaster and tax collector in Georgetown. He was married to Ella Moses Hart on October 25, 1797. (*EJMC*, 7; *EJSC*, 127, *et passim; MSGC*)

COHEN, Solomon.[2] 1782, London—January 24, 1824. Son of Joseph Cohen, he was married to Mary Isaacs. (*MSGC*)

COHEN, Solomon.[3] In Philadelphia in 1782. (*MIPR*)

COHEN, Solomon.[4] 1777, Charlestown—April 6, 1850. Also known as Solomon Jacob Cohen. This son of Isaac Cohen[3] served as an ensign in the War of 1812. He was married to Eleanor B. (*ELODN*, 29; *MSGC; Reznikoff*, 104f)

COHEN, Solomon I. Born 1791, Richmond. Son of Israel I. Cohen, he lived in Richmond. (*MHM*, XVIII, 370)

COHEN, Solomon Myers. About 1744—February 15, 1796, New York City. Son of Abraham Myers Cohen,[1] he was married to Belle Simon. (*PAJHS*, XVIII, 99; XXXIII, 210)

COHEN, William. This son of Jacob Cohen[4] lived in Alexandria, Virginia. He probably did not profess Judaism. (*WAJA*)

COHEN, Wolf Levy. In Philadelphia in 1784. (*MIPR*)

COHEN, Yitlah. Born June, 1769, New York City. Daughter of Jacob Cohen.[1] (*SIR*)

COHEN, Zachariah. In 1735 he was married to Eleanor Phillips, in Newport, by Reverend James Searing. He was a gunner on a privateer. (*JNEB*, 8; *PAJHS*, XXXV, 293)

COHN, Friedrich. A merchant in Philadelphia in 1779. (*PAJHS*, III, 149)

COHON, Mrs. In Boston in 1790. (*PAJHS*, XXIII, 86)

COHON, Simon. In Halifax, North Carolina with his family in 1790. It is doubtful that he was Jewish. (*Census A, North Carolina*)

COLEMAN, Byla. Granddaughter of Isaac Levy,[1] she was in New York City in 1744. (*NYHSW*, IV, 57; *PAJHS*, XXIII, 152)

COLEMAN, Coleman. Grandson of Isaac Levy,[1] he was in New York City in 1744. (*NYHSW*, IV, 57; *PAJHS*, XXIII, 152)

COLEMAN, Solomon. In Philadelphia in 1783. (*MIPR*)

COLLMUS. This family of three is known to have come to Baltimore from Bohemia in 1798. (*UJE*, II, 53)

COLLY, Cox'n. An itinerant, he lived in Philadelphia in 1735. He was connected with the Frank family. (*LIL*, 3, *et passim*)

COLLY, Rachel. Wife of Cox'n Colly, she was in New York City in 1749 about to leave for Curaçao. (*LIL*, 3f; *PAJHS*, XXI, 60)

COLMAN, Solomon. Also listed as Collman Salomons. On August 26, 1736, he arrived in Savannah from London. In 1729 he was in New York City. He was a merchant shipper associated with Abraham Minis. Cf.

Collman Salomons. (*Coulter*, 68; *MEAJB*, 292, 321)

COMIGLE, Dinah. Wife of Moses Cohen[2] of Charlestown. After his death she was married to Joseph David in Charlestown, about 1763. (*EJSC*, 45; *MSGC*; *Wills*, 37)

COMPASS, Isaac. In Georgia about 1735. He was married to Rebecca Young. (*Coulter*, 68f)

COMPASS, Jacob. In Georgia about 1735. (*Coulter*, 69)

COMPOS, Manual Rodriques. A merchant in New York City in 1746. (*MSP*)

COOTY, Rabba. In 1666 he was a merchant in New York City. (*AJAM*, III, 5)

CORAES, Aaron. In New York City in 1789. (*SIR*)

CORAES (CORAER), Joseph. In New York City in 1789. (*SIR*)

CORDEA, Hester. In Maryland in 1674. It is doubtful that she was Jewish. (*AJAM*, III, 5)

CORDEVA, Moses de. In New York City about 1740. (*PAJHS*, XXI, 45)

CORDOVA, Mr. de. Son of Ralph de Cordova, he was in Philadelphia before 1800. (*MIPR*)

CORDOVA, Emanuel de. In the French and Indian War he served with the British. In 1768 he was in Montreal, engaged in fur trading. (*HSIM*, 11; *PAJHS*, I, 117; *UJE*, II, 651)

CORDOVA, Jacob Haim de. A stranger in New York City in 1762. (*SIR*)

CORDOVA, Mrs. Jacob Haim de. In New York City in 1762. (*SIR*)

CORDOVA, Joseph. In Philadelphia in 1783. (*MIPR*)

CORDOVA, Myer. In Philadelphia in 1783. (*MIPR*)

CORDOVA, Ralph. In Philadelphia before 1800. (*MIPR*)

CORDOVA, Simha. Born February 16, 1762, New York City. Daughter of Jacob Haim de Cordova. (*SIR*)

CORIELL, Abraham. In 1702 he was a merchant, probably in America. (*GAV*, 72)

CORREA, Manuel Alvares. A merchant from the West Indies, he appeared in a Newport court about 1747. (*JNEB*, 11; *PAJHS*, XXXVII, 392)

CORTISSOZ, Imanuel. A merchant in Charlestown in 1762. (*EJSC*, 43)

COSTA, Dr. da. Buried in New York City about 1789. (*Pool*, 309)

COSTA, Mr. da.[1] Born October 22, 1762, South Carolina. Son of Isaac da Costa.[1] (*JRMP*)

COSTA, Mr. da.[2] About 1776—March, 1790, Charleston. Son of Isaac da Costa,[1] he died of a dogbite. (*MSGC*; *SCHGM*, XXI, 28)

COSTA, Mrs. da. In New York City in 1795. (*PAJHS*, XXVII, 59)

COSTA, Aaron da. Son of Isaac da Costa.[2] (*EJSC*, 279; *MSGC*)

COSTA, Abraham da. By 1750 he was in South Carolina, and in Georgetown, South Carolina, he became a merchant. In 1791 he applied for admission to Congregation Mikveh Israel in Savannah, and he is reported to have cut his throat in Savannah in 1785. He was married to Rebecca Pimenta about 1765. (*EJSC*, 32, et passim; *MISR*; *PAJHS*, XII, 44; *SRB*)

COSTA, Benjamin Mendes da. In Philadelphia about 1780. (*MIPR*)

COSTA, Daniel Nunes da. A merchant in New York City in 1728. (*Pool*, 14, 309; *SIR*)

COSTA, Mrs. Esther da. Died June 6, 1766, New York City. (*Pool*, 309; *SIR*)

COSTA, Isaac da.[1] About 1721, probably England—November 23, 1783, Charleston. In 1750 he came to Charlestown from London, and became the first hazzan of Congregation Beth Elohim. He was probably the most outstanding Jew of Charlestown before the Revolution. An ardent patriot, he supported the American side during the Revolution. He left Charleston during the British occupation. A merchant, he was very active in the Masons as well as being a leader in the general community. He was married to Sarah Pimenta. (*Coldoc*, 116, *et passim*; *EJSC*, 32, *et passim*; *EOJCC*, 105; *MEAJA*, 139f; *MEAJB*, 226, *et passim*; *UJE*, III, 115, 118, 444; *WAJA*)

COSTA, Isaac da, Jr.[2] 1746—July 20, 1809, Charleston. Nephew of Isaac da Costa,[1] he lived in Charleston for about forty years. (*Coldoc*, 116, *et passim*; *EJSC*, 91, *et passim*; *EOJCC*, 106; *MIPR*)

COSTA, Isaac de. In Georgia in 1733. (*Coulter*, 71)

COSTA, Isaac Gomez da. In New York City in 1795. (*PAJHS*, XXVII, 58)

COSTA, Jacob da. In 1746 he was in New York City and was buried there on February 10, 1780. (*PAJHS*, XXI, 79; *Pool*, 309)

COSTA, John da. In New York City in 1738. (*NYHSW*, V, 115)

COSTA, Jona de. In New York City in 1775. (*PAJHS*, XI, 84)

COSTA, Jose de. In New York City about 1788. (*PAJHS*, XXVII, 43)

COSTA, Joseph. In 1780 he was a benefactor of Harvard University. It is highly doubtful that he was Jewish. (*PAJHS*, XIX, 110)

COSTA, Joseph da. 1759, Charlestown—December 21, 1809, Kingston, Jamaica. Son of Isaac da Costa,[1] he was a merchant. He was married to Rebecca de Paz on March 21, 1786. (*ELODN*, 33; *MSGC*; *Reznikoff*, 16)

COSTA, Joseph de. A merchant in New Amsterdam in 1655 (*AJAM*, III, 5)

COSTA, Joseph R. Probably from Kingston, Jamaica. In 1792 he was in Philadelphia. (*MIPR*)

COSTA, Manuel de. In 1728 he was in New York City. A man named Manuel Vaz de Costa left London for New York City about 1722. (*PAJHS*, XXX, 33; XXXV, 176; XLII, 74)

COSTA, Matthias. In Maryland in 1671. It is doubtful that he was Jewish. (*AJAM*, III, 5)

COSTA, Moses da. Son of Isaac de Costa.[2] (*MSGC*)

COSTA, Rachel da.[1] Daughter of Isaac da Costa,[1] she was married to Abraham Sasportas in Charlestown in September, 1778. (*EJMC*, 5)

COSTA, Rachel da.[2] 1761, Newport—July 30, 1808, New York City. Daughter of Jacob da Costa, she was married to Baruch Hays in New York City on April 13, 1783. (*MIPR*; *MSP*; *Pool*, 309)

COSTA, Rachel de. In May, 1775, she was married to Jacob Tobias in Charlestown. (*EJMC*, 5)

COSTA, Rebecca da. Daughter of Isaac da Costa.[2] (*MSGC*)

COSTA, Samuel da. Died September 16, 1794, Savannah. This son of Isaac da Costa[1] was a Charlestown merchant. In 1785 he was in Philadelphia. On February 12, 1794, he was married to Esther de Pass in Savannah. (*EOJCC*, 103; *MIPR*; *Reznikoff*, 16; *SRB*)

COSTA, Samuel Noe. A servant in Georgia in 1733. (*Coulter*, 91)

COSTA, Sarah da.[1] May have been a daughter of Isaac da Costa.[1] In April, 1779, she was married to Colonel David Maysor. (*MSGC*)

COSTA, Sarah da.[2] 1767—December 19, 1816. Wife of David Sarzedas. (*MSGC*)

COSTAR, Isaac de. In 1750 he was elected as constable in New York City. It is doubtful that he was Jewish. (*MCCCNY*, V, 308)

COSTELLO, Moses. In New York City in 1794. (*SIR*)

COSTER, Ezekiel de. In Boston in 1790. It is doubtful that he was Jewish. (*PAJHS*, XXIII, 87)

COSTER, Mrs. Ezekiel de. In Boston in 1790. It is doubtful that she was Jewish. (*PAJHS*, XXIII, 87)

COSTER, Isaac de. On November 2, 1699, he was married to Mary Temple in Massachusetts. It is doubtful that he was Jewish. (*AJAM*, III, 5)

COURLANDER, Jacob Judah. In a receipt book of Isaac Moses dated about 1785, he is listed as Judah Jacob Courlander. In 1786 he was in Philadelphia and in New York City. (AJA; MIPR; PAJHS, XXI, 159)

COUTINHO, Issac. A merchant in New York City in 1676. (AJAM, III, 5)

COWAN, Dr. Barnet. Also known as Barnett Coan and Bernard Cowen. In New York City in 1786. (PAJHS, XXII, 162)

COWEN, Jacob. In Charlestown about 1771. It is doubtful that he was Jewish. (SCHGM, XLIV, 175)

CRASTO, Abraham de. In New York City in 1744. Cf. below. (PAJHS, XXI, 47)

CRASTO, Abraham Mendes de. In New York City in 1746. Cf. above. (PAJHS, XXI, 48f)

CRASTO, Benjamin. In New York City in 1794. (SIR)

CRASTO, Daniel Mendez de. In New York City about 1740. (PAJHS, XXI, 45, 55)

CRASTO, Jacob Lopes de. In 1733 he was in Savannah. In 1737 he married Zipporah, the former wife of the late David Lopez de Pax. Crasto was naturalized in Jamaica, B.W.I., about 1740. (Coulter, 71; CRG, II, 185; Hugsoc, XXIV, 2)

CRASTO, Judith de. Born April 2, 1738, Savannah. Daughter of Jacob Lopes de Crasto. (SRB)

CRASTO, Rachel. Born July 26, 1736, Savannah. Daughter of Jacob Lopes de Crasto. (SRB)

CRASTO, Ralph. Born June 12, 1739, Savannah. Son of Jacob Lopes de Crasto. (SRB)

CRASTO, Solomon da. In Philadelphia in 1792; in New York City in 1794. (MIPR; PAJHS, XXVII, 59)

CRASTO, Mrs. Zipporah. Wife of Jacob Lopes de Crasto, she had been married previously to David Lopez de Pax. Cf. Mrs. Zipporah de Pax. (Coulter, 71; CRG, II, 185)

CRATE, Daniel de. In New York City in 1746. Cf. Daniel Mendez de Crasto. (PAJHS, XXI, 51)

CRESSON, Warder. July 13, 1798, Philadelphia—November 6, 1860, Jerusalem. After studying many Christian sects he converted to Judaism and changed his name to Michael C. Boaz Isreal. His conversion shocked his family so greatly that they challenged his sanity. At the ensuing trial he successfully defended his sanity. Influenced by Isaac Leeser, he wrote extensively on Jewish themes. He was the first U.S. Consul to Palestine, and eventually founded and settled in an agricultural settlement there. (UJE, III, 410; WW, 238; JE, IV, 354f)

CUNICA, Isaac de. On July 12, 1737, he came to Georgia from London. (Hyamson, 158; PAJHS, X, 82; SRB)

CUSHELL, Fanny, 1749—August 1/15, 1809, New York City. Her first husband was Samuel Lazarus, in March, 1777; her second husband was Michael Isaacs, after 1798. (MSGC; PAJHS, XVIII, 109; XXVII, 373; Pool, 278, et passim; SIR; Wills, 5)

D

DAIKLAIN, Mayer. In Philadelphia in 1782. Cf. Myer Derkeim. (*Morais*, 15)

DANDRADA, Salvador. In 1655 he was a trader in New Amsterdam. (*AJAM*, III, 5)

DANIEL, Henry. About 1743—August 18, 1799, New York City. A learned man, he was in business in New York City. (*PAJHS*, XVIII, 104; *Pool*, 279; *SIR*)

DANIEL, the Jew. In New York City in 1696. (*AJAM*, III, 5)

DANIELS, Henry. Died about 1798, New York City. A glass grinder. (*Pool*, 279)

DARMSTADT, Joseph. Died about 1820, Richmond. He came to America as a Hessian sutler with the British Revolutionary forces, and was captured by the Continental forces. He settled in Richmond, where he was engaged as a merchant and a dealer in country produce. A well known public figure, he was prominent in Masonic and social circles. (*ELJR*, 26, *et passim*; *MEAJB*, 219f)

DAVEGA. An additional unlisted member of the Davega family. In Charleston in 1800. (*Census B, South Carolina*)

DAVEGA, Isaac. December 25, 1796, probably in Charleston—January 21, 1835. Son of Moses Davega, he was married to Grace Labatt on June 28, 1815. (*MSGC*)

DAVEGA, Moses. About 1760—July 27, 1833, Charleston. In Charleston by 1788. (*MSGC*)

DAVEGA, Mrs. Sol. 1771, Gibraltar—January 19, 1828, Charleston. Wife of Moses Davega, she lived in South Carolina for forty years. (*EOJCC*, 28; *MSGC*)

DAVID, Baruch. In New York City in 1791. (*SIR*)

DAVID, Brandile Abigail. May 25, 1762—1840. Daughter of Lazarus David, she was married to Andrew Hays[1] in 1778. In 1798 she was in Montreal. (*MSGC; SIR*)

DAVID, David.[1] In North Carolina in 1750. It is highly doubtful that he was Jewish. (*PAJHS*, XXIX, 141; *UJE*, VIII, 237)

DAVID, David.[2] October 14, 1764, Montreal—November 30, 1824, Montreal. Son of Lazarus David, he was a prominent Montreal businessman who was one of the founders of the Bank of Montreal, and a charter member of the Montreal Board of Trade. During the War of 1812 he was a quartermaster in the British army. (*JE*, IV, 458; *UJE*, III, 485)

DAVID, Frances (Fanny). Born 1770. Daughter of Lazarus David of Montreal, she was married to Myer Michaels.[2] (*HSIM*, 15; *MSGC*)

DAVID, Isaac Moses. In Philadelphia in 1782. (*MIPR*)

DAVID, the Jew. A trader in Connecticut in 1659. (*AJAM*, III, 5)

DAVID, Joseph. Died about 1811, Charleston. In 1763 he came from Koenigsburg, Germany, to Charlestown, where he married Dinah Comigle, the widow of Moses Cohen. (*EJSC*, 45, 278; *Wills*, 76)

DAVID, Lazarus. 1734, Swansea, Wales—October 22/30, 1776, Montreal. In 1761 he was married to Phoebe Samuel in Rhode Island. He was a prominent merchant in Montreal. (*JE*, IV, 458f; *PAJHS*, I, 117f)

DAVID, Moses.[1] In Philadelphia in 1784; in New York City in 1786. (*MIPR; PAJHS*, XXI, 160)

DAVID, Moses.[2] 1767, Montreal—September 26, 1814, Sandwich, Ontario. This son of Lazarus David was active in political affairs. He was married to Charlotte Hart. (*JE*, IV, 459; *MSGC*)

DAVID, Rabbi Moses bar. Born 1720, Apta, Poland. In 1772 he met Ezra Stiles while sojourning in Newport. He was probably an itinerant money collector, either for himself or for a Jewish institution. (*PAJHS*, X, 18f)

DAVID, Samuel. October 22, 1766, Montreal—January 3, 1824. This son of Lazarus

David was a Montreal merchant who served in the War of 1812, attaining the rank of lieutenant colonel. He was married to Sarah Hart. (*Coldoc*, 111, *et passim*; *MSGC*; *UJE*, III, 485)

DAVIDS, David. In Philadelphia in 1783. (*MIPR*)

DAVIDS, Hyam. In New York City in 1756. In 1759 he did business with Michael Gratz. (*Byars*, 43; *PAJHS*, XXI, 73)

DAVIS, David. In Philadelphia in 1786. Cf. David Davids. (*MIPR*)

DAVIS, Henry. In New York City in 1792. (*PAJHS*, XXVII, 51; *SIR*)

DAVIS, Israel. In Charleston in 1800. (*EJSC*, 134)

DAVIS, Joseph. In Savannah in 1798. (*MISR*)

DAVIS, Moses. 1759—1843. In 1787 he was in New York City. He then went to Richmond, where he was a tobacco manufacturer. In March, 1813, he was married to Hannah Stork. (*ELJR*, 80f; *Wills*, 42)

DAVIS, Samuel. A native of Quebec, he became a business partner of Baruch Hays in Quebec in 1783. (*Coldoc*, 283)

DEABOAB, Joshua. In New York City in 1748. (*PAJHS*, XXI, 58)

DEAS, Mr. In 1734 he came to Savannah from London. (*SRB*)

DELANY, Mr. In Philadelphia in 1783. (*MIPR*)

DELIEBEN, Israel. 1740, Prague—January 28, 1807, Charleston. In 1770 he came to America, and settled in Charlestown as a merchant. He was briefly in Northumberland, Pennsylvania, in 1774. In 1774 he was shohet and hazzan for Congregation Mikveh Israel in Philadelphia. He served in the Revolutionary army. About 1790 he settled in Savannah. (*EJSC*, 95, *et passim*; *Fish*, 32; *JRMP*; *MSP*; *PAJHS*, XIX, 84; *Reznikoff*, 57, *et passim*; *SRB*; *WW*, 124f)

DEPAZE, Dubec jeune. Son of Samuel, he came to America from Bordeaux in 1797. (*SZ*, 121)

DEPAZE, Marianne Rodrigue Henrique. In 1797 she came from Bordeaux. She was the wife of Samuel. (*SZ*, 121)

DEPAZE, Samuel. In 1797 he came to America from Bordeaux. (*SZ*, 121)

DEPIVEA, Aaron. In Georgia in 1733. Cf. Mr. Pavias. (*JRMP*; *PAJHS*, X, 73)

DERIBERA, Rodrigo. In New York City in 1736. Cf. Rodrigo de Rivera. (*PAJHS*, XXIII, 151)

DERKEIM, Abram. Born 1791, Petersburg, Virginia. Son of Myer Derkeim. (*ELJR*, 33)

DERKEIM, David. Son of Myer Derkeim. (*MSGC*)

DERKEIM, Eliezer. Born 1789, Richmond. Son of Myer Derkeim. (*ELJR*, 33)

DERKEIM, Eliza. Daughter of Myer Derkeim. (*MSGC*)

DERKEIM, Mayer Solomon. Born April 10, 1799. Son of Myer Derkeim. (*ELJR*, 33)

DERKEIM, Mordecai (Marcus). Born May 9, 1788, Richmond. Son of Myer Derkeim. (*ELJR*, 33)

DERKEIM, Moses. Born February 22, 1774. Son of Myer Derkeim. (*ELJR*, 33)

DERKEIM, Myer. About 1748—August 2, 1818, Philadelphia. He came to America from Germany by way of England. He traveled throughout the colonies as an itinerant circumciser. When he was not traveling, he was engaged as a petty merchant. In the middle 1780s he came to Richmond, and settled more or less permanently in Richmond, Charleston, and Philadelphia. He was married to Sarah. Cf. Mayer Daiklain. (*ELJR*, 32f; *MEAJB*, 216f; *MIPR*; *PAJHS*, VI, 109; XIX, 87)

DERKEIM, Rachel. Daughter of Myer Derkeim, she was married to Abraham de Pass in Charleston in August, 1798. (*EJMC*, 7)

DERKEIM, Mrs. Sarah. 1754—September 9, 1825, Philadelphia. Wife of Myer Derkeim. (*ELJR*, 34; *MEAJB*, 217; *PAJHS*, VI, 110)

DERVALL, Rachel. Wife of Joseph Bueno, she was in New York City in 1708. (PAJHS, XXIII, 149; POFNW, 468)

DESMA, Abraham le. Born July 27, 1733, Georgia. Son of Moses le Desma. (*Coulter*, 82)

DESMA, Mrs. Hester le. Wife of Moses le Desma, she was in Savannah in 1733. (*Coulter*, 82)

DESMA, Isaac le. In New York City about 1740. (PAJHS, XXI, 45)

DESMA, Moses le. In Savannah in 1733. Cf. Moses Lidesmo. (*Coulter*, 82)

DESMA, Rachel le. Daughter of Moses le Desma, she was born in Georgia after 1733. (*Coulter*, 82)

DESMA, Rebecca le. Born July 12, 1735/7. Daughter of Moses le Desma. (*Coulter*, 82; SRB)

DESMA, Samuel le. Son of Moses le Desma, he was in Georgia in 1733. (*Coulter*, 82)

DESMA, Ralph le. Born July 25, 1733, Savannah. Son of Moses le Desma. (SRB)

DIAS, Abraham Lopes. In 1796 he came to Louisiana from Bordeaux. (SZ, 121)

DIAS, Daniel Lopes. In 1796 he came to Louisiana from Bordeaux. (SZ, 121)

DIAS, Isaac Fernandas. In New York City as early as 1695. He was either a freeman or a freeholder. (AJAM, III, 6; MCCCNY, II, 163; POFNW, 469)

DINIS, Moses Joseph. Died December 2, 1779, Montreal. (MSP)

DORMISTED, Zodak. In Philadelphia in 1782. (*Morais*, 15)

DORWORA, Abraham B. In New York City in 1727. (*Wills*, 6)

DOUGHLASS. Son of Abraham Doughlass. (SRB)

DOUGHLASS, Abraham. On November 1, 1785, he arrived in Savannah from London, but soon left for Charleston. (SRB)

DOUGHLASS, Mrs. Abraham. Wife of Abraham Doughlass. (SRB)

DOUGHLASS, Jacob. Born December 8, 1785, Savannah. Son of Abraham Doughlass. (SRB)

DUBOIS, Abraham. A French Jew, he was in Pennsylvania in 1744. He seems to have been quite learned in the Hebrew Bible. (ITAH, 34f; MEAJB, 9)

DURASSE, Jacob. In New York City in 1748. (PAJHS, XXI, 58)

DURMIN. In New York City in 1787. (PAJHS, XXVII, 42)

DWOFSIN, Meyer. Exact spelling of this name is uncertain. In Lancaster with his gentile wife and daughter. (AJA)

E

ELCAN, Lyon. In Richmond in 1797. (*PAJHS*, XIX, 61)

ELCAN, Marcus. About 1757—1808, Richmond. He came from Germany, and settled in Richmond by 1782. A wealthy merchant and a leading citizen, he was well read and possessed a fine library in both Jewish and secular literature. He was the first president of Congregation Beth Shalome, and was prominent in Masonic affairs. His wife was Philah. (*ELJR*, 21, *et passim*; *MEAJB*, 188, *et passim*; *PAJHS*, XIX, 61)

ELCAN, Mrs. Philah. About 1760—May 1, 1820, Boston. Wife of Marcus Elcan, she had lived in Richmond. (*Gutstein*, 301; *PAJHS*, XXVII, 206)

ELEAZER, Moses. In South Carolina in 1780. (*EJSC*, 278; *PAJHS*, XIX, 77)

ELIAS, Benjamin. Died 1732, New York City. A merchant, he also acted as a Hebrew teacher and shohet for Congregation Shearith Israel in New York City. (*FEAJ*, 69; *NYHSW*, II, 276; III, 88f; *PAJHS*, XXI, 4, *et passim*)

ELIAS, David. Son of Benjamin Elias, he was naturalized in New York City in 1723. (*NYHSW*, II, 276; *PAJHS*, VI, 105)

ELION, Engel. In Philadelphia in 1797. Cf. Angel Elkin. (*MIPR*)

ELIZER, Bilhah. Born July 17, 1765, Newport. Daughter of Isaac Elizer. (*MSGC*)

ELIZER, Eleazer. October 7, 1761, Newport—September 20, 1821, Charleston. Son of Isaac Elizer, he was postmaster in Greeneville, South Carolina in 1784. In 1813 he was a justice of the peace. (*EJSC*, 128, 141; *ELODN*, 43; *MSGC*)

ELIZER, Frances (Fanny). November 11, 1774, Newport—August 11, 1796, Charleston. Daughter of Isaac Elizer. (*ELODN*, 43; *MSGC*)

ELIZER, Hannah. Born May 21, 1763. Daughter of Isaac Elizer. (*MSGC*)

ELIZER, Isaac. About 1720—January 2, 1807, Charleston. He was a merchant shipper in Newport, where he was also engaged in the slave trade. For a time he was in partnership with Samuel Moses. On July 23, 1763, he was naturalized in New York City. His wife was Richa Isaacs.[1] He died impoverished. (*EJSC*, 134; *Gutstein*, 159; *Hugsoc*, XXIV, 37; *MEAJA*, 125f; *MSGC*)

ELIZER, Josie. Daughter of Isaac Elizer. (*MSGC*)

ELIZER, Moses. Born August 27, 1772, Newport, died Charleston. Son of Isaac Elizer. (*MSGC*)

ELIZER, Priscilla. August 14, 1777, Newport—August, 1796, Charleston. Daughter of Isaac Elizer. (*ELODN*, 43; *MSGC*)

ELKIN, Angel. In Philadelphia in 1786. Cf. Engel Elion. (*MIPR*)

ELKIN, Jonas. In New York City in 1788; in Savannah in 1797. (*MISR*; *SIR*)

ELKIN, Mordecai. In Philadelphia in 1784. (*MIPR*)

ELLIS, Mrs. Mother of Myer J. Ellis, she was in New York City in 1794. (*MSP*)

ELLIS, Jonah. In New York City in 1794. (*SIR*)

ELLIS, Josiah (Yishi). Died October 8, 1798, New York City. Also known as Isaiah. He was a merchant. (*MIPR*; *PAJHS*, XVIII, 103; *Pool*, 276f)

ELLIS, Myer J. 1794, New York City—September 1, 1829, New Orleans. On August 30, 1821, he was married to Frances Polock. He lived also in Charleston. (*ELODN*, 43)

ELVIN, Mr. A Jewish convert to Christianity, he was in Philadelphia in 1763. (*JRMP*)

EMANUEL, Charlotte Jane. 1799—December 1, 1820, Georgetown, South Carolina. Daughter of Michael Emanuel. (*MSGC*)

EMANUEL, Emanuel. In Charleston in 1800. (*EHCBE*, 4)

EMANUEL, Isaac. In 1720 he had a business in Freehold, New Jersey. In 1722 he absconded, leaving many debts. (*PAJHS*, XXXV, 173-181)

EMANUEL, Michael. Died October 19, 1801, Charleston. In New York City in 1800. (*MSGC*)

EMANUEL, Mrs. Michael. In New York City in 1800. (*MSGC*)

EMANUEL, Nathan. Son of Michael Nathan, he was married to Sarah Gomez[2] on February 14, 1816. (*MSGC*)

EMANUEL, Sarah. Born 1800, New York. Daughter of Michael Emanuel, she was married to Jacob Judah Joseph. (*MSGC*)

EN REQUES, Joshua Mordekay. In 1656 he was a merchant in New Amsterdam. (*AJAM*, III, 6)

EPHRAIM, Lyon. In Philadelphia in 1786. (*MIPR*)

ESPINOSA, Isaac. In New York City in 1749. (*PAJHS*, XXI, 60)

ETTING, Asher. Died about 1752. This son of Reuben Etting[1] was a merchant in New York City. He was married to Ritzel Adolphus. (*MSGC*; *PAJHS*, XXI, 45; *Pool*, 268)

ETTING, Benjamin.[1] Died May 24, 1778, Norwalk, Connecticut. This son of Asher Etting was a New York merchant and goldsmith who was naturalized in 1740. In 1769 he became a freeman of New York City. A patriot, he fled before the British occupied New York City. (*PAJHS*, II, 66; *UJE*, IV, 188)

ETTING, Benjamin.[2] March 25, 1798, Baltimore—March 27, 1875, Philadelphia. This son of Reuben Etting[3] was active in public life in Philadelphia. He was a director of the Philadelphia Public Schools, the Secretary of the Mercantile Library, and an active member in the Musical Society of Philadelphia. On October 13, 1830, he was married to Harriet Marx. (*MSGC*; *UJE*, IV, 189; *WW*, 315)

ETTING, Bilhah. December 12, 1785—February 12, 1786. Daughter of Solomon Etting.[1] (*MSGC*)

ETTING, Elijah.[1] August 10, 1724, Frankfort-on-the-Main, Germany—July 3, 1778, York, Pennsylvania. In 1758 he came to America, and on September 24, 1765, he was naturalized. He was a merchant and an Indian trader. On January 5, 1759, he was married to Shinah Solomon. (*Blum*, 3; *Hugsoc*, XXIV, 109; *MSGC*; *PAJHS*, 1, 67; *UJE*, IV, 188)

ETTING, Elijah.[2] September 30, 1784, Lancaster—August 31, 1854, Baltimore. Son of Solomon Etting.[1] (*MSGC*)

ETTING, Elijah Gratz. July 14, 1795, Baltimore—May 25, 1849, Baltimore. This son of Reuben Etting[3] was graduated from the University of Pennsylvania in 1812, and was admitted to the bar as an attorney in 1816. He was the district attorney for Cecil County, Maryland. (*MIPR*; *Morais*, 393)

ETTING, Elizabeth. November 24, 1773—December 27, 1860, Emmitsburg, Missouri. Daughter of Elijah Etting,[1] she was married to Robert Mickle about 1795. (*MSGC*)

ETTING, Esther. Died 1793. Daughter of Asher Etting, she was married to David Hays,[2] in New York City on May 23, 1764. (*MSGC*; *SIR*; *Trachtenberg*, 50)

ETTING, Fanny. October 2, 1766, York, Pennsylvania—January 20, 1828. Daughter of Elijah Etting,[1] she was married to Robert Taylor on March 7, 1793. (*JRMP*; *MSGC*)

ETTING, Frances Gratz. February 16, 1794—August 24, 1854. Daughter of Solomon Etting.[1] (*MSGC*)

ETTING, Henry. May 20, 1799, Baltimore—February 15, 1876, Philadelphia. This son of Reuben Etting[3] was in the U.S. Navy from 1818 until 1871, and retired with the rank of commodore. (*JE*, V, 263; *Morais*, 470; *UJE*, IV, 189)

ETTING, Hetty. March 4, 1770—September 13, 1847. Daughter of Elijah Etting.[1] (*MSGC*)

ETTING, Isabella. September, 1796—January 6, 1800. Daughter of Reuben Etting.[3] (*MSGC*)

ETTING, Joseph.[1] November 17, 1778—1781. Son of Elijah Etting.[1] (*MSGC*)

ETTING, Joseph.[2] January 2, 1788, Lancaster—February 19, 1856. Son of Solomon Etting,[1] he was in New York City about 1793. (*MIPR; MSGC; PAJHS*, XXVII, 55)

ETTING, Judah. Died November 16, 1773. He died at sea on his way to Surinam from New York City. (*SIR*)

ETTING, Kitty.[1] September 15, 1763—April 12, 1837/8. Daughter of Elijah Etting.[1] (*MSGC*)

ETTING, Kitty.[2] November 25, 1799—April 26, 1837, Baltimore. Daughter of Solomon Etting,[1] she was married to Benjamin I. Cohen on December 15, 1819. (*MHM*, XIX, 56; *MSGC*)

ETTING, Miriam. January 27, 1787, Lancaster—August 24, 1808, Georgetown, South Carolina. Daughter of Solomon Etting, she was married to Jacob Myers[7] on July 31, 1806, in Baltimore. (*EVJC*)

ETTING, Moses. Died about 1778, Easton, Pennsylvania. Son of Asher Etting, he was a merchant. (*PAJHS*, II, 66)

ETTING, Richea Gratz. September 18, 1792—June 19, 1881. Daughter of Solomon Etting.[1] (*MSGC*)

ETTING, Rebecca. March 28, 1798—August 5, 1799, Oakland, Maryland. Daughter of Solomon Etting.[1] (*MSGC*)

ETTING, Reuben.[1] Died August 29, 1770, Philadelphia. (*SIR*)

ETTING, Reuben.[2] About 1760—1780, probably in Charlestown. This son of Asher Etting was a bank clerk in Baltimore. He fought in the Revolution, and was captured by the British. He died soon after his release. (*PAJHS*, II, 66; *UJE*, IV, 188)

ETTING, Reuben.[3] June 6, 1762, York, Pennsylvania—June 3, 1848, Philadelphia. This son of Elijah Etting[1] fought in the Revolutionary army, and, in 1794, in the Whiskey Insurrection in western Pennsylvania. He attained the rank of captain before he retired in 1803, but later fought in the War of 1812. In 1801 he was appointed U.S. marshal of Maryland by Thomas Jefferson. In 1804 he settled as a merchant in Philadelphia, where he was prominent in civic affairs. On September 17, 1794, he was married to Frances Gratz in Philadelphia. (*MIPR*; Morais, 393, 459; *UJE*, IV, 188f; *WW*, 50, *et passim*)

ETTING, Sally. September 12, 1776—June 2, 1863. Daughter of Elijah Etting.[1] (*MSGC*)

ETTING, Samuel. January 17, 1796—May 18, 1862. This son of Solomon Etting[1] was wounded in the War of 1812. He was the first president of Congregation Beth Israel in Baltimore. On November 5, 1828, he was married to Ellen Hays. (*MIPR*; *MSGC*; *UJE*, IV, 190)

ETTING, Solomon.[1] July 28, 1764, York, Pennsylvania—August 6, 1847, Baltimore. This son of Elijah Etting[1] moved to Baltimore in 1787, and then to Lancaster, where he became a merchant in partnership with Joseph Simon. He founded a Masonic lodge in Lancaster. He later moved to Philadelphia, and then to Baltimore, where he was a certified shohet. An abolitionist, he was also active in the movement to permit Jews to hold public office in Maryland. In 1826 he became the first Jew to be elected to public office, when he was elected a member of the City Council of Baltimore. He later became president of that body. One of the promoters of the Baltimore and Ohio Railroad, he served on the first board of directors of that company. Etting's first wife was Rachel Simon, September 1, 1783; his second wife was Rachel Gratz,[1] October 26, 1791. (*Markens*, 93f; *MIPR*; Morais, 270, 393; *MSGC*; *PAJHS*, XIX, 58; *UJE*, II, 53; IV, 188; V, 85; *WW*, 125, *et passim*)

ETTING, Solomon.[2] In Baltimore in 1773. (*PAJHS*, VI, 155)

ETTING, William. In Baltimore in 1800. (*Census B, Maryland*)

EZEKIEL, Mr. A resident of New York City, he was married to Esther Lazarus in 1784. (*Douville*, 117)

EZEKIEL, Rabbi. In 1774 he was sent to St. Eustatius from New York City. (*POFNW*, 344)

EZEKIEL, Elizabeth. 1755—February 6, 1837. On March 27, 1775, she was married to Samuel Judah[1] in London. (*MSGC*)

F

FALK, Rebecca. About 1653—January 22, 1740, New York City. Daughter of Rabbi Jerachmeal Falk, she was married to Asher Michaels. (*PAJHS*, XVIII, 121; XXI, 11; Pool, 216f)

FARO, Benjamin. Born April 2, 1687. Son of Isaac Gabay Faro. (*MSGC*)

FARO, Bilhah Gabay. Died 1694, New York City. (*MSGC*)

FARO, Isaac Gabay. A peddler, he was in New York City in 1686 and in 1701. He was married to Esther Bueno de Mesquito. Cf. Isaac Gabay. (*FEAJ*, 66f; *Pool*, 447, 450f)

FARO, Jacob. Born September 18, 1694. Son of Isaac Gabay Faro. (*MSGC*)

FARO, Solomon. Born November 18, 1701, New York City. Son of Isaac Faro. (*Pool*, 451)

FARIERES, Charlotte. On April 23, 1742, she was naturalized in New York City. (*Hugsoc*, XXIV, 30)

FEIS, Moses. Born 1791, Norfolk. Son of Uri Feis. (*ELJR*, 33)

FEIS, Uri. In Norfolk in 1791. (*ELJR*, 33)

FEIS, Mrs. Uri. In Norfolk in 1791. (*ELJR*, 33)

FERERA, David. In 1655 he was in New Amsterdam. An attorney, he also lived in Maryland, and was confined in prison there. (*AJAM*, III, 6; *Grollman, no.* 133)

FERNANDES, Jacob Nunes. In New York City in 1709. (*MEAJA*, 53; *PAJHS*, XXIII, 150; *Pool*, 200)

FERNANDO, Judith. Sister of Abraham Molina, she was in Georgia in 1733. (*Coulter*, 73)

FERREIRA, Elizabeth. In 1798 she came from Bordeaux to America. (*SZ*, 121)

FERRO, Jacob, Jr. About 1740 he was naturalized in New York City. (*PAJHS*, V, 116; XXI, 43)

FLORENTINE, Abraham. Before the Revolution he was in Nova Scotia. About 1780 he was a merchant in New York City. In 1783 he went to England, but returned in 1829 to New York City, where he was a street inspector. (*PAJHS*, XXXVIII, 105f)

FLORES, Abraham Rodriguez. In New York City about 1740. (*PAJHS*, XXI, 43)

FLORES, Isaac. In New York City in 1750. (*PAJHS*, XXI, 61)

FLOUR, Aaron. In 1794 he came to Philadelphia from Bordeaux. (*SZ*, 121)

FONSECA, Abraham. Son of Jacob Fonseca, he was in New York City in 1729. (*PAJHS*, XXI, 21; *WAJA*)

FONSECA, Elias Lopez de. Born New York City. Son of Moses Lopez de Fonseca. (*Emanuel*, 316)

FONSECA, Esther. Daughter of Jacob Fonseca, she was in New York City in 1728. (*WAJA*)

FONSECA, Fernandez de. In Montreal in 1768. (*PAJHS*, I, 117)

FONSECA, Isaac. Son of Jacob Fonseca, he was in New York City in 1728. (*WAJA*)

FONSECA, Isaac Lopez de. Born New York City. Son of Moses Lopez de Fonseca, he was in New York City in 1732. (*Emanuel*, 267f)

FONSECA, Jacob. Died about 1728, probably in New York City. In 1728 he was a merchant in New York City. His wife was Rebecca. (*PAJHS*, XXI, 9; *WAJA*)

FONSECA, Johebet Lopez de. Daughter of Moses Lopez de Fonseca. (*Emanuel*, 316)

FONSECA, Joseph. Son of Jacob Fonseca, he was probably in New York City in 1728. (*WAJA*)

FONSECA, Judith. Daughter of Jacob Fonseca, she may have been in New York City in 1728. (*WAJA*)

FONSECA, Moses Lopez da. Born Barbados. This son of Hakham Lopes of

FONSECA

Curaçao came to New York City to start a business. From 1728 until 1736 he was the reader for Congregation Shearith Israel in New York City. He left there to serve the Jewish community in Curaçao as hazzan. He was married to Miriam Naftali in New York City, and to Rachel Israel in Curaçao. (*Emanuel*, 315f; *Pool*, 206; *UJE*, IV, 355)

FONSECA, Rachel. Daughter of Jacob Fonseca, she was probably in New York City in 1726. (*WAJA*)

FONSECA, Mrs. Rebecca. Wife of Jacob Fonseca, she was in New York City in 1729. (*PAJHS*, XXI, 18; *WAJA*)

FONSECA, Sarah. Daughter of Jacob Fonseca, she was probably in New York City in 1728. (*WAJA*)

FONSECA, Simna Lopez de. Daughter of Moses Lopez de Fonseca. (*Emanuel*, 316)

FORST, Abraham.[1] Came to America from London. In 1782 he left for London but returned later. A prominent Mason, he attained high office, and traveled throughout the colonies, organizing and meeting with local Masonic groups. He was also a merchant in Philadelphia. From 1784 until 1811 he served as shohet for Congregation Mikveh Israel there. He was married to one of the daughters of Jacob R. Cohen. (*MIPR*; *Morais*, 18; *PAJHS*, XIX, 45, et passim)

FORST, Abraham.[2] About 1782—1848. Son of Abraham Forst.[1] (*MIPR*)

FRANCES, Joseph. In 1660 he was a merchant in New Amsterdam for a short time. (*AJAM*, III, 6)

FRANCKFORT, Abraham. In 1683 he was involved in the sale of a slave in Brooklyn, New York. (*Essays*, 63f)

FRANCO, Solomon. The first known Jew in the North American Colonies, on May 2, 1649, he was given funds for passage to Holland. (*AJAM*, III, 6)

FRANK, Abraham. Died February 24, 1792, Philadelphia. Cf. Abraham Franks.[2] (*MIPR*)

FRANKLIN, Judah. In Philadelphia in 1785. (*MIPR*)

A Biographical Dictionary

FRANKS.[1] A child of Joshua Franks, he was expelled with his parents from Boston in 1756. It is doubtful that he was Jewish. (*JNEA*, 25)

FRANKS.[2] Son of Isaac Franks,[2] he died an infant. (*PAJHS*, V, 10)

FRANKS.[3] Son of Isaac Franks,[2] he died an infant. (*PAJHS*, V, 10)

FRANKS, Miss. May 14, 1761, New York City—January 16, 1762. Daughter of Moses B. Franks. (*MSGC*; *SIR*)

FRANKS, Aaron. December 8, 1732—July 21, 1738, New York City. Son of Jacob Franks.[1] (*MSGC*; *PAJHS*, XVIII, 121)

FRANKS, Abigail. January 6, 1744—September 11, 1798. Daughter of David Franks, she was baptized, and was married to Andrew Hamilton III on January 6, 1768. (*MSGC*; *PAJHS*, I, 58)

FRANKS, Abraham.[1] 1721—1797, Montreal. A prominent Canadian merchant, he lived in Quebec until about 1771, when he moved with his family to Montreal. (*HSIM*, 26; *MEAJA*, 251; *SIMR*)

FRANKS, Abraham.[2] A tobacconist and snuff manufacturer from London, he was in Philadelphia in 1772. Cf. Abraham Frank. (*Exponent*, 13; *PAJHS*, XIX, 46)

FRANKS, B. In Philadelphia in 1784. (*MIPR*)

FRANKS, Becca. In America in 1745. (*ILI*)

FRANKS, Benjamin. About 1649—1716. This son of Aaron Franks lived in Barbados. In 1696 he was a jeweler in New York City, and may have been there yet in 1700. He may have been the first Frank in America. He served with Captain William Kidd's pirates but left their ship in India. His wife was Rachel. (*MSGC*; *PAJHS*, XXXI, 229f; *POFNW*, 469; *Shilstone*, xi)

FRANKS, Butzie. In America in 1745.(*ILI*)

FRANKS, David. September 23, 1720, New York City—October 7, 1793, Philadelphia. In 1748 this son of Jacob Franks[1] was elected to the provincial assembly. In his early years he was very active in land speculation in Pennsylvania, Virginia, and some western lands. Although he was an assimilationist, he did maintain some contact with the Jewish community throughout his life. A prominent merchant shipper, he was in partnership with Nathan Levy and many others, both Jewish and gentile. He was also engaged in general merchandising, fur trading, and army purveying, and it was in the latter that he gained prominence. During the French and Indian War, he was occupied in this practice, and also during the Revolution, when he was the chief supplier for the British prisoners of the American forces. Suspected of being a loyalist, he was relieved of his commissary rights by the United States government, and was twice tried for being a Tory. He finally found refuge in New York City. After a short visit to England he returned to New York. He then went to Philadelphia, where he died in a yellow fever epidemic, a poor and obscure figure. On December 17, 1743, he was married to Margaret Evans. (*Coldoc*, 7, *et passim*; *MEAJB*, 7, *et passim*; *MSGC*; *PAJHS*, XVIII, 213f; *Trachtenberg*, 32f; *UJE*, IV, 417; V, 85, 229; VII, 15; VIII, 426f, 545; *WW*, 26, *et passim*)

FRANKS, David Salisbury. Born Philadelphia, died 1793, Philadelphia. This son of Abraham Franks[1] was a merchant in Montreal, where he was president of Congregation Shearith Israel in 1775. He supported the American forces in Canada monetarily and with supplies. When these forces retreated he was forced to flee. While serving as an officer with the Revolutionary army, he was attached to the military staff of Benedict Arnold. Though Franks was under suspicion after Arnold's defection, Franks was eventually completely vindicated. For his services in the Revolution, he was granted four hundred acres of land. After the Revolution he served as a courier for the government, a position he filled in many foreign countries. He was Vice-consul in Marseilles. In 1786 he aided in the negotiation of the treaty of peace with the Emperor of Morocco. He was later associated with the Bank of North America, and was a member of the Pennsylvania Society of Cincinnati. (*Coldoc*, 83, *et passim*; *MEAJA*, 251f; *MEAJB*, 508f; *PAJHS*, I, 57, *et passim*; IV, 81, *et passim*; V, 157, *et passim*; X, 101, *et passim*; XVI, 25f; *UJE*, IV, 418; VIII, 287f; *WW*, 42, *et passim*)

FRANKS, Henry Benjamin. Died 1758. This son of Jacob Franks[1] was naturalized in Yorktown, Pennsylvania, in 1755. His will was filed in Trenton, New Jersey, in 1758. Cf. Naphtali Franks. (*Hugsoc*, XXIV, 51; *PAJHS*, XXV, 125f)

FRANKS, Isaac.[1] Son of Naphtaly Hart Franks, he was in Montreal in 1776. (*MSGC*; *SIMR*)

FRANKS, Isaac.[2] May 27, 1759, New York City—March 4, 1822, Philadelphia. This son of Moses Benjamin Franks enlisted in the American Revolutionary forces in 1776. He served in various capacities including quartermaster and foragemaster. He is known to have rented his house in Germantown to George Washington. He settled in Philadelphia, and was engaged in land speculation with Benjamin Rush. In 1794 he was appointed lieutenant colonel of the second regiment of Philadelphia. In 1795 he was appointed a justice of the peace. In 1819 he became the chief clerk of the Pennsylvania Supreme Court. An active Mason, he was an assimilationist and apparently had no interest in Jews or Judaism. He was married to a gentile, Mary Davidon, on July 9, 1782. (*Coldoc*, 267, *et passim*; *MSGC*; *PAJHS*, IV, 201; V, 7, *et passim*; X, 168f; XIX, 41, *et passim*; *UJE*, IV, 417f; VIII, 433, 477; IX, 322; *WW*, 97, *et passim*)

FRANKS, Isaac.[3] A merchant in Savannah in 1795. (*MISR*; *SRB*)

FRANKS, Jacob.[1] 1688, Germany—January 16, 1769, New York City. This son of Naphtali Franks came to America about 1710, and soon became a freeman of New York City. One of the most prominent merchant shippers of the city in this period, he was the King's agent for New York and the northern colonies, and handled troop supplies. Prominent in Jewish communal affairs, he served in a variety of offices in Congregation Shearith Israel, including the office of president in 1729. He contributed to the building of the steeple of Trinity Church in New York City. In 1712 he was married to Bilhah Abigail Levy. (*Coldoc*, 30, *et passim*; *MEAJA*, 46, *et passim*; *MEAJB*, 6, *et passim*; *MSGC*; *PAJHS*, IV, 189, *et passim*; IX, 33f; XI, 82, *et passim*; *UJE*, IV, 416)

FRANKS, Jacob.[2] Born about 1766. He came to America from England, and was sent to Green Bay as an agent for Igilvy, Gillespie, and Company in 1792. By 1797 he was in business for himself. He established the first sawmills and gristmills in that area. Because he remained loyal to the British during the War of 1812, his property was pillaged. One of the earliest pioneers in the Wisconsin area, he helped develop that area. (*MEAJB*, 410, 506; *PAJHS*, IX, 151f; XIII, 53f; XVI, 27; *UJE*, IV, 418; VII, 534; X, 532)

FRANKS, Jacob (John).[3] January 7, 1747, Philadelphia—May 11, 1814, England. This son of David Franks was baptized on March 20, 1747. He was married to Priscilla Franks, probably in England. (*PAJHS*, I, 58; IV, 199; XVI, 189; XVIII, 214)

FRANKS, Jacob, Jr.[4] Son of Jacob Franks,[2] he was a trader. He was married to Mary Solomons. (*HSIM*, 28f; *JE*, III, 525; *PAJHS*, XIII, 52)

FRANKS, Jacob.[5] About 1787 he was a student in Lancaster at Franklin College. It is doubtful that he was Jewish. (*PAJHS*, XIX, 122f)

FRANKS, John, Jr. In Philadelphia in 1769. He settled finally in Canada, where he became a prominent merchant. (*Coldoc*, 83f; *WW*, 51, 395)

FRANKS, Joshua. In 1756 he was expelled from Boston. It is doubtful that he was Jewish. (*JNEA*, 25)

FRANKS, Mrs. Joshua. In 1756 she was expelled from Boston. It is doubtful that she was Jewish. (*JNEA*, 25)

FRANKS, Mary. January 25, 1748, Philadelphia—August 26, 1754, Philadelphia. Daughter of David Franks, she was baptized on April 7, 1748. She was known also as Polly. She was buried in Christ Churchyard. (*MSGC*; *PAJHS*, I, 58; V, 204f; XVIII, 214)

FRANKS, Michael. In 1754 he served under Colonel George Washington in Virginia. It is doubtful that he was Jewish. (*JPP*, 16; *PAJHS*, II, 180f; XX, 90)

FRANKS, Moses.[1] January 1, 1718, New York City—April 2, 1789, London. This son of Jacob Franks[1] served in the New York militia as early as 1738. He was involved in land speculation in the Illinois country, and was a partner in the Grand Ohio Company. By 1741 he formed a brief partnership with his brother, David. He then moved to London, where he joined his brother, Naphtali, and became a member of the firm of Colebrook, Nesbitt, and Franks. This firm provided supplies to the British forces during the French and Indian War. He moved in high government circles, procuring contracts and seeking financial and political aid for his brother. While maintaining his loyalty to Judaism, he moved in the highest society of London. (*Coldoc*, 11, *et passim*; *MEAJB*, 8, *et passim*; *PAJHS*, I, 56, 71f; II, 92; IX, 33f; XVIII, 213f; XIX, 116f; *UJE*, IV, 416f; X, 371; *WW*, 26, *et passim*)

FRANKS, Moses.[2] Born about 1743, died before 1812. This son of David Franks was engaged in land speculation in the Illinois territory. He studied abroad and at the University of Pennsylvania in 1761. An attorney, he served as attorney general of the Bahamas. He was a Tory. (*JRMP*; *MSGC*; *PAJHS*, IX, 33f; XVIII, 213; XIX, 107; 120)

FRANKS, Moses.[3] A patriot during the Revolution. (*FPNL*, 71f)

FRANKS, Moses Benjamin. Died February 24, 1792, Philadelphia. This son of Benjamin Franks was a tailor in New York City. On October 18, 1748, he was naturalized there, and was made a freeman in 1751. (*JRMP*; *MEAJB*, 137f; *MIPR*; *MSGC*; *PAJHS*, VI, 102)

FRANKS, Myer. A Tory during the Revolution, in 1781 he lived in Ninety-Six, South Carolina. It is doubtful that he was Jewish. (*EJSC*, 104f)

FRANKS, Naphtali (Hart). July 1, 1715, New York City—October 31, 1796, England. This son of Jacob Franks[1] left America for England by 1737. There he became a prominent and powerful merchant shipper and army purveyor. He was active in Jewish and civic affairs, and probably never returned to America. On November 24, 1742, he was married to his cousin, Phila Franks. (*Coldoc*, 241, *et passim*; *MEAJA*, 58, *et passim*; *MEAJB*, 8, *et passim*; *MSGC*)

FRANKS, Naphtali (Henry) Benjamin. Son of Benjamin Franks, he was in New York City in 1728. He was buried there on December 14, 1758. Cf. Henry Benjamin Franks. (*MSGC; NYHSW*, XI, 72; *Pool*, 501)

FRANKS, Phila. Born June 19, 1722. Daughter of Jacob Franks,[1] in 1742 she eloped with Oliver de Lancey, a member of one of New York's outstanding families. She was loyal to the British cause during the Revolution. (*MEAJA*, 66f; *MEAJB*, 104, *et passim; PAJHS*, I, 103)

FRANKS, Rachel (Richa).[1] Daughter of Jacob Franks,[1] in 1769 she went to London to join her brothers after the death of her father. (*MEAJA*, 66, 70; *MEAJB*, 8, 116; *PAJHS*, XXII, 39f; *UJE*, IV, 416)

FRANKS, Mrs. Rachel.[2] Died 1774. Wife of Benjamin Franks, she may have been in America. (*MSGC*)

FRANKS, Rachel.[3] February 16, 1762—January 27, 1818. Daughter of Moses Benjamin Franks, she was married first to Haym Salomon on July 6, 1777; then to David Heilbron on August 24, 1786. Cf. Ritzel Franks. (*MIPR; MSGC*)

FRANKS, Rebecca.[1] Died March 27, 1812. Daughter of Abraham Franks, she was married to Levy Solomons of Canada on May 31, 1775. (*HSIM*, 26; *MEAJA*, 255; *MSGC*)

FRANKS, Rebecca.[2] 1760, Philadelphia—March, 1823, Bath, England. This daughter of David Franks was reared as an Anglican. She was an ardent Tory during the Revolution. One of the leading socialites of Philadelphia, she moved to England and continued in social prominence there. On January 17, 1782, she was married to Sir Henry Johnson. (*MEAJB*, 96, *et passim; MSGC; UJE*, IV, 417; VIII, 477; *WW*, 63, *et passim*)

FRANKS, Rebecca.[3] Probably the daughter of John Franks, she was in Philadelphia in 1799. (*Coldoc*, 83f)

FRANKS, Ritzel. Born May 6, 1762, New York City. Daughter of Moses Benjamin Franks. Cf. Rachel Franks.[3] (*SIR*)

FRANKS, Samuel D. 1783—1831. Son of Isaac Franks,[2] he was a judge in Pennsylvania. He was probably baptized at birth. In 1804 he was married to Sarah May. (*MSGC; PAJHS*, V, 10f)

FRANKS, Sarah.[1] Died November 30, 1733, New York City, at the age of two. Daughter of Jacob Franks.[1] (*Pool*, 209)

FRANKS, Sarah.[2] Died January 12, 1767. Daughter of Abraham Franks, she was married to Moses Benjamin Franks. (*PAJHS*, IV, 201; *Pool*, 502; *SIR*)

FRANKS, Sarah Eliza. Daughter of Isaac Franks,[2] she was probably baptized at birth. On September 9, 1806, she was married to John Huffnagle. (*PAJHS*, V, 7f)

FRANKS, Simon. A wigmaker, he became a freeman of New York City in 1748. (*PAJHS*, VI, 102)

FRAZON (FRAZIER), Joseph. Died February 4, 1703/4. He probably came to North America from Brazil, where his family had lived for about two generations. A shipowner, he had property in Charlestown, Massachusetts. As early as 1697 he lived in Boston, where Cotton Mather attempted to convert him to Christianity. He did extensive trade with the West Indies. He was buried in Newport. (*FEAJ*, 6; *MEAJA*, 105; *PAJHS*, XI, 79; XX, 54f; *UJE*, II, 481; VII, 402)

FRAZON, Moses. A merchant in Boston in 1702. (*JNEA*, 14)

FRAZON (FRAZIER), Samuel. Brother of Joseph Frazon, he was engaged in trade with the West Indies. On one voyage to the West Indies he was captured by Indians, but was finally ransomed. He lived in Boston as early as 1697. (*AJAM*, III, 6; *JNEA*, 14; *MEAJA*, 105f; *UJE*, VII, 402)

FREEZE, Mrs. Abigail de. Wife of Nathan de Freeze, she was in New York City in 1775. (*Pool*, 480)

FREEZE, Nathan de. About 1723—July 22, 1775, New York City. A merchant, he came from Surinam to New York City. His wife was Abigail. Cf. Nathan de Vriest. (*PAJHS*, XVIII, 122; *Pool*, 480; *SIR*)

FROCIS, David. In Georgia about 1735. His wife was Hester. (*Coulter*, 74)

FROCIS, Mrs. Hester. Wife of David Frocis, she was with him in Georgia about 1735. (*Coulter*, 74)

FROIS, Joshua. In New York City in 1747. (*PAJHS*, XXI, 54)

FURTADO, Jacob. A resident of Bordeaux, he was in New York City in 1800. (*Census B, New York*; SZ, 121)

FURTADO, Joseph. A Mason, he was in New York City in 1799. (*PAJHS*, XIX, 32)

FURTH, Susanna. In 1767 she was a midwife in Quebec. It is doubtful that she was Jewish. (*MEAJA*, 223)

G

GABAY, Mr. In Philadelphia in 1796. (*MIPR*)

GABAY, Isaac. Cf. Isaac Gabay Faro.

GABAY, Moses. In June, 1788, he was in Savannah for a short time, but later returned to Jamaica. (*SRB*)

GABAY, Solomon. Born November 18, 1701, New York City. Son of Isaac Gabay. (*MSP*)

GABRIEL, Benjamin Rodrigues. In New York City in 1747. (*PAJHS*, XXI, 55)

GABRIEL, Judah. In Philadelphia in 1786. (*MIPR*)

GABRIEL, Solomon. In New York City in 1788. (*SIR*)

GARCIA, Daniel. In New York City in 1787. (*SIR*)

GARCIA, Hananiel. In Montreal about 1760. He was an army supply man during the French and Indian War. (*HSIM*, 11; *Sack*, 52)

GAST. Son of Hayyim Gast, in 1771 he was a rogue living in Philadelphia. (*MEAJB*, 46f)

GATES, Manuel. In New York City in 1787. (*MIPR*; *PAJHS*, XXVII, 41, 253)

GEDALIA, Isaac. In New York City in 1799. (*PAJHS*, XIX, 33)

GETTING, Isaac. In Philadelphia in 1786. (*MIPR*)

GIDEON, Benjamin. In Hampstead, Georgia, in 1733. (*Coulter*, 75)

GIDEON, Moses. In New York City in 1731. (*PAJHS*, XXI, 27f)

GIDEON, Rowland. In Boston in 1674. (*AJAM*, III, 6)

GOLDSMITH, Benjamin. In 1750 he was a peddler in New York City. (*PAJHS*, XXVII, 246)

GOLDSMITH, Hyam. In New York City in 1788. (*SIR*)

GOLDSMITH, Sarah. Died 1792, Philadelphia. (*PAJHS*, VI, 108)

GOMEZ.[1] Child of Isaac Gomez, Jr.,[6] he died an infant. (*MSGC*)

GOMEZ.[2] Child of Isaac Gomez, Jr.,[6] he died an infant. (*MSGC*)

GOMEZ, Miss.[1] Born about 1794. Daughter of Isaac Gomez, Jr.,[2] she lived only fifteen days. (*MSGC*)

GOMEZ, Miss.[2] Daughter of Lewis Moses Gomez. (*PAJHS*, XI, 141)

GOMEZ, A. I. In New York City in 1798. (*SIR*)

GOMEZ, Aaron L. Probably born before 1800, Wilmington, North Carolina—1860. Son of Moses Mordecai Gomez, he was married to Hetty Hendricks on May 20, 1821. (*MSGC*; *PAJHS*, XVII, 197)

GOMEZ, Abraham.[1] 1742—September 12, 1808, New York City. Son of Mordecai Gomez.[1] (*PAJHS*, XVII, 197; *SIR*)

GOMEZ, Abraham.[2] A resident of Bordeaux, he was in New York City in 1795. He later returned to Bordeaux with his wife, Richa Henricks, and his family. (*PAJHS*, XXVII, 58, 286)

GOMEZ, Abraham M. In New York City in 1795. (*PAJHS*, XXVII, 58)

GOMEZ, B. M. In New York City in 1795. (*PAJHS*, XXVII, 59)

GOMEZ, Benjamin.[1] April 11, 1711, New York City—August 8, 1772, New York City. This son of Lewis Moses Gomez was a New York City merchant and importer. He also lived in Charlestown. He was married to Esther Nunes of Barbados. (*PAJHS*, XXVII, 283, 288; *Pool*, 476f; *SIR*)

GOMEZ, Benjamin.[2] In 1785 in Philadelphia; in New York City in 1787. His wife may have been named Esther. (*MIPR*; *SIR*)

GOMEZ, Benjamin.[3] September 11, 1769, New York City—August 14, 1828, New York City. This son of Matthias Gomez[3] was a bookseller in New York City, where he published at least twenty-one books. On September 13, 1794, he was married to Charlotte Hendricks. (*PAJHS*, XVII, 198; XXX, 99; *SIR*; *UJE*, V, 50)

GOMEZ, Catherine. In New York City in 1798. (*NYHSW*, XV, 121)

GOMEZ, Charlotte. Born before 1800. A granddaughter of Mordecai Gomez.[1] (*Wills*, 6)

GOMEZ, Cynthia. Born March 16, 1795. Daughter of Isaac Gomez, Jr.,[6] she was married to Mordecai Frois on February 7, 1816. (*MSGC*)

GOMEZ, Daniel.[1] June 23, 1695—July 28, 1780, Philadelphia. This son of Lewis Moses Gomez was a merchant who became a freeman in New York City in 1727, and was naturalized there in 1740. He was married first to Rebecca de Torres in Jamaica, B.W.I., February 10, 1724; and then to Esther Levy,[1] May 31, 1753. (*MIPR*; *MSGC*; *PAJHS*, XVII, 198; XLI, 107-125)

GOMEZ, Daniel.[2] March 13, 1759, New York City—August 27, 1784, New York City. Son of Moses Gomez,[1] he served in the Revolutionary army. (*PAJHS*, XXVII, 282, *et passim*; *Pool*, 481; *SIR*)

GOMEZ, David.[1] August 14, 1694/1697—July 15/16, 1769, New York City. Son of Lewis Moses Gomez, he was a fur trader and a merchant who was naturalized in New York City about 1740. He was married to Rebecca de Leon (Sielva). (*PAJHS*, V, 116; *Pool*, 474f; *SIR*)

GOMEZ, David.[2] September/November 15, 1761, New York City—December 7, 1761, New York City. Son of Isaac Gomez, Jr.[2] (*Pool*, 501; *SIR*)

GOMEZ, David.[3] In Philadelphia in 1780. (*MIPR*)

GOMEZ, Deborah. January 13, 1766, New York City—October 5, 1783, Philadelphia. Daughter of Matthias Gomez.[3] (*PAJHS*, XVII, 198; *SIR*)

GOMEZ, Eleanor. A sister of Lewis Moses Gomez, she may have been in New York City in 1730. (*PAJHS*, XI, 143)

GOMEZ, Elias. In Charleston sometime between 1783 and 1800. (*EJSC*, 279)

GOMEZ, Esther.[1] August 8, 1739, Barbados—August 7, 1822, New York City. Daughter of Isaac Gomez,[1] she was married to Moses Gomez[1] on May 14, 1755, in New York City. (*PAJHS*, XVII, 198; *Pool*, 413)

GOMEZ, Esther.[2] 1743—June 24, 1775, New York City. Also known as Eve Esther. Daughter of Mordecai Gomez,[1] she was married to Uriah Hendricks on June 30, 1762, in New York City. (*PAJHS*, XVII, 197; XVIII, 122; *Pool*, 479; *SIR*)

GOMEZ, Esther.[3] July 19, 1768, New York City—before 1807, Virginia. Daughter of Matthias Gomez,[3] she was married to Mr. Meeks. (*PAJHS*, XVII, 198; XXVII, 288; *SIR*)

GOMEZ, Esther.[4] March 29, 1791, New York City—November 22, 1871. Daughter of Isaac Gomez, Jr.,[6] she was married to Solomon M. Seixas on February 1, 1815. (*MSGC*; *PAJHS*, IV, 211)

GOMEZ, Esther.[5] In New York City in 1795. (*PAJHS*, XXVII, 59)

GOMEZ, I. Phillip. In New York City in 1792. (*PAJHS*, XXVII, 51)

GOMEZ, Isaac.[1] July 13, 1705, New York City—August 28, 1770, New York City. This son of Lewis Moses Gomez was married to Deborah de Leon in 1738. (*MSGC*; *PAJHS*, XI, 141; XVII, 198; *Pool*, 502; *SIR*)

GOMEZ, Isaac, Jr.[2] In New York City in 1746. (*PAJHS*, XXI, 51)

GOMEZ, Isaac.[3] March 23, 1763, New York City—September 1, 1764, New York City. Son of Moses Gomez.[1] (*PAJHS*, XXVII, 282; *Pool*, 502; *SIR*)

GOMEZ, Isaac.[4] Died November 9, 1764, Curaçao. This son of Mordecai Gomez[1] was in New York City in 1730. His wife was Esther Jessurun. (*MSGC*; *Pool*, 213; *SIR*)

GOMEZ, Isaac.[5] June 24, 1767, New York City—December 4, 1810, New York City. Also listed as Isaac Matthias Gomez. Son of Matthias Gomez,[3] he was a broker. (*MSGC*; *PAJHS*, XXVII, 291; *Pool*, 319; *SIR*)

GOMEZ, Isaac, Jr.[6] July 28, 1768, New York City—December 5, 1831, New York City. This son of Moses Gomez[1] wrote poetry and prose, and prepared a book for his children entitled *Selections of a Father in Prose and Verse*. He was prominent in Jewish communal affairs. On May 26, 1790, he was married to Abigail Lopez.[1] (*MSGC; PAJHS*, XI, 139f; XVII, 198; XXI, 187f; *Pool*, 434; *SIR; UJE*, V, 50)

GOMEZ, Jacob.[1] Died 1722. Son of Lewis Moses Gomez, he was killed by Spaniards while on a trading voyage. (*PAJHS*, XVII, 197; XXXVIII, 47; *WW*, 21)

GOMEZ, Jacob.[2] Died September 8, 1763, New York City. Son of Mordecai Gomez,[1] he became insane. (*PAJHS*, XVII, 197; *Pool*, 501; *SIR*)

GOMEZ, Jacob.[3] In Charleston in 1800. (*EJSC*, 135)

GOMEZ, John. In New York City in 1787 and in 1799. (*NYHSW*, XV, 134; *SIR*)

GOMEZ, Joseph. 1729—September 26, 1734, New York City. Son of Daniel Gomez.[1] (*PAJHS*, XVII, 198; *Pool*, 210)

GOMEZ, Joseph de Torres. February 10/14, 1766, New York City—April 2, 1769, New York City. Son of Moses Gomez.[1] (*MSGC; Pool*, 204; *SIR*)

GOMEZ, Lebanah. September 27, 1770, New York City—July 3, 1772, New York City. Daughter of Matthias Gomez.[1] (*Pool*, 502; *SIR*)

GOMEZ, Lewis. 1793—November 15, 1827. Also listed as Lewis Mordecai Gomez. Son of Moses Mordecai Gomez, he lived in Wilmington, North Carolina. He died while at sea, and was buried at St. Augustine. (*PAJHS*, XXVII, 285, 294, 309)

GOMEZ, Lewis (Louis) Moses. About 1660, Madrid—March 31, 1740, New York City. This son of Isaac Gomez was the head of one of the most powerful Jewish families in the eighteenth century. When the situation of the Jews became difficult in Spain, he was sent to Bordeaux. After the revocation of the Edict of Nantes, and religious disturbance in France, he took his family to England and finally to America. He was the founder of the Gomez family in America. An Indian trader and merchant shipper, he exported to Portugal and the West Indies. In 1730 he was president of Congregation Shearith Israel in New York City. In 1695 he was married to Esther Markaze. (*Coldoc*, 313f; *MEAJA*, 53, *et passim; MSGC; PAJHS*, XI, 140f; XVII, 197; XLI, 107f; *UJE*, V, 49f; VIII, 209)

GOMEZ, Manuel. In Montreal about 1760. (*HSIM*, 11; *Sack*, 52)

GOMEZ, Maria. May have been born before 1800. Daughter of Moses M. Gomez, she was married to Samuel Peixotto on February 26, 1817. (*MSGC; PAJHS*, XXVII, 264, *et passim*)

GOMEZ, Mary Ann. March 3, 1799—November 15, 1847. Daughter of Isaac Gomez, Jr.,[6] she was married to Joshua Lopez on June 29, 1836. (*MSGC; PAJHS*, XXVII, 284, *et passim*)

GOMEZ, Matthias.[1] About 1742—May 5, 1781, Philadelphia. (*MIPR; PAJHS*, XXVII, 284, *et passim*)

GOMEZ, Matthias.[2] Died May 5, 1783, Philadelphia. Cf. above. (*PAJHS*, XXVII, 291)

GOMEZ, Matthias.[3] Died May 5, 1786, Philadelphia. Son of Isaac Gomez,[1] he was married to Rachel Gomez[1] on February 6, 1765. (*MSGC; PAJHS*, XVII, 198)

GOMEZ, Mordecai.[1] 1688, British West Indies—November 1, 1750, New York City. This son of Lewis Moses Gomez was a merchant. In 1723 he was elected a collector of New York City, and became a naturalized citizen there about 1740. Gomez' first wife was Esther Campos; his second wife was Rebecca de Lucena on May 4, 1741. (*MCCCNY*, III, 327; *MSGC; PAJHS*, V, 116; XVII, 197; *Wills*, 4f)

GOMEZ, Mordecai.[2] Born October 20, 1786, New York City. Son of Moses Gomez.[1] (*PAJHS*, XXVII, 281)

GOMEZ, Moses.[1] May 29, 1728, New York City—April 12, 1789, New York City. Son of Daniel Gomez,[1] he was married to Esther Gomez[1] on May 14, 1755, in New York City. (*PAJHS*, XVII, 198; *Pool*, 29, *et passim*)

GOMEZ, Moses.[2] Listed as Moses de (or bar) Daniel Gomez. He may have been one of the other Gomezes. In 1728 he was in New York City. (*PAJHS*, XXI, 11, *et passim*)

GOMEZ, Moses.[3] Listed as Moses de Mordy Gomez. He may have been one of the other Moses Gomezes. In 1730 he was in New York City. (*PAJHS*, XXI, 23)

GOMEZ, Moses.[4] On May 27, 1759, he was buried in New York City. (*Pool*, 501)

GOMEZ, Moses.[5] January 19, 1772, New York City—August 17, 1772, New York City. Son of Matthias Gomez.[1] (*MSGC*; *Pool*, 502; *SIR*)

GOMEZ, Moses.[6] Born about 1792, died an infant. Son of Isaac Gomez, Jr.[6] (*PAJHS*, XXVII, 288)

GOMEZ, Moses.[7] Son of Isaac Gomez, Jr.,[6] he died in 1795, an infant. (*MSGC*)

GOMEZ, Moses, Jr. A loyalist auctioneer, he was in New York City in 1776. (*Coldoc*, 194f; *PAJHS*, III, 83)

GOMEZ, Moses Mordecai. January 23, 1744, New York City—May 29, 1826, New York City. Son of Mordecai Gomez,[1] he was married to Esther Lopez. He manufactured chocolate. (*PAJHS*, XXVII, 306; *Pool*, 425; *MSGC*)

GOMEZ, Rachel.[1] Died April 16, 1776, Newark, New Jersey. Daughter of Benjamin Gomez,[1] she was married to Matthias Gomez[3] on February 6, 1765. (*PAJHS*, XVII, 198; XXVII, 283; *Pool*, 503; *SIR*)

GOMEZ, Rachel.[2] About 1739—January 22, 1809, England. Daughter of Mordecai Gomez,[1] she was married to Abraham Wagge on July 4, 1770. (*MSGC*; *PAJHS*, XVII, 197; *SIR*)

GOMEZ, Rachel.[3] August 9, 1800—1836. Daughter of Isaac Gomez, Jr.[6] Her first husband was Aaron Judah,[2] February 3, 1819; her second husband was Mr. Wood. (*PAJHS*, XXVII, 113, *et passim*)

GOMEZ, Rebecca.[2] May 10, 1761, New York City—October 12, 1762, New York City. Daughter of Moses Gomez.[1] (*MSGC*; *Pool*, 501; *SIR*)

GOMEZ, Reyna. Died July 24, 1740, New York City, at the age of seventy-seven. (*Pool*, 224)

GOMEZ, Sarah.[1] February 8, 1763, New York City—July 18, 1763, New York City. Daughter of Isaac Gomez.[1] (*MSGC*; *Pool*, 501; *SIR*)

GOMEZ, Sarah.[2] September 12, 1793—April 5, 1852, Charleston. Daughter of Isaac Gomez, Jr.,[6] she was married to Nathan Emanuel on February 14, 1816. (*PAJHS*, XXVII, 285f; *MSGC*)

GOMEZ, Sebana. Born September 27, 1770, died an infant. Daughter of Matthias Gomez.[3] (*MSGC*)

GOMPAZ, Isaac. On July 12, 1737, he arrived in Savannah with his wife and her brother. (*SRB*)

GOMPERTS, Gompert S. In New York City in 1800. (*SIR*)

GONSALEZ, Isaac. In New York City in 1728. (*PAJHS*, XXI, 10)

GONSALEZ, Jacob. In New York City in 1728. (*PAJHS*, XXI, 10)

GOTATUS, Abraham. A merchant, he came from London to Boston in 1716. (*JNEA*, 17; *PAJHS*, XII, 101)

GOTTSCHALKSON, Solomon. Cf. Solomon Gutshalkson.

GRADES, Moses. Also known as Moïse Gradis. In 1794 he came from Bordeaux, and was in Philadelphia in 1796. (*MIPR*; *SZ*, 121)

GRAHAM, Dr. In 1787 he was in New York City. He owed a debt to the charity fund of Congregation Shearith Israel. It is doubtful that he was Jewish. (*PAJHS*, XXVII, 42)

GRANADA, Benjamin. A merchant in New York City in 1707. (*Pool*, 453)

GRANADA, Isaac Henriques. Died May 5, 1717, New York City. In 1688 he became a freeman of New York City. He was a butcher. His wife was Sarah. (*Pool*, 447, 453)

GRANADA, Mrs. Sarah Henriques. Died March 21, 1708, New York City. Wife of

Isaac Henriques Granada, she was in New York City in 1695. (AJAM, III, 6; Pool, 453)

GRATZ, Barnard. April, 1738, Langendorf, Germany—April 20, 1801, Baltimore. Son of Solomon Gratz, as a youth he went from Germany to London, where he was employed as a clerk. In January, 1754, he made the journey to Philadelphia. He was the first Jewish resident in Pittsburgh. After a short employment with David Franks he went into business as a merchant. About 1760 he formed a lasting partnership with his brother Michael. Before the Stamp Act and the successive Non-Importation Agreements, he was engaged chiefly in coastwise and West Indian trade. He was among the signers of the Non-Importation resolutions adopted on October 2, 1765. During the French and Indian War he supplied the British forces, but during the Revolution he sided with the American cause and supplied the Revolutionary forces. Along with many others he shared in opening the West through trade and investments. He was an original shareholder in the Illinois Company. In addition to land speculation he was engaged in extensive fur and Indian trade. He also served as banker for William Franklin. He laid the cornerstone of the first synagogue in Philadelphia on June 16, 1782, and was the first recorded president of Congregation Mikveh Israel of Philadelphia. On December 10, 1760, he was married to Richea Myers Cohen. (Byars; Coldoc, 33, et passim; DAB, VII, 504; Feldman, 4; MEAJB, 12, et passim; PAJHS, I, 14f; XXXIII, 210; UJE, V, 85, 538; VII, 361, 392; VIII, 428, 545; WW, 36, et passim)

GRATZ, Benjamin. September 4, 1792, Philadelphia—March 17, 1884, Lexington, Kentucky. This son of Michael Gratz was one of the first Jewish settlers in Kentucky. He was graduated from the University of Pennsylvania in 1811 and was admitted to the bar in 1815. He served as a lieutenant in the War of 1812. In 1830 he aided in the organization of the Lexington and Ohio Railroad and was chosen its second president. In 1835 he was one of the founders of the Lexington branch of the Bank of Kentucky. He helped organize the Lexington Public Library. He was also in the hemp industry, and in 1850 he was made the first president of the Kentucky Agricultural and Mechanical Association. In 1832 he was a member of the first city council of Lexington. He was a close friend of Henry Clay, into whose family one of his daughters married. Gratz' first wife was Maria Gist on November 24, 1819; his second wife was Anne Marie Boswell on July 6, 1843. (JE, VI, 82; Morais, 26, et passim; MSGC; UJE, V, 87; VI, 362; VII, 591; WW, 180, et passim)

GRATZ, Fanny. Born October 9, 1761. Daughter of Barnard Gratz, she died an infant. (MSGC)

GRATZ, Frances. June 18, 1771—September 21, 1852, Philadelphia. Daughter of Michael Gratz, she was married to Reuben Etting[3] in Philadelphia on September 17, 1794. (JCES; MIPR; Morais, 270)

GRATZ, Hyman. September 23, 1776, Philadelphia—January 27, 1857, Philadelphia. This son of Michael Gratz took over the family's wholesale grocery business when his father became ill. He was an active worker for the Federalist Party. He became a director of the Pennsylvania Company for Insurance on Lives and Granting Annuities. He was one of the founders of the Pennsylvania Academy of Fine Arts and one of the managers of the first Jewish Publication Society, which was organized in Philadelphia in 1845. From 1824 until 1856 he was treasurer of Congregation Mikveh Israel in Philadelphia. (Morais, 270f; UJE, V, 85; WW, 36, et passim)

GRATZ, Jacob. December 20, 1789, Baltimore—December 24, 1856, Philadelphia. This son of Michael Gratz was graduated from the University of Pennsylvania in 1807. He received his M.A. there in 1811. He was in business with his brothers but left them to form his own dry goods concern. He later became president of the Union Canal Company. In 1824 he was elected to the Pennsylvania legislature, and to the state senate in 1839. He was one of the first directors of the Philadelphia Institution for the Instruction of the Deaf and Dumb, and was one of the first directors of the Athenaeum in 1814, and its treasurer in 1816. He had a gentile wife or mistress. (MIPR; Morais, 25, et passim; UJE, V, 87; VIII, 433; IX, 462; WW, 218, et passim)

GRATZ, Jonathan. Son of Michael Gratz, he died an infant. (*Morais*, 270; *MSGC*)

GRATZ, Joseph. February 22, 1785, Philadelphia—October 25, 1858, Philadelphia. This son of Michael Gratz was active in the affairs of Congregation Mikveh Israel in Philadelphia as well as various public organizations. He served on the original board of directors of the Philadelphia Institution for the Deaf and Dumb, and was a director of the Atlantic Insurance Company. An active Federalist, he nevertheless joined a cavalry unit in the War of 1812. (*Morais*, 270; *MSGC*; *UJE*, V, 86f; IX, 462; *WW*, 218, *et passim*)

GRATZ, Michael. 1740, Langendorf, Germany—September 8, 1811, Philadelphia. Son of Solomon Gratz, he clerked in London for a short time and spent 1758 in India. In 1759 he came to Philadelphia. He was a prominent merchant who engaged in extensive Indian and fur trade and land speculation in the West. In 1784 he was president of Congregation Mikveh Israel in Philadelphia. On June 20, 1769, he was married to Miriam Simon in Lancaster. (*Byars*; *Coldoc*, 18, *et passim*; *DAB*, VII, 504f; *MEAJB*, 14, *et passim*; *Morais*, 13, *et passim*; *MSGC*; *PAJHS*, I, 59, *et passim*; XXXIII, 210; *WW*, 39, *et passim*)

GRATZ, Rachel.[1] October 9, 1764—December 25, 1831. Daughter of Barnard Gratz, she was married to Solomon Etting[1] on October 26, 1791. (*MIPR*; *MSGC*; *PAJHS*, XXXIII, 210)

GRATZ, Rachel.[2] January 25, 1783—September 29, 1823, Philadelphia. Daughter of Michael Gratz, she was married to Solomon Moses[2] on June 24, 1806. (*JCES*; *MIPR*; *MSGC*; *PAJHS*, VI, 110; *SIR*)

GRATZ, Rebecca. March 4, 1781, Philadelphia—August 27, 1869, Philadelphia. Daughter of Michael Gratz, she was the outstanding Jewess in America in her time. A woman of culture, she was friendly with many outstanding literary figures, including Washington Irving. She was a prolific letter-writer. In 1801 she was secretary of the Female Association for the Relief of Women and Children in Reduced Circumstances. She helped found the Philadelphia Orphan Asylum, which she served until 1859. She also aided in the foundation of the Female Hebrew Benevolent Society in 1819, and in 1838 she founded the Hebrew Sunday School Society, which she served as president until 1864. She is erroneously reputed to have been the prototype of Rebecca in Sir Walter Scott's *Ivanhoe*. (*Byars*; *Coldoc*, 57, *et passim*; *DAB*, VII, 505f; *Memoirs* I, 2, *et passim*; *Morais*, 25, *et passim*; *MSGC*; *UJE*, IV, 188; V, 86; VIII, 13, 477; *WW*, 3 *et passim*)

GRATZ, Richea. October 1, 1774—November 22, 1858, Philadelphia. This daughter of Michael Gratz went to Marshall College, Lancaster, Pennsylvania. She was probably the first Jewish girl to go to college in the United States. She was married to Samuel Hays[1] on January 8, 1794. (*Coldoc*, 60, *et passim*; *JCES*; *GBMIP*; *MSGC*; *PAJHS*, XIX, 123)

GRATZ, Sarah (Sally). June 11, 1779—February 20/21, 1817, Philadelphia. Daughter of Michael Gratz. (*JCES*; *MIPR*; *MSGC*; *PAJHS*, VI, 109)

GRATZ, Simon. January 14, 1773—July 14, 1839, Philadelphia. This eldest son of Michael Gratz was a merchant who took over the firm of Benjamin and Michael Gratz. He spent time in Richmond but returned to Philadelphia, where he was active in Jewish and civic functions: in Congregation Mikveh Israel; in the Pennsylvania Academy of Fine Arts; and in the Pennsylvania Botanical Garden, of which he was director. He was married to a gentile, Mary Smith, and their children were raised as Christians. (*ELJR*, 281; *MIPR*; *Morais*, 270f; *MSGC*; *WW*, 181, *et passim*)

GRATZ, Solomon. 1770—1772. Son of Michael Gratz. (*Morais*, 270; *MSGC*)

GRIMLE, Solomon. A brother-in-law of Abraham Cassell, he was probably in Philadelphia in 1776. (*WAJA*)

GUTIEREZES. In Newport about 1670. (*Gutstein*, 38)

GUTSHALKSON, Solomon. On March 30, 1797, he was married to Sarah Hays[1] in Philadelphia. Cf. Solomon Gottschalkson. (*Coldoc*, 82; *MIPR*)

GUTTERES, Aaron. A merchant in South Carolina in 1734. (*EJSC*, 27, 277)

H

HACHAR, Catherine. Died before 1740. She was from Curaçao and was married to Moses Michaels. (*MSGC*)

HAIM, Henry (Uriah). In New York City in 1728. (*PAJHS*, XXI, 9, *et passim*)

HALBOURNE, Haim. In New York City about 1788. Cf. Hayman Heilbron. (*PAJHS*, XXVII, 43)

HAMMER, Moses. In Pennsylvania in 1775. It is highly doubtful that he was Jewish. (*Morais*, 458)

HAMBURG, M. M. In Philadelphia in 1790. (*Coldoc*, 172; *MIPR*)

HANNAY, Mrs. Hannah. About 1756, Philadelphia—December 23, 1840, Charleston. (*EOJCC*, 31)

HARBY, George Washington. Born October 12, 1797, Charleston. Son of Solomon Harby, he was a playwright who lived in Charleston and New Orleans. (*EJSC*, 135f, 190f; *PAJHS*, XXXII, 46)

HARBY, Henry Jefferson. October 4, 1799, Charleston—September 14, 1841, Charleston. This son of Solomon Harby was active in Charleston politics. (*EJSC*, 168, *et passim*; *EOJCC*, 119; *PAJHS*, XXXII, 46; *Wills*, 40f)

HARBY, Isaac. November 4/9, 1788, Charleston—December 14, 1828, New York City. This son of Solomon Harby attended Dr. Best's academy and studied law but later turned to education. He established a school on Edisto Island and opened an academy in Charleston. He edited the *Quiver*, the *Investigator*, and the *Southern Patriot*, and contributed to the *Mercury* and the *Courier*. He also wrote for the *City Gazette* and for the *Commercial Daily Advertiser*. In addition he wrote numerous plays, poems, and essays. His first play, *Alexander Severus*, was written when he was only seventeen years old. In 1824 he was one of the founders of the Reformed Society of Israelites in Charleston, a group which was the forerunner of the American Jewish Reform movement. He introduced the English sermon in the regular Jewish religious service in America. In 1828 he moved to New York City, where he opened a school and contributed to many periodicals. He was married to Rachel Mordecai about 1809. (*DAB*, VIII, 239; *Moïse*; *PAJHS*, VI, 114; XXXII, 46f; *UJE*, III, 117, 251; V, 213; VI, 51; VIII, 237; X, 233)

HARBY, Levy Myers. September 21, 1793, Georgetown (or Charlestown)—December 3, 1870, Galveston. This son of Solomon Harby commanded a Confederate ship in the Civil War, fought in the War of 1812, and aided Texas in its struggle for independence. In 1838 he was married to Leonora de Lyon. (*PAJHS*, II, 146f; XXXII, 46; *UJE*, V, 213f)

HARBY, Rachel. Born May 4, 1791, Georgetown, South Carolina. Daughter of Solomon Harby, she was married to Abraham Cohen. (*PAJHS*, XXXII, 46f)

HARBY, Samuel da Costa. October 12, 1795, Charleston—October 12, 1799, Charleston. Son of Solomon Harby. (*PAJHS*, XXXII, 46f)

HARBY, Solomon. 1762, London—March 14, 1805. This son of Isaac Harby was in Jamaica from 1778 to 1781. He was married to Rebecca Moses[1] in Charleston in 1787. (*EJSC*, 135, *et passim*; *PAJHS*, XXXII, 45f)

HARRIS, Mrs. Probably the wife of Alexander Harris. In 1796 she was a widow in New York City. (*SIR*)

HARRIS, Alexander. Died August 14, 1796, New York City. Son of Zebi Harris, he came from Halberstadt, Germany, to New York City, where he was shohet briefly for Congregation Shearith Israel. (*POFNW*, 240; *Pool*, 264)

HARRIS, Andrew. In Charleston in 1800. (*EJSC*, 135)

HARRIS, Henry. In 1783 he was a tailor in Charleston. (*EJSC*, 99; *Reznikoff*, 50, 53)

HARRIS, Hyam. 1774, England—June 1, 1828, New Orleans. In Charleston in 1800.

He was married to Catherine Nathan in London. (*EJSC*, 135; *MSGC*)

HARRIS, Jacob.[1] Died January 9, 1837, Charleston. He came to Charleston from Holland about 1797. (*EJSC*, 135; *MSP*)

HARRIS, Jacob, Jr.[2] In Charleston in 1800. (*EJSC*, 135)

HARRIS, Mordecai. In Charlestown sometime between 1750 and 1783. (*EJSC*, 278)

HARRIS, Moses. In Charlestown during the Revolution. (*EJSC*, 91)

HARRIS, Sarah. 1776—April 20, 1821, Charleston. Daughter of Lazarus Harris, she was married to Samuel Mendes Marks in 1797. (*MSGC*; *Wills*, 56)

HART.[1] Son of Solomon Hart, he was a child in New York City in 1743. (*MEAJA*, 71)

HART.[2] Born April 30, 1768, Newport. Son of Naphtaly Hart.[2] (*NHM*, II, 208)

HART.[3] Born 1771, Newport. Daughter of Naphtaly Hart.[2] (*NHM*, II, 208)

HART.[4] Born before 1800. Son of Myer Hart. (*MSGC*)

HART.[5] Died by 1793, Savannah. (*MISR*)

HART, Aaron.[1] 1724, London—December 28, 1800, Three Rivers, Canada. He came to America as a sutler with the English army. During the French and Indian War, he aided the English in Canada, probably as a sutler. He lived for a time in New York City, but finally settled at Three Rivers, where he continued as a purveyor of army supplies and was also engaged in the fur trade. The wealthiest Jew in Canada, he was a large landholder who owned or controlled the seigneuries of Becancour, Ste. Marguerite, and the fief of Marquisat-Dusable. During the Revolution he did business with the American soldiers stationed near his home. He was one of the first Jews of America to become a Mason. On February 7, 1768, he was married to Dorothy Catherine Judah. (*Coldoc*, 48, *et passim*; *Douville*; *MEAJA*, 203, *et passim*; *MSGC*; *UJE*, II, 651; V, 223; VI, 194, 232; IX, 622)

HART, Aaron.[2] Died January 29, 1777, New York City. On November 20, 1774, he was married to Richea, the widow of David Jacobs. (*MSP*)

HART, Aaron Asher. 1783—December 9, 1800/2. Son of Ephraim Hart. (*MSGC*)

HART, Abraham.[1] In New York City in 1747. (*PAJHS*, XXI, 53)

HART, Abraham de.[2] In Easton in 1785. (*Trachtenberg*, 29)

HART, Abraham.[3] In Bedford, New York, about 1785. It is doubtful that he was Jewish. (*HDB*)

HART, Abraham.[4] In New York City in 1796. (*PAJHS*, VI, 154)

HART, Mrs. Abraham. In Savannah in 1795. (*MISR*)

HART, Abraham Levy. Died August/September, 1796, Charleston. Son of Levy Hart, he committed suicide. (*MSGC*; *MSP*; *WAJA*)

HART, Abraham Luria. December 21, 1789, Easton—August 20, 1872, Philadelphia. Son of Michael Hart,[1] he was a merchant in Belvedere, New Jersey. On October 11, 1813, he was married to Louisa Barnett. (*MIPR*; *MSGC*; *PAJHS*, VIII, 133)

HART, Alexander. January 31, 1782, Three Rivers—September 16, 1835. Son of Aaron Hart,[1] he was in Philadelphia in 1790. (*Douville*, 103; *MSGC*)

HART, Alexander Moses. Died about September, 1797, Charleston. Son of Moses Hart. (*WAJA*)

HART, Asher.[1] A Mason, in 1795 he was in New York City. (*PAJHS*, XIX, 32)

HART, Asher.[2] Born January 31, 1782, Three Rivers. Son of Aaron Hart.[1] (*MIPR*)

HART, Asher.[3] About 1783—December 9, 1802, New York City. Son of Ephraim Hart. (*Pool*, 289)

HART, B. D. In Philadelphia in 1793. (*MIPR*)

HART, Balthazar de. In New York City in 1732. It is doubtful that he was Jewish. (*NYHSW*, III, 222)

HART, Barnet (Baruch). Son of Michael Hart,[1] he was in New York City in 1787. (PAJHS, XXVII, 41; MSGC)

HART, Benjamin.[1] In Connecticut in 1762. It is highly doubtful that he was Jewish. (JRMP)

HART, Benjamin.[2] In Three Rivers in 1773. (PAJHS, VI, 155)

HART, Benjamin.[3] August 10, 1779, Three Rivers—February 28, 1855, New York City. This son of Aaron Hart[1] was a prominent merchant who was very active in Jewish affairs in Montreal. He was president of Congregation Shearith Isreal for many years. He was one of the founders of the Montreal General Hospital. In the War of 1812 he attained the rank of lieutenant colonel. In 1837 he was a magistrate in Montreal. On April 1, 1806, he was married to Harriet Hart. (Coldoc, 48f; MEAJA, 281f; MSGC; MSIR; UJE, V, 224f)

HART, Benjamin.[4] Born March 9, 1800, died Philadelphia. Son of Jacob Hart,[4] he was married to Delphine. (MSGC)

HART, Bernard.[1] December 25, 1763, London—July 19, 1855, New York City. This son of Menachem Hart settled in New York City in 1780. He served as quartermaster in the state militia in 1787 and was a divisional quartermaster during the War of 1812. From 1831 to 1853 he was secretary of the New York Stock Exchange. He was the grandfather of Bret Harte. Hart's first wife was Catherine Brett in 1799; his second wife was Rebecca B. Seixas in New York City, on August 13, 1806. (Coldoc, 196, et passim; MSGC; PAJHS, XXI, 167; SIR; UJE, V, 225; VIII, 180, 428; IX, 623)

HART, Bernard.[2] In Charleston sometime between 1783 and 1800. (EJSC, 279)

HART, Betsy. Daughter of Moses Hart, she was married to Benjamin Wolf on September 27, 1795, probably in Philadelphia. (MIPR; Wills, 62)

HART, Betty. On January 11, 1792, she was married to Moses Nathan[1] in Philadelphia. Cf. Sarah Abrahams. (MIPR)

HART, Bilhah.[1] Died December 16, 1762, New York City. Daughter of Moses Hart. (Pool, 501; SIR)

HART, Bilhah.[2] Born March 27, 1783. Daughter of Aaron Hart.[1] (MSGC)

HART, Brinah. Born April 30, 1761, Newport. Daughter of Naphtali Hart.[1] (MSGC)

HART, Catherine. January 24, 1776, Three Rivers—February 14, 1859, New York. Daughter of Aaron Hart,[1] she was married to Bernard S. Judah on August 30, 1797. (MEAJA, 283; MSGC)

HART, Charlotte. Born 1777. Daughter of Aaron, she was the wife of Moses David. (MSGC)

HART, Daniel, Sr.[1] In New York City in 1773. It is doubtful that he was Jewish. (HDB)

HART, Daniel.[2] Born Mannheim, Germany, died May, 1811, Charleston. In 1792 he was in Charleston. His wife was Bella Levy.[2] (EJSC, 117; EOJCC, 76)

HART, David.[1] Nephew of Isaac Levy,[1] he was in New York City in 1745. (NYHSW, IV, 57)

HART, David.[2] July 4, 1785, Baltimore—October, 1854. This son of Jacob Hart[4] was in New York City about 1793. (MSGC; PAJHS, XXVII, 55)

HART, Elias. In New York City in 1787. (PAJHS, XXVII, 41)

HART, Mrs. Eliza. In New York City in 1784. She may have been the wife of Lyon Hart. (SIR)

HART, Elizabeth. Probably May 15, 1770—September, 1843. Daughter of Aaron Hart.[1] (MSGC)

HART, Ella. October 11, 1787, New York—November 8, 1860, New York. Daughter of Jacob Hart,[4] she was married to Hyam M. Salomon in 1809. (MSGC)

HART, Ella Moses. Daughter of Moses Hart, she was married to Solomon Cohen[1] in Charleston in October, 1797. (EJMC, 7; WAJA)

HART, Ephraim. 1747, Fürth, Bavaria—July 16, 1825, New York City. This son of Samuel Hart (Herz) was in New York City by 1773. During the Revolutionary War he lived in Philadelphia while the British occupied New York City. He returned to New York City, became a stockbroker, and was one of the original members of the Board of Stockbrokers in New York. One of the wealthiest Jews in New York, he was a large land speculator. In 1810 he became a state senator. He was very active in the Jewish community and was the president of Congregation Shearith Israel in 1794. In 1783 he was married to Frances Noah. (*Coldoc*, 73f; *EJSC*, 279; *JE*, VI, 240; *MSGC*; *PAJHS*, IV, 215f; VI, 155; *Pool*, 289f; *UJE*, V, 226)

HART, Esther (Hetty).[1] Born before 1787. Daughter of Joshua Hart, she lived in Charleston. (*MEAJB*, 254f; *MSGC*)

HART, Esther (Hetty).[2] December 5, 1792/3—November 2, 1852/3. Daughter of Jacob Hart,[4] on July 10, 1816, she was married to Alexander Marks[2] in Charleston. (*MSGC*)

HART, Esther (Betty).[3] About 1767—April 16, 1843, Philadelphia. Also known as Hetty. Daughter of Myer Hart, she was married to Isaac Marks[3] on March 15, 1797, in Philadelphia. (*GBMIP*; *MIPR*; *MSGC*; *WW*, 226)

HART, Ezekiel. May 15, 1770, Three Rivers—September 16, 1843. This son of Aaron Hart[1] was a merchant and large landholder who succeeded his father as seigneur of Becancour. In 1807 he was the first Jew to be elected to the Canadian Assembly. The House of Commons refused to permit him to take his seat because he declined to take the oath "on faith of a Christian." He was elected a second time but was again barred. He served as an officer in the War of 1812. His wife was Frances Lazarus. (*MSGC*; *Sack*, 66, *et passim*; *UJE*, II, 652; V, 223; IX, 26)

HART, Frances. July, 1740, Hague, Holland—October 25, 1820, Beaufort, South Carolina. Daughter of Moses Hart, she was married to Mordecai Sheftall[1] on October 28, 1761, in Charlestown. (*EJSC*, 40; *SRB*; *Wills*, 79)

HART, Hannah. Died November 25, 1779. Daughter of Michael Hart,[1] she was the wife of Isaac Hart. (*MSGC*; *Pool*, 503; *SIR*)

HART, Harriet Judith. Born May 20, 1786, New York City. This daughter of Ephraim Hart was married to Benjamin Hart[3] on April 1, 1804/6, in New York City. (*MSGC*; *PAJHS*, IV, 217)

HART, Hart Moses. 1764—July 12, 1795, Charleston. A Charleston broker. (*EOJCC*, 58; *WAJA*)

HART, Hendle Moses. In Charleston in 1795. (*WAJA*)

HART, Henry.[1] 1797, Charleston—March 11, 1834, New Orleans. Son of Simon Moses Hart. (*MSGC*)

HART, Henry.[2] Born February 1, 1800. Son of Bernard Hart. (*MSGC*)

HART, Henry (Harry).[3] Brother of Aaron Hart of Three Rivers, he was a merchant in Albany in 1786. (*Douville*, 60f; *MEAJA*, 276f)

HART, Henry S. April 10, 1796—1841. Son of Michael Hart.[1] (*PAJHS*, VIII, 133)

HART, Hermann Fisher. In 1794 he may have been in Albany. A nephew of Aaron Hart of Three Rivers, he may have been the son of Henry (Harry) Hart.[3] (*Douville*, 178)

HART, Hymon. About 1760, Germany—November 2, 1791, Charleston. A merchant, he was married to Hannah Stork. (*EOJCC*, 81; *WAJA*)

HART, Isaac.[1] Died 1780, Long Island. He settled in Newport about 1750. He became a prominent merchant in business with his brothers, and was one of the foremost citizens of the colony. He contributed much to the building of the old Newport synagogue. He was interested in privateering and was associated with Governor Wanton in this enterprise during the French and Indian War. Because of his Tory sentiments during the Revolutionary War he was banished from Newport. He was finally shot and killed in an attack by Continental soldiers, supposedly in Long Island. On June 1, 1763, he was married to Hannah Polock.[2] (*Coldoc*, 88, *et passim*; *MEAJA*, 154f; *MSP*; *UJE*, V, 227; X, 348)

HART, Isaac.[2] In Philadelphia in 1782. (*MIPR*)

HART, Isaac.[3] Born March 16, 1794, Philadelphia. Son of Michael Hart. (*MIPR*)

HART, Isaac.⁴ Born November 5, 1763, Newport. Son of Naphtaly Hart.² (NHM, II, 207)

HART, J. N. In Georgetown, South Carolina, in 1780. It is doubtful that he was Jewish. (EJSC, 106)

HART, Jacob.¹ In New York City in 1730. (PAJHS, XXI, 23, et passim)

HART, Jacob.² Died November 3, 1784, England. A loyalist, he lived in Newport and in Stamford, Connecticut. His wife was Esther Levy.² (MSGC)

HART, Jacob.³ Born about 1775. Son of Michael Hart,¹ he was an Indian trader. (PAJHS, VIII, 132)

HART, Jacob.⁴ 1746, Fürth, Bavaria—May 9, 1822, New York City. When he first came to America in 1775, he settled in Baltimore. He was a patriotic merchant who advanced money to Lafayette and supplied Lafayette's soldiers with clothing and shoes. On November 4, 1778, he was married to Leah Nathan in Philadelphia. (Pool, 411f; UJE, II, 53; V, 228)

HART, Jacob.⁵ A Child in New York City about 1793. (PAJHS, XXVII, 55)

HART, Captain Jacob de.⁶ In 1744 he may have been in New York City. (PAJHS, XXVII, 246)

HART, Jane. 1795, Charleston—March 8, 1858. Daughter of Daniel Hart,² she was married to William Warner on August 31, 1814. (MSGC)

HART, Mrs. Jenny. In Georgetown, South Carolina, in 1797. (MSP)

HART, Joel. September 14, 1784, Philadelphia—June 14, 1842, New York City. This son of Ephraim Hart studied medicine in England and was graduated by the Royal College of Surgery in London. A prominent Mason, he was a charter member of the Medical Society of the county of New York. President James Madison appointed him consul at Leith, Scotland, in 1817, a position he held until 1832. On May 2, 1810, he was married to Louisa Levien in London. (PAJHS, IV, 217f; UJE, V, 228; VII, 269; IX, 29)

HART, Joseph.¹ Fought in Virginia in the Revolution. It is doubtful that he was Jewish. (PAJHS, XX, 99)

HART, Joseph.² In Newport in 1773. (JNEB, 39)

HART, Joseph.³ In Philadelphia in 1780. (PAJHS, I, 59; VI, 51)

HART, Joshua. Died July 10, 1787, Charleston. Son of Moses Hart of the Hague, he was a merchant in Charlestown as early as 1762. He did business with Aaron Lopez. His wife was Rebecca. (EJSC, 43; MEAJB, 249f; MSGC)

HART, Judah. In Connecticut in 1762. It is highly doubtful that he was Jewish. His wife was Sarah. (JRMP)

HART, Judith.¹ February 22, 1762—February 25, 1844, Philadelphia. Daughter of Myer Hart,¹ she was married to James Pettigrew by an Army chaplain in 1782. They were later remarried according to Jewish law. (GBMIP; MSGC; WW, 128f)

HART, Judith.² A child in New York City about 1793. (PAJHS, XXVII, 55)

HART, Levy. A New York merchant, he was naturalized on October 27, 1763. (Hugsoc, XXIV, 37)

HART, Love. Born September 14, 1762, Newport. Daughter of Naphtaly Hart.² (NHM, II, 207)

HART, Lyon.¹ Died about 1794. He lived in New York City, Richmond, and Philadelphia in the years after 1783. (ELJR, 77, 240; MIPR; PAJHS, XXI, 142; SIR)

HART, Lyon.² December 7, 1797—October 11, 1869. Son of Jacob Hart.⁴ (MSGC; Pool, 412)

HART, Maria. Born December 18, 1797. Daughter of Nathan Hart,³ she died an infant in Georgetown, South Carolina. (MSP)

HART, Michael.¹ 1738, Germany—March 23, 1813/5, Easton. A shopkeeper in Easton, he acquired considerable real estate. In 1780 he was one of the largest taxpayers in Easton. He was a pious Jew and served as his own shohet. He fought in the Revolutionary army. In 1772 he was married to Leah Marks. After her death he was married to Esther Cohen[3] on February 7, 1787. (*MIPR; MSGC; PAJHS*, VIII, 127f; *Trachtenberg*, 68-82; *UJE*, V, 228f; VIII, 427f; X, 470)

HART, Michael.[2] A clerk to Joseph Salvador, he was in Charleston in 1786. (*EJSC*, 116f)

HART, Miriam.[1] Born August 28, 1753. Daughter of Jacob Hart,[2] she was married to Montague Blackwell of the British Army. (*MSGC*)

HART, Miriam.[2] Born December 6, 1772. Daughter of Aaron Hart.[1] (*MSGC*)

HART, Miriam.[3] 1792—April 14, 1828. Daughter of Daniel Hart,[2] she was married to Jacob Lazarus in October, 1812. (*MSGC*)

HART, Mrs. Miriam. Wife of Uriah Hart. (*MSGC*)

HART, Mordecai. Born June 22, 1791, Philadelphia. Son of Michael Hart. (*MIPR*)

MART, Moses.[1] A merchant, in 1713 he became a freeman of New York City. He may have been married to Miriam Levy.[1] (*NYHSW*, II, 189; *PAJHS*, VI, 101; XXXIV, 61; *Pool*, 194)

HART, Moses.[2] In Charlestown sometime between 1750 and 1783. (*EJSC*, 278)

HART, Moses.[3] Born May 3, 1748. This son of Jacob Hart[2] was a trader in Boston in 1769, and in Rhode Island in 1780. (*FEAJ*, 14; *JRMP; MSGC*)

HART, Moses.[4] November 26, 1768—1852. This son of Aaron Hart[1] succeeded his father in business as a merchant and banker, and as seigneur of Ste. Marguerite, and Courval, and the fief of Marquisat-Dusable. He was one of the pioneers of steam navigation in Canada and operated several boats between Montreal, Three Rivers, and Quebec. In 1835 he established a bank at Three Rivers. A deist, he wrote a tract on *Modern Religion* in an effort to create a universal faith. On April 10, 1799, he was married to Sarah Judah.[4] (*Douville*, 141; *MEAJA*, 274, *et passim; MSGC; UJE*, V, 224)

HART, Moses.[5] Born March 28, 1783, died Paris. Son of Jacob Hart.[4] (*MSGC*)

HART, Moses.[6] A child in New York City about 1793. (*PAJHS*, XXVII, 55)

HART, Moses.[7] Brother of Aaron Hart of Three Rivers, he was married to Esther Solomon. (*Douville*, 130)

HART, Myer (de Texeira). Died August 14, 1797, Philadelphia. In Easton by 1752, he was naturalized there on April 3, 1764. He was a leading merchant and banker in Easton, a community which he helped establish. An agent of David Franks during the Revolution, he cared for American prisoners quartered in Easton. In 1782 he moved to Philadelphia. He was married to Rachel de Lyon. (*MIPR; Trachtenberg*, 55-67; *UJE*, III, 618; V, 229; VIII, 427; *WW*, 87, *et passim*)

HART, Myer. June 2, 1779—August 16, 1779. Son of Nathan Hart.[1] (*PAJHS*, XXVII, 348)

HART, Naphtaly.[1] 1716—August 22, 1786, New York City. This son of Aaron Hart was a merchant in New York City by 1742. Cf. below. (*MSGC; PAJHS*, XXVII, 350)

HART, Naphtaly.[2] This son of Moses Hart[1] came from England and was a merchant in Newport in 1760. He was a loyalist during the Revolution. His wife was Sheprah Barnett. Cf. above. (*NHM*, II, 207; *PAJHS*, XXXVII, 163-169)

HART, Naphtaly.[3] Died 1828, Philadelphia. This son of Michael Hart[1] was married to Mrs. Elizabeth Barnett on February 21, 1799, in Easton. (*GBMIP; MIPR; MSGC*)

HART, Naphtaly.[4] 1800, Charleston—May 2, 1832. Son of Daniel Hart,[2] he was married to Sarah Oppenheim in January, 1823. (*MSGC*)

HART, Naphtaly, Jr. In Newport in 1761 with his family; in Tiverton, Rhode Island in 1779. (*JRMP; MSP; Newport Historical Society, Lopez Letters; PAJHS*, XXVII, 154)

HART, Mrs. Naphtaly, Jr. In Rhode Island in 1768. (*PAJHS*, XXVII, 154)

HART, Nathan.[1] In New York City in 1779. His wife was Grace Isaacs.[3] (*PAJHS*, XXVII, 348; *Pool*, 317; *SIR*)

HART, Nathan.[2] Born May 11, 1768; Rhode Island. Son of Naphtaly Hart, Jr.,

[54]

he was in Newport in 1777. (*Kohut*, 35; *PAJHS*, XXVII, 154)

HART, Nathan.[3] In Georgetown, South Carolina, in 1791; in Charleston sometime between 1783 and 1800. (*EJSC*, 243, 279)

HART, Nathan.[4] December 7, 1797, New York City—April 29, 1857, New York. Son of Jacob Hart.[4] (*MSGC*; *Pool*, 412)

HART, Philip. 1727, Hamburgh, Germany —February 1/4, 1796, Charleston. A mohel and a merchant, he was in America by 1750. He fought in the Revolution and furnished supplies to the state commissary. (*EJSC*, 41; *EOJCC*, 58; *Occident*, I, 336; *UJE*, III, 115; *Wills*, 41)

HART, Rachel.[1] 1790—January 8, 1869. Daughter of Daniel Hart,[2] she was married to Nathan Hart in December, 1807. (*MSGC*; *WAJA*)

HART, Rachel.[2] October 5, 1795, New York—September 1, 1889, New York. Daughter of Jacob Hart,[4] she was married to Angel Jacob on July 3, 1822, in New York. (*MSGC*)

HART, Rebecca.[1] About 1768—December 22, 1836, Philadelphia. Daughter of Myer Hart, she was married to Elias Polock on August 21, 1806. (*GBMIP*; *MIPR*; *MSGC*)

HART, Rebecca.[2] Born November 14, 1791, New York. Daughter of Jacob Hart,[4] she was married to Moses Seixas Phillips on November 6, 1822, in New York. (*MSGC*)

HART, Rebecca.[3] Born November 20, 1766, Newport. Daughter of Naphtaly Hart.[2] (*NHM*, II, 207)

HART, Mrs. Rebecca. Wife of Joshua Hart, she was in Charleston by 1766. (*MSGC*; *PAJHS*, XX, 160)

HART, Reyna. August 27/September 2, 1779, Philadelphia—February 2, 1867, New York. Daughter of Jacob Hart.[4] (*MSGC*)

HART, Richea. Daughter of Joshua Hart, she lived in Charlestown. She was married to Abraham M. Seixas[3] on November 18, 1777. (*EJSC*, 43; *PAJHS*, XXVII, 161)

HART, Mrs. Sally. Wife of Moses Hart, she was in Charleston about 1795. (*WAJA*)

HART, Sally (Sarah). August 2, 1763— August 11, 1823. Daughter of Myer Hart, she was married to Isaac N. Cardozo[1] on January 10, 1798, in Philadelphia. (*MIPR*; *MSGC*)

HART, Samuel.[1] Died October 15, 1773, Barbados. This son of Moses Hart was a well known merchant who was in New York City in 1746. In 1768 he was president of Congregation Shearith Israel in New York City. (*AJAM*, V, 18; *JRMP*; *PAJHS*, XXI, 51)

HART, Samuel.[2] A Rhode Island merchant, he joined with the British during the Revolution. Cf. Samuel Hart, Jr. (*JRMP*; *PAJHS*, XXIII, 166f)

HART, Samuel.[3] Born October 15, 1749. Son of Jacob Hart.[2] (*MSGC*)

HART, Samuel.[4] Born May 6, 1774. Son of Aaron Hart.[1] (*MSGC*)

HART, Samuel.[5] Died October 7, 1795, New York City. Son of Ephraim Hart, he lived in New York City. (*MSGC*; *PAJHS*, XXVII, 274)

HART, Samuel.[6] May have been the son of Michael Hart. He was prominent in politics. (*MSP*)

HART, Samuel.[7] Born 1773, Easton. Son of Myer Hart. (*MSGC*)

HART, Samuel, Jr. In Newport in 1780; in New York City in 1792. Cf. Samuel Hart.[2] (*PAJHS*, XXVII, 51, 448)

HART, Samuel D. In Philadelphia in 1800. (*MIPR*)

HART, Samuel Isaac. In New York City in 1795. (*SIR*)

HART, Samuel Judah. 1789—1802. Son of Uriah Hart. (*MSGC*)

HART, Sarah. Born January 9, 1765, Newport. Daughter of Naphtaly Hart.[2] (*NHM*, II, 207)

HART, Mrs. Sarah. Wife of Judah Hart, she was in Connecticut in 1762. It is highly doubtful that she was Jewish. (*JRMP*)

HART, Seymour. In 1783 he pledged his loyalty to the Continental Congress in

Philadelphia. It is doubtful that he was Jewish. (*UJE*, VIII, 477)

HART, Shankey. June 5, 1766, Charlestown—January 24, 1804. Daughter of Joshua Hart, she was married to Abraham Jacobs[1] on October 19, 1785. (*Wills*, 80)

HART, Mrs. Sheprah. Wife of Naphtali Hart. (*MSGC*)

HART, Simeon. 1771—January 14, 1846, Paterson, New Jersey. Son of Michael Hart,[1] he was married to Elizabeth. (*MSGC*; *Trachtenberg*, 71)

HART, Simon. In Charlestown in 1762. (*EJSCB*, 11)

HART, Simon I. In New York City in 1795. (*JRMP*)

HART, Simon Moses. 1763—December 22, 1840, New Orleans. In 1797 he was a merchant in Charleston. (*WAJA*; *Wills*, 41)

HART, Mrs. Simon Moses. Married to Simon Moses Hart, probably before 1800. (*MSP*)

HART, Solomon. A shohet, he was in New York City in 1736 with his wife and child. In 1743 he absconded, leaving his family. (*MEAJA*, 71; *PAJHS*, II, 48)

HART, Solomon, Jr. About 1740 he was naturalized in New York City. (*Hugsoc*, XXIV, 30)

HART, Uriah. Born August 24, 1771. Son of Aaron Hart,[1] he was married to Miriam. (*MSGC*)

HART, Zipporah. September 5, 1789—March 16, 1875. Daughter of Jacob Hart,[4] she was married to Eleazer S. Lazarus on November 1, 1809. (*MSGC*)

HAYES, Mordecai. In 1797 he was a joiner in Petersburg, Virginia. (*Ginsberg*, 11)

HAYMAN, Jacob. In Philadelphia in 1785. (*MIPR*)

HAYMAN, Moses. Also known as Moses Heyman and Moses Heymann. He was in New York City in 1747, and was known as a merchant in Philadelphia in 1761. He was married to Rebecca. (*PAJHS*, XXI, 55; XXXIV, 77; *WW*, 41)

HAYMAN, Nathan. In 1718 he left Boston for Antigua. (*JNEA*, 24)

HAYMAN, Mrs. Rebecca. Wife of Moses Hayman, she was in Philadelphia in 1761. (*PAJHS*, XXXIV, 77)

HAYS. Died July, 1796, Philadelphia, probably an infant. (*MIPR*)

HAYS, Aaron Burr. 1800—May, 1881. Son of Jacob Hays,[3] he was married to Sarah Foreman. (*MSGC*)

HAYS, Abigail.[1] Daughter of Jacob Hays,[1] she was married to Michael S. Hays on July 23, 1766. (*MSGC*; *SIR*)

HAYS, Abigail.[2] Daughter of David Hays,[2] she was married after 1812 to Mr. Conkling. (*PAJHS*, II, 71)

HAYS, Abraham.[1] In New York City in 1731. (*PAJHS*, XXI, 28f, 31)

HAYS, Abraham.[2] Died Long Island. This son of Michael Hays[1] fought in the Revolution. (*JE*, VI, 271; *MSGC*)

HAYS, Andrew.[1] Born 1742. This son of Solomon Hays[1] was a silversmith who came from Holland about 1763 and went to Montreal. One of the first Jews in Canada in the 1770s, he was an early member of Congregation Shearith Israel. In 1778 he was married to Abigail David. (*JRMP*; *MSGC*; *PAJHS*, I, 117; *Sack*, 62, 66; *UJE*, V, 256)

HAYS, Andrew.[2] Son of Michael Hays,[1] he was in New York City and Philadelphia from 1781 through 1797. (*MIPR*; *MSGC*; *SIR*)

HAYS, Asher.[1] September 13, 1760, New York City—February 22, 1761, New York City. Son of Isaac Hays.[1] (*PAJHS*, XXVII, 151; *Pool*, 501; *SIR*)

HAYS, Asher.[2] Born April 25, 1775, Bedford, New York. Son of David Hays.[2] (*PAJHS*, XXVII, 330; *SIR*)

HAYS, Baruch. Died April 13, 1845, West Indies. This son of Solomon Hays[1] became a freeman of New York City in 1768. During the Revolution he served with the loyalist forces. He later went to Canada, where he sought his livelihood as a merchant and auctioneer. On April 16, 1783, he was married to Rachel da Costa[2] in New York City. (*Coldoc*, 98, *et passim*; *JRMP*; *MIPR*; *MSGC*; *PAJHS*, VI, 102; XVI, 27; XXI, 104; XLV, 54f)

HAYS, Basha (Bertha). 1737—March 4, 1741, New York City. Daughter of Judah Hays.[1] (*MSGC*; *PAJHS*, XVIII, 121; *Pool*, 466)

HAYS, Benjamin.[1] A member of the Revolutionary army, he was in Philadelphia in 1783. (*JE*, VI, 270; *MIPR*)

HAYS, Benjamin.[2] October, 1796—October, 1872. Son of Jacob Hays.[3] (*MSGC*)

HAYS, Benjamin.[3] Died July, 1816. Son of Jacob Hays.[1] (*MSGC*)

HAYS, Benjamin Etting. December, 1779, Bedford, New York—August 13, 1858, Pleasantville, New York. This son of David Hays[2] was a shohet and farmer. He was charitable and beloved by his neighbors, Jewish and non-Jewish. On March 23, 1814, he was married to Sarah Myers.[2] (*MSGC*; *PAJHS*, II, 63; *UJE*, V, 256)

HAYS, Catherine.[1] October 3, 1776, Boston —January 2, 1854, Richmond. Daughter of Moses Michael Hays. (*PAJHS*, XII, 105, 109; XXVII, 194)

HAYS, Catherine.[2] 1780—February 14, 1861, Montreal. Daughter of Andrew Hays,[1] she was married to James Solomons. (*MSGC*)

HAYS, Caty. Daughter of Judah Hays,[1] she was married first to Abraham Sarzedas in 1753, and in 1775 to Jacob Jacobs[2] in Savannah. (*MSGC*; *PAJHS*, X, 94)

HAYS, Charity.[1] September, 1722—June 18, 1773, New York City. Daughter of Michael Hays,[1] she was married to Isaac Adolphus. (*PAJHS*, XVIII, 122; XXXIII, 210; *SIR*)

HAYS, Charity.[2] 1740—January 19, 1813, New York City. Daughter of Jacob Hays,[2] she was married to Jacob Cohen[2] on September 3, 1760, in New York City. (*Pool*, 331f; *SIR*)

HAYS, Charity.[3] March 14, 1782, Bedford, New York—July 20, 1839, New York. Daughter of David Hays,[2] she was married to David de Silvasolis on April 24, 1811. (*MSGC*)

HAYS, Daniel. In Bedford, New York, in 1775. He may have been a son of David Hays.[2] (*HDB*)

HAYS, David.[1] Died June, 1778. This son of Michael Hays[1] was a merchant in New York City by 1728. He became a freeman there in 1735, and a constable in 1736, and was naturalized in 1740. In 1751 he was president of Congregation Shearith Israel. On April 28, 1735, he married Grace Mears,[1] his second wife. (*MCCCNY*, IV, 346; *MSGC*; *PAJHS*, XXI, 10, *et passim*; *UJE*, V, 256)

HAYS, David.[2] February 19, 1732, Rye, New York—October 17, 1812, Mt. Pleasant, New York. This son of Jacob Hays[1] was in Bedford as a merchant by 1771. He was also a farmer and storekeeper. During the French and Indian War he served in the New York contingent. On May 23, 1764, he was married to Esther Etting in New York City. (*MSGC*; *PAJHS*, XVIII, 111; *Pool*, 329f; *SIR*; *UJE*, IV, 188; V, 255)

HAYS, Elinor E. November 11, 1770—1858. Daughter of David Hays.[2] (*MSGC*)

HAYS, Ellen. June 18, 1800, Philadelphia —November 23, 1855, Baltimore. Daughter of Samuel Hays,[1] she was married to Samuel Etting on November 5, 1828. (*GBMIP*; *MSGC*)

HAYS, Fannie. October 24, 1794—August 9, 1796. Daughter of Samuel Hays.[1] (*MSGC*)

HAYS, Gitlah. Born March 18, 1772, New York City. Daughter of Michael Solomon Hays. (*SIR*)

HAYS, H. About 1756 he was buried in New York City. (*Pool*, 89, 501)

HAYS, Hannah. April 15, 1768, New York City—before 1812. Daughter of David Hays,[2] she was married to Benjamin Myers.[1] (*MSGC*; *PAJHS*, II, 71; *SIR*)

HAYS, Henry. In New York City in 1797. It is doubtful that he was Jewish. (*PAJHS*, XIX, 33f)

HAYS, Hetty. Died before 1803. Daughter of David Hays,[2] she was married to Isaiah Isaacs.[1] (*ELJR*, 14; *PAJHS*, II, 69)

HAYS, Isaac.[1] Died September 18, 1765, New York City. This son of Michael Hays[1] came to America from the Hague in 1720. A tallow chandler, he was naturalized and became a freeman in 1748. His wife was Rebecca Judah.[1] *(MSGC; PAJHS, VI, 102; Pool, 502; SIR; UJE, V, 256)*

HAYS, Isaac.[2] In Philadelphia in 1783. *(MIPR)*

HAYS, Isaac.[3] July 5, 1796, Philadelphia—April 13, 1879, Philadelphia. This son of Samuel Hays[1] had a distinguished career in medicine. In 1812 he entered the University of Pennsylvania and received his M.D. in 1820. He was a staff physician of the Pennsylvania Infirmary for Diseases of the Eye and Ear. One of the first to study color blindness and to detect astigmatism, he was one of the foremost ophthalmologists in the country, and was the first president of the Ophthalmological Society of Philadelphia. He was also an outstanding medical editor and author in the medical sciences. He wrote the code of ethics for the American Medical Association, which he helped found, and he was a leader in the Academy of Natural Sciences of Philadelphia. On May 7, 1834, he was married to Sarah Ann Minis. *(DAB, VIII, 462f; Morais, 50, et passim; UJE, V, 257; VIII, 526; WW, 275, et passim)*

HAYS, Jacob.[1] Died September 3, 1760. This son of Michael Hays[1] was a merchant who became a freeman about 1725. He was married to Hetty Adolphus. *(MSGC; PAJHS, VI, 101; XXXIII, 210)*

HAYS, Jacob.[2] Born June 19, 1768, Claverack, New York. Son of Michael Solomon Hays. *(SIR)*

HAYS, Jacob.[3] May 5, 1772, Bedford, New York—June 20, 1850, New York City. This son of David Hays[2] came to New York City in 1798 and was appointed city marshal. From 1802 until 1849 every mayor appointed him high constable (chief of police). His reputation as a detective was worldwide. Hays' second wife was Katherine Conroy; his third wife was Mary Post. He was a convert to Christianity. *(MSGC; PAJHS, II, 64, et passim; UJE, V, 255f)*

HAYS, Jacob.[4] Died 1798, New York City. A conveyancer. *(Pool, 271)*

HAYS, Jacob.[5] June 5, 1791, New York City—June 20, 1801. Son of Baruch Hays. *(MSGC; PAJHS, XXVII, 349)*

HAYS, John. Born August 7, 1768, New York City. This son of Michael Hays[3] was mayor of Cumberland, Maryland. He was probably reared as a Christian. His wife was Anne Maria Wright. *(MSGC)*

HAYS, John Jacob. 1766/1770, New York City—February, 1836, Cahokia, Illinois. This son of Baruch Hays went to the northwest as a young man and engaged in the Indian trade. One of the first Jewish settlers in what is today Illinois, about 1793 he settled in Cahokia, where he became postmaster. From 1809 until 1834 he was sheriff of St. Clair County. In 1813 Hays was appointed collector of internal revenue for the Indian territory, and in 1822 he was appointed Indian agent at Fort Wayne. He was married to a Christian, Mary Louise Brouillet, in Vincennes, October, 1801, and his children were reared as Christians. *(Coldoc, 282f; JE, VI, 271; PAJHS, XLV, 54f; UJE, III, 134; V, 256, 538, 557; VII, 269)*

HAYS, Joseph. In New York City in 1738. *(PAJHS, II, 92)*

HAYS, Joseph Lopez. July 1, 1792—October 11, 1834, Philadelphia. Son of Baruch Hays, he was married to Mary Ann Levy on January 19, 1817. *(MSGC)*

HAYS, Josse. Died March 14, 1808. Daughter of Judah Hays,[1] she was married to Joseph Pinto on November 6, 1765, in New York City. *(PAJHS, XXI, 81; SIR; Wills, 5)*

HAYS, Judah.[1] 1703, Holland—August 19, 1764, New York City. This son of Michael Hays[1] came from Holland to New York City, where he became a freeman in 1735 and was naturalized about 1740. A distinguished merchant, he was elected constable in 1736. He was a shipowner and had privateers in service of the British during the French and Indian War. About 1734 he was married to Rebecca Michaels.[1] *(Coldoc, 12f; MSGC; PAJHS, II, 82; III, 81f; V, 116; VI, 102; XXXIII, 210; Pool, 471f; UJE, V, 257)*

HAYS, Judah.[2] April 16, 1770, Newport—May 1, 1832, St. Augustine, Florida. This son of Moses Michael Hays was a prominent

Boston merchant. In 1805 he was elected as fire warden of Boston, probably the first Jew to be elected to a public office in Boston. He was one of the founders of the Boston Athenaeum, the first library association in the United States. (*MSGC; PAJHS,* XXVII, 195; *SIR; UJE,* VII, 404)

HAYS, Judith. September 2, 1767—February 4, 1844. Daughter of Moses Michael Hays, she was married to Samuel Myers[3] on September 21, 1796. (*MSGC; PAJHS,* XII, 105, 109)

HAYS, Kitty. 1784, Montreal—November 30, 1872, New York. Daughter of Baruch Hays. (*MSGC*)

HAYS, Lazarus. Born about 1784. Son of Andrew Hays,[1] he was a silversmith in Montreal. (*JRMP*)

HAYS, Michael.[1] Died 1740, New York City. Son of Solomon Hays. (*PAJHS,* XVIII, 121)

HAYS, Michael.[2] Born June 29, 1750. Son of Isaac Hays.[1] (*MSGC*)

HAYS, Michael.[3] 1753, Westchester, New York—1799. This son of Jacob Hays[1] was a farmer who was elected assessor of Mt. Pleasant, New York. He later owned shops in Oblong, New York, and in Bedford, New York. (*MSGC; PAJHS,* II, 64, 67-70; *UJE,* V, 255)

HAYS, Michael (Meleg). Son of Judah Hays,[1] he was buried in New York City on February 26, 1759. (*Pool,* 472, 501)

HAYS, Michael Solomon. Son of Solomon Hays,[1] in 1800 he was unable to support himself because of his crippled condition. On July 23, 1766, he was married to Abigail Hays[1] in New York City. (*SIR*)

HAYS, Miriam Gratz. July 4, 1798—July 2/3, 1826, Philadelphia. Daughter of Samuel Hays.[1] (*JCES; PAJHS,* VI, 110)

HAYS, Moses.[1] Son of Jacob Hays,[1] he was born before 1766. (*MSGC*)

HAYS, Moses.[2] 1789—October 22, 1857, Pleasantville, New York. Son of David Hays.[2] (*PAJHS,* XXVII, 330)

HAYS, Moses I. Son of Isaac Hays.[1] (*MSGC*)

HAYS, Moses Michael. March 9, 1739, New York City—May 9, 1805, Boston. This son of Judah Hays[1] was a watchmaker who became a freeman of New York City in 1769. That same year he went to Newport to build and freight ships in partnership with Myer Polock. He was also interested in the China trade and in banking. Late in 1782 he went to Boston and started an insurance business as a maritime underwriter. A member of numerous business and civic organizations, he held many high positions with the Masons. In 1768 he was appointed deputy inspector general of Masonry for North America; in 1791 he was grand master of the Massachusetts grand lodge while Paul Revere was the deputy grand master. On August 13, 1766, he was married to Rachel Myers.[1] (*Coldoc,* 13, *et passim; MEAJA,* 152, *et passim; MEAJB,* 60, *et passim; MSGC; PAJHS,* VI, 102; XII, 104, 107; XIX, 5, *et passim; UJE,* II, 481; V, 257; VII, 404; X, 284, 427, 471)

HAYS, Peter. Died 1798. Infant son of Jacob Hays.[3] (*MSGC*)

HAYS, Phila. 1738—April 2, 1808, New York City. Daughter of Judah Hays,[1] she was married to Daniel Nunez on January 21, 1767. (*MSGC; SRB*)

HAYS, Phoebe. 1779—July 30, 1841. Daughter of Andrew Hays,[1] she was married to Isaac Valentine on August 30, 1820. (*MSGC*)

HAYS, Rachel.[1] Born September 17, 1765, New Rochelle, New York. Daughter of David Hays,[2] she was married to Benjamin Myers[1] on March 25, 1804. (*PAJHS,* XXVII, 330; *SIR*)

HAYS, Rachel.[2] Died May 2, 1768, Quebec. Daughter of Judah Hays,[1] she was married to Levy Michaels in 1759. (*MSGC*)

HAYS, Rachel.[3] 1782—April 15, 1844, Montreal. Daughter of Andrew Hays,[1] she was married to Phillip Hofstetter. (*MSGC*)

HAYS, Rachel.[4] Daughter of a Judah Hays, she was married to Abraham Lazarus and was in New York City in 1760. (*NYHSW,* VI, 339f)

HAYS, Rebecca. February 1, 1769, New York City—July 23, 1802, Boston. Daughter of Moses Michael Hays. (*Gutstein*, 315; *PAJHS*, XII, 109; *SIR*)

HAYS, Reyna.[1] 1743—September 28, 1787, Boston. Daughter of Judah Hays,[1] she was married to Isaac Touro in Newport in 1773. (*MEAJA*, 193; *PAJHS*, XII, 104f)

HAYS, Reyna.[2] November 17, 1757—August 30, 1835, Philadelphia. Daughter of Isaac Hays.[1] (*MSGC*)

HAYS, Sally. May 14, 1772, Newport—August 3, 1832. Daughter of Moses Michael Hays, she was married to Moses Myers[3] on September 21, 1796. (*MSGC*)

HAYS, Samuel.[1] January 30, 1764, New York City—September 26, 1838, Philadelphia. This son of Isaac Hays[1] was a prominent merchant and broker who served his apprenticeship under Haym Salomon. He was an active Mason. On January 8, 1794, he was married to Richea Gratz. (*MSGC*; *PAJHS*, I, 21; II, 175; VI, 50; XIX, 40, *et passim*; *UJE*, V, 256f)

HAYS, Samuel.[2] Son of Michael Hays.[1] (*MSGC*)

HAYS, Sarah.[1] June 16, 1755—March 20, 1799, Philadelphia. Daughter of Isaac Hays,[1] she was also known as Sally. On March 30, 1797, she was married to Solomon Gutshalkson in Philadelphia. (*JCES*; *MIPR*; *MSGC*)

HAYS, Sarah.[2] Born before 1764. Daughter of Judah Hays.[1] (*MSGC*)

HAYS, Slowey. June 29, 1779, Kingston, Jamaica, B.W.I.—October 19, 1836, Richmond. Daughter of Moses Michael Hays. (*MSGC*; *PAJHS*, XII, 105, 109)

HAYS, Solomon.[1] A West Indies merchant, he was a shohet and merchant in New York City by 1736. In 1742 he became a freeman of New York City. (*JE*, VI, 271; *PAJHS*, II, 48; VI, 102; XXI, 6, *et passim*)

HAYS, Solomon.[2] Born March 21, 1770, New York City. Son of Michael Solomon Hays. (*SIR*)

HAYS, Thomas. Born probably before 1800, Maheata, Ohio. Son of Michael Hays,[3] he was reared as a Christian. (*JRMP*; *MSGC*)

HAYS, William. In New York City in 1799. It is highly doubtful that he was Jewish. (*PAJHS*, XIX, 33)

HAYS, Yitlah.[1] July 9, 1774, New York City—February 3, 1816, New York. Daughter of Michael Solomon Hays, she was married to Mark Salomon. (*MSGC*; *SIR*)

HAYS, Yitlah.[2] Born March 11, 1778. Daughter of David Hays.[2] (*PAJHS*, XXVII, 330)

HEGA, Rachel Mendez. December 25, 1781, Bordeaux—February 3, 1839. Wife of Aaron Soria, she came to New York City in 1794. (*MSGC*; *Pool*, 407)

HEIDEK, Mr. A Jewish convert to Christianity, he came to Charleston from Europe in 1787. He attempted to convert Indians. (*Kohut*, 47)

HEILBRON, David. On August 24, 1786, he was married to Rachel Franks in Philadelphia. (*MIPR*)

HEILBRON, Hannah. June 15, 1787, New York—1866, Philadelphia. Daughter of David Heilbron, she was married to Jacob Monnheimer on December 29, 1819, in New York. (*GBMIP*; *MSGC*)

HEILBRON, Hayman. In Philadelphia in 1786. Cf. Haim Halbourne. (*Essays*, 116; *MIPR*)

HEILBRON, Jonas. 1790, Philadelphia—1808, Philadelphia. Son of David Heilbron. (*MIPR*)

HEILBRON, Jonathan (Jonas). April 1, 1799, Philadelphia—1808. Son of David Heilbron. (*MIPR*; *MSGC*)

HELBERT, Sarah. Born probably in England, died February 24, 1749, New York City. Daughter of Philip Helbert, she was the second wife of Baruch Judah.[1] (*Pool*, 242)

HENDRICKS, Aaron.[1] Died March 21, 1771, New York City. Son of Chaim Hendricks, he came to New York City from London about 1758. (*MSGC*)

HENDRICKS, Aaron.[2] Born April 13, 1772, New York City. Son of Uriah Hendricks, he was dead by 1775. (*Pool*, 479; *SIR*)

HENDRICKS, Abraham. In Hamshire County, Virginia, in 1784. It is highly doubtful that he was Jewish. (*PAJHS*, XX, 100)

HENDRICKS, Charlotte. September 26, 1773, New York City—December 2/3, 1849, New York City. Daughter of Uriah Hendricks, she was married to Benjamin Gomez[3] on September 13, 1797. (*MSGC*; *PAJHS*, XVII, 198; *Pool*, 432; *SIR*)

HENDRICKS, Esther. June 18, 1775—January 28, 1848, New York. Daughter of Uriah Hendricks, she was married to Naphtali Judah on November 11, 1801. (*MSGC*; *PAJHS*, XXVII, 286, 289; *Pool*, 479; *SIR*)

HENDRICKS, Hannah. January 2, 1768, New York City—July 19, 1839, Camden, South Carolina. Daughter of Uriah Hendricks, she was married to Jacob de Leon on October 4, 1789, in New York City. (*MSGC*; *SIR*)

HENDRICKS, Harmon (Menachem). March 3/10, 1771, New York City—April 3, 1838, New York City. This son of Uriah Hendricks was a merchant reputed to have established the first copper-rolling mill in America about 1813. He aided the government financially during the War of 1812. A prominent member of the Jewish community of New York City, he was president of Congregation Shearith Israel from 1824 to 1827. On June 4, 1800, he was married to Frances Isaacs.[3] (*MSGC*; *PAJHS*, IV, 90; VI, 133; IX, 36; XIII, 140; XVIII, 105; *POFNW*, 49, *et passim*; *Pool*, 479; *SIR*; *UJE*, V, 314; VIII, 177)

HENDRICKS, Jochebed Sarah. October 9/November 7, 1766, New York City—March 25, 1821, New York City. Daughter of Uriah Hendricks. (*MSGC*; *PAJHS*, XVIII, 118; XX, 164; *Pool*, 479; *SIR*)

HENDRICKS, Matilda. Died by 1775. Daughter of Uriah Hendricks. (*Pool*, 479)

HENDRICKS, Mordecai. Born October 5, 1769, New York City. Son of Uriah Hendricks, he died while on a sea voyage. (*PAJHS*, XXVII, 154; *et passim*; *Pool*, 479; *SIR*)

HENDRICKS, Rebecca. October 18, 1764, New York City—November 9, 1829, Charleston. Daughter of Uriah Hendricks, she was married to Solomon Hyam Levy in 1789. (*MSGC*; *PAJHS*, XXVII, 286; *SIR*)

HENDRICKS, Richa. Born October 18, 1763, New York City. Daughter of Uriah Hendricks, she was married to Abraham (Arnet) Gomez[2] in 1798. (*PAJHS*, XXVII, 286; *Pool*, 479; *SIR*)

HENDRICKS, Rosy. Daughter of Chaim Hendricks, she was in New York City in 1758. (*MSGC*)

HENDRICKS, Uriah. 1731/7, Holland—September 27, 1798, New York City. About 1750 this son of Aaron Hendricks was the first of his family to come to America from Holland. He settled in New York City as a merchant and an importer. He then established a successful metal business. During the Revolution he was a loyalist. A devoted member of the Jewish community, he served as president of Congregation Shearith Israel. (*Coldoc*, 11, *et passim*; *MSGC*; *PAJHS*, III, 83; XIII, 140; XX, 163f; XXI, 73, *et passim*; *POFNW*, 46, *et passim*; *SIR*; *UJE*, V, 314)

HENRICUS, I. In New York City in 1795. (*PAJHS*, XXVII, 63)

HENRICUS, Jacob. In New York City in 1795. (*PAJHS*, XXVII, 58)

HENRIQUES, Abraham Nunes. 1674—June 9, 1741, New York City. His wife was Esther. (*PAJHS*, XVIII, 121; *Pool*, 227f)

HENRIQUES, Elias, Jr. He came from Bordeaux to New York City in 1797. (*SZ*, 121)

HENRIQUES, Mrs. Esther Nunes. In New York City in 1741. She may have been the wife of Abraham Nunes Henriques. (*PAJHS*, XXVII, 246; *Pool*, 227f)

HENRIQUES, Hetty. In New York City in 1800. (*SIR*)

HENRIQUES, Isaac Fernandez. In New York City in 1739. (*PAJHS*, XXI, 40)

HENRIQUES, Isaac Nunes. Died July 7, 1767, Philadelphia. A merchant, he was in Georgia in 1733 and in Lancaster in 1747. In 1741 he was naturalized in New York City. Cf. Isaac Ricus. (*LCHS*, V, 93;

MIPR; PAJHS, II, 48f; V, 117; X, 73; XXI, 45, et passim)

HENRIQUES, Mrs. Isaac Nunes. Wife of Isaac Nunes Henriques. Cf. Mrs. Abigail Nunes. (PAJHS, X, 73)

HENRIQUES, Jacob Cohen. A baker, he arrived in New Amsterdam about 1655. (Grollman, 115; POFNW, 468)

HENRIQUES, Moses. In New York City in 1740. (PAJHS, XXI, 42)

HENRIQUES, Nathaniel. In Newport about 1790. (PAJHS, XXVII, 185, 190)

HENRIQUES, Shem. Son of Isaac Nunez Henriquez, he was in Georgia in 1733. (PAJHS, X, 73; XVII, 168)

HENRIQUEZ, Abraham. In Philadelphia in 1782. (Morais, 15)

HENRIQUEZ, Isaac. On June 2, 1687, he was made a freeman in New York City. (AJAM, III, 6f)

HENRIQUEZ, Jacob. A child in New York City about 1793. (PAJHS, XXVII, 55)

HENRIQUIS, I. Abba. His book, Reason and Faith, was published in Philadelphia in 1791. (ALDINE)

HENRY, Aaron.[1] In Charlestown in 1779; in Richmond in 1790. (PAJHS, XIX, 152; XX, 104)

HENRY, Aaron.[2] In New York City in 1792. (PAJHS, XXVII, 51)

HENRY, Barnard.[1] Also listed as Bernal and Barnet Henry. Son of Aaron Henry,[1] he was United States consul in Gibraltar in 1788, and an officer in the U.S. Navy. (PAJHS, XII, 164; XVIII, 209; XIX, 152)

HENRY, Barnard.[2] Born November 6, 1783, Savannah. Son of Lyon Henry. (SRB)

HENRY, Mrs. Catherine. Died September 4, 1812. First wife of Jacob Henry.[2] (MSGC; SCHGM, XXXVII, 160)

HENRY, Mrs. Esther. 1787, Beaufort, South Carolina—July 16, 1823, Charleston. Second wife of Jacob Henry.[2] (MSGC)

HENRY, I. P. In Savannah in 1790. (MISR)

HENRY, Isaac. November 18, 1785, Savannah—November, 1843. Son of Lyon Henry, he was married to Anna Myers. (MSGC; SRB)

HENRY, Jacob.[1] About 1729—March 20, 1761, Philadelphia. A merchant, he was in business in New York City and in Newport. He was active in Congregation Mikveh Israel. (MIPR; PAJHS, VI, 108; WW, 37, et passim)

HENRY, Jacob.[2] This son of Joel Henry was elected in 1808 to the North Carolina legislature. Attempts were made to unseat him because he was a Jew. Henry's first wife was Catherine; his second wife was Esther. (PAJHS, XII, 53, 164; XVI, 46, et passim; UJE, V, 317; WW, 220f)

HENRY, Jacob.[3] Born August 17/18, 1782, Newport. Son of Lyon Henry, he was married to Marie (Miriam) Myers. (MSGC; PAJHS, XXVII, 349)

HENRY, Joel. In 1787 he lived in Beaufort, South Carolina. His wife was Ann Amelia. (MSGC)

HENRY, Mrs. Joel. (probably Ann Amelia) In Beaufort, South Carolina, in 1787. (MSGC)

HENRY, John L. In New York City in 1800. (SIR)

HENRY, Joseph.[1] Died February 24, 1792, Philadelphia. In 1785 he came to Philadelphia from London, and lived with his uncles Barnard and Michael Gratz. (MIPR; WW, 182)

HENRY, Joseph.[2] In Philadelphia in 1797. (MIPR)

HENRY, Judah. Died 1788, Vainsborough, Georgia. Infant son of Lyon Henry. (SRB)

HENRY, Lyon. Died about 1790, Vainsborough, Georgia. In 1783 he arrived in Savannah from Newport, and was in New York City in 1782. (MSGC; PAJHS, XXVII, 349; SRB)

HENRY, Moses. One of the first Jews to own land in Pittsburgh in 1768. It is highly doubtful nevertheless that he was Jewish. (UJE, XIII, 545)

HENRY, Philip Minis. 1789—October 2, 1799, Savannah. Probably the son of Lyon Henry. (*SRB*)

HENRY, Solomon. In New York City in 1798. (*SIR*)

HERTZ, Mrs. Isabella. 1769, Charlestown—January 24, 1824, Charleston. Wife of Handel Moses Hertz. (*MSP; Wills*, 43)

HEUMAN (HEYMANN), Isaac. In 1772 he was an indentured servant who had arrived in Philadelphia from Rotterdam. (*WW*, 57)

HEYMAN, Moses. Cf. Moses Hayman. (*PAJHS*, XXXIV, 77)

HEYMAN, Mrs. Rebecca. Wife of Moses Heyman, she was in Philadelphia in 1761. (*PAJHS*, XXXIV, 77)

HEYMES, Isaac. In New York City in 1794. It is doubtful that he was Jewish. (*PAJHS*, XIX, 31)

HINOZY, Joseph. Died May 12, 1793, Philadelphia. (*MIPR*)

HIRSCH, Alexander. In New York City in 1795. He tried to establish contact with the Jews of China. (*POFNW*, 317)

HOFFMAN, Jacob. In Reading, Pennsylvania, in 1759. It is highly doubtful that he was Jewish. (*PAJHS*, XXXIV, 77)

HOMBERG, Mrs. Ann. Wife of Moses Homberg, she continued his business after his death. (*GBMIP; WW*, 446)

HOMBERG, Moses. Died 1793, Philadelphia. In 1788 he was in New York City but eventually settled in Philadelphia, where he was a merchant and tavernkeeper. His wife was Ann. (*Coldoc*, 448f; *GBMIP; PAJHS*, XXVII, 43; *WW*, 172, *et passim*)

HOMBERTZ, Moses. In New York City in 1787. Cf. above. (*PAJHS*, XXVII, 42)

HUGENIN, Ann Sarah. Died 1835. A convert to Judaism, she was married first to Mr. Irby, and then to Abraham Alexander, Sr., on December 26, 1784. (*Alexander*, 15f; *EJSC*, 44; *MSP*)

HYAMS, Catherine. Born Ireland, died January 7, 1844, London. Daughter of Moses Hyams, she may have come to America. On October 2, 1799, she was married to Anthony Broglio in Venice. (*MSGC*)

HYAMS, David. Son of Moses Hyams, he was in Charleston in 1800. His wife was Rebecca da Costa Maysor. (*EJSC*, 135; *MSGC*)

HYAMS, Hannah. Daughter of Moses Hyams, she was married to Montague Jackson on February 27, 1811. (*MSGC*)

HYAMS, Isaac. 1762—December 26, 1830. Son of Moses Hyams, he was married to Catherine in January, 1785. (*MSGC*)

HYAMS, Joseph. Born 1767, New York City. Son of Moses Hyams. (*MSGC*)

HYAMS, Judah. Born 1768, New York City. Son of Moses Hyams. (*MSGC*)

HYAMS, Judith. May 13, 1800—August 10, 1840, Barcelona. Daughter of Samuel Hyams. (*MSGC*)

HYAMS, Moses. Born Poland. In New York City in 1767. His wife was Judith Isaacs.[3] (*MSGC*)

HYAMS, Moses David. July 20, 1798, Charleston—May 29, 1868, Charleston. Husband of Susanna Jackson. (*EOJCC*, 36; *MSGC*)

HYAMS, Moses Kosciusko. April 8, 1798—August 18, 1836, Pointe Coupée, Louisiana. Son of Samuel Hyams. (*MSGC*)

HYAMS, Samuel. June 9, 1776, London—May 30, 1843, Natchitoches, Louisiana. In 1795 he came to Charleston from England and was married to Miriam Levy[3] about this time. (*EJSC*, 35, *et passim*; *JRMP*; *MSGC*)

HYAMS, Solomon M. 1753, Dublin, Ireland—July 28, 1837. This son of Moses Hyams lived in Charleston for about fifty years. He was married to Mrs. Samuel Jacobs on June 20, 1811. (*EOJCC*, 37; *MSGC*)

HYAMS, Uriah. Died about 1740. He was a New York City chandler. (*PAJHS*, XXIII, 151)

HYMAN. In America in 1760, serving in the English army. (*PAJHS*, XXXV, 10f)

HYMAN, Moses. Died 1765, Philadelphia. In New York City in 1750; in Lancaster in 1751. He died leaving a widow. (*GBMIP; LCHS*, V, 93; *PAJHS*, XXI, 61)

HYMAN, Perla. On June 21, 1786, she was married to Joseph Benjamin in Philadelphia. (*MIPR*)

HYMES, Henry. An entertainer, lately with Sadler's Wells, he was advertising his balancing act in New York City in 1767. (*Arts & Crafts*, 288f)

HYNEMAN, Henry. In Philadelphia in 1779. (*Morais*, 23)

I

ISAACS. Died July 1, 1764. Daughter of Isaac Isaacs. (*SIR*)

ISAACS, A. M. In Charleston in 1800. (*EJSC*, 135)

ISAACS, Aaron.[1] August 15, 1724, Hamburg, Germany—September 11, 1798, Easthampton, Long Island. This son of Aaron Isaacs converted himself to Christianity, and his ten or eleven children were baptized at birth. A merchant, landowner, and ardent patriot, he fled to Connecticut during the Revolution. He helped found the Clinton Academy in Easthampton. In 1750 he was married to Mary Hedges. (*Coldoc*, 408f; *MEAJA*, 91f; *MSGC*)

ISAACS, Aaron.[2] In 1748 he was a member of Congregation Shearith Israel in New York City. Cf. above. (*PAJHS*, XXI, 58)

ISAACS, Aaron.[3] Born July 11, 1752, Easthampton, Long Island. Son of Aaron Isaacs,[1] he was reared as a Christian. He was married to Esther Mulford. (*MEAJA*, 91f; *MSGC*)

ISAACS, Aaron Lopez. Born August 10, 1778, Norwalk, died an infant. Son of Moses Isaacs.[1] (*MSGC*)

ISAACS, Abigail. August 5, 1782, Newport—September 8, 1855, New York City. Daughter of Moses Isaacs.[1] (*MSGC*; *PAJHS*, XXXIII, 210)

ISAACS, Abraham.[1] In New York City in 1710. (*WAJA*)

ISAACS, Abraham.[2] Born Emden, Germany, died September 24, 1743, New York City. A merchant who came to America about 1698, he became a freeman of New York City on September 6, 1723, and was naturalized in the same year. In 1725 he was elected constable. His wife was Hannah Mears. (*MCCCNY*, III, 374; *MSGC*; *NYHSW*, IV, 55; *PAJHS*, XXXIII, 210; *Pool*, 231f)

ISAACS, Abraham.[3] Died February 25, 1835, Montgomery, Alabama. Son of Jacob Isaacs, he was married to Rebecca Cohen.[3] (*MSGC*; *PAJHS*, XXXIII, 210)

ISAACS, Abraham.[4] In Charleston sometime between 1783 and 1800. (*EJSC*, 279)

ISAACS, Abraham.[5] In Wilmington, North Carolina, in 1798. (*PAJHS*, XXIX, 145)

ISAACS, Abraham.[6] Died February 15, 1803. A native of Prussia, he was a merchant in Portsmouth, New Hampshire, in 1798. He was a Mason as well as an observant Jew. (*PAJHS*, XI, 98f; XIX, 26; *UJE*, VIII, 165)

ISAACS, Abraham, Jr.[1] Died March 20, 1815. Son of Abraham Isaacs,[2] he was in New York City in 1737. (*MSGC*; *PAJHS*, XXI, 38)

ISAACS, Abraham, Jr.[2] In Charleston in 1800. (*EJSC*, 135)

ISAACS, Mrs. Abraham. Wife of Abraham Isaacs,[6] she lived in New Hampshire before 1800. (*PAJHS*, XI, 98)

ISAACS, Abraham Mears. November 17, 1765, Swansea, Massachusetts—October 29, 1814, Charleston. Son of Moses Isaacs,[1] he was married to Rebecca Simson[2] in New York City on June 18, 1806. (*EOJCC*, 74; *MSGC*; *PAJHS*, XX, 158; XXXIII, 210)

ISAACS, Abram. In New York City in 1792. (*PAJHS*, XXVII, 51)

ISAACS, Asher. Son of Asher Isaacs, he may have been in Charlestown in 1751. (*PAJHS*, XII, 167; *WAJA*)

ISAACS, Catherine.[1] Born February 5, 1751, Easthampton, Long Island, died an infant. Daughter of Aaron Isaacs.[1] (*MSGC*)

ISAACS, Catherine.[2] July 4, 1781, Newport—May 12, 1854, New York. Daughter of Moses Isaacs.[1] (*MSGC*; *PAJHS*, XXXIII, 210)

ISAACS, David.[1] About 1760, Frankfort-on-the-Main, Germany—February 28, 1837, Charlottesville, Virginia. He lived in Richmond but settled in Charlottesville as a merchant in 1802. He supported Thomas Jefferson in his efforts to establish a college in Virginia. (*ELJR*, 240, 281, 297; *PAJHS*, XIX, 70; *Wills*, 22)

ISAACS, David.[2] Son of Isaiah Isaacs,[1] he was probably born before 1800 and died very young. (*ELJR*, 15; *PAJHS*, XIX, 70; XX, 100)

ISAACS, Elizabeth. Born December 18, 1755, Easthampton, Long Island. Daughter of Aaron Isaacs,[1] she was baptized. Her husband was Elisha Jones. (*MSGC*)

ISAACS, Esther.[1] May 18, 1762, Easthampton, Long Island—September 28, 1848, New York City. Daughter of Aaron Isaacs,[1] she was baptized. (*MSGC*)

ISAACS, Esther.[2] March 20, 1780—November 27, 1841, New York. Daughter of Moses Isaacs,[1] she was married to Isaac Moses[4] on March 6/July 2, 1800. (*MSGC*; *PAJHS*, XXXIII, 210)

ISAACS, Eve Deborah. About 1791—September 16, 1807, New York City. Daughter of Nathaniel Isaacs. (*Pool*, 306)

ISAACS, Frances.[1] February 11, 1774, New York City—March 15, 1848, Yonkers. Daughter of Moses Isaacs,[1] she was married to Joseph Simson[2] on June 4, 1806. (*MSGC*; *PAJHS*, XXXIII, 210)

ISAACS, Frances.[2] Daughter of Isaiah Isaacs, she was married to Abraham Block on October 2, 1811. (*ELJR*, 15; *PAJHS*, XX, 100)

ISAACS, Frances.[3] June 9, 1783, Lancaster—May 1, 1854, New York. Daughter of Joshua Isaacs,[3] she was married to Harmon Hendricks on June 4, 1800. (*MSGC*; *PAJHS*, IX, 36)

ISAACS, Frumet. Born February 11, 1774, New York City. Daughter of Moses Isaacs.[1] (*PAJHS*, XXVII, 372; *SIR*)

ISAACS, Gitlah.[1] Born 1775, New York City. Daughter of Abraham Isaacs. (*PAJHS*, XXVII, 373)

ISAACS, Gitlah.[2] Born April 20, 1776, New York City. Daughter of Abraham Isaacs. (*SIR*)

ISAACS, Grace.[1] Daughter of Joshua Isaacs.[1] (*PAJHS*, XXIII, 152)

ISAACS, Grace.[2] May 13, 1788, New York City—June 14, 1848, New York City. Daughter of Joshua Isaacs.[3] (*MSGC*)

ISAACS, Grace.[3] Died October 14, 1781, Jamaica, Long Island. Wife of Nathan Hart.[1] (*Pool*, 503; *SIR*)

ISAACS, Grace.[4] Daughter of Jacob Isaacs.[2] (*PAJHS*, XXXIII, 210)

ISAACS, Hannah.[1] March 14, 1769, Newport—October 1, 1837, New York City. Daughter of Moses Isaacs.[1] (*MSGC*)

ISAACS, Hannah.[2] Born Newport or Jamaica, B.W.I., died March 8, 1798, Martinique. Daughter of Jacob Isaacs,[2] she was married to Jacob Phillips[1] on August 13, 1785. (*MSGC*; *PAJHS*, XXXII, 125; XXXIII, 210)

ISAACS, Hannah.[3] 1785—June 9, 1859. Daughter of Abraham Isaacs, Jr.,[1] she was married to Tobias Ezekiel on June 7, 1810. (*MSGC*)

ISAACS, Hannah.[4] July 7, 1792, New York City—November 17, 1867, New York City. Daughter of Joshua Isaacs.[3] (*MSGC*)

ISAACS, Hayes. Probably born before 1800. Son of Isaiah Isaacs.[1] (*ELJR*, 15)

ISAACS, Henrietta. Probably born before 1800. Daughter of Isaiah Isaacs.[1] (*PAJHS*, XIX, 70)

ISAACS, Henry.[1] Probably in New York City in 1709. (*EJSC*, 23)

ISAACS, Henry.[2] Born March 7, 1765, New York City. Son of Isaac Isaacs. (*PAJHS*, XXVII, 152)

ISAACS, Henry.[3] A merchant in Charlestown in 1765. (*EJSCB*, 13)

ISAACS, I. A. In New York City in 1795. (*PAJHS*, XXVII, 58)

ISAACS, Isaac.[1] In New York City in 1750. (*PAJHS*, XXI, 64, *et passim*)

ISAACS, Isaac.[2] January 17, 1764, Easthampton, Long Island—June 22, 1809, Newburgh, New York. This son of Aaron Isaacs[1] was baptized. His first wife was

Lucretia Wickham on November 17, 1782; his second wife was Fanny Dennison. (MSGC)

ISAACS, Isaac.[3] Born July 20, 1774, New York City. Son of Abraham Isaacs. (PAJHS, XXVII, 373; SIR)

ISAACS, Isaac.[4] In Savannah in 1788 and in 1802. (SRB)

ISAACS, Isaiah.[1] 1747, Germany—April, 1806, Charlottesville, Virginia. He came to America, probably from England. By 1769 he was in Richmond, and may have been the first permanent Jewish settler in Virginia. A silversmith, he then became a prominent merchant in partnership with Jacob I. Cohen, dealing in merchandising, real estate, and slave trading. In 1785 he was appointed clerk of the market; later he became a tax assessor and a councilman. His first wife was a Christian, Mary; his second wife was Hetty Hays. (ELJR, 13, et passim; MEAJB, 182, et passim; MSGC; PAJHS, XX, 100)

ISAACS, Isaiah.[2] Son of Isaiah Isaacs,[1] he lived in Richmond. (PAJHS, XX, 100)

ISAACS, Jacob.[1] In 1703 he was a merchant in New York City. (PAJHS, II, 82)

ISAACS, Jacob.[2] About 1718, New York City—March 20, 1798, Newport. This son of Abraham Isaacs[2] lived in New York City until 1743 and then moved to Newport. A merchant and ship broker with scientific interests, he presented to Congress a method for converting salt water to fresh water. On December 8, 1760, he was married to Rebecca Mears, probably in New York City. (Coldoc, 212, et passim; PAJHS, II, 111f; VI, 77f; VIII, 124; XIX, 18; XXI, 25, et passim; XXXIII, 210; SIR; UJE, V, 598; X, 470)

ISAACS, Jacob.[3] About 1752 he arrived in New York City, where he was addressed as "doctor." (PAJHS, XXII, 161)

ISAACS, Jacob.[4] April 25, 1785, Newport —March 16, 1786. Son of Moses Isaacs.[1] (PAJHS, XXVII, 349)

ISAACS, Joheveth. June 17, 1767, Swansea, Massachusetts/Norwalk, Connecticut—January 17, 1852. This daughter of Moses Isaacs was married to Michael Marks on October 11, 1786, at Newport. She settled with her husband in Sing Sing, New York, and gave birth to ten children. (Morais, 242; PAJHS, XXII, 182)

ISAACS, Jonathan. In New York City in 1740. (NYHSW, III, 321)

ISAACS, John.[1] Fought in the Virginia line in the Revolution. It is highly doubtful that he was Jewish. (PAJHS, XX, 99)

ISAACS, John.[2] Born May 9, 1758, Easthampton, Long Island. Son of Aaron Isaacs,[1] he was baptized. His wife was Kate Havens. (MSGC)

ISAACS, Joseph.[1] 1659—May 25, 1737, New York City. A butcher, he became a freeman of New York City on August 23, 1698. He served in King William's War in 1690. His wife was Rebecca. (AJAM, III, 7; MEAJA, 45f; PAJHS, VI, 101; XVIII, 121; POFNW, 469)

ISAACS, Joseph.[2] Born February 8, 1763, Jamaica, Long Island. Son of Isaac Isaacs. (PAJHS, XXVII, 152, 372; SIR)

ISAACS, Joseph.[3] In 1799 he was president of Congregation Shearith Israel in New York City. Cf. above. (PAJHS, XXI, 167)

ISAACS, Joseph.[4] March 21, 1782, Lancaster—July 20, 1783. Son of Joshua Isaacs.[3] (MSGC)

ISAACS, Josey. Daughter of Jacob Isaacs.[2] (PAJHS, XXXIII, 210)

ISAACS, Joshua.[1] Died July, 1744. This son of Joseph Isaacs was a merchant in New York City as early as 1730. He left funds for a Hebrew School for poor children. His wife was Hannah Levy.[1] (NYHSW, IV, 11f; PAJHS, XXI, 27; et passim; XXXIII, 210; POFNW, 213)

ISAACS, Joshua.[2] Son of Asher Isaacs, he was probably in Charlestown in 1751. (PAJHS, XII, 167)

ISAACS, Joshua.[3] September 17, 1744, Grenada, W. I.—February 17, 1810, New York City. This son of Joshua Isaacs[1] was a merchant who served in the Revolutionary army. On March 28, 1781, he was married to Brandly Lazarus in Lancaster. (*MSGC*; *Pool*, 317f)

ISAACS, Judah.[1] Born November 20, 1775, New York City, died an infant. Son of Moses Isaacs.[1] (*PAJHS*, XXVII, 373; XXXIII, 203; *SIR*)

ISAACS, Judah.[2] Died Charleston. Son of Jacob Isaacs.[2] (*PAJHS*, XXXIII, 203, 210)

ISAACS, Judith.[1] 1723, New York City—September 25, 1802, Charleston. Daughter of Abraham Isaacs.[2] (*MSGC*)

ISAACS, Judith.[2] Daughter of Asher Isaacs, she was probably in Charlestown in 1751. (*PAJHS*, XXI, 167)

ISAACS, Judith.[3] Born Germany. Wife of Moses Hyams. (*MSGC*)

ISAACS, Lazarus. In 1773 he was a glasscutter in Philadelphia, hired by William H. Stiegel of Lancaster County. (*PAJHS*, XXVIII, 255f; *WW*, 60)

ISAACS, Lion. In New York City in 1787. (*SIR*)

ISAACS, Martha. Born probably before 1800. Daughter of Isaiah Isaacs. (*PAJHS*, XX, 100)

ISAACS, Mary.[1] Born October 27, 1754, Easthampton, Long Island, died an infant. Daughter of Aaron Isaacs,[1] she was baptized. (*MSGC*)

ISAACS, Mary.[2] Born December 18, 1768, Easthampton, Long Island. Daughter of Aaron Isaacs,[1] she was baptized. (*MSGC*)

ISAACS, Mrs. Mary (Molly).[3] Died about 1784. Born a Christian, she was the first wife of Isaiah Isaacs.[1] (*ELJR*, 14)

ISAACS, Mrs. Mary.[4] After the death of her husband, Solomon Isaacs,[3] in 1798, she was married to Judah King. (*Pool*, 298)

ISAACS, Michael. Son of Abraham Isaacs,[2] he was in New York City about 1800. He was married to Mrs. Fanny Lazarus. (*MSGC*; *SIR*)

ISAACS, Moses.[1] March 25, 1737, New York City—August 31, 1798, New York City. This son of Abraham Isaacs[2] was a merchant and broker who lived in Newport and Norwalk, Connecticut. He served in the Revolutionary army. On August 30, 1764, he was married to Rachel Mears in Philadelphia. (*Morais*, 241f; *PAJHS*, XXV, 123; *UJE*, V, 599; X, 470)

ISAACS, Moses.[2] In Charleston sometime between 1783 and 1800. (*EJSC*, 280)

ISAACS, Nathaniel. About 1762—September 25, 1798, New York City. Son of Isaac Isaacs. (*PAJHS*, XVIII, 103; *Pool*, 270)

ISAACS, Patsey. Probably born before 1800. Daughter of Isaiah Isaacs.[1] (*ELJR*, 15)

ISAACS, Philip. Died about 1755. He was an East Chester, New York, merchant, who was in New York City in 1728. (*FEAJ*, 77; *PAJHS*, XXI, 9, et passim; XXVII, 1)

ISAACS, Rachel.[1] Daughter of Asher Isaacs, she was probably in Charlestown in 1751. (*PAJHS*, XII, 167)

ISAACS, Rachel.[2] 1781—September 22, 1803. Daughter of Jacob Isaacs,[2] she lived in Charleston and Cheraw, South Carolina. (*MSGC*; *PAJHS*, XXXIII, 210)

ISAACS, Mrs. Rachel.[3] Widow of S. Isaacs, she was in New York City in 1799. (*SIR*)

ISAACS, Ralph. Died Norwalk, Connecticut. Reputedly of Jewish origin. On March 7, 1725, he was married to Mary Rumsey. (*JRMP*; *MSGC*; *PAJHS*, XXXV, 188)

ISAACS, Rebecca.[1] Daughter of Joseph Isaacs, she was married to Joseph Simson sometime between 1712 and 1722 in Wilton, Connecticut. (*MEAJA*, 163; *PAJHS*, XXXIII, 210)

ISAACS, Rebecca.[2] Daughter of Asher Isaacs, she may have been in Charlestown in 1751. (*PAJHS*, XII, 167)

ISAACS, Rebecca.[3] September 16, 1772, Newport—April 15, 1775. Daughter of Moses Isaacs.[1] (*MSGC*)

ISAACS, Mrs. Rebacca. Wife of Joseph Isaacs.[1] (*POFNW*, 469)

ISAACS, Richa.[1] 1733—August 9, 1796, Charleston. Daughter of Abraham Isaacs,[2] she was married to Isaac Elizer in Newport in 1760. (*MSGC*)

ISAACS, Richa.[2] Born January 3, 1784, Newport. Daughter of Moses Isaacs.[1] (*MSGC*)

ISAACS, Richa.[3] Daughter of Abraham Isaacs, Jr.,[1] she was married to Abraham Levy on June 7, 1810. (*MSGC*)

ISAACS, Ruth. Born March 23, 1771, Easthampton, Long Island. Daughter of Aaron Isaacs,[1] she was baptized. (*MSGC*)

ISAACS, Sampson. August 29, 1790, New York City—August 10, 1791, New York City. Son of Joshua Isaacs.[3] (*MSGC*)

ISAACS, Samson Mears.[1] March 6, 1777, Norwalk, Connecticut—November 27, 1859, Charleston. Son of Moses Isaacs,[1] he was married to Catherine Cohen in Charleston on March 25, 1807. (*MSGC; PAJHS*, XXXIII, 210)

ISAACS, Samson Mears.[2] December 27, 1779, New York City—January 20, 1780, New York City. Son of Jacob Isaacs.[2] (*PAJHS*, XXVII, 349)

ISAACS, Samson Mears.[3] June 13, 1783, New York City—June 29, 1783. Son of Jacob Isaacs.[2] (*MSGC; PAJHS*, XXVII, 349)

ISAACS, Samuel.[1] In 1770 he was naturalized in New York City. (*JRMP*)

ISAACS, Samuel.[2] Born May 5, 1766. Son of Isaac Isaacs. (*MSGC*)

ISAACS, Samuel M. In New York City in 1796. (*PAJHS*, XXVII, 64)

ISAACS, Sarah.[1] In 1709 she may have been in New York City. (*EJSC*, 23)

ISAACS, Sarah.[2] August 19, 1760, Easthampton, Long Island—June 18, 1807, Boston. Daughter of Aaron Isaacs,[1] she was baptized. About 1779 she was married to William Payne. Her son William Howard Payne wrote *Home Sweet Home*. (*MEAJA*, 92; *MSGC*)

ISAACS, Sarah.[3] Died Charleston. Daughter of Abraham Isaacs.[1] (*MSGC*)

ISAACS, Sarah.[4] November, 1790—January 30, 1811, New York City. Also known as Sarah Haya. Daughter of Abraham Isaacs, Jr.,[1] she was married to Abraham L. Phillips on July 11, 1810. (*MSGC; Pool*, 321)

ISAACS, Sarah Lopez. December 24/26, 1770, Newport—April 23, 1860, New York. Daughter of Moses Isaacs,[1] she was married to Judah Myers[1] on October 21, 1821, in Richmond. (*MSGC; PAJHS*, XXXIII, 203)

ISAACS, Solomon.[1] This son of Joseph Isaacs was a merchant in Freehold, New Jersey, and was in Boston in 1737. (*PAJHS*, XXIII, 84; XXXV, 173f; *Pool*, 317)

ISAACS, Solomon.[2] Died about 1757, Charlestown. This son of Asher Isaacs was a merchant in New York City and Charlestown. (*EJSC*, 28, *et passim; PAJHS*, XII, 167)

ISAACS, Solomon.[3] Died 1798, New York City. A shopkeeper. (*Pool*, 271)

ISAACS, Solomon J. February 26, 1786, New York City—January 13, 1855, New York City. Son of Joshua Isaacs,[3] he was married to Elkaleh Kursheedt in New York City on May 21, 1829. (*MSGC*)

ISRAEL, A. E. In Philadelphia in 1783. (*MIPR*)

ISRAEL, Abigail. Daughter of Michael Israel, she was reared as a Christian. (*MSGC*)

ISRAEL, Abram. In New Amsterdam in 1654. (*AJAM*, III, 7)

ISRAEL, Bela. In 1787 he was involved in a law suit in Frederick County, Maryland. (*Records of Frederick County Court*, 123, 124; Hall of Records, Annapolis, Maryland)

ISRAEL, Benjamin.[1] A soapmaker in 1699, he was a qualified voter in New York City about 1701. (*AJAM*, III, 7; *MCCCNY*, II, 177)

ISRAEL, Benjamin.[2] In New York City in 1787. (*PAJHS*, XXVII, 42)

ISRAEL, David.[1] In New Amsterdam in 1654. (*AJAM*, III, 7)

ISRAEL, David.[2] On October 4, 1790, he arrived in Philadelphia from Amsterdam. (*MIPR*)

ISRAEL, Eleanor. Daughter of Solomon Israel, she was married to John Wood. It is doubtful that she was Jewish. (*MSP*)

ISRAEL, Eliau. In New York City in 1738. (*PAJHS*, XXI, 39f)

ISRAEL, Eliza. May 10, 1784, London—February 11, 1860, New York City. On February 16, 1803, she was married to Benjamin S. Judah. (*MSGC*)

ISRAEL, Hannah. Died August 20, 1825, New York City. Daughter of Gomperts Israel, she was married to Benjamin Jacobs. (*JRMP*; *MSGC*; *Pool*, 327)

ISRAEL, Isaac.[1] In 1655 he was a trader in New Amsterdam. (*AJAM*, III, 7)

ISRAEL, Isaac.[2] Fought in the Virginia line during the Revolution. It is doubtful that he was Jewish. (*PAJHS*, I, 122)

ISRAEL, Isaac.[3] In Philadelphia in 1783. (*MIPR*)

ISRAEL, Israel.[1] October 20, 1744, Philadelphia—March 17, 1822, Philadelphia. This son of Michael Israel was reared as a Christian. In 1746 he was baptized and became a member of the Universalist church in Philadelphia. At twenty-one he went to Barbados, where he amassed a fortune. An ardent patriot, he served in the Revolutionary army and was captured by the British in 1777. In 1800 he became high sheriff of Philadelphia, where he was a tavernkeeper. He was a prominent Mason. His wife was Hannah Erwin. (*Link*, 57, 121f; *MSGC*; *Rosenbach*, 43f; *UJE*, V, 619; *WW*, 31)

ISRAEL, Israel.[2] Died 1798, New York City. (*PAJHS*, XXVII, 68)

ISRAEL, John. In Philadelphia and Pittsburgh in 1800. In Pittsburgh he published the *Tree of Liberty*, a weekly newspaper. He was married to the daughter of David Reddick. It is highly doubtful that he was Jewish. (*PAJHS*, XXXVIII, 135f; *UJE*, VIII, 545)

ISRAEL, Joseph.[1] Died September 4, 1804. This son of Michael Israel was reared as a Christian. In 1800 he was in Norfolk. A member of the Revolutionary army, he later was a midshipman in the U.S. Navy.
(*MSGC*; *PAJHS*, XIX, 61, 70; *Rosenbach*, 43)

ISRAEL, Joseph.[2] A "Rabby" visiting in America, in 1765 he was on his way to Newport. From there he went to Surinam. (*PAJHS*, XXI, 91)

ISRAEL, Judah Levy. In 1738 he was a loyalist merchant in Newport. From 1759 until 1779 he was shammas of Congregation Shearith Israel in New York City. (*PAJHS*, XXI, 79; XXIII, 85; *POFNW*, 286f)

ISRAEL, Levy. Died June 27, 1779, New York City. He was shammas for Congregation Shearith Israel in New York City. (*Pool*, 503; *SIR*)

ISRAEL, Michael.[1] An early settler in Virginia, he fought in the Albermarle County, Virginia militia, against the Indians in 1758 and later in the Revolution. He finally settled in Philadelphia, where he was naturalized in 1752 as "Midrach Israel." His first wife was Sarah; his second wife was Mary J. Paxton. He reared his children as Christians. (*MSGC*; *PAJHS*, XIX, 70; XX, 90; *WW*, 31f)

ISRAEL, Michael.[2] Died 1798, New York City. A nephew of Isaac Adolphus, he came to America from Germany and practiced fur trading. About 1740 he was in New York City. (*PAJHS*, XXI, 45, et passim; XXIII, 157; XXV, 123)

ISRAEL, Moses. Born August 5, 1762, New York City. Son of Samuel Moses. (*PAJHS*, XXI, 142; *SIR*)

ISRAEL, Rose. In Norwalk, Connecticut, sometime between 1763 and 1789. It is doubtful that she was Jewish. (*JRMP*)

ISRAEL, Samuel.[1] In New York City in 1770. (*PAJHS*, XXI, 107, et passim; *SIR*)

ISRAEL, Samuel.[2] In 1765 he was a merchant in Mobile. He also lived in New Orleans. (*UJE*, VII, 206, 603)

ISRAEL, Mrs. Sarah. Wife of Michael Israel,[1] she was in Virginia in 1779. It is doubtful that she was Jewish. (*PAJHS*, XX, 90)

ISRAEL, Saul. In 1786 he was in New York, listed as a "curer of deafness." (*PAJHS*, XXII, 162)

ISRAEL, Saunders. In Philadelphia in 1786; in New York City in 1784. (*MIPR; POFNW*, 261)

ISRAEL, Solomon.[1] Probably in New York City in 1708. (*NYHSW*, XI, 2)

ISRAEL, Solomon.[2] In Virginia in 1764. He was related to Michael Israel.[1] (*PAJHS*, XX, 90)

ISRAELLS, Ansel. In 1757 he was in Maryland—one of the few Jews in Maryland in the eighteenth century. (*PAJHS*, V, 116)

ISSACKE, Joseph. On March 9, 1636, he became a freeman in Boston. It is doubtful that he was Jewish. (*AJAM*, III, 7)

ISSACS, Jacobus. On August 23, 1698, he became a freeman in New York City, where he was a carpenter. (*AJAM*, III, 7)

ISSACS, Rebecca. In 1695 she was a widow in New York City. (*AJAM*, III, 7)

J

JACOB, Mr. In Hickorytown, Pennsylvania, in 1761. (*PAJHS*, XXXIV, 82)

JACOB(S), Barnard Itzhak. In 1765 he was naturalized in Heidelberg, Pennsylvania. He lived also in Lancaster, where he was a shopkeeper, active in the civic life of Lancaster. He served as a wandering mohel or circumciser. His first wife was Clara; his second wife was Judica, the widow of Isaac Levy.[2] (*Hugsoc*, XXIV, 131; *MSGC*; *PAJHS*, IX, 30; *Wills*, 26; *WW*, 32, *et passim*)

JACOB, Mrs. Clara. First wife of Barnard Jacob(s). (*MSGC*)

JACOB, Henry. During the Revolution he was taken prisoner by the British while fighting in Charlestown, and was kept on the prison ship *Torbay*. It is doubtful that he was Jewish. (*SCHGM*, XXXIII, 283)

JACOB, Isaac.[1] Born Surinam, died October 28, 1782, Newport. Son of Jacob Jacob. (*MSP*)

JACOB, Isaac.[2] In 1770 he came from Ireland to Philadelphia. His whereabouts were unknown in 1772. (*PAJHS*, XXVIII, 255)

JACOB, John I. 1777, Baltimore—1852, Louisville, Kentucky. Although he married two Christian women and raised his children as Christians, he was reputed to have been a Jew. He lived in Shepherdsville and in Louisville. It is highly doubtful that he was Jewish. (*PAJHS*, I, 99f)

JACOB, Mordecai. In New York City in 1786. He operated a vendue and commission store. (*JRMP*)

JACOB, Moses.[1] In Richmond in 1791. (*PAJHS*, XX, 105)

JACOB, Moses.[2] In Philadelphia in 1784. (*MIPR*)

JACOB, Rebecca. Daughter of R. Jacob. (*PAJHS*, XXXIV, 62)

JACOBS. Born before 1800. Daughter of Israel Jacobs. (*MSP*)

JACOBS, Abigail.[1] Died April 19, 1721, Connecticut. Daughter of Isaac Jacobs. (*JRMP*)

JACOBS, Abigail.[2] Died by 1799, New York City. (*SIR*)

JACOBS, Abraham.[1] July 31, 1755—April 1, 1834. This son of Raphael Jacobs was a merchant in New York City, Charleston, and Savannah. On October 19, 1785, he was married to Shankey Hart. (*MISR*; *PAJHS*, XIX, 9, *et passim*; *Wills*, 80)

JACOBS, Abraham.[2] Born September, 1770, New York City. Son of Myer Jacobs.[1] (*MSP*)

JACOBS, Abraham.[3] Grandson of Joseph Simson, he was in New York City in 1781. (*Wills*, 8)

JACOBS, Abram. In 1742 he was a merchant in New York City. (*MSP*)

JACOBS, Augusta. August 20, 1799, Augusta, Georgia—August 4, 1800. Daughter of Abraham Jacobs.[1] (*MSGC*)

JACOBS, Barnard. In Charleston in 1800. Cf. Barnard Itzhak Jacob(s). (*EJSC*, 135)

JACOBS, Belah. In Newport with his family of six in 1790. It is doubtful that he was Jewish. (*Census A, Rhode Island*)

JACOBS, Benjamin.[1] 1661—October 13, 1739, New York City. Son of Jacob Schwab of Amsterdam, he was married to Rebecca Hadassah. (*Pool*, 215f)

JACOBS, Benjamin.[2] Son of Raphael Jacobs, he was a shohet in New York City in 1790. (*Pool*, 326)

JACOBS, Benjamin.[3] 1738/1747, Surinam —December 13/15, 1811, New York City. This son of Jacob Jacobs was a merchant who came to America in 1776. His wife was Hannah Israel. (*MSGC*; *PAJHS*, XVIII, 110; *Pool*, 325f)

JACOBS, Benjamin.[4] In Wilmington, North Carolina, in 1799. It is doubtful that he was Jewish. (*PAJHS*, XIX, 75)

[72]

JACOBS, Benjamin.[5] In Vermont in 1782. It is doubtful that he was Jewish. (PAJHS, XI, 96)

JACOBS, Benjamin.[6] Born May, 1786, New York City. Son of Joseph Jacobs. (PAJHS, XXVII, 349)

JACOBS, Benjamin.[7] Born May 14, 1793, Philadelphia. Son of Moses Jacobs. (MIPR)

JACOBS, Benjamin I. In 1784 he was in New York City, planning marriage to a Christian woman. (PAJHS, XXI, 143; XXVII, 29; Pool, 325f)

JACOBS, Daniel.[1] Fought in the Revolution in Charlestown. It is doubtful that he was Jewish. (PAJHS, XII, 55)

JACOBS, Daniel.[2] May have been the son of Barnard Jacobs.[1] His wife was Richa. (MSGC)

JACOBS, David. Died by 1773. Husband of Richa Simson, he was in New York City in 1764. (PAJHS, XXVII, 152; Wills, 9)

JACOBS, Dufty. In New York City in 1784. It is doubtful that he was Jewish. (PAJHS, XIX, 33)

JACOBS, Eleanor. Daughter of Joseph Jacobs,[4] she was in New York City in 1774. It is highly doubtful that she was Jewish. (PAJHS, XXIII, 157)

JACOBS, Mrs. Elinor. Wife of Joseph Jacobs, she was in New York City in 1774. It is highly doubtful that she was Jewish. (PAJHS, XXIII, 157)

JACOBS, Mrs. Elizabeth. Wife of Benjamin I. Jacobs, she left him in 1786. (Pool, 326)

JACOBS, Frances. February 2, 1789, Kingston, Jamaica, B.W.I.—November 23, 1874, New York City. Daughter of Abraham Jacobs,[1] she was in America by 1790. (SRB; Wills, 80)

JACOBS, Frederick. In the Charlestown Revolutionary militia in 1780. (EJSC, 92)

JACOBS, Georgina. March 27, 1791, Savannah—July 2, 1859, New York. Daughter of Abraham Jacobs.[1] (MSGC; Wills, 80)

JACOBS, Hart. In New York City in 1774. He refused to perform military duty on the Sabbath and was excused. (PAJHS, X, 163; XXI, 115, et passim; SIR; UJE, VIII, 177)

JACOBS, Hyam. In Charleston in 1800. (EJSC, 135)

JACOBS, Isaac.[1] In New York City in 1722. In 1726 he was in the fishing industry in Branford, Connecticut. (JRMP; PAJHS, XXXV, 181)

JACOBS, Isaac.[2] He came to America from Germany by way of Ireland. In 1772 he was a peddler in Philadelphia and its environs. At this same time, he was sought by creditors, who advertised in the newspapers to find him. (WW, 57f)

JACOBS, Isaac.[3] 1783—September 15, 1784, New York City. Son of Joseph Jacobs. (PAJHS, XXVII, 349)

JACOBS, Israel. About 1741, London—March 3, 1810, Philadelphia. In 1739 he came to America and became a shopkeeper. He was married to Zipporah Nunez, the widow of David Mendez Machado. (MSP; SIR; WW, 30, 388)

JACOBS, Jacob.[1] In the fishing industry in Connecticut in 1723. It is doubtful that he was Jewish. (JRMP)

JACOBS, Jacob.[2] 1742—November 1, 1797, Charleston. By 1763 he was in business in Charlestown. On February 1, 1764, he arrived in Savannah. His wife was Caty Hays. (EJSC, 43, et passim; SRB; Wills, 44)

JACOBS, Jacob.[3] Died September 7, 1771, New York City. Son of Michael Jacobs. (Pool, 502; SIR)

JACOBS, Jacob.[4] Born August 25, 1764, New York City. Son of David Jacobs. (PAJHS, XXVII, 152)

JACOBS, Jacob.[5] Nephew of Jacob Jacobs,[2] he passed through Savannah in November, 1790, on his way to Charleston. (SRB)

JACOBS, Mrs. Jacob. Wife of Jacob Jacobs.[5] (SRB)

JACOBS, James Levy. Son of Samuel Jacobs[1] of Montreal, he studied medicine but did not complete his studies. (WAJA)

JACOBS, Jean-Baptiste. Son of Samuel Jacobs[1] of Montreal. (WAJA)

JACOBS, Joel. Son of Joseph Jacobs.[4] It is highly doubtful that he was Jewish. (PAJHS, XXIII, 157)

JACOBS, Johanan. In 1759 he was a shohet in New York City. (PAJHS, XXI, 80)

JACOBS, Mrs. Johanan. In New York City in 1771. (SIR)

JACOBS, Joseph. Born New York City, died 1778. A silversmith and a shohet, he lived in Newport. His wife was Bilhah Polock. (MSP; PAJHS, XXVII, 211, 445, 450)

JACOBS, Joseph.[2] He may be one of the other Joseph Jacobs. Son of Joseph Jacobs,[4] he was in New York City in 1774. It is highly doubtful that he was Jewish. (NYHSW, XVII, 331)

JACOBS, Joseph.[3] Son of Raphael Jacobs. (PAJHS, XXV, 90)

JACOBS, Joseph.[4] Died about 1774, New York City. It is highly doubtful that he was Jewish. (PAJHS, XXIII, 157)

JACOBS, Joseph.[5] In New York City in 1792. (PAJHS, XXVII, 51, et passim)

JACOBS, Joseph.[6] In Baltimore in 1796. (Blum, 4)

JACOBS, Joseph R. In New York City in 1795. (PAJHS, XXVII, 62)

JACOBS, Joshua. Fought in the Revolutionary army in Charlestown. It is doubtful that he was Jewish. (EJSC, 106)

JACOBS, Judah. Assisted by Aaron Lopez after he went bankrupt, he left America for England about 1767. (Newport Historical Society, Lopez Letters)

JACOBS, Judith. Born March 27, 1791, Savannah. Daughter of Abraham Jacobs.[1] (SRB)

JACOBS, Judith Hadassah. 1758—December 25, 1832. Daughter of Raphael Jacobs, she was married to Manuel Myers. (MSP; Pool, 267; SIR)

JACOBS, Levi. Born before 1800. Son of Jacob Jacobs, he was in New York City in 1811. (Wills, 7)

JACOBS, Malcha. Born April 10, 1771, New York City. Daughter of Johanan Jacobs. (SIR)

JACOBS, Maria. April 26, 1795, Savannah —August 4, 1876, New York. Daughter of Abraham Jacobs.[1] (MSGC; Wills, 80)

JACOBS, Marie-Ann. Daughter of Samuel Jacobs[1] of Montreal, she was baptized. (JRMP; WAJA)

JACOBS, Marie-Genevieve. Daughter of Samuel Jacobs[1] of Montreal, she was baptized. Her husband was Captain Vigneau. (JRMP; WAJA)

JACOBS, Mark. A shopkeeper, he was in New York City in 1773. He went to debtor's prison. (PAJHS, XXVII, 29)

JACOBS, Michael. A shopkeeper, he was imprisoned for a debt. On March 22, 1780, he was buried in New York City. (Coldoc, 100; PAJHS, XXI, 117; Pool, 503)

JACOBS, Mrs. Michael. In New York City in 1772. (SIR)

JACOBS, Moses.[1] August 27, 1772, New York City—January 13, 1802, Maryland. Son of Michael Jacobs, he was living in Baltimore in 1791. (Blum, 4; JRMP; MIPR; SIR)

JACOBS, Moses.[2] In Kent, Rhode Island, in 1790. It is doubtful that he was Jewish. (Census A, Rhode Island)

JACOBS, Myer.[1] In New York City in 1772. (MSP)

JACOBS, Myer.[2] Born July 5, 1791, Philadelphia. Son of Moses Jacobs,[1] he was married to Rebecca Lazarus on February 17, 1817. (MIPR; MSGC)

JACOBS, Nathaniel. In Rhode Island with his family of seven in 1790. It is doubtful that he was Jewish. (Census A, Rhode Island)

JACOBS, Oliver. Son of Joseph Jacobs,[4] he was in New York City in 1774. It is highly doubtful that he was Jewish. (PAJHS, XXIII, 157)

JACOBS, Perla. June 28, 1798, Washington, Georgia—July 10, 1798. Infant daughter of Abraham Jacobs.[1] (*MSGC*)

JACOBS, Philip. In 1787 he was a merchant in New York City. He was in Charleston about the same time. (*EJSC*, 278; *PAJHS*, X, 164)

JACOBS, Prudence. Daughter of Joseph Jacobs,[4] she was in New York City in 1774. It is highly doubtful that she was Jewish. (*PAJHS*, XXIII, 157)

JACOBS, Rachel.[1] 1754—November 1, 1821, Philadelphia. Daughter of Israel Jacobs, she was married to Jacob I. Cohen[1] on November 3, 1807. (*BGMIP*; *MSGC*; *PAJHS*, II, 49f)

JACOBS, Rachel.[2] On October 4, 1786, she was married to Cushman Polock. (*SRB*)

JACOBS, Rachel.[3] February 20, 1793, Savannah—November 18, 1870, New York. Daughter of Abraham Jacobs,[1] she was married to Samuel A. Barnett on November 13, 1822, in New York. (*MSGC*)

JACOBS, Rachel Alia. Wife of Mayer Polonies. (*Pool*, 160; *Wills*, 8)

JACOBS, Raphael. Born January 23, 1782, New York City. Son of Joseph Jacobs. (*PAJHS*, XXVII, 349)

JACOBS, Raphael (Ralph). August 9, 1711—September 16, 1796, New York. This son of Benjamin Jacobs[1] was a shopkeeper and farmer who was in New York City as early as 1733. He was married to Sarah Simson. (*MSGC*; *PAJHS*, XVIII, 101; XXI, 31, *et passim*; XXVII, 22, *et passim*; *Pool*, 267, *et passim*)

JACOBS, Sally. Daughter of Abraham Jacobs,[1] she was living in Savannah in 1790. (*SRB*)

JACOBS, Samuel.[1] Died 1786. A shipowner, who had come to Canada with the English during the French and Indian War, he supplied the British forces. He was also a general merchant who operated from St. Denis in the province of Quebec. One of the largest wheat buyers in the area, he had numerous commercial contracts in Canada and in the colonies. During the Revolution he operated a commissary for the English troops. He married Marie-Josie Audet Lapoint, a Catholic, and his family were reared as Christians. (*Coldoc*, 21, *et passim*; *MEAJA*, 203, *et passim*; *WAJA*)

JACOBS, Samuel.[2] Born 1764. This son of Samuel Jacobs[1] was baptized. For a time he entered his father's business in the West Indies. (*JRMP*; *MEAJA*, 270f; *WAJA*)

JACOBS, Samuel.[3] Born February 8, 1767, New York City. Son of David Jacobs, he was married to Catherine whose second husband was Solomon Hyams. (*MSGC*; *PAJHS*, XXVII, 153)

JACOBS, Samuel.[4] In Lancaster in 1798. It is doubtful that he was Jewish. (*PAJHS*, XIX, 48)

JACOBS, Samuel.[5] In Baltimore in 1798. It is doubtful that he was Jewish. (*PAJHS*, XIX, 57)

JACOBS, Samuel, Jr. 1764, New York City—September 18, 1810, Charleston. Son of Samuel Jacobs, he was married to Catherine in Charleston in April, 1805. (*EOJCC*, 44; *MSP*)

JACOBS, Samuel, Sr. In Charleston in 1797. (*WAJA*)

JACOBS, Sarah. July 29, 1786, Charleston —December 18, 1861, New York. Daughter of Abraham Jacobs.[1] (*MSGC*)

JACOBS, Solomon.[1] 1777, Heidelberg, Pennsylvania—November 3, 1827, Richmond. This son of Barnard Jacob(s) was a Richmond businessman who became recorder and acting mayor of that city. In 1813 he was a member of the Richmond assembly. The first Jew to become grand master of the Masons of Virginia, he was also president of Congregation Beth Shalome in Richmond. An agent for the French government in the tobacco market, he was the Richmond representative for the European banking house of Rothschild. On May 28, 1815, he was married to Esther Nones. (*ELJR*, 41, *et passim*; *UJE*, VI, 20; *Wills*, 26f)

JACOBS, Solomon.[2] Fought in the Revolutionary army in Connecticut. It is doubtful that he was Jewish. (*PAJHS*, XI, 91)

JACOBS, Thomas. Brother of Samuel Jacobs,[1] he lived in Montreal, and was married to Angelique Mosse on February 26, 1781, in a Roman Catholic church. (*Malchelosse*, 171; *WAJA*)

JACOBS, Yittah. Born February 14, 1769, New York City. Daughter of David Jacobs. (*SIR*)

JACQUES, Gershom R. In 1800 he was a surgeon's mate in the U.S. Navy. (*MSP*)

JESURUN, David, Jr. In New York City in 1754. (*AJA*)

JEWEL, Benjamin. In 1790 he was living in Savannah, married to a French Catholic woman. Cf. Benjamin Edgar Joel. (*SRB*)

JEWEL, Elizabeth. October, 1759—July 11, 1835, New York City. Wife of David Valentine.[2] (*MSGC*)

JOEL, Benjamin Edgar. A member of the Revolutionary army, he was in New York City in 1790. (*PAJHS*, XXV, 113; *SIR*)

JOEL, Mrs. B. In 1793 she was a merchant in Savannah. (*MISR*)

JOEL, Israel. In New York City in 1798. (*PAJHS*, XXVII, 68)

JOEL, Phillip. In Philadelphia in 1797. (*MIPR*)

JOEL, Solomon. In Georgia in 1764. It is doubtful that he was Jewish. (*JRMP*)

JONAS, Henry. June 20, 1780, New York City—June 28, 1780, New York City. Infant son of Lyon Jonas. (*Pool*, 503; *SIR*)

JONAS, Hyam. May 22, 1779, New York City—June 22, 1779, New York City. Infant son of Lyon Jonas. (*Pool*, 503; *SIR*)

JONAS, Jessie. About 1737, London—May 29, 1818, New York City. Daughter of Alexander Jonas, she was married to Samuel Judah[2] on December 19, 1759, in New York City. (*PAJHS*, XI, 154; *Pool*, 392; *SIR*; *Wills*, 5)

JONAS, Joshua. In Philadelphia in 1786; in New York City in 1790; in Charleston sometime between 1783 and 1800. (*Census A, New York*; *EJSC*, 280; *MIPR*)

JONAS, Lyon. A Tory who had come from London, he was a furrier in New York City in 1779. (*PAJHS*, VI, 51, *et passim*; *Pool*, 94; *SIR*)

JONAS, Mrs. Lyon. In New York City in 1779. (*SIR*)

JONES, Abraham. About 1713—about December, 1807, Charleston. He came to America about 1767. For fifteen years he served as sexton for Congregation Beth Elohim in Charleston, and filled the same position in Savannah for Congregation Mikveh Israel. In 1792 he was married to the widow of Mr. Nathan. (*EJMC*, 6; *ELODN*, 79; *JRMP*; *SCHGM*, XXXI, 320)

JONES, Emil. In Charleston in 1798. It is doubtful that he was Jewish. (*PAJHS*, XIX, 87)

JONES, Joseph. In New York City in 1766. (*PAJHS*, XXI, 92)

JONES, Joshua. In Charlestown in 1780. It is doubtful that he was Jewish. (*EJSC*, 106)

JONES, Mrs. Judith. Died February 26, 1767, New York City. Wife of Joseph Jones. (*Pool*, 502; *SIR*)

JONES, Mrs. Maria. Born May 25, 1798, Mt. Pleasant, New York. She was married to Alfred T. Jones. (*JRMP*)

JONES, Samuel. About 1737—January 6, 1809, Charleston. Son of Elisha Jones, he came to Charlestown about 1763. (*EJSC*, 91; *EOJCC*, 62; *MSGC*)

JOSEPH, Aaron. In New York City in 1795. He was married to Frances Jacobs on April 15, 1807. (*MSP*; *PAJHS*, XXVII, 60)

JOSEPH, Abraham.[1] In New York City in 1740. (*PAJHS*, XXI, 42)

JOSEPH, Abraham.[2] In New York City in 1800. (*SIR*)

JOSEPH, Barnard. In Philadelphia in 1792. (*MIPR*)

JOSEPH, Betsy. From London. On April 5, 1797, she was married to Moses Tabarre in Charleston. (*SCHGM*, XXIV, 32f)

JOSEPH, Eleanor. November 9, 1794, Black Mingo, South Carolina—February 6, 1856. Probably the daughter of Lizar Joseph, she was married to Israel Solomons. (*MSGC*)

JOSEPH, Eleazar (Lazarus). 1763, Germany—November 23, 1817, Richmond. Husband of Gertrude. (*MSGC*)

JOSEPH, Mrs. Gertrude. 1769, Germany—May 22, 1842, New York. Wife of Eleazar (Lazarus) Joseph. (*MSGC*)

JOSEPH, Isaac Jacob. In Storeworth, Connecticut, in 1722. It is doubtful that he was Jewish. (*JRMP*)

JOSEPH, Israel.[1] 1733, Germany—June 9, 1804, Charleston. He was born in Mannheim-on-the-Rhine, Germany, and became a merchant in Charlestown and in Savannah, where he lived for about forty years. He was a prominent patriot during the Revolution. His wife was Miriam Levy.[2] (*EJSC*, 117, *et passim*; *EOJCC*, 82; *MISR*; *Wills*, 41)

JOSEPH, Israel.[2] Sometime before 1760 he absconded to Holland from New York City. (*White*, 469f)

JOSEPH, Joseph. In Charleston in 1800. (*EJSC*, 136)

JOSEPH, Joseph Lazarus. 1797, Germany—June 5, 1858, New York City. Son of Eleazar Joseph, he was married to Frances Levy on May 16, 1824. (*MSGC*)

JOSEPH, Leah. Died November 25, 1799, South Carolina. Wife of Lyon Levy. (*Wills*, 46)

JOSEPH, Lizar. 1762, Mannheim, Germany—June 25, 1827, Georgetown, South Carolina. Husband of Sarah Judah.[6] (*MSGC*)

JOSEPH, Miriam. 1791—April 15, 1863, Sumter, South Carolina. Daughter of Israel Joseph,[1] she was married to Levy Moses in February, 1809. (*MSGC*)

JOSEPH, Nathan. In New York City in 1787. (*PAJHS*, XXVII, 41)

JOSEPH, Samuel. In Charleston in 1800. (*Census B, South Carolina*)

JOSEPH, Simon. In Philadelphia in 1784. (*MIPR*)

JOSEPH, Solomon I. August 7, 1799, Richmond—September 26, 1866, New York. Son of Eleazar Joseph, he was married to Emily Cohen. (*MSGC*)

JOSEPH, Solomon Moses. In Charleston in 1800. (*EHCBE*, 15; *EJSC*, 136)

JOSEPHS, Aaron. In South Carolina in 1771. (*MSP*)

JOSEPHS, Mrs. Frances L. 1796, Georgetown, South Carolina—September 15, 1827, Charleston. Wife of Levy L. Josephs. (*MSGC*; *MSP*)

JOSEPHS, Israel. In New York City in 1759. (*PAJHS*, XXI, 79)

JOSEPHSON, Miss. Daughter of Myer Josephson. (*PAJHS*, XXXIV, 77)

JOSEPHSON, Amiel. In Philadelphia in 1786. (*MIPR*)

JOSEPHSON, Mrs. Esther. Wife of Meyer Josephson. (*PAJHS*, XXXIV, 77)

JOSEPHSON, Joseph. Son of Meyer Josephson. (*PAJHS*, XXXIV, 77)

JOSEPHSON, Manuel. About 1729, Germany—January 30, 1796, Philadelphia. During the French and Indian War he was a sutler who later settled in New York City as a merchant and trader. He was a cultured man and had a good Hebrew education. In 1762 he was president of Congregation Shearith Israel in New York City. In the post Revolutionary period he settled in Philadelphia, where he was active as a Jewish leader of the community. He sought to unite six American Jewish congregations in sending a congratulatory message to President Washington; he succeeded in presenting such a letter personally in behalf of four of the six congregations. In 1759 he was married to Rebecca Judah in New York City. (*Coldoc*, 55, *et passim*; *MEAJA*, 76f; *MEAJB*, 43, *et passim*; *MIPR*; *SIR*; *WW*, 57, *et passim*)

JOSEPHSON, Meyer. Came to America from Germany before 1756. From 1756 to 1773 he was a trader in Reading, Pennsylvania. His first wife was Esther; his second wife was a gentile. (*Essays*, 116; *PAJHS*, XXXIV, 76f; *WW*, 392)

JUDAH, Miss. Born October 6, 1762, New York, died an infant. Daughter of Samuel Judah. (*SIR*)

JUDAH, Aaron.[1] Born before 1749. Son of Baruch Judah.[1] (*MSGC*)

JUDAH, Aaron.[2] June 16, 1775, New York City—June 28, 1834. Son of Samuel Judah,[2] he was married to Rachel Gomez[3] on February 3, 1819. (*MSGC*; *PAJHS*, XXVII, 303; *SIR*)

JUDAH, Abigail. November 17, 1742—September 1, 1819, Richmond. (*PAJHS*, VI, 111)

JUDAH, Abraham.[1] In Boston in 1736. Cf. Abraham Judah.[8] (*JNEA*, 20)

JUDAH, Abraham.[2] Died about 1762, Philadelphia. In 1758 he liquidated his merchant business in Wilmington to move to Philadelphia. He was the first known Jew in Wilmington. His wife was Bridget. (*GBMIP*; *Wills*, 19; *WW*, 39)

JUDAH, Abraham.[3] About 1714—September 2, 1784, New York City. This son of Uriah Judah was a merchant who lived in Newport, Boston, and New York City. (*PAJHS*, XVIII, 122; XXI, 42; XXIII, 85)

JUDAH, Abraham.[4] July 15, 1774, Newport—January 12, 1827, Wilmington. Son of Hillel Judah, he was a physician. (*MSGC*; *PAJHS*, XI, 155; *SIR*)

JUDAH, Abraham.[5] In Montreal in 1778. (*SIMR*)

JUDAH, Abraham.[6] Born March 8, 1781, Montreal. Son of Isaac Judah.[1] (*MIPR*)

JUDAH, Abraham.[7] A child in New York City about 1793. (*PAJHS*, XXVII, 55)

JUDAH, Abraham.[8] Born New York City, died Baltimore. Son of Samuel Judah,[1] he was a physician. (*MSGC*)

JUDAH, Amelia. September 12, 1761—April 22, 1849. Daughter of Samuel Judah.[2] Cf. Mink Judah. (*MSGC*)

JUDAH, Ann. Daughter of Abraham Judah.[2] (*Wills*, 19)

JUDAH, Anna. Died 1822, New York City. Daughter of Naphtali Judah. (*JE*, VII, 331)

JUDAH, Andrew. In 1761 he was a physician in New York City. In 1764 he was in Charlestown, where he stated that he was from London and Holland. (*EJSC*, 43; *PAJHS*, XXVII, 22)

JUDAH, Barnueb S. In Philadelphia in 1782. (*Morais*, 15)

JUDAH, Barnebas S. In New York City in 1796. Cf. Bernard S. Judah. (*PAJHS*, XIX, 32)

JUDAH, Barrett. Noted in Connecticut. It is doubtful that he was Jewish. (*CPR*, VII, 30)

JUDAH, Baruch.[1] About 1678, Breslau, Germany—January 12, 1774, New York City. About 1700 he arrived in New York City, was a freeman in 1716, and was elected a constable in 1732. In 1738 he was in the New York City militia. He was a merchant. His first wife was Rachel Jochanan; his second wife was Sarah Helbert whom he married in Brookhaven, Connecticut, about 1701. (*MSGC*; *PAJHS*, IV, 196; VI, 101, 127; XI, 154f; XVIII, 122; *Pool*, 241, *et passim*; *SIR*)

JUDAH, Baruch.[2] Born December 7, 1760, New York City. Son of Samuel Judah. (*SIR*)

JUDAH, Baruch H. June 21, 1763, New York City—September 26, 1830, Richmond. Son of Hillel Judah, he was prominent in Richmond Jewry. He was librarian of the Richmond Library Company. (*ELJR*, 55, *et passim*; *PAJHS*, XI, 154; *SIR*; *UJE*, VI, 231)

JUDAH, Bella. September 29, 1770—January 16, 1847, New York. Daughter of Samuel Judah.[2] (*MSGC*)

JUDAH, Benjamin. Died 1763, Philadelphia. In 1758 he liquidated his business in Georgetown, Maryland, to move to Philadelphia. (*GBMIP*; *WW*, 39)

JUDAH, Benjamin S. October 6, 1760—December 24, 1831. This son of Samuel Judah[2] was a prominent merchant in Philadelphia and New York City. He helped found the New York Tontine. He suffered financial bankruptcy in the War of 1812.

On February 16, 1803, he was married to Eliza Israel. (*MSGC; NYHSW*, XIII, 390; *PAJHS*, III, 120; *UJE*, VI, 232)

JUDAH, Berlah. On February 13, 1781, he was married to Fanny Judah in Montreal. (*MIPR*)

JUDAH, Bernard S. June 8, 1777, London —May 21, 1831, New York. This son of Samuel Judah[1] was a physician living in New York City. On August 30, 1797, he was married to Catherine Hart. (*MEAJA*, 282f; *MSGC; NYHSW*, XV, 17; *PAJHS*, XIX, 32, 34; *UJE*, VI, 232)

JUDAH, Bilah. Born before 1730. Daughter of Baruch Judah.[1] (*MSGC*)

JUDAH, Bilhah. Born September 30, 1769, New York City. Daughter of Samuel Judah. (*SIR*)

JUDAH, Mrs. Bridget. Wife of Abraham Judah,[2] she lived in Philadelphia. (*Wills*, 19)

JUDAH, Cary J. September 14, 1766, New York City—February 16, 1837. Son of Samuel Judah,[2] he lived in New York City. (*MSGC; PAJHS*, XXVII, 59; *SIR*)

JUDAH, Catherine. January 1, 1788, New York—July 30, 1860. Daughter of Samuel Judah.[1] (*MSGC*)

JUDAH, David.[1] This son of Abraham Judah[2] attended the University of Pennsylvania in 1760. (*PAJHS*, XIX, 120; *Wills*, 19)

JUDAH, David.[2] Died 1833. Son of Rabbi Michael Judah, he was married to Esther Taylor of Westport, Connecticut, about 1780. (*MSGC*)

JUDAH, David.[3] November 15, 1756—1824, Fairfield, Connecticut. This son of Michael Judah fought in the Revolution. A merchant, he was a prominent citizen of Fairfield, where he became completely assimilated in the Christian community and was given a Christian burial. His wife was Constance (Charity) Bennet. (*Jacobus*, II, 110f, 556, 559; *JE*, VII, 331; *MEAJA*, 175f; *PAJHS*, XXVII, 151)

JUDAH, David.[4] May 10, 1789—May 29, 1866. He may have been born in America. (*MSGC*)

JUDAH, Dorothy Catherine. 1747, Portsmouth, England—August, 1827. Daughter of Abraham Judah, she was married to Aaron Hart[1] on February 7, 1768. (*MEAJA*, 279f; *MSGC*)

JUDAH, Eliezer B. In New York City in 1740. (*PAJHS*, XXI, 42)

JUDAH, Elizabeth. 1763—October 19, 1823, Montreal. Her first husband was Chapman Abrahams; her second husband was Moses Myers[1] on March 22, 1787. (*MSGC*)

JUDAH, Emanuel. July 15, 1769, Newport —November 8, 1834, Baltimore. This son of Hillel Judah was a merchant who married Grace Seixas[4] on February 1, 1815. (*ELJR*, 44, *et passim; MSGC; PAJHS*, IV, 21, 23; XI, 155; *UJE*, VI, 231; IX, 159; *SIR*)

JUDAH, Mrs. Fanny. On February 13, 1781, she was married to Berlah Judah in Montreal. (*MIPR*)

JUDAH, Fanny (Frumet). May 6, 1771—February 14, 1833. Daughter of Samuel Judah.[2] (*MSGC; SIR*)

JUDAH, Gershom Seixas. Born October 12, 1767, Charlestown/Richmond. Son of Hillel Judah, he was a well known merchant. (*ELJR*, 38, *et passim; MSGC; PAJHS*, XI, 154f; *SIR*)

JUDAH, Grace. 1780—July 4, 1867. Daughter of Hillel Judah, she was married first to Judah Myers, and then to Hayman (Henry) Marks. (*GBMIP; MSGC; PAJHS*, XI, 155)

JUDAH, Hannah. Daughter of Abraham Judah.[2] (*Wills*, 19)

JUDAH, Henry. About 1790 he worked for Moses Myers in Norfolk. (*MSP*)

JUDAH, Hillel (Hilliard). About 1730—about 1815. This son of Baruch Judah was a shohet in Newport, who supplied kosher meat to the Jews in that area. He was also a merchant in New York City. In 1759 he was married to Abigail Seixas.[1] (*Gutstein*, 194, 198; *MEAJB*, 217f; *MSGC; PAJHS*, IV, 202; XI, 154; *SIR; UJE*, VI, 231)

JUDAH, Isaac.[1] In Montreal in 1778. (*Malchelosse*, 171; *SIMR*)

JUDAH, Isaac.[2] July 10, 1761—May 2, 1827, Richmond. This son of Hillel Judah was known as Reverend Isaac H. Judah and was probably the first reader in Congregation Beth Shalome in Richmond. He was also a merchant. (*ELJR*, 35, *et passim*; *PAJHS*, XI, 154; *SIR*; *UJE*, VI, 231)

JUDAH, Jacob.[1] About 1740 he was a merchant in New York City, and later in Newport. (*JNEB*, 8; *PAJHS*, XXI, 45)

JUDAH, Jacob.[2] Born May 4, 1765, Charlestown. Son of Hillel Judah. Cf. Jacob Judah.[5] (*PAJHS*, XI, 154; *SIR*)

JUDAH, Jacob.[3] Died 1781, Philadelphia. (*GBMIP*; *MIPR*)

JUDAH, Jacob.[4] October 7, 1767, New York City—June 20, 1783, Philadelphia. Son of Baruch Judah.[2] (*MSGC*; *PAJHS*, VI, 108; XXVII, 153; *SIR*)

JUDAH, Jacob.[5] In Charleston in 1800. Cf. Jacob Judah.[2] (*EJSC*, 136)

JUDAH, Margaret. Died 1793, Philadelphia. (*GBMIP*)

JUDAH, (Rabbi) Michael. Died 1786, New York. He was a merchant who lived in Norwalk and Hartford, Connecticut, and New York City. An observant Jew, he left his estate to the Jews of New York to be divided among the synagogue and widows and orphans. He married a Christian woman, Martha Raymond. (*Jacobus*, II, 559; *MEAJA*, 175f; *MSGC*; *PAJHS*, XI, 90, 93; XXVII, 247)

JUDAH, Mink. Born November 12, 1761, New York City. Daughter of Samuel Judah. Cf. Amelia Judah. (*SIR*)

JUDAH, Miriam. Died 1779, probably in Philadelphia. Daughter of Abraham Judah, she was married to David Manuel about 1766. (*MIPR*; *MSGC*)

JUDAH, Moses.[1] 1735—September 25, 1822, New York City. Son of Baruch Judah, he was a merchant who became a freeman of New York City in 1768. He later served in the Revolutionary army. (*PAJHS*, VI, 102; *Pool*, 418)

JUDAH, Moses.[2] An embroiderer from London, he was in Philadelphia in 1784. (*WW*, 184, 434)

JUDAH, Moses.[3] March, 1779—August 17, 1813. Son of Hillel Judah. (*MSGC*; *PAJHS*, XXVII, 170)

JUDAH, Naphtali. June 1/6, 1774—September 16, 1855, New York. This son of Samuel Judah[2] was a merchant in New York and a famous printer and publisher. He was a member of Tammany society and was a prominent Mason. In addition he was active in the Jewish community and served as president of Congregation Shearith Israel in New York City. On November 11, 1801, he was married to Esther Hendricks. (*MSGC*; *PAJHS*, VI, 132; XIX, 32f; XXVII, 62, *et passim*; XXX, 113f; *POFNW*, 49, *et passim*; *Pool*, 47, *et passim*)

JUDAH, Rachel.[1] 1732—February 12, 1797, Philadelphia. Daughter of Baruch Judah,[1] she was married to Manuel Josephson in 1759. (*MSGC*; *PAJHS*, VI, 108; XI, 155)

JUDAH, Rachel.[2] September 12, 1768, New York City—April 29, 1770, New York City. Daughter of Samuel Judah.[2] (*SIR*)

JUDAH, Rachel.[3] May 11, 1772, New York City—February 8, 1836. Daughter of Samuel Judah.[2] (*MSGC*; *SIR*)

JUDAH, Rachel.[4] July 3, 1772, New York City—May 1, 1863, New York City. Daughter of Hillel Judah, she was married to Zalma Rehine on January 15, 1800. (*MSGC*; *PAJHS*, XI, 155; *SIR*)

JUDAH, Rebecca.[1] 1727—March 24, 1817, Philadelphia. Daughter of Baruch Judah,[1] she was married to Isaac Hays. (*MSGC*)

JUDAH, Rebecca.[2] July 12, 1765—December 19, 1846, New York. Daughter of Samuel Judah.[2] (*MSGC*; *SIR*)

JUDAH, Rebecca.[3] August 30, 1782, Newport—January 13, 1867, New York. Daughter of Hillel Judah, she was married to Isaac B. Seixas on May 31, 1809. (*MSGC*; *PAJHS*, IV, 211)

JUDAH, Sally (Sarah). March 6, 1760, New York City—February 10, 1842, Baltimore. Daughter of Hillel Judah, she was married to Ralph de Paz in August, 1798, in Newport. (*MSGC*; *PAJHS*, XI, 154; *SIR*)

JUDAH, Samuel.[1] 1725—1789, New York City. This son of Abraham Judah was a merchant in Montreal by 1761. He later moved to Three Rivers, where he was in partnership with his brother-in-law, Aaron Hart. He traded in the Detroit area. During the Revolution he was sympathetic to the American cause. On March 27, 1775, he was married to Elizabeth Ezekiel. (*MEAJA*, 272f; *MSGC*; *PAJHS*, IV, 224; *UJE*, VI, 232)

JUDAH, Samuel.[2] August 19, 1728, New York City—October 19, 1781, Philadelphia. This son of Baruch Judah[1] was a businessman who became a freeman in New York City in 1769. Late in his life he moved to Philadelphia. On December 19, 1759, he was married to Jessie Jonas. (*MSGC*; *PAJHS*, XI, 154; *Pool*, 393; *UJE*, VI, 321f; VIII, 177)

JUDAH, Samuel.[3] Died June 20, 1783, Philadelphia. (*MIPR*)

JUDAH, Samuel.[4] July 10, 1798/July 18, 1799, New York City—April 29, 1869, Vincennes, Indiana. This son of Bernard S. Judah was graduated from Rutgers College in 1816 and was admitted to the bar in the same year. He settled in Vincennes, Indiana, but practiced law nationally. He was elected to the Indiana legislature and was in the House of Representatives from 1827 to 1829, and again from 1839 to 1841. In 1840 he was Speaker of the House. In 1830 he held the post of United States Attorney in Indiana. On June 22, 1825, he was married to Harriet Brandon in Picqua, Ohio. (*DAB*, X, 227f; *MSGC*; *PAJHS*, XII, 164; *UJE*, V, 557)

JUDAH, Samuel B. H. 1799, New York City—July 21, 1876, New York City. This son of Benjamin S. Judah was a lawyer who was admitted to the bar in 1825 and practiced in New York City. He was also an author, a playwright and poet, whose first play *The Mountain Torrent* was a failure. He was once imprisoned for libelous remarks in one of his books. (*DAB*, X, 228f; *PAJHS*, VI, 114; XI, 154; XXX, 190, *et passim*; *UJE*, VI, 232; X, 223)

JUDAH, Sarah.[1] October 6, 1762—before December, 1763. Daughter of Samuel Judah.[2] (*MSGC*)

JUDAH, Sarah.[2] Died October 30, 1780, perhaps in Philadelphia. (*MIPR*)

JUDAH, Sarah.[3] December 14, 1763, New York City—October 12, 1795, New York City. Daughter of Samuel Judah,[2] she was married to Samuel Myers[3] on October 22, 1794. (*MSGC*; *Pool*, 393; *SIR*)

JUDAH, Sarah.[4] Died November 14, 1826. Daughter of Uriah Judah, she was married to Moses Hart[4] on April 10, 1799. (*Douville*, 142; *MSGC*)

JUDAH, Sarah.[5] Daughter of Abraham Judah.[2] (*Wills*, 19)

JUDAH, Sarah.[6] 1776—October 8, 1820, Georgetown, South Carolina. Daughter of Jacob Judah, she was married to Lizar Joseph. (*MSGC*)

JUDAH, Sarah.[7] March 6, 1760—February 10, 1842. In 1798 she was married to Ralph de Pass. (*MSGC*)

JUDAH, Uriah.[1] 1714—August 2, 1782. This son of Abraham Judah came to Montreal about 1768. He was a member of the Aaron Hart clan. A merchant at Vercheres, Quebec, he served also as prothonotary of Three Rivers. (*Douville*, 141; *MEAJA*, 270, *et passim*; *PAJHS*, I, 117)

JUDAH, Uriah.[2] Born April 5, 1782, Canada. (*MIPR*)

JUDAH, Walter Jonas. April 4, 1778, New York City—September 15, 1798, New York City. This son of Samuel Judah[2] entered Columbia College in 1795 and subsequently attended the Medical School there. He died while attending the sick during the yellow fever epidemic in 1798. His epitaph describes him as the ideal physician. (*MSGC*; *PAJHS*, XVIII, 102; XIX, 120; *Pool*, 269; *UJE*, VI, 232)

JUDAH, William. Son of Abraham Judah.[2] (*Wills*, 19)

JUDD, Eliza. About 1766—October 19, 1823, Montreal. Wife of Moses Myers[1] on March 22, 1787. (*MSGC*)

JUDITH, Benjamin S. In Philadelphia in 1786. Cf. Benjamin S. Judah. (*MIPR*)

K

KALMUS (COLLMUS), Levi. When he arrived from Bohemia in Baltimore in 1798 he was fifteen years old. (*Blum*, 4)

KARPELLES, I. W. In Philadelphia in 1785. (*MIPR*)

KATZ, Asher. In Richmond in 1790. (*ELJR*, 33)

KATZ, Mrs. Asher. In Richmond in 1790. (*ELJR*, 33)

KATZ, Henry. In Philadelphia in 1779. It is doubtful that he was Jewish. (*Morais*, 23)

KATZ, Isaac. In 1772 he arrived in Philadelphia as an indentured servant. In 1795 he was a cooper in Philadelphia. (*Exponent*, 13; *WW*, 184, 435)

KATZ, Jacob. Born 1790, Richmond. Son of Asher Katz. (*ELJR*, 33)

KATZ, Michael. In 1772 he arrived in Philadelphia as an indentured servant. In 1794 he was a leather worker in Philadelphia. (*Exponent*, 13; *WW*, 184, 435)

KAUFMAN, Solomon. In Lancaster in 1797. It is highly doubtful that he was Jewish. (*LCHS*, V, 94)

KEYSER. Son of Rabbi Keyser, he was in New York City in 1774. (*POFNW*, 344)

KEYSER, Aaron. In New York City in 1776. (*Schappes*, 52)

KEYSER, Rabbi Samuel bar Isaac. In 1774 he was in New York City for a month on his way to London or Jamaica. (*POFNW*, 344)

KEYZER, Jacob. In New York City in 1739. (*PAJHS*, XXI, 41f)

KING, Isaac. 1799—November 6, 1824, Philadelphia. Son of Jacob King, he was a merchant in Richmond. (*MSGC*)

KING, Jacob. 1774—October 22, 1824, Richmond. In 1798 he was in New York City. He was married to Mary, the widow of Solomon Isaacs. (*PAJHS*, XVIII, 108; VI, 111; *SIR*)

KISTEDT, Jacob. A Mason from South Carolina, he was visiting Boston on his way to New York City in 1722. It is highly doubtful that he was Jewish. (*JNEA*, 24)

KOHN, Joseph Solomon. A loyalist merchant, he was in Philadelphia about 1760. (*JE*, IX, 671; *PAJHS*, I, 61; *Rosenbach*, 12)

KUHN, A. In Philadelphia in 1800. It is doubtful that he was Jewish. (*PAJHS*, I, 114)

KUHN, Jacob. In 1778 he was chief commissioner of police in Montreal. (*HSIM*, 36)

KURSHEEDT, Israel Baer. April 6, 1766, Germany—April 30, 1852, New York City. He studied in a Yeshiva in Frankfort and then became an army contractor for the Prussian Army. In 1796 he landed in Boston. Shortly thereafter he went to New York City, and then to Richmond, where he lived from 1812 until 1824. There he was reader in Congregation Beth Shalom. A prominent merchant and broker, he returned to New York City, and in 1834 established the Hebrath Terumath Hakodesh, a society for the relief of the poor in Palestine. He was president of the Hebrew Mutual Benefit Society of New York and of Congregation Shearith Israel. During the Damascus Affair he was chairman of the Committee of Israelites of the City of New York. An outstanding Hebraist, he was an authority on religious matters. On January 18, 1804, he was married to Sara Sexias.[1] (*Coldoc*, 198f; *ELJR*, 86, *et passim*; *MSP*; *PAJHS*, IV, 208; VIII, 142f; *POFNW*, 187, *et passim*; *Pool*, 47, *et passim*; *UJE*, VI, 491)

L

LABAT, Mrs. Catherine. 1773—January 2, 1846, New Orleans. Wife of David Labat. (*MSGC*)

LABAT, David. In Charleston with his wife, Catherine, and his family in 1800. (*Census B, South Carolina; EJSC*, 136)

LABAT, Grace. 1799—July 29, 1872. Daughter of David Labat, she was married to Isaac Davega on June 28, 1815. (*MSGC*)

LANDA, Joseph de. In Portsmouth, New Hampshire in 1781. It is highly doubtful that he was Jewish. (*PAJHS*, XXIII, 175)

LANEY, Joseph. In 1759 he was a merchant in North Carolina, and was still there in 1784. (*MEAJB*, 249; *PAJHS*, XXII, 183; XXIX, 141f; *UJE*, VIII, 237)

LARA, Jacob de. About 1722 he left London for New York City, and was in New York City in 1728. (*PAJHS*, XXX, 33; XLII, 74)

LARAH, Aron de. In New York City about 1740. (*PAJHS*, XXI, 43)

LARAH, Isaac Cohen de. In 1699 he was a trader in New York City. (*AJAM*, III, 5)

LARAH, Moses Cohen de. On February 28, 1784, he arrived in Savannah, but left soon for Charleston. In 1796 he was in Philadelphia. (*SRB*)

LASKEY, E. In Philadelphia in 1800. It is doubtful that he was Jewish. (*PAJHS*, I, 114)

LAZARE, Abigail. In Lancaster in 1761. She may have been the daughter of Jacob Leazar. (*Essays*, 111)

LAZARUS. December 3, 1788—December 12, 1788. Son of Marks Lazarus. (*MSGC*)

LAZARUS, Aaron. August 26, 1777, Charlestown—October 2, 1841, Petersburg, Virginia. This son of Marks Lazarus was a director of the Wilmington and Weldon Railroad. His first wife was Esther Cohen,[4] May 10, 1803; his second wife was Rachel Mordecai, March 2, 1821, in Richmond. (*ELJR*, 299; *MSGC*; *PAJHS*, VI, 48; XIX, 75; *UJE*, VI, 568; VII, 644; VIII, 238)

LAZARUS, Abraham. Husband of Rachel Hays, he was in New York City in 1760. (*NYHSW*, VI, 340)

LAZARUS, Bella (Isabella). July 29, 1785 —July 18, 1862. Daughter of Marks Lazarus, she was married to Aaron Phillips on November 14, 1821. (*MSGC*)

LAZARUS, Benjamin. Born November 20, 1779, died an infant. Son of Marks Lazarus. (*MSGC*)

LAZARUS, Benjamin Dores. July 5, 1800 —November 23, 1875. Son of Marks Lazarus, he was married to Cornelia Cohen on April 1, 1840. (*MSGC*)

LAZARUS, Brandly. October 16, 1752— February 16, 1825, New York City. Daughter of Sampson Lazarus, she was married to Joshua Isaacs[3] on March 28, 1781, at Lancaster. (*MSGC*; *PAJHS*, IX, 36; *Pool*, 424)

LAZARUS, Caroline. January 18, 1790— July 21, 1818. Daughter of Marks Lazarus, she was married to Aaron Phillips on February 25, 1808. (*MSGC*; *Wills*, 45)

LAZARUS, Daniel. Born about January, 1795, died an infant. Son of Marks Lazarus. (*EOJCC*, 27; *JRMP*)

LAZARUS, Eleazar. Died 1777, New York City. (*MSGC*)

LAZARUS, Eleazar S. February 2, 1788— March 28, 1844, New York City. This son of Samuel Lazarus was a city assessor in New York City for many years. He edited the Hebrew text of the first Hebrew prayer book published in North America. On November 1, 1809, he was married to Zipporah Hart. (*MSGC*; *SIR*; *UJE*, VI, 568)

LAZARUS, Emma. May 21, 1798, Charleston—August 21, 1865, Charleston. Daughter of Marks Lazarus. (*EOJCC*, 31; *JRMP*)

LAZARUS, Esther. In February, 1784, she was married to Ezekiel Hart of New York City. (*Douville*, 117)

LAZARUS, Hannah. September 23, 1783— October 3, 1835, Hilton Head, South Carolina. Daughter of Marks Lazarus, she was married to Isaac Clifton Levy on November 3, 1802. (*MSGC*)

LAZARUS, Henry. In Maryland before 1800. (*JRMP*)

LAZARUS, Isaac. Died April 25, 1779, New York City. (*Pool*, 503; *SIR*)

LAZARUS, Joshua. March 18, 1796—June 1, 1861. Son of Marks Lazarus, he lived in Cheraw, South Carolina, after his marriage to Phebe Yates on October 28, 1835, in Liverpool, England. (*JRMP*; *Memoirs*, III, 137; *MSGC*)

LAZARUS, Leah. October 19, 1778— February 26, 1844. Daughter of Marks Lazarus, she was married to Mordecai Cohen in 1795. (*EOJCC*, 32; *JRMP*; *MSGC*; *Wills*, 37)

LAZARUS, Liepman. A child in New York City about 1793. (*PAJHS*, XXVII, 55)

LAZARUS, Marks. February 22, 1757, Charlestown—November 1, 1835, Charleston. This son of Michael Lazarus[1] fought in the Revolution and attained the rank of sergeant major. Later a merchant, he was married to Rachel Benjamin on December 11, 1776. (*EJSC*, 40, *et passim*; *EOJCC*, 32; *Wills*, 45)

LAZARUS, Michael.[1] A Charlestown merchant in 1750, he was reputed to have been the first secretary of Congregation Beth Elohim there. (*EJSC*, 32, *et passim*; *UJE*, VI, 570; *Wills*, 45)

LAZARUS, Michael.[2] December 19, 1786 —September 8, 1862, Charleston. This son of Marks Lazarus was one of the founders of the Reform Society of Israelites in Charleston. He was the first to open navigation by steamship between Charleston and Augusta. (*EJSC*, 161, *et passim*; *EOJCC*, 31; *JRMP*; *UJE*, VI, 570)

LAZARUS, Mrs. Michael. Wife of Michael Lazarus,[1] she was in Charlestown in 1757. (*Wills*, 45)

LAZARUS, Moses. Son of Eleazar Lazarus, he was a shohet in New York City in 1771. (*PAJHS*, XXVII, 28; *Pool*, 278)

LAZARUS, N. Fought in the Revolution and was in Georgia in 1780. It is doubtful that he was Jewish. (*PAJHS*, XVII, 99, 106)

LAZARUS, Peter. In Lancaster in 1778. It is doubtful that he was Jewish. (*LCHS*, V, 93f)

LAZARUS, Rachel. April 27, 1781—1785. Daughter of Marks Lazarus. (*MSGC*)

LAZARUS, Rebecca. October 7, 1791— November 9, 1869. Daughter of Marks Lazarus, she was married to Myer Jacobs[2] on February 17, 1817. (*MSGC*)

LAZARUS, Sampson. Died November 28, 1788, New York City. This son of Eleazar Lazarus came to New York City from England in 1748. By 1757 he was a shopkeeper in Lancaster. His wife was Frumet Cohen. (*LCHS*, V, 93; *PAJHS*, IX, 30; XXI, 58; XXVII, 43; *Pool*, 503)

LAZARUS, Samuel. Died October 11, 1798, New York City. Son of Eleazar Lazarus, he was a merchant. On March 25/26, 1777, he was married to Fanny Cushell. (*PAJHS*, XXV, 123; XXVII, 43; *Pool*, 277; *SIR*; *Wills*, 5)

LAZARUS, Simon. In Charleston in 1800. (*EJSC*, 136)

LAZARUS, Solomon David. July 12, 1793 —September 12, 1808. Son of Marks Lazarus. (*EOJCC*, 26; *MSP*)

LEALTAR, Moses. Expenses were paid by Congregation Shearith Israel of New York City to send him to South Carolina in 1775. (*PAJHS*, XX, 134)

LEAS, Abraham de. On October 23, 1741, he was naturalized in New York City. (*PAJHS*, V, 117)

LEAZAR, Jacob. In Lancaster in 1757 and 1778. (*LCHS*, V, 93)

LEBETH, Abraham. A money collector, in 1775 he arrived from London. (*POFNW*, 344)

LEION, David. In 1799 he was president of Congregation Mikveh Israel in Savannah. On April 17, 1798, he was married to Hannah Minis; he was divorced from her on August 22, 1799. He was a Tory. (*MISR; PAJHS,* XVII, 105; *SRB*)

LENEIRA, David de. In Georgia in 1733. (*Coulter,* 71)

LEON, de. Born July 1, 1772, died at birth. Daughter of Abraham de Leon.[2] (*MSGC*)

LEON, Abigail de. November 26, 1783—November 24, 1850, New York City. Daughter of Abraham de Leon,[2] she was married to Joseph Henriques in 1802. (*GBMIP; MSGC*)

LEON, Abraham de.[1] Born May 8, 1702. Probably the son of Jacob de Leon. On August 25, 1732, he was married to Esther (Nunes) in Jamaica, B.W.I. The following year he came to Savannah. (*MSGC*)

LEON, Abraham de.[2] September 21, 1734—December 26, 1786. Son of Abraham de Leon.[1] (*MSGC*)

LEON, Abraham de.[3] Son of Abraham de Leon.[2] (*MSGC*)

LEON, Abraham de.[4] July 16, 1790, Philadelphia—November 12, 1847, Charleston. This son of Jacob de Leon[2] served as a surgeon's mate in the War of 1812. A prominent Mason, he later conducted a drug business in Camden, South Carolina, and practiced medicine in Charleston. On September 27, 1815, he was married to Isabella Nones in Philadelphia. (*EOJCC,* 23; *MSGC; UJE,* III, 116, 498)

LEON, Abraham Rodriques de. In New City in 1789. (*SIR*)

LEON, Mrs. Abraham de. Died January 10, 1792. Wife of Abraham de Leon.[1] (*MSGC*)

LEON, Almeria de. About 1798, Philadelphia—February 23, 1879/84. Daughter of Jacob de Leon,[2] she was married to Hyam Levy in Charleston on November 24, 1819. (*MSGC*)

LEON, Benjamin de. Born March 16, 1771, died an infant. Son of Abraham de Leon.[2] (*MSGC*)

LEON, Benjamin Marache de. In New York City in 1746. (*PAJHS,* XXVII, 247)

LEON, David de.[1] Born August 19, 1751. Son of Abraham de Leon.[1] Cf. below. (*MSGC*)

LEON, David de.[2] In Savannah in 1793. Cf. David Leion. (*MISR*)

LEON, Deborah de. November 26, 1713—August 6, 1801. In 1738 she was married to Isaac Gomez.[1] She was from Barbados. (*MSGC; PAJHS,* XXVII, 288)

LEON, Eleazer. In Lancaster in 1778. (*LCHS,* V, 93)

LEON, Esther de.[1] March 19, 1740—1785, Philadelphia. Daughter of Abraham de Leon.[1] (*MSGC*)

LEON, Esther de.[2] March 11, 1785—November 20, 1803. Daughter of Abraham de Leon.[2] (*MSGC*)

LEON, Hannah de. Granddaughter of Mordecai Gomez.[1] (*Wills,* 6)

LEON, Henrietta de. Probably born before 1800. Daughter of Jacob de Leon,[2] she was a convert to Christianity. (*MSGC*)

LEON, Isaac de. Born November 18, 1738. Son of Abraham de Leon.[1] (*MSGC*)

LEON, Jacob de.[1] Born November 3, 1746. Son of Abraham de Leon.[1] (*MSGC*)

LEON, Jacob de.[2] September 7, 1764—September 29, 1828, Columbia, South Carolina. This son of Abraham de Leon[2] was in Georgia in 1780, and in New York City in 1795; he also lived in Charleston for a short time. He served in the Revolutionary army. He was prominent in Masonry. On October 4, 1789, he was married to Hannah Hendricks. (*EJSC,* 84, *et passim; EVJC; MSGC; PAJHS,* XVII, 102; XXVII, 60, 286)

LEON, Jacob de, Jr. In New York City in 1789. (*SIR*)

LEON, Mrs. Jacob de, Jr. In New York City in 1791. (*SIR*)

LEON, Leah Abigail de. Born January 15, 1779, died an infant. Daughter of Abraham de Leon.[2] (*MSGC*)

LEON, Louisa. Probably born before 1800. Daughter of Jacob de Leon.[2] (MSGC)

LEON, Mordecai Hendricks de. November 12, 1791, perhaps in Charleston—October 29, 1848, Charleston. This son of Jacob de Leon[2] practiced chiefly in Columbia, South Carolina, and was a surgeon in the War of 1812. He was married to Rebecca Lopez.[2] (EJSC, 134, et passim; MSGC; Wills, 40)

LEON, Moses de. Born October 3, 1736. Son of Abraham de Leon,[1] he was in New York City in 1798. On September 9, 1828, he was buried there. (MSGC; Pool, 504; SIR)

LEON, Moses Rod(rigues) de. In New York City in 1764. (PAJHS, XXVII, 247)

LEON, Rachel de.[1] December 30, 1749—1793, Philadelphia. Daughter of Abraham de Leon,[1] she was married to Myer Hart. (MSGC)

LEON, Rachel de.[2] December 29, 1780—October 11, 1811. Daughter of Abraham de Leon.[2] (MSGC)

LEON, Rachel de.[3] In 1792 she came to Philadelphia from Bordeaux. She was the wife of Joseph R. Pereyra. (SZ, 121)

LEON, Rebecca de.[1] June, 1705—September 23, 1761. Came to America from Barbados. Widow of de Sielva, she was married to David Gomez.[1] (PAJHS, XVIII, 121; Pool, 470, 474; SIR)

LEON, Rebecca de.[2] Born September 8, 1748. Daughter of Abraham de Leon.[1] (MSGC)

LEON, Rebecca de.[3] Born November 16, 1765. Daughter of Abraham de Leon.[2] (MSGC)

LEON, Samuel. In 1754 he was given a grant of land in Georgia. (PAJHS, X, 88)

LEON, Sarah (Abigail). October 29, 1743—November 30, 1803, Philadelphia. Daughter of Abraham de Leon.[1] (MSGC)

LEON, Sarah de. October 4, 1768—September 8, 1841, New York City. Daughter of Abraham de Leon,[2] she was married to Aaron Correa. (MSGC)

LEONARD, Jacob. In New York City in 1800. (SIR)

LEPINE, Joseph. In New York City in 1795. It is highly doubtful that he was Jewish. (JRMP)

LEVAREZ, Rod(riguez). In Newport in 1760. Cf. Rodriguez Alvarez. (PAJHS, X, 8)

LEVENSTENE, Hheym (Haym). In Baltimore in 1796. (Blum, 4; UJE, II, 53)

LEVI. In 1658 he is said to have arrived in Newport from Holland. He became a Mason. (AJAM, III, 7)

LEVI, Abraham.[1] From Lissa, Poland. In 1770 he was in Newport, but left shortly thereafter for Jamaica, B.W.I. (Kohut, 27; PAJHS, XXXIV, 70)

LEVI, Abraham.[2] In Charleston sometime between 1783 and 1800. (EJSC, 280)

LEVI, Barnet. A merchant in Easton until 1790. Cf. Barnet Levy. (PAJHS, VIII, 129; Trachtenberg, 28, 228)

LEVI, Benjamin.[1] In 1768 he may have been in Philadelphia. (PAJHS, XIX, 121)

LEVI, Benjamin.[2] Died July 19, 1737, South Carolina. Son of Benjamin Levi. (SCHGM, XII, 138)

LEVI, Benjamin.[3] In Savannah about 1733. It is doubtful that he was Jewish. (Coulter, 82)

LEVI, Bernard. A merchant in Easton in 1780. Cf. Barnet Levy. (Trachtenberg, 228)

LEVI, Hulda. In Guilford, Connecticut, in 1772. It is doubtful that she was Jewish. (PAJHS, XI, 89)

LEVI, Isaac. In New York City in 1794. (PAJHS, XXVII, 56)

LEVI, Jacob. In 1798 he lived in Maryland. He was married to Mary Margaret and probably converted to Christianity. (PAJHS, V, 203)

LEVI, John.[1] A servant in Georgia about 1733. It is doubtful that he was Jewish. (Coulter, 82)

LEVI, John, Jr. This son of Hannah Britain came from Carolina and was in Georgia in

1733. It is doubtful that he was Jewish. (*Coulter*, 82)

LEVI, Joseph. Died 1798, New York City. A soldier. It is doubtful that he was Jewish. (*PAJHS*, XXV, 123)

LEVI, Juda. Fought in the Revolution in Virginia. (*PAJHS*, XX, 99)

LEVI, Lazarus. In Philadelphia in 1777. Cf. Levy Andrew Levy. (*PAJHS*, VI, 51)

LEVI, Mrs. Lazarus. In Philadelphia in 1777. (*PAJHS*, VI, 51)

LEVI, Mrs. Mary Margaret. Died April 8, 1798, Maryland. Wife of Jacob Levi, she was probably a Christian. (*PAJHS*, V, 203)

LEVI, Nathan.[1] In Georgia in 1757. (*CRG*, VII, 531)

LEVI, Nathan.[2] In 1768 he entered the University of Pennsylvania. (*PAJHS*, XIX, 121)

LEVI, Pomp. In Newport in 1790. It is doubtful that he was Jewish. (*Census A, Rhode Island*)

LEVI, Simson. In New York City in 1738. (*PAJHS*, XXI, 39f)

LEVI, Solomon. In Charlestown about 1765. (*EJSC*, 44)

LEVI, Thomas. In Savannah about 1733. It is doubtful that he was Jewish. (*Coulter*, 82)

LEVI, William. In 1777 he was a private in the Continental regiment from New Hampshire. It is doubtful that he was Jewish. (*PAJHS*, XI, 98)

LEVIE, Alexander. In 1778 he served with the Continental forces in Maryland. It is highly doubtful that he was Jewish. (*MTAR*, 135)

LEVINE, John. Died about 1773. He was an oculist in New York City. It is highly doubtful that he was Jewish. (*NYHSW*, VIII, 371; XVII, 344)

LEVISON, David. In New York City in 1776. (*Schappes*, 52)

LEVY. Died October 19, 1770, New York City. Daughter of Eleazar Levy.[1] (*SIR*)

LEVY, Miss.[1] Daughter of Eleazar Levy of Holland, she was married to Samuel Hyams in Charleston about 1795. (*JRMP*)

LEVY, Miss.[2] Daughter of Eleazar Levy,[1] she was in Philadelphia in 1771. (*AJA*)

LEVY (LEVI), Mr. A London Jew, he was converted to Christianity in America about 1775. (*Kohut*, 22)

LEVY, Mr. A fur trader, he traded between Pittsburgh and Detroit in 1763. Cf. Levy Andrew Levy. (*PAJHS*, XXXV, 15f)

LEVY, Aaron.[1] 1742, Amsterdam—February 23, 1815, Philadelphia. This son of Aaron Levy came to America about 1760. He was a merchant in Philadelphia and Lancaster. An active land agent, he established the town of Aaronsburg, Pennsylvania. A close business acquaintance of the Gratzes, he was a partner of Joseph Simon, and at one time worked for Robert Morris. During the Revolution he furnished supplies to the colonial troops and loaned money to the Continental Congress. In 1796 he settled in Philadelphia and lived there until his death. Sometime after 1760 he married Rachel Phillips.[1] (*Fish; PAJHS*, I, 89; II, 157f; IX, 30f; *UJE*, VII, 6; *WW*, 57, et passim)

LEVY, Aaron.[2] Born August 6, 1760, Spotswood, New Jersey. Son of Myers Levy. (*PAJHS*, XXVII, 151)

LEVY, Aaron.[3] June 30, 1771, New York City—October 24, 1852. This son of Hayman Levy was an army officer serving as paymaster as early as 1800. He served again as paymaster in the War of 1812 but by 1816 was promoted to lieutenant colonel. In 1819 he retired from the army. Thereafter he worked as an auctioneer for Isaac Moses and was a land speculator in the Lake George region. He was prominent in the Jewish society of New York City. On February 12, 1800, he was married to Richea Moses in New York City. (*PAJHS*, XXVII, 168, et passim; *SIR*; *UJE*, VII, 6; VIII, 196)

LEVY, Aaron, Jr. 1774—August 3, 1852. Nephew of Aaron Levy,[1] he was in Philadelphia in 1800. On June 10, 1801, he was married to Fanny Joseph. (*MIPR; MSGC; WW*, 226)

LEVY, Abigail.¹ Identical with Bilhah Levy.¹

LEVY, Abigail.² August 12, 1760—August 4, 1820. Daughter of Benjamin Levy,² she was married to Dr. Lyde Goodwin on March 17, 1779, in Baltimore; and to Dr. John Worthington on November 12, 1807. (*MSGC*)

LEVY, Abraham.¹ June 6, 1767, New York City—September 20, 1767, New York City. Infant son of Hayman Levy. (*PAJHS*, IV, 210; *SIR*)

LEVY, Abraham.² Died August 7, 1786, Philadelphia. (*PAJHS*, VI, 108)

LEVY, Abraham.³ In Philadelphia in 1796. (*JRMP*)

LEVY, Abraham.⁴ Died July 21, 1785, Philadelphia. Son of Judah Levy.³ (*MSGC*)

LEVY, Abraham.⁵ A trader, he arrived in Philadelphia with his family in 1768. Cf. Abraham Levy² and Abraham Levy.³ (*WW*, 51)

LEVY, Abraham Isaac. In Philadelphia in 1785. (*MIPR*)

LEVY, Abraham L. August 5, 1796—October 9, 1829. Son of Lyon Levy, he was married to Rebecca Benjamin in Charleston on November 29, 1826. (*MSGC*)

LEVY, Abram. On August 24, 1786, he was married to Janet Moris in Philadelphia. (*MIPR*)

LEVY, Amelia. 1793—April 7, 1867. Daughter of Michael Levy.³ It is highly doubtful that she was Jewish. (*MSGC*)

LEVY, Amran. In 1788 he applied for aid from Congregation Shearith Israel in New York City. (*SIR*)

LEVY, Anne. On July 21, 1728, she was married to John Connant in South Carolina. It is doubtful that she was Jewish. (*SCHGM*, XXIII, 128)

LEVY, Ansell Samuel. In New York City in 1684. He may have been married to the widow of Asser Levy.¹ (*AJAM*, III, 7)

LEVY, Asher.¹ Son of Moses Levy,¹ he may not have been in America. (*PAJHS*, XXIII, 158)

LEVY, Asher.² Died August, 1785, Philadelphia. Son of Isaac Levy,⁶ he may have been in Philadelphia in 1783. (*PAJHS*, X, 165)

LEVY, Asser.¹ Died 1681. Probably the most prominent Jew in the North American colonies in the seventeenth century, he came to New Amsterdam in 1654. His full name, Asser Levy Van Schwelm, indicates that his family came from Schwelm, Westphalia. A poor laborer, he petitioned against the special tax exacted of Jews in lieu of military service. Later he turned to trade and became wealthy. He was considered the Jewish good will ambassador to the non-Jews. As a butcher he built a public slaughterhouse in 1678. His wife was Miriam. (*AJAM*, III, 7)

LEVY, Asser.² Probably the son of Asser Levy.¹ In 1724 he was in Connecticut. His wife was Margaret. (*PAJHS*, VIII, 22f)

LEVY, Asser.³ May have been a grandson of Asser Levy.¹ He was an ensign in the First New Jersey regiment in the Revolution. (*PAJHS*, I, 122; VIII, 23)

LEVY, Barnard. Died 1783. A merchant in Easton about 1780. His wife was Rebecca de Lyon. (*GBMIP*; *MSGC*; *Trachtenberg*, 228)

LEVY, Barnet. From 1772 until 1790 he was a merchant in Easton. Cf. Barnet Levi and Bernard Levi. (*Trachtenberg*, 28, 43f)

LEVY, Bella (Arabella).¹ November 22, 1761—December 17, 1810. Daughter of Samson Levy,¹ she was in Philadelphia in 1781. On June 24, 1784, she was married to James Morris Jones. (*MSGC*; *Wills*, 21)

LEVY, Bella.² 1762, London—November 6, 1851, Charleston. Wife of Daniel Hart,² she came to Charleston in 1786. (*EOJCC*, 35; *MSP*)

LEVY, Benjamin.¹ 1692—December 30, 1787, New York City. Husband of Judith. (*PAJHS*, XXVII, 347; XXXIII, 210)

LEVY, Benjamin.² September 5, 1726, New York City—February 3, 1802, Baltimore. This son of Moses Levy¹ enjoyed great social status as a prominent merchant and Indian trader in Philadelphia and Baltimore. He was involved early in pro-American activity, beginning with the Non-Importation Agreement of 1765. A friend of Robert Morris, he signed government bills of credit and certificates. In 1758 he was married to Rachel Levy. (*MSGC; PAJHS*, I, 60, 86; XXXIII, 210; *UJE*, II, 53; VII, 8f; VIII, 476; *WW*, 31, *et passim*)

LEVY, Benjamin.[3] Probably born before 1800. Son of Simeon Levy,[2] he was married to a gentile in Baltimore. He died in New Orleans. (*MSGC; PAJHS*, IV, 213)

LEVY, Benjamin.[4] Son of Michael Levy.[3] (*MSGC*)

LEVY, Benjamin.[5] Born 1782, Lancaster, Pennsylvania. Son of Judah Levy.[3] (*MSGC*)

LEVY, Bernard. 1789, Charleston—May 23, 1869. In December, 1841, he was married to Mary Ann Suares. (*MSGC*)

LEVY, Bilhah.[1] Born about 1717. Daughter of Samuel Levy,[1] she was an orphan in Boston, cared for by an uncle, Michael Asher. Cf. Abigail Levy.[1] (*PAJHS*, XXIII, 150; *SCMCNYC*, 189)

LEVY, Bilhah.[2] 1742—February 3, 1781, Newport. Daughter of Benjamin Levy.[1] (*PAJHS*, IV, 213)

LEVY, Bilhah.[3] Probably born before 1800. Daughter of Simeon Levy,[2] she was married to John Hart. (*PAJHS*, IV, 213)

LEVY, Bilhah Abigail. November 26, 1696, London—May 16, 1756/65, New York City. Daughter of Moses Levy,[1] she was married to Jacob Franks[1] in 1712/9. She was a well read woman. (*MEAJA*, 58, *et passim*; *MSGC; PAJHS*, IV, 190; *UJE*, IV, 416)

LEVY, Chapman. 1787, Camden, South Carolina—1850, Camden, Mississippi. In 1806 he was admitted to the bar in South Carolina. He served in the War of 1812, attaining the rank of colonel. During the years 1829 till 1833, and 1836 till 1838, he was in the state legislature of South Carolina. He was also a planter in the Mississippi Territory. (*EJSC*, 136, *et passim*; *JRMP; PAJHS*, XII, 163f; XVIII, 209; *UJE*, VII, 9)

LEVY, Colonel. He was involved in the Carolina Insurrection of 1711 and was executed. It is doubtful that he was Jewish. (*PAJHS*, XX, 89; *UJE*, X, 426)

LEVY, Daniel.[1] Born January, 1765, Jamaica, Long Island. Son of Moses Levy.[3] (*MSP*)

LEVY, Daniel.[2] Died May 12, 1844. In 1791 he became a member of the bar in Philadelphia. (*Morais*, 411)

LEVY, Daniel.[3] Born September 22, 1766. Son of Samson Levy,[1] he was in Philadelphia by 1781. Cf. above. (*MSGC; Wills*, 21)

LEVY, David.[1] On September 7, 1761, he was married to Margaret Ashbaugh. (*PA*, II, 176)

LEVY, David.[2] In 1776 he served with the Continental forces in Maryland. (*MTAR*, 263)

LEVY, David.[3] In 1789 he arrived in New York City from Jamaica, B.W.I. (*SIR*)

LEVY, David.[4] A child in New York City about 1793. (*PAJHS*, XXVII, 55)

LEVY, David.[5] Born February 20, 1793, Philadelphia. Son of Moses Nathan Levy. Cf. David Nathan.[3] (*MIPR*)

LEVY, David Jacob. Died April 29, 1771, St. Eustatia. On December 2, 1761, he was married to Richa Simson. In 1762 he was a merchant in New York City. (*PAJHS*, XXV, 90; *SIR*)

LEVY, Deborah.[1] Born April 17, 1761, New York City, died an infant. Daughter of Hayman Levy. (*PAJHS*, XXVII, 168; *SIR*)

LEVY, Deborah.[2] June 2, 1762—August 30, 1821. Daughter of Hayman Levy. (*PAJHS*, XXVII, 168)

LEVY, Eleazar.[1] This son of Hayman Levy was a merchant in Quebec and traded in that area, probably supplying the British during the French and Indian War. He was closely associated with Aaron Hart of Three Rivers. He later moved to New York City and changed his allegiance to the American cause. During the Revolution he was such an ardent patriot that he moved to Philadelphia, where he became friendly with Haym Salomon. At one time he held a mortgage on West Point. He died impoverished. (*MEAJA*, 211, *et passim*; *MEAJB*, 146, *et passim*; *Pool*, 53, *et passim*)

LEVY, Eleazar.[2] In 1780 he was a merchant in Charlestown. His wife was Judith. (*EOJCC*, 110; *MSP*)

LEVY, Eleazar.[3] Born 1789, Easton. Son of Simeon Barnard Levy. (*MIPR*)

LEVY, Mrs. Eleazar. Wife of Eleazar Levy,[1] she was with him in Philadelphia in 1771. (*AJA*)

LEVY, Elias. September 18, 1791, probably in Charleston—February 6, 1856, Charleston. Son of Lyon Levy, he was married to Rachel Moïse on June 13, 1821. (*Wills*, 46)

LEVY, Eliza. Daughter of Michael Levy.[3] (*MSGC*)

LEVY, Emmanuel. 1794, Charleston—August 31, 1867, Charleston. (*MSGC*)

LEVY, Esther.[1] About 1701—May 31, 1753, New York City. Wife of Daniel Gomez,[1] she came to New York City from Curaçao. (*PAJHS*, XVIII, 121; *Pool*, 237f)

LEVY, Esther.[2] February 28, 1721—June 26, 1785, England. Daughter of Moses Levy,[1] she was married to Jacob Hart.[2] (*PAJHS*, XXXIII, 210)

LEVY, Esther.[3] On December 27, 1786, she was married to Isaac Simons in Easton. (*MIPR*)

LEVY, Esther.[4] A child in New York City about 1793. (*PAJHS*, XXVII, 55)

LEVY, Esther.[5] 1789, Charleston—February 18, 1871, New Orleans. On August 30, 1815, she was married to Henry Nathan. (*MSGC*)

LEVY, Esther (Henrietta). Daughter of Isaac Levy,[6] she was married to Matthias Williamson. (*MSGC*; *PAJHS*, XXIII, 160)

LEVY, Ezekiel.[1] This son of Abraham Levy arrived in Philadelphia in 1768. In 1776 he was employed as shohet, hazzan, and Hebrew teacher by Congregation Mikveh Israel in Philadelphia. In 1777 he was in Northumberland in the employ of Aaron Levy. A trader, he returned to Philadelphia in 1782. He was married and had a family. (*MEAJB*, 68, 149f, 393; *Morais*, 15; *WW*, 51)

LEVY, Ezekiel.[2] In 1779 he was in Charlestown, where he served in Captain Lushington's "Jew Company." (*EJSC*, 278; *PAJHS*, XIX, 152)

LEVY, Ezekiel.[3] Probably a converted Jew, in the late 1780s he was a vestryman in the Protestant Episcopal Church in Williamsburg, Virginia. (*MEAJB*, 150)

LEVY, Figlah. Daughter of Jacob Levy, she was married to Joseph Simon[2] on October 15, 1769, probably in New York City. (*SIR*)

LEVY, Gershom. A merchant in Canada and in the Detroit area, he traded with the Indians and supplied the English during the French and Indian War. He was probably captured by Indians but was later released. (*MEAJA*, 208, *et passim*)

LEVY, Hagima. In Philadelphia in 1782. (*Morais*, 15)

LEVY, Haim. 1739—July 12, 1789. Son of Benjamin Levy,[2] he was a merchant who was married to Grace Mears[2] on July 26, 1768, in Newport. (*PAJHS*, IV, 213; XXXIII, 203; *MSGC*)

LEVY, Haim Eleazar. In Philadelphia in 1783. (*MIPR*)

LEVY, Hannah.[1] September 22, 1723—April 3, 1751. Daughter of Moses Levy,[1] she was married to Joshua Isaacs.[1] (*MSGC*; *PAJHS*, XXIII, 159; XXXIII, 210)

LEVY, Hannah.[2] On May 13, 1767, she was married to Charles Davis. (*PA*, II, 176)

LEVY, Hannah.[3] About 1758, Holland—November 20, 1849, Philadelphia. Daughter of Isaac Levy,[6] she was married to Eleazar Lyons at Harrisburg on May 29, 1776. (*MSGC*)

LEVY, Hannah.[4] 1783—July 5, 1863, Washington. Daughter of Simeon Levy.[2] (*MSGC*; *PAJHS*, IV, 213)

LEVY, Mrs. Hannah.[1] Died 1761, Philadelphia. Wife of Isaac Levy.[3] (*GBMIP*)

LEVY, Mrs. Hannah.² Died November 8, 1772, New York City. Wife of Joshua Levy.¹ (SIR)

LEVY, Hays Sara. Died May 5, 1763, New York City. Daughter of Hayman Levy. (PAJHS, IV, 210; SIR)

LEVY, Hart. In Charleston before 1783. He was the sexton of Congregation Beth Elohim. (EJSC, 136, 278, 288)

LEVY, Hayman. January 15, 1721, Hanover, Germany—August 20, 1789, New York City. This son of Moses Levy was naturalized on November 24, 1750, and became a freeman of New York City on December 20, 1750. He was an outstanding merchant and fur trader, trading throughout the colonies and the West Indies, and was a purveyor of army materials. During the French and Indian War he owned a privateer. A zealous Revolutionary patriot, he moved to Philadelphia during the British occupation of New York City. A prominent participant in the Jewish life of New York City, he served as president of Congregation Shearith Israel in New York City. On May 15/26, 1751, he was married to Sloe Myers. (Coldoc, 14, et passim; MEAJA, 73, et passim; MEAJB, 11, et passim; PAJHS, IV, 210f; XXVI, 237; XXVII, 168; POFNW, 249, et passim; Pool, 39, et passim; SIR; UJE, VII, 10; VIII, 177)

LEVY, Hester.¹ Daughter of Joshua Levy,¹ she was married to Simeon Levy.² (MSGC; PAJHS, XVIII, 117; XXXIII, 210)

LEVY, Hester.² Daughter of Moses Levy,¹ she was living in Philadelphia in 1744. (Morais, 41f)

LEVY, Hester.³ Probably born before 1800. Granddaughter of Nathan Levy, she lived in Baltimore in 1812. (PAJHS, I, 22)

LEVY, Hetty.¹ 1761—about 1816. Daughter of Benjamin Levy.² (MSGC)

LEVY, Hetty.² October 21, 1768—September 13, 1780. Daughter of Samson Levy.¹ (MSGC)

LEVY, Hetty Grace. 1793—March 17, 1826. Daughter of Solomon Levy.² (PAJHS, XXVII, 286)

LEVY, Hezekiah. Before 1771 he was a member of a Masonic lodge in Fredericksburg, Virginia. George Washington was a member of the same lodge. Levy may have been a convert to Christianity. (PAJHS, XIX, 58f; UJE, X, 426)

LEVY, Haim. Died September, 1795, Philadelphia. (MIPR)

LEVY, Hyam. Died 1865. Son of Solomon (H) Levy,² he was in Charleston sometime between 1783 and 1800. In 1819 he was married to Almira de Leon. (EJSC, 280; MSGC)

LEVY, Hyam E. In Charleston sometime between 1783 and 1800. (EJSC, 280)

LEVY, Hyman, Jr. In 1765 he was a merchant in Philadelphia. (PAJHS, I, 60; Schappes, 40)

LEVY, Isaac.¹ Died 1745. Lived in New York City. (PAJHS, XXIII, 152f)

LEVY, Isaac.² In 1755 he came to Philadelphia from Rotterdam. He was divorced from Judica and was married to Miss Jacobs. (MSP)

LEVY, Isaac.³ Died 1761, Philadelphia. Husband of Hannah. (MSP)

LEVY, Isaac.⁴ About 1762 he was a merchant in Quebec. (MEAJA, 208, 232, 234)

LEVY, Isaac.⁵ Died 1764, Philadelphia. (MIPR)

LEVY, Isaac.⁶ July 19, 1706, New York City—March, 1777, Philadelphia. This son of Moses Levy¹ was a merchant who lived in New York City, Philadelphia, and Boston. He was married to Elizabeth Pue. (JNEA, 20; MSP; PAJHS, XXIII, 85, 158f)

LEVY, Isaac.⁷ Born November 15, 1761, New York City. Son of Joshua Levy.¹ (MSGC; SIR)

LEVY, Isaac.⁸ A provisioner for the Virginia Revolutionary forces, he also acted as a physician. He played an important role in opening the Illinois country. (PAJHS, XX, 95f)

LEVY, Isaac.⁹ Born early eighteenth century, New York City. A merchant and trader, he was naturalized in New York City on November 18, 1740. In 1752 he went to England but returned to Philadelphia in 1756. He was last heard of in Boston in 1769. (*PAJHS*, IX, 57-62)

LEVY, Isaac.[10] On August 31, 1736, he arrived in Savannah from London. He may be one of the other Isaac Levys. (*SRB*)

LEVY, Isaac.[11] Born August 18, 1800, in Philadelphia. A son of Michael Levy.[3] (*MIPR*)

LEVY, Isaac.[12] Born before 1772. Son of Joseph Levy.[1] (*MSGC*)

LEVY, Isaac (H). October 15, 1763, New York City—April 19, 1854. Son of Hayman Levy, he was a merchant. (*PAJHS*, IV, 210; XXVII, 39, *et passim*; *SIR*)

LEVY, Isaac Jacob. About 1770—October 15, 1846, Philadelphia. In Philadelphia in 1783. He was married to Hester Polock on February 16, 1809. (*GBMIP*; *MIPR*)

LEVY, Isaac Tobias. December 11, 1792—February 18, 1811. Son of Lyon Levy, he lived in Charleston. (*MSGC*; *Wills*, 46)

LEVY, Isaiah.[1] In Philadelphia in 1791. (*MIPR*)

LEVY, Isaiah.[2] Born March 18, 1795, Philadelphia. Son of Moses Nathan Levy. Cf. Isaiah Nathan.[2] (*MIPR*)

LEVY, Israel. In 1759 he was a merchant in Charlestown. (*EJSC*, 42)

LEVY, J. H. In New York City in 1795. Cf. Isaac (H) Levy. (*PAJHS*, XIX, 31)

LEVY, Jacob.[1] A merchant, he was in New York City about 1740. (*PAJHS*, XXI, 45; *Public Notary Records*, V, 229; *Rhode Island State Archives*)

LEVY, Jacob.[2] Born August 26, 1764, New York City. Son of David Jacob Levy. (*SIR*)

LEVY, Jacob.[3] One of the first Jews in Baltimore in 1773, he served with the Continental troops in Maryland in 1779. (*MTAR*, 270; *UJE*, I, 232)

LEVY, Jacob.[4] Born August 22, 1790, Philadelphia. Son of Moses Nathan Levy. Cf. Jacob Nathan. (*MIPR*)

LEVY, Jacob.[5] November 4, 1793—about 1814. Son of Lyon Levy, he was in Charleston in 1800. He was married to Rachel Moïse Abraham. (*MSGC*; *Wills*, 46)

LEVY, Jacob Clarisse (or Clavius). December 19, 1788, Charleston—June 10, 1785, Savannah. Son of Moses Clava Levy, he was married to Fannie Yates in Liverpool, England, on October 21, 1817. (*MSGC*)

LEVY, Jacob F. Son of Benjamin Levy,[2] he was a stockholder in a newly organized bank in Baltimore in 1796. (*MSGC*; *UJE*, II, 53)

LEVY, Jacob J. Died June, 1773, Philadelphia. Son of Nahman Levy. (*JCES*)

LEVY, Mrs. Jacob. Widow of Jacob Levy,[1] she was in New York City in 1747. (*PAJHS*, XXI, 55)

LEVY, Jochebed.[1] January 12, 1746—October 26, 1828. Daughter of Benjamin Levy,[1] she was married to Moses Mendes Seixas[1] on October 3, 1770, in Newport. (*PAJHS*, IV, 203; XXVII, 346)

LEVY, Jochebed.[2] 1794—February 28, 1819. Daughter of Simeon Levy.[2] (*PAJHS*, IV, 213; XVIII, 117)

LEVY, Joh. From St. Thomas. In 1795 he was in New York City. (*PAJHS*, XXVII, 62)

LEVY, John.[1] In Virginia in 1648. It is doubtful that he was Jewish. (*AJAM*, III, 7f)

LEVY, John.[2] About 1780 he lived in Warwick County, Virginia. It is doubtful that he was Jewish. (*PAJHS*, XX, 100)

LEVY, Joseph.[1] June 12, 1728, New York City—1772, South Carolina. This son of Moses Levy[1] became a freeman of New York City on November 7, 1752. He was married to Esther. (*MSGC*; *PAJHS*, VI, 102; XXXIII, 210)

LEVY, Joseph.[2] In 1757 he was a lieutenant in the South Carolina militia. From 1762 through 1772 he was a businessman in Charlestown. (*EJSC*, 42)

LEVY, Joseph.[3] Lived in Cushing, Maine, with his family of eight. It is doubtful that he was Jewish. (*Census A, Maine*)

LEVY, Joseph.[4] In New York City in 1795. (PAJHS, XXVII, 58)

LEVY, Joseph.[5] In 1796 he was leaving America from Richmond. (ELJR, 35)

LEVY, Joseph.[6] Born December 10, 1758, Philadelphia, died an infant. Son of Samson Levy.[1] (MSGC)

LEVY, Joseph.[7] Born 1779, Lancaster. Son of Judah Levy.[3] (MSGC)

LEVY, Joshua.[1] Died before 1807. In New York City in 1759. His wife was Hannah. (MSGC; PAJHS, XXI, 79)

LEVY, Joshua.[2] In New York City in 1792. (PAJHS, XXVII, 51)

LEVY, Juda. Niece of Isaac Lopes, she came from Bordeaux to New York City in 1793. (SZ, 121)

LEVY, Judah.[1] In 1774 he was in New York City and was shammas of Congregation Shearith Israel. (PAJHS, XXI, 131)

LEVY, Judah.[2] By 1764 he lived in Philadelphia and Lancaster. (MSGC)

LEVY, Judah, Jr. In New York City in 1749. (PAJHS, XXI, 60)

LEVY, Judah Mears. June 18, 1778—Havana. Son of Haim Levy. (MSGC; PAJHS, XXXIII, 203)

LEVY, Mrs. Judica. Divorced wife of Isaac Levy,[2] she was married to Bernard Jacobs. (Wills, 26)

LEVY, Judith. Died March 17, 1833. Daughter of Haim Levy. (PAJHS, IV, 213)

LEVY, Mrs. Judith.[1] 1702—October 23, 1788. Wife of Benjamin Levy.[1] (PAJHS, IV, 213)

LEVY, Mrs. Judith.[2] Wife of Eleazar Levy,[2] she was in Charlestown in 1780. (EOJCC, 110)

LEVY, Julia. 1789/1790, New York City—November 23, 1862, Washington, D.C. Daughter of Simeon Levy,[2] she was married to John Solomons on January 1, 1818. (MSGC; PAJHS, IV, 213)

LEVY, Lawrence. In New York City in 1719. (Coldoc, 323; NYHSW, II, 189)

LEVY, Lazarus. In Easton in 1773. During the Revolution he served in the Philadelphia militia. In 1792 he was a glasscutter in Philadelphia. (MIPR; Trachtenberg, 28; WW, 96)

LEVY, Lev. Born 1764, Lancaster. Son of Judah Levy.[3] (MSGC)

LEVY, Levy Andrew. A trader in Lancaster, in 1760 he founded a trading house at Fort Pitt. He was also engaged in land speculation and took part in the development of the Illinois country. He formed a partnership with Joseph Simon and the Gratzes. During the French and Indian War he was held prisoner for a short time by the Indians, but was later released. His wife was Susannah Simon. Cf. Lazarus Levi and Mr. Levy. (MEAJA, 228; MSGC; PAJHS, II, 157; VI, 51; IX, 30; UJE, V, 538; VIII, 545)

LEVY, Louis. Son of Michael Levy.[3] (MSGC)

LEVY, Lyon. July, 1764, Woolwich, England—March 20, 1835, Charleston. An attorney, he was Justice Q.U. in 1806, and the South Carolina state treasurer from 1817 through 1822. His first wife was Leah Joseph; his second wife was Sarah N. Cardozo on May 1, 1801. (EJSC, 136, et passim; EOJCC, 14; PAJHS, XII, 163; Wills, 46)

LEVY, M. M. In Philadelphia in 1784. (MIPR)

LEVY, Magnus. In Philadelphia in 1784. (MIPR)

LEVY, Mary Ann Barbara. Died April 9, 1797. Infant daughter of David Levy. (PAJHS, V, 203)

LEVY, Mary Asser. Born Philadelphia, died 1841. On February 1, 1804, she was married to Judah Eleazar Lyons in New York City. (MSP; PAJHS, XXI, xxiii)

LEVY, Meshach. In Montreal in 1774. (Malchelosse, 169)

LEVY, Michael.[1] Born July 10, 1709. Son of Moses Levy,[1] he lived in New York City in 1740. (MSGC; PAJHS, XXI, 39f; XXIII, 158f)

LEVY, Michael.[2] In Charlestown sometime between 1750 and 1782. (*EJSC*, 278)

LEVY, Michael.[3] 1755—1812. A merchant, he served in the Revolutionary army. His wife was Rachel; he was the father of Uriah P. Levy. (*MSGC*; *UJE*, VII, 17; VIII, 477)

LEVY, Michael.[4] In 1772 he arrived in Philadelphia from Germany as an indentured servant. (*WW*, 57)

LEVY, Mrs. Michal. Widow of Nathan Levy,[1] she was in Philadelphia in 1754. (*GBMIP*)

LEVY, Michel. 1741—October 1, 1826. Daughter of Nathan Levy.[1] (*MSGC*)

LEVY, Miriam.[1] February 11, 1720—February 4, 1748. Daughter of Moses Levy,[1] she was married to Moses Hart. (*MSGC*; *PAJHS*, XXXIII, 210; XXXIV, 61)

LEVY, Miriam.[2] 1752—February 7, 1814, Charleston. Wife of Israel Joseph.[1] (*MSP*; *Wills*, 41)

LEVY, Miriam.[3] 1780, Charlestown—January 19, 1821, Charleston. Daughter of Eleazar Levy,[2] she was married to Samuel Hyams. (*EOJCC*, 110)

LEVY, Miriam.[4] 1793—February 29, 1880. Daughter of Simeon Levy.[2] (*PAJHS*, IV, 213)

LEVY, Mrs. Miriam.[1] Widow of Samuel Levy, she was in New York City in 1762. (*PAJHS*, XXV, 90)

LEVY, Mrs. Miriam.[2] Wife of Asser Levy,[1] she was in New York City in 1681. (*AJAM*, III, 7f)

LEVY, Mordecai.[1] Died October 29, 1783, Philadelphia. In 1773 he was a merchant in Philadelphia. Just previous to the Revolution he was a loyalist, but in 1775 he pledged his allegiance to the American Congress. He was one of the founders of Congregation Mikveh Israel in Philadelphia. (*MIPR*; *PAJHS*, I, 59f; X, 163; *WW*, 79)

LEVY, Mordecai.[2] In Charleston sometime between 1783 and 1800. (*EJSC*, 280)

LEVY, Morton Phillips. Son of Michael Levy.[3] (*MSGC*)

LEVY, Moses.[1] About 1665—June 14, 1728, New York City. On June 5, 1695, he became a freeman of New York City. In 1719 he was elected constable there. He was a prominent merchant, distiller, real estate investor, and shipowner. Levy's first wife was Rycha Asher; his second wife was Grace Mears.[1] (*AJAM*, III, 9; *MEAJA*, 50, *et passim*; *MCCNY*, III, 210, 214; *PAJHS*, II, 82; IV, 189f; V, 117; XXVIII, 237; *Pool*, 12, *et passim*)

LEVY, Moses.[2] Died about 1763, Rhode Island. Son of Isaac Levy, he was in New York City in 1732. (*JRMP*; *PAJHS*, XXI, 29)

LEVY, Moses.[3] 1704—June 18, 1792, Newport. This son of Moses Levy[1] was a wealthy merchant who lived in Newport and New York City. (*PAJHS*, IV, 213)

LEVY, Moses.[4] August 9, 1756, Philadelphia—May 9, 1826, Philadelphia. This son of Samson Levy[1] was graduated from the University of Pennsylvania in 1772. On March 19, 1778, he was admitted to the bar. From 1802 through 1822 he was recorder of Philadelphia; from 1822 through 1825 he was city and county judge of Philadelphia; he also served in the Pennsylvania legislature. He was a trustee of the University of Pennsylvania. The Federalist Party attacked Levy as a Jew although he neither considered himself a Jew (he became an Episcopalian) nor took part in the Jewish life of the community. On June 26, 1791, he was married to Mary Pearce. (*Morais*, 38, *et passim*; *MSGC*; *PAJHS*, IX, 35; XIX, 121; *UJE*, VII, 15; VIII, 428, 433; X, 371; *WW*, 31, *et passim*)

LEVY, Moses.[5] Born November 20, 1763, New York City. Son of Joshua Levy.[1] (*SIR*)

LEVY, Moses.[6] Born March 4, 1772, Newport, died England. Son of Haim Levy, he was married to Rosetta Almund in Bristol, England. (*MSGC*; *PAJHS*, IV, 213; XXXIII, 203, 210)

LEVY, Moses B. In New York City in 1729. (*PAJHS*, XXI, 16)

LEVY, Moses Clava. About 1750, Zobnau, Poland—March 20, 1839, Charleston. About 1783 he came to Charleston and became a merchant and an active Mason. His wife was Sarah. (*EJSC*, 117, *et passim*; *MSGC*; *Wills*, 47)

LEVY, Moses Hyman. In New York City in 1750. (*MSP*)

LEVY, Moses Nathan. In Philadelphia in 1782. He was probably Moses Nathan the Levite. Cf. Moses Nathan.[1] (*MIPR*)

LEVY, Moses Sim. In Charlestown sometime between 1750 and 1782. (*EJSC*, 278)

LEVY, Myer. May 30, 1771, New York City—November 28, 1771, New York City. (*SIR*)

LEVY, Myers. In 1756 he arrived in New Jersey from Surinam with his wife and children. A trader in Spotswood until 1760, he fled leaving large debts to the Gratzes, Franks, and many gentile merchants. (*MEAJB*, 51; *PAJHS*, XVII, 39; XXVII, 151)

LEVY, Mrs. Myers. Wife of Myers Levy, she came to New Jersey with her family from Surinam in 1756. (*PAJHS*, XVII, 39; XXVII, 151)

LEVY, Nathan.[1] February 18, 1704, London—December 2, 1753, Philadelphia. This son of Moses Levy[1] sailed from London on the *Myrtilla*, the ship that brought the Liberty Bell to Philadelphia. He became a merchant, trading with the Indians in the West, and was a renowned shipowner. In 1737 he settled in Philadelphia and was the founder of the Jewish community there. He established the first Jewish cemetery in Philadelphia and bequeathed his excellent library to the community. His wife was Michal. (*GBMIP*; *Morais*, 200f; *MSGC*; *PAJHS*, I, 20f; IV, 193f; V, 203f; VI, 108; XXIII, 158f; XXVI, 235f; *WW*, 23, *et passim*)

LEVY, Nathan.[2] In 1772 he was a physician in Charlestown. (*EJSC*, 129, 136)

LEVY, Nathan.[3] In 1769 he was a shopkeeper in New Jersey. (*PAJHS*, XVII, 40)

LEVY, Nathan.[4] August 15, 1754, Philadelphia—October 12, 1756. Son of Samson Levy.[1] (*MSGC*; *Wills*, 14)

LEVY, Nathan.[5] July 21, 1759—February 1, 1846. Son of Benjamin Levy.[2] (*MSGC*)

LEVY, Nathan.[6] Born 1779, Lancaster. Son of Judah Levy.[2] (*MSGC*)

LEVY, Nathaniel. A member of the First Baltimore Cavalry under General Lafayette, he fought in the Revolution. (*UJE*, VII, 392)

LEVY, Rachel.[1] Died by 1745, New York City. Wife of Samuel Myers Cohen.[1] (*PAJHS*, XI, 191f)

LEVY, Rachel.[2] Died August 21, 1749, New York City. (*PAJHS*, XVIII, 121)

LEVY, Rachel.[3] February 27, 1719, London—May 12, 1797, New York City. Daughter of Moses Levy,[1] she was married to Isaac M. Seixas about 1740. (*MSGC*; *PAJHS*, XXVII, 161)

LEVY, Rachel.[4] 1739, Philadelphia—November 11, 1794, Baltimore. Daughter of Nathan Levy,[1] she was married to Benjamin Levy.[2] (*MSGC*; *PAJHS*, I, 21f; XXXIII, 210)

LEVY, Rachel.[5] Born February 22, 1766, New York City. (*SIR*)

LEVY, Rachel.[6] 1768—February 13, 1843, Baton Rouge. Daughter of Joshua Levy,[1] she was married first to Phillips, and then to Jacob Mendez Seixas on December 28, 1807. (*MSGC*)

LEVY, Rachel.[7] February 26, 1771—December 28, 1862. Daughter of Samson Levy,[1] she was baptized and lived in Philadelphia. (*MSGC*; *Wills*, 14, 21)

LEVY, Rachel Debora. April 17, 1761—August 30, 1821. Daughter of Hayman Levy. (*PAJHS*, IV, 210)

LEVY, Rebecca.[1] Died October 2, 1762, New York City. Daughter of Joshua Levy.[1] (*SIR*)

LEVY, Rebecca.[2] Granddaughter of Mordecai Gomez,[1] she was alive in 1801. (*Wills*, 6)

LEVY, Reuben. In Charleston in 1800. (*EJSC*, 136)

LEVY, Reyna. April 15, 1753—June 24, 1824. Daughter of Hayman Levy, she was married to Isaac Moses on August 8, 1770, in New York City. (*PAJHS*, IV, 210; *SIR*)

LEVY, Richa. January 3, 1770—October 5, 1788, New York City. Daughter of Hayman Levy. (PAJHS, IV, 210; SIR)

LEVY, Ritzy. Daughter of Isaac Levy,[1] she was in New York City in 1745. (NYHSW, IV, 57)

LEVY, Robert Morris. Born 1763. Son of Benjamin Levy.[2] (MSGC)

LEVY, Mrs. Rose. 1727—May 9, 1812, Charleston. Wife of Solomon Levy, she lived in Charleston for fifty years. (MSGC)

LEVY, Samson.[1] August 19, 1722—March 22, 1781, Philadelphia. This son of Moses Levy[1] was a merchant who enjoyed a high social position. He apparently had little to do with the Jewish community, and was converted to Christianity. On November 3, 1753, in Old Swede's Church in Philadelphia, he was married to Martha Lampley, the widow of James Steel Thompson. (MSGC; PAJHS, XXXIII, 210; Schappes, 40; UJE, VII, 15; VIII, 476; Wills, 13f; WW, 31)

LEVY, Samson.[2] May 1, 1764, Philadelphia—December 15, 1831, Philadelphia. This son of Samson Levy[1] was admitted to the bar on June 9, 1787, and was known for his bizarre method of practicing law. He was one of the incorporators of the Pennsylvania Academy of Fine Arts. On September 28, 1780, he was baptized. On September 5, 1793, he was married to Sarah Corts. (Morais, 39, et passim; MSGC; UJE, VII, 17)

LEVY, Samuel.[1] Died May 5, 1719. Also known as Samuel Zanwill Levy. Merchant son of Isaac Levy, he was elected constable in New York City in 1718. His wife was Rachel Asher. (MCCCNY, III, 186; PAJHS, XXXIII, 210; XXXIV, 60f; Pool, 162f)

LEVY, Samuel.[2] A merchant in New York City, he was elected constable there in 1736, but was ineligible since he was not a freeman or a freeholder. In 1740 he was naturalized there. In 1736 he was president of Congregation Shearith Israel. (PAJHS, XIII, 6; XXI, 11, et passim; MCCCNY, IV, 346, 351)

LEVY, Samuel.[3] In 1741 he was a merchant in Charlestown. (EJSC, 24)

LEVY, Samuel.[4] About 1781—June 20, 1799, Camden/Charleston, South Carolina. (EOJCC, 109)

LEVY, Samuel.[5] Born October 4, 1772, New York City. Son of Eleazar Levy. (SIR)

LEVY, Samuel.[6] Born Germany. He may have come to America with the Hessians. In 1782 he went to Charlestown from New York City and became a merchant. In June, 1796, he was married in Charleston to Hannah Abrahams. (EJMC, 6; EJSC, 98, 136, 278)

LEVY, Samuel.[7] In 1776 he served with the Continental forces in Maryland. It is doubtful that he was Jewish. (MTAR, 41)

LEVY, Samuel.[8] Born August 31, 1787, Philadelphia. Son of Joseph Levy. (MIPR)

LEVY, Samuel Eleazer. In New York City in 1772. (PAJHS, XXI, 113)

LEVY, Sarah(?).[1] Wife of Abraham Myers Cohen.[1] (MSGC)

LEVY, Sarah.[2] September 21, 1762, New York City—September 20, 1763, New York City. Daughter of David Jacob Levy. (SIR)

LEVY, Sarah.[3] October 1, 1768, New York City—April 11, 1855. Daughter of Hayman Levy. (PAJHS, XXVII, 168; SIR)

LEVY, Sarah.[4] Niece of Isaac Lopes. When she was a child in 1793, she came from Bordeaux to New York City. (PAJHS, XXVII, 55; SZ, 121)

LEVY, Simeon.[1] In Georgia in 1737. (JRMP)

LEVY, Simeon.[2] 1748—December 23, 1825, New York City. Son of Benjamin Levy,[1] he was married to Hester Levy.[1] (PAJHS, IV, 213; XXXIII, 210)

LEVY, Simon. A prominent Canadian merchant, he was in Canada in 1760 and in Montreal in 1778. (MEAJA, 207; SIMR)

LEVY, Simon Magruder. Born Maryland, died 1807. He was in the first class of West Point Military College in 1802. It is doubtful that he was Jewish. (JRMP; UJE, X, 371)

LEVY, Solomon. In 1783 he lived in Amherst County, Virginia. It is doubtful that he was Jewish. (PAJHS, XX, 100)

LEVY, Solomon, Jr. In 1762 he was married to Rose in Charlestown. (EJSC, 280; MSGC)

LEVY, Solomon (H). December 18, 1764, New York City—January 7, 1841. Son of Hayman Levy, he was a merchant who was married to Rebecca Hendricks. (MSGC; PAJHS, IV, 210; XXVII, 168; SIR)

LEVY, Captain Stephen. In 1790 he lived in Kettery, Maine, with his family of two. It is doubtful that he was Jewish. (Census A, Maine)

LEVY, Uriah Phillips. April 22, 1792, Philadelphia—March 22, 1862, New York City. This son of Michael Levy shipped out as a cabin boy at the age of ten. He entered naval school and was captain of a ship before he was twenty. During the War of 1812 he was appointed as assistant sailing master to the brig Argus. He was taken prisoner during this war. He served on many other missions, including suppression of piracy and extermination of the slave trade along Honduras Bay. During his career in the Navy he frequently met anti-Semitic prejudice, and he encountered repeated difficulties in his service career because of this, and because of his pride and his shipmates' contempt for his having risen from the ranks. In one of his duels his opponent was slain. Court-martialed six times and twice dismissed from the Navy, he was reinstated finally through a special court of inquiry, and was given the titular rank of commodore, the highest rank in the U.S. Navy at the time of his retirement. While he was working toward his command he fought the practice of flogging. His admiration for Thomas Jefferson led him to purchase the Monticello home. Late in his life he married Virginia Lopez. (DAB, XI, 203f; Morais, 469f; UJE, VI, 51; VII, 17f)

LEVY, William. In Baltimore in 1761; in North Carolina in 1768. It is doubtful that he was Jewish. (PAJHS, XXIX, 142; JRMP)

LEVY, Zachariah. In Charleston in 1800. (EJSC, 136)

LEVY, Zipporah. January 15, 1760, New York City—August 21, 1832. Daughter of Hayman Levy, she was married to Benjamin M. Seixas[2] about 1778. (MEAJA, 161f; PAJHS, IV, 210f; XXVII, 336; SIR)

LEWIS, Rachel. Died before 1737. A benefactor of New York's Mill Street Synagogue, she was also known as Rachel Luiza. (PAJHS, XXI, 37; POFNW, 108, 110, 113)

LIDESMO, Moses. In Georgia in 1737. Cf. Moses le Desma. (CRG, II, 347)

LIEBEN, Israel. Cf. Israel Delieben.

LINDO, Abraham. In 1792 he was in Savannah. He was a member of the St. George society in Philadelphia. (SIMR; WW, 265)

LINDO, Moses. 1712, England—about 1774, Charlestown. In 1756 he arrived in South Carolina from London, where he had been a merchant. A shipowner, he sold privately such commodities as indigo, and was inspector general and surveyor of indigo, drugs, and dyes for South Carolina. He experimented scientifically with dyes. (EJSC, 47-67; PAJHS, II, 51f; Reznikoff, 23-34)

LION, Barnet. In Montreal in 1778. Cf. Benjamin Lyon(s). (MSIR)

LION, Hart. In 1786 he was a merchant in New York City. (JRMP)

LIPMAN. In New York City about 1740. (PAJHS, XXI, 45)

LOMRAH, Mr. In New York City in 1796. Cf. Moses Cohen de Lorah and Henry Somrah. (SIR)

LONG, Hyman Isaac. Came to America from Jamaica, B.W.I. A physician, in 1795 he was in need of assistance in New York City. Later he became prominent in Masonic circles in Virginia and South Carolina. (PAJHS, XIX, 34, et passim)

LOPES, Isaac. In 1793 he came from Bordeaux to New York. (SZ, 121)

LOPES, Joseph. In 1793 he came from Bordeaux to Baltimore. (SZ, 121)

LOPEZ, Aaron.[1] About 1731, Portugal—May 28, 1782, Scott's Pond, Rhode Island. This son of Diego Jose Lopez came to

Newport with his family from Portugal, where he had secretly practiced Judaism but publicly professed Christianity. He was denied naturalization in Rhode Island but obtained it in Massachusetts in 1762. In 1763 he laid the cornerstone of the old Newport synagogue. In partnership with Jacob R. Rivers he was engaged in the whaling, fishing, and chandling industry, in which he pioneered in the manufacture of the spermaceti candle. In the 1770s he became the outstanding merchant shipper of Newport, owning as many as thirty ships engaged in foreign trade, but at the time of the Revolution he lost most of his wealth. After Newport was evacuated because of the British occupation, he lived in Philadelphia and Leicester, Massachusetts. Ezra Stiles paid homage to him after his death. Lopez' first wife was Abigail (or Ann); his second wife was Sarah Rivera.[1] (*Coldoc*, 3, *et passim*; *DAB*, XI, 402f; *MEAJA*, 79, *et passim*; *PAJHS*, II, 101f; IV, 88, 204; V, 202; VI, 69, *et passim*; VIII, 124f; IX, 147; X, 8, *et passim*; XI, 81f)

LOPEZ, Aaron.[2] Born February 4, 1757, New York City. Son of Moses Lopez. (*PAJHS*, XXVII, 151)

LOPEZ, Aaron.[3] In Charleston in 1800 with his family. Cf. above. (*Census B, South Carolina*; *EJSC*, 136; *MSGC*)

LOPEZ, Aaron.[4] March 3, 1800, Charleston —August 19, 1874, Memphis. This son of David Lopez[4] was prominent in public affairs in Georgetown, South Carolina. On January 23, in the 1820s, he was married to Eleanor Cohen. (*EJSC*, 194, *et passim*; *MSGC*)

LOPEZ, Abigail.[1] About 1770—August 2, 1851. Daughter of Aaron Lopez,[1] she was married to Isaac Gomez, Jr.,[6] on May 26, 1790. (*PAJHS*, II, 104; XVII, 198)

LOPEZ, Abigail.[2] Daughter of Moses Lopez.[1] (*PAJHS*, II, 104)

LOPEZ, Mrs. Abigail (Ann).[1] About 1726, Portugal—May 14, 1762, Newport. First wife of Aaron Lopez.[1] (*PAJHS*, XXVII, 202)

LOPEZ, Mrs. Abigail (Joana).[2] About 1710 —October 10, 1792, Newport. Wife of Abraham Lopez.[1] (*PAJHS*, II, 105; XXVII, 207)

LOPEZ, Abraham. In Charleston in 1800. He may be identical with Abram Lopez who was in Charleston in 1800. (*EJSC*, 136)

LOPEZ, Abraham (Michael). This son of Diego Jose Lopez fled the inquisition in Portugal to come to America. By 1767 he settled in Newport, where he was a merchant. In 1773 he translated a Spanish sermon which Haim Isaac Carigal preached in Newport. His wife was Abigail. (*MEAJA*, 81f, 138f; *PAJHS*, II, 104f; III, 123; XXVII, 153)

LOPEZ, Daniel.[1] Son of Moses Lopez.[1] (*PAJHS*, II, 104)

LOPEZ, Daniel.[2] July 16, 1798, Charleston —September 17, 1798, Charleston. Son of David Lopez.[4] (*MSGC*)

LOPEZ, David.[1] About 1714—December 19, 1797, Boston. Son of Diego Jose Lopez, he came to America from Portugal and was an early member of the Masons. (*FEAJ*, 20, *et passim*; *PAJHS*, II, 104; XIX, 18f; XXIII, 88f)

LOPEZ, David.[2] In Georgia in 1733. (*PAJHS*, XVII, 168)

LOPEZ, David.[3] Died March 26, 1775, Newport. (*PAJHS*, X, 17f)

LOPEZ, David.[4] March, 1750, Newport— January 15, 1811, Charleston. Merchant son of Moses Lopez,[1] he was a Mason in Newport. He was the first president of the Hebrew Orphan Society in Charleston. His first wife was Rachel Lopez;[2] his second wife was Priscilla Moses whom he married on September 20, 1793, in Charleston. (*EJSC*, 122, *et passim*; *EOJCC*, 75; *Gutstein*, 310; *PAJHS*, XIX, 18; XXVII, 208; *Reznikoff*, 57, 155)

LOPEZ, Mrs. David. Wife of David Lopez,[2] she was in Georgia in 1733. (*PAJHS*, XVII, 168)

LOPEZ, Deborah. Niece of David Lopez,[1] she is mentioned in his will. (*PAJHS*, XXIII, 89)

LOPEZ, Delia. Daughter of Aaron Lopez.[1] (*PAJHS*, II, 105)

LOPEZ, Elias. In 1728 he was in New York City. He may have been the son of Moses Lopez Fonseca. Cf. Elias Lopez de Fonseca. (*PAJHS*, XXI, 11, et *passim*)

LOPEZ, Esther. About 1758—January 3, 1811, New York City. Daughter of Aaron Lopez,[1] she was married to Moses Mordecai Gomez. (*PAJHS*, XVII, 197)

LOPEZ, Grace. Daughter of Aaron Lopez.[1] (*PAJHS*, II, 105; XXIII, 89)

LOPEZ, Hannah. Daughter of Aaron Lopez,[1] she was married to Abraham R. Rivera.[2] (*PAJHS*, II, 104; *Pool*, 402)

LOPEZ, Isaac.[1] A prominent merchant, he came to Boston from London in 1716. In 1721 he was elected constable in Boston, but declined the office. He returned to London, apparently having absconded. (*FEAJ*, 7; *JNEA*, 17f; *PAJHS*, XII, 101; XXIII, 81)

LOPEZ, Isaac.[2] May 1, 1762—November 10, 1762. Infant son of Moses Lopez.[1] (*PAJHS*, XXVII, 151, 203)

LOPEZ, Isaac.[3] A child in New York City about 1793. (*PAJHS*, XXVII, 55)

LOPEZ, Jacob.[1] About 1752—March 18, 1822, Newport. Son of Abraham Lopez,[2] he was one of the last Jews remaining in Newport. (*Gutstein*, 309; *PAJHS*, II, 105; XXVII, 306)

LOPEZ, Jacob.[2] Son of Aaron Lopez,[1] he died an infant in Newport. (*PAJHS*, II, 104)

LOPEZ, Jacob.[3] Son of Aaron Lopez,[1] he died an infant in Newport. (*PAJHS*, II, 104)

LOPEZ, Jacob.[4] About 1755—1764. Son of Moses Lopez.[1] (*PAJHS*, XXVII, 203)

LOPEZ, John Immanuel. In 1760 he was master of the ship *Young Moses* in Salem. It is doubtful that he was Jewish. (*FEAJ*, 13)

LOPEZ, Joseph.[1] In New York City in 1740. (*PAJHS*, XXI, 43)

LOPEZ, Joseph.[2] Circumcised on February 12, 1757, died November 22, 1822, New York City. Son of Aaron Lopez.[1] (*PAJHS*, XXVII, 151, 306; *Pool*, 419f)

LOPEZ, Joshua. Son of Aaron Lopez,[1] he was married to Rebecca Touro. (*PAJHS*, II, 105; XIII, 95)

LOPEZ, Judith. Niece of Daniel Lopez,[1] she was probably in America in 1797. (*PAJHS*, XXIII, 89)

LOPEZ, Juliet. Daughter of Aaron Lopez,[1] she was probably married to Mr. Levy. (*PAJHS*, II, 104)

LOPEZ, Maria. Died July 22, 1812, Wilmington, North Carolina. Daughter of Aaron Lopez,[1] she was married to Jacob Levy in 1805 in Stamford, Connecticut. (*Pool*, 327f)

LOPEZ, Matthias. A child in New York City about 1793. (*PAJHS*, XXVII, 55)

LOPEZ, Moses.[1] About 1706—April 6, 1767, Newport. This son of Diego Jose Lopez came to America from Portugal and was a merchant in Newport and New York City, where he was naturalized in 1740, and made a freeman on July 23, 1741. He was given a patent to manufacture potash in Rhode Island; he also manufactured candles. He translated documents for the Rhode Island assembly. His wife was Rebecca Rivera. (*Coldoc*, 7, et *passim*; *MEAJA*, 81, et *passim*; *PAJHS*, II, 102f; VI, 72f, 102; XXVII, 199)

LOPEZ, Moses.[2] About 1744, Portugal—April 1, 1830, New York City. A merchant, he lived in New York City and in Newport for sixty years. (*Gutstein*, 309; *PAJHS*, XXVII, 201)

LOPEZ, Moses.[3] Born about 1739. Son of Abraham Lopez,[1] he lived in Tiverton. (*PAJHS*, II, 105; XXVII, 153)

LOPEZ, Moses.[4] August 31, 1796, Charleston—September 16, 1849, Charleston. Son of David Lopez.[4] (*EJSC*, 137, 170, 187; *MSGC*)

LOPEZ, Rachel.[1] About 1758—August 26, 1789, Newport. Daughter of Aaron Lopez,[1] she was married to David Lopez.[4] (*Gutstein*, 310f)

LOPEZ, Rachel.[2] June 9, 1794, Charleston —June 1, 1833. Daughter of David Lopez,[4] she was married to Jacob Cohen⁷ on February 19, 1816. (*MSGC*)

LOPEZ, Mrs. Rachel. She came from St. Domingo, where she was a confectioner. In 1796 she was married to Francis Lecat in Charleston. (*SCHGM*, XXIII, 152)

LOPEZ, Rebecca.¹ 1760—February 20, 1844, New York City. Daughter of Aaron Lopez,¹ she was married to Uriah Hendricks. (*MSGC*)

LOPEZ, Rebecca.² June 9, 1797, Charleston —February 7, 1868, Washington. Daughter of David Lopez,⁴ she was married to Mordecai de Leon. (*MSGC*; *Wills*, 40)

LOPEZ, Samuel.¹ Born about 1743. Son of Abraham Lopez,¹ he lived in Tiverton. (*PAJHS*, XXVII, 153)

LOPEZ, Samuel.² Son of Aaron Lopez,¹ he was married to Judith Seixas and was living in Newport in 1818. (*PAJHS*, II, 104; IV, 204; VI, 138)

LOPEZ, Samuel.³ In Charleston in 1800. (*EJSC*, 137, 246)

LOPEZ, Samuel A. In New York City in 1788. (*PAJHS*, XXVII, 43)

LOPEZ, Sarah. Daughter of Aaron Lopez,¹ she was married to Abraham Pereira Mendes. In 1776 she was in Portsmouth, Rhode Island. (*PAJHS*, II, 104; XXVII, 348)

LORAH, Moses Cohen de. In New York City in 1789. Cf. Mr. Lomrah and Henry Somrah. (*SIR*)

LOUISA, Rachel. Died about 1787. In Philadelphia about 1780. (*MIPR*; *MSP*)

LOUZADA, Aaron. About 1693—December 27, 1764, Bound Brook, New Jersey. This son of Jacob Louzada¹ was a wealthy merchant and shopkeeper in New York City and New Jersey. His wife was Blume Michaels. (*MSGC*; *PAJHS*, XVIII, 121; *Pool*, 238f; *SIR*)

LOUZADA, Abigail. Daughter of Moses Louzada. (*MSGC*)

LOUZADA, Mrs. Abigail. Wife of David Louzada. (*MSGC*)

LOUZADA, Benjamin. Son of Moses Louzada, he was in New York City about 1756. (*Pool*, 239)

LOUZADA, Catherine. Born about 1756. Daughter of Aaron Louzada, she was married to Abraham Loxley in 1779. (*MSGC*)

LOUZADA, David. Died 1800, Middlesex County, New Jersey. Son of Aaron Louzada, he was married to Abigail. (*MSGC*)

LOUZADA, Elkaly Esther. 1722—January 22, 1789, New York City. Daughter of Moses Louzada, she was married to Abraham Isaac Abrahams. (*Pool*, 239; *SIR*)

LOUZADA, Mrs. Hannah. Wife of Moses Louzada, she was a widow in New York City in 1750, receiving charity from Congregation Shearith Israel for many years. In 1761 she was in New Brunswick, New Jersey. (*PAJHS*, XXI, 61, *et passim*; XXVII, 21; *Pool*, 239)

LOUZADA, Jacob.¹ Died June 12, 1729, New York City. A merchant. (*Pool*, 202)

LOUZADA, Jacob.² Died 1738, New York City. (*PAJHS*, XVIII, 121)

LOUZADA, Jacob.³ About 1737—July 3, 1744, New York City. (*PAJHS*, XVIII, 121; *Pool*, 467)

LOUZADA, Jacob.⁴ About 1743—January 2, 1791, New York City. Son of Moses Louzada, he was mentally deranged. (*Pool*, 239; *SIR*)

LOUZADA, Moses. Died 1750. Son of Jacob Louzada, he lived in New York City and New Jersey. His wife was Hannah. (*PAJHS*, XXI, 10, *et passim*; *Pool*, 239)

LOUZADA, Rachel. Died 1790, New York City. Daughter of Moses Louzada, she was married to Haym Myers. (*PAJHS*, XXVII, 150; *Pool*, 239)

LOUZADA, Sarah. Daughter of Aaron Louzada, she was in New Jersey in 1739. (*MSGC*)

LUCENA, Miss de. Third wife of Abraham Rodriquez de Rivera.¹ (*Pool*, 196)

LUCENA, Mr. Son of Abraham Haim de Lucena, he was in New York City in 1703. (*Pool*, 458)

LUCENA, Abraham. A merchant, he arrived in New Amsterdam in 1654. He acted as spokesman for the Jewish community. He was married, probably to a gentile. (*AJAM*, III, 5f; *Grollman*, 156)

LUCENA, Abraham Haim de. Died August 4, 1725, New York City. This son of Abraham Lucena served as minister of Congregation Shearith Israel in New York City. A prominent merchant, he became a freeman there on July 6, 1708. During Queen Anne's War he was a supplier of the American expedition. In 1699 he was married to Rachel. (*FEAJ*, 68; *MSP*; *PAJHS*, VI, 126; XVIII, 105; *POFNW*, 160f)

LUCENA, Esther. Daughter of Abraham Haim de Lucena. (*PAJHS*, XXIII, 150)

LUCENA, Francis. Brother of James Lucena, in 1761 he was practicing as a physician in Newport. (*GLT*, 12)

LUCENA, Jacob. In 1654 he arrived in New Amsterdam. He was married and became a trader in New York and Connecticut. He was arrested for lascivious behavior with women. (*AJAM*, III, 9; *Grollman*, 17)

LUCENA, James. Portuguese cousin of Aaron Lopez, in 1761 he introduced a method for making Castile soap in Newport. He was in Savannah in the same year, where he was engaged in shipping and the slave trade. In 1766 he was a justice of the peace. He was a Tory. Born a Catholic, he died a nominal Catholic, and finally returned to Portugal. (*Coldoc*, 208f; *MEAJA*, 89, 128; *MEAJB*, 321, et passim)

LUCENA, John Charles. About 1750—June 2, 1813. This son of James Lucena was a loyalist merchant with his father in Rhode Island and Savannah. During the Revolution he went to London and ultimately became a consul general for the Court of Portugal. He was born and died a Catholic, but while in the colonies he was an Anglican. His wife was Mary Anne Lancaster. (*JRMP*; *MEAJB*, 325, et passim; *PAJHS*, XXXVIII, 93)

LUCENA, Joseph de. In Boston and Newport about 1735. (*PAJHS*, XXIII, 84)

LUCENA, Judith de. Daughter of Abraham Haim de Lucena. (*PAJHS*, XXIII, 150)

LUCENA, Matantta. Godmother of Moses M. Gomez, she was in New York City about 1744. (*PAJHS*, XXVII, 281)

LUCENA, Moses.[1] In 1658 he was an interpreter and butcher in New Amsterdam. (*AJAM*, III, 9)

LUCENA, Moses.[2] Born October 30, 1723, New York City. Son of Abraham Haim de Lucena. (*Pool*, 458)

LUCENA, Mrs. Rachel de. Wife of Abraham Haim de Lucena. (*PAJHS*, XXIII, 150)

LUCENA, Rebecca de. July, 1713, New York City—June 25, 1801, New York City. Daughter of Abraham Haim de Lucena, she was married to Mordecai Gomez[1] on May 4, 1741. (*PAJHS*, XXVII, 291, 304; *Wills*, 4f)

LUCENA, S. D. de. In July, 1789, he was buried in New York City. Cf. below. (*Pool*, 503)

LUCENA, Samuel de. Born January 2, 1711, New York City. This son of Abraham Haim de Lucena became a freeman in New York City on July 3, 1759. He was a merchant there and in Philadelphia. During the Revolution he became involved in the search for sulphur to be used for gunpowder, but he was never paid for any efforts he may have made. Cf. above. (*MIPR*; *PAJHS*, I, 24, 68f; VI, 102; XXIII, 150; *Pool*, 458; *SIR*)

LURIA, Rebecca. About 1740, England—October 14, 1815, Philadelphia. About 1764 she was married to Jacob Raphael Cohen in London. (*MIPR*; *Morais*, 18; *MSGC*)

LYNES, Lewis. In New York in 1705. It is doubtful that he was Jewish. (*NYHSW*, I, 322)

LYON.[1] Daughter of Moses de Lyon (or of his wife and another man), she died in March, 1775. (*SIR*)

LYON.[2] Child of Mordecai Lyon, he was in Charleston in 1783. (*MSP*)

LYON, Abraham. A baker in New York City, he became a freeman there on May 29, 1750. (*PAJHS*, VI, 102)

LYON, Abraham de.[1] A Portuguese refugee, he was farming in Savannah in 1733. Through his knowledge of the cultivation of vines, he attempted to pioneer viticulture in Georgia. After leaving Savannah he settled for a short time in Charlestown, but returned again to Savannah, where he died. Cf. Abraham de Leon[1] and below. (*MEAJB*, 299f; *PAJHS*, I, 10f; X, 69, *et passim*; *UJE*, IV, 536; VII, 254)

LYON, Abraham de.[2] Son of Isaac de Lyon, he was in Charlestown in 1776. Cf. above and Abraham de Leon.[1] (*WAJA*)

LYON, Abraham de.[3] Died October 10, 1835, Savannah. Son of Isaac de Lyon,[1] he was a surgeon in the Revolution. On June 1, 1785, he was married to Sarah Sheftall. (*MSGC*)

LYON, Abraham de.[4] April 24, 1793—March 27, 1840. Son of Isaac de Lyon,[1] he was married to Hannah Sheftall on March 21, 1827. (*MSGC; SRB*)

LYON(S), Benjamin. A prominent merchant and fur trader, he supplied the British during the French and Indian War. He traded in the Mackinac region and had contacts in the colonies. An active participant in civic affairs and in the Montreal Jewish community, he was among the first Jewish merchants in Montreal in 1760. He was alive in 1800. Cf. Barnet Lion. (*Katz*, 12, *et passim*; *MEAJA*, 225, *et passim*)

LYON, Benjamin. In Baltimore in 1796. (*Blum*, 4)

LYON, Benjamin de. July, 1797, Savannah—September 13, 1802, Savannah. Son of Abraham de Lyon.[4] (*SRB*)

LYON, David. In Bedford, New York, in 1790. It is doubtful that he was Jewish. (*HDB*)

LYON, Emanuel. From London. In 1769 he was the first Jew to offer Hebrew lessons in Philadelphia. A peddler and merchandiser in the soap industry, he was sought by his Philadelphia creditors in 1772. In 1774 he is noted in Lancaster. (*JRMP; MIPR; WW*, 54, 58)

LYON, Enoch. About 1765 he came to America from England. A clerk and an agent for Aaron Lopez,[1] he did business in New York, Philadelphia, and Virginia. About 1790 he may have settled permanently in Gloucester County, Virginia. (*MEAJB*, 169f)

LYON, Mrs. Esther de. Wife of Abraham de Lyon,[1] she was in Savannah in 1733 and left in 1740. About 1761 she is noted in Easton. (*Coulter*, 71; *Trachtenberg*, 39f)

LYON, Esther de. Born August 9, 1762, Savannah. Daughter of Isaac de Lyon,[1] she was married to Barnard Moses on September 23, 1777, in Savannah. (*SRB*)

LYON, Hannah. November 1, 1798, Savannah—1872. Daughter of Abraham de Lyon.[3] (*MSGC; SRB*)

LYON, Isaac.[1] In August, 1767, he left Philadelphia for the West Indies. (*WW*, 51)

LYON, Isaac.[2] About 1779 he was a merchant who came to Charlestown. During the Revolution he was a loyalist. (*EJSC*, 86, *et passim*)

LYON, Isaac.[3] In Bedford, New York, in 1770, and again in 1791. It is doubtful that he was Jewish. (*HDB*)

LYON, Isaac de.[1] Born January 28, 1739, Savannah. About 1766 he was in Charlestown. He was married to Rinah Tobias. (*EJSC*, 44; *MSGC*)

LYON, Isaac de.[2] February 16, 1786—February 16, 1856. Son of Abraham de Lyon.[3] (*MSGC; SRB*)

LYON, Jacob. 1777, Posen, Poland—November 29, 1851, Richmond. He was named Posnanski in Poland. About 1790 he came to Richmond and became a merchant. He was married three times; his last wife was Eliza White. (*ELJR*, 51, *et passim*)

LYON, Jacob de. April 6, 1795, Savannah—October 13, 1795, Savannah. Infant son of Abraham de Lyon.[3] (*SRB*)

LYON, Jonas. A well known Tory, he was a furrier in New York City in 1786. (*JRMP*)

LYON, Joseph. On June 11, 1776, he was married to Mary Underwood in Newport. (*NHM*, III, 24)

LYON, Joseph de. Born September 17, 1800, Savannah. Son of Abraham de Lyon.³ (SRB)

LYON, Judith de.¹ 1748—November, 1816, Charleston. She may have been the daughter of Abraham de Lyon. Her first husband was Moses Cohen in 1774; her second husband was Joseph Abrahams.⁴ (MSGC; SRB; Wills, 75)

LYON, Judith de.² Born February 19, 1764, Savannah. Daughter of Isaac de Lyon.¹ (SRB)

LYON, Mrs. Judith. 1747—November 19, 1815. Wife of Mordecai Lyon. (MSP; Wills, 47)

LYON, Levi Sheftall de. Son of Abraham de Lyon,³ he was married first to Rebecca de la Motta, and then to Leonora. He was a judge. (MSGC)

LYON, Levy Warburg. In Charleston in 1795. (WAJA)

LYON, Mordecai. About 1735, Poland—October 3, 1818, Charleston. About 1782 he arrived in Charlestown and became a tailor. (EJSC, 98, et passim; MSP)

LYON, Mrs. Mordecai. In Charlestown in 1782. (EJSC, 98)

LYON, "Rabbi" Moses. He came to America from Poland. On October 2, 1762, he was buried in New York City. (Pool, 501)

LYON, Moses de. As early as 1753, and as late as 1798, he is noted in New York City. On May 22, 1771, he was married to Rose Solomons in New York City. (PAJHS, XXVII, 247; SIR)

LYON, Philip.¹ In Berkeley County, South Carolina, in 1724. It is highly doubtful that he was Jewish. (WAJA)

LYON, Philip.² In Philadelphia in 1782. (MIPR)

LYON, Rachel de. Born August 2, 1734, Savannah. Daughter of Abraham de Lyon,¹ she was married to Myer Hart in 1752. (Coulter, 71; SRB; Trachtenberg, 40)

LYON, Rebecca. Born Savannah. Daughter of Abraham de Lyon,¹ she was married to Barnard Levy. (Coulter, 71; MSGC; SRB)

LYON, Samuel Solomon. In America about 1785. (JRMP)

LYON, Sarah de. Daughter of Abraham de Lyon,³ she was married to Samuel Russell in Savannah on March 26, 1806. (MSGC)

LYON (LION), Solomon. In Philadelphia, New York City, and Baltimore between 1785 and 1796. (MIPR; PAJHS, XXVII, 43; SIR)

LYON, Zipporah (Sipra) de. February 10, 1738, Savannah—April 6, 1806. Daughter of Abraham de Lyon,¹ she was married to Mordecai M. Mordecai. (MSGC; SRB)

LYONS, Catherine. July 23, 1792, Surinam—December 9, 1868, Philadelphia. Daughter of Eleazar Lyons, she was married to Jacob Moss in Philadelphia on August 19, 1812. (MSGC)

LYONS, Eleazar. 1729, Holland—October 1, 1816, Philadelphia. A Dutch Jew, in 1772 he started his own business. On May 29, 1776, he was married to Hannah Levy³ at Harrisburg. (AJA; Essays, 113; MSGC)

LYONS, Esther. December 6, 1786, Baltimore—May 18, 1846. Daughter of Eleazar Lyons, she was married to Isaac Lazarus on May 10, 1805, in Philadelphia. (MSGC)

LYONS, J. In Philadelphia in 1783. (MIPR)

LYONS, Judah. July 17, 1779, Philadelphia—August 29, 1849, New York City. This son of Eleazar Lyons also lived in Surinam. On February 29, 1804, he was married to Mary Levy in New York City. (MSGC; PAJHS, XXI, xxiii; XXVII, 74)

LYONS, Lovi. In Philadelphia sometime in the 1700s. (Essays, 120)

LYONS, Mordecai. July 23, 1792, Surinam—January 19, 1845. Son of Eleazar Lyons, he was married to May Bausman in Baltimore on July 23, 1812. (MSGC)

LYONS, Rebecca. May 10, 1777, Lancaster—August 24, 1864. Daughter of Eleazar Lyons, she was married to John Moss in Philadelphia on February 15, 1797. (GBMIP; MIPR; MSGC)

LYONS, Samuel. October 5, 1781, Baltimore—March 17, 1858, Philadelphia. Son of Eleazar Lyons, he was married to Dinah

Levy on June 29, 1810, in Surinam; and then to Sarah Marks in Philadelphia on March 14, 1821. (MSGC)

LYONS, Solomon. In 1785 he was a shopkeeper in Philadelphia. On April 11, 1802, he was married to Rebecca Abraham, a convert. Cf. Solomon Lyon (Lion). (*Morais*, 444; *Wills*, 17; WW, 430)

LYONS, Uriah. April 15, 1784, Baltimore —July 3, 1832. Son of Eleazar Lyons, he was married to Mary Ann Alexander in Surinam. (MSGC)

LYTE, E. In 1796 he was the clerk of Congregation Shearith Israel in New York City. (PAJHS, XXVII, 64)

M

MACAUDO, Solomon. In New York City in 1787. Either he had come from Surinam or had just left for Surinam. He left a debt in Congregation Shearith Israel in New York City. (*PAJHS*, XXVII, 42)

MACHADO, Aaron. A distiller, he became a freeman in New York City on July 10, 1739. (*PAJHS*, VI, 102)

MACHADO, Benjamin Mendez. In New York City in 1728. (*PAJHS*, XXI, 11)

MACHADO, David Mendez. Died December 4, 1747, New York City. A native of Portugal, he became a merchant in New York City. About 1734 he was the hazzan of Congregation Shearith Israel; he also taught school there. His wife was Zipporah Nunez. (*GBMIP*; *PAJHS*, II, 45-61; XXVII, 281; *POFNW*, 162f)

MACHADO, Rebecca. November 17/26, 1746, New York City/Reading—June 21/25, 1831, Philadelphia. Daughter of David Mendez Machado, she was married to Jonas Phillips on November 10, 1762, in Philadelphia. (*MSGC*; *PAJHS*, II, 49; VI, 110; *SIR*)

MACHADO, Sara. 1747, New York City—March 12, 1810, Charleston. Daughter of David Mendez Machado, she was married to Philip Moses.[2] (*MSGC*; *PAJHS*, II, 49)

MACHORO, David. In New York City in 1670. (*POFNW*, 468)

MADEIRA, Isaac. In Philadelphia in 1782. (*Morais*, 15)

MADEIRA, Joseph. In Philadelphia in 1782. (*Morais*, 15)

MADINA, Moses. About 1708 he owned land in Goose Creek, South Carolina, and probably lived there. (*SCHGM*, XXIX, 273)

MADUHY, Haim. Probably an itinerant money collector, in 1761 he arrived in America from Palestine. (*PAJHS*, XXIV, 289)

MALACH, Moses. In Boston in 1800. (*JRMP*)

MALKI, Rabbi Moses. Born Safed, Palestine. Probably an itinerant money collector, he was in Newport and New York City in 1759. (*PAJHS*, X, 18; *POFNW*, 397)

MANDELLS, Joshua H. In New York City in 1786. (*PAJHS*, XXVII, 42)

MANHEIM, Sol. In Charleston in 1800. (*EJSC*, 137)

MANUEL, Catherine.[1] In America in 1766. (*MSP*)

MANUEL, Catherine.[2] January 1, 1768, London—March 29, 1852, New York City. Daughter of David Manuel, she was married to Levy Solomons on July 29, 1801. (*MSGC*; *PAJHS*, XXVII, 376)

MANUEL, David.[1] In Georgia about 1757. It is doubtful that he was Jewish. (*CRG*, XVIII, 185)

MANUEL, David.[2] Probably lived in Philadelphia. Before 1766 he was married to Miriam Judah. (*MIPR*; *MSGC*)

MANUEL, Hannah (Anne). October, 1766—March 16, 1856, Philadelphia. Daughter of David Manuel, she was the second wife of Gershom M. Seixas on November 1, 1789. Congregation Shearith Israel of New York City gave her a pension after Seixas' death. (*MSGC*; *PAJHS*, IV, 208; XXVII, 97, *et passim*)

MANUEL, Mordecai. July, 1785, Philadelphia—March 22, 1851, New York City. On November 28, 1827, he was married to Rebecca Esther Jackson in New York City. (*MSP*)

MARACHE, Benjamin. In New York City in 1746. (*PAJHS*, XXI, 58)

MARACHE, Esther. February 20, 1768, Newport—January 17, 1820, Charleston. Daughter of Solomon Marache, she was married to Joseph Mordecai on October 25, 1786. (*MIPR*; *MSGC*)

MARACHE, Mrs. Esther. Mother of Solomon Marache, she was a widow in New York City in 1749. (*Schappes*, 31f)

MARACHE, Hannah. Daughter of Solomon Marache, she was married to John V. Cowell on November 4, 1823, in Philadelphia. (*MSGC*)

MARACHE, Henrietta. Daughter of Solomon Marache, she was married to Thomas Armstrong in May, 1806. (*MSGC*)

MARACHE, Jacob. In New York City in 1746. (*PAJHS*, XXI, 51)

MARACHE, Judith. February 26, 1770, Newport—September 4, 1855, New York City. Daughter of Solomon Marache. (*MSGC*)

MARACHE, Moses. In New York City in 1746; in Philadelphia in 1792. (*MIPR; PAJHS*, XXI, 51)

MARACHE, Solomon. In 1749 he was an apprentice to Isaac Hays. He then became a merchant in New York City, where he held many offices in Congregation Shearith Israel. Later he lived in Philadelphia and was one of the founders of Congregation Mikveh Israel there. He was an abolitionist. In his last years he had little to do with Jews. Marache's first wife was Rebecca Myers in New York City on August 13, 1766; his second wife was a gentile called Mary. (*Coldoc*, 116, *et passim*; *PAJHS*, I, 24; II, 57; III, 82; XXI, 51, *et passim*; *Schappes*, 30f; *UJE*, VIII, 476f; *WW*, 61, *et passim*)

MARCUS, Isaac. In 1774 he was a shohet in New York City who had come from Holland. Cf. Isaac Mark(s).[3] (*PAJHS*, XXI, 123, 125)

MARCUS, Lazarus. In New York City in 1786. (*JRMP*)

MARCUS, Samuel. On June 18, 1732, he was married to Priscilla Burnly in Berkeley County, South Carolina. It is doubtful that he was Jewish. (*JRMP*)

MARK, Philip. In New York City in 1786. (*JRMP*)

MARKESS, Joseph. A member of the Revolutionary army, he was in Charlestown in 1780. Cf. Joseph Marques (Marquise). (*EJSC*, 106)

MARKS. Born February 20, 1787, Easton. Stillborn son of Michael Marks. (*MSGC*)

MARKS. Two daughters of Isaac Marks[1] and an unmarried girl arrived in Savannah on October 5, 1738. (*SRB*)

MARKS, Miss. Daughter of Joseph Marks, she was in Philadelphia in 1757. Cf. Fanny Marks. (*PAJHS*, I, 54)

MARKS, Abraham.[1] October 19, 1748—1766. Son of Mordecai Marks,[1] he may have been a convert to Christianity. (*JRMP*)

MARKS, Abraham.[2] Born March 12, 1792, Tarrytown. Son of Michael Marks. (*MSGC*)

MARKS, Alexander.[1] In New York City in 1749. (*PAJHS*, XXI, 60)

MARKS, Alexander.[2] August 4, 1788, Charleston—September 14, 1861, New Orleans. Son of Humphrey Marks, on July 10, 1816, he was married to Esther Hart[2] in Charleston. (*MSGC*)

MARKS, Anna. March 30, 1800, Sing Sing, New York—June 30, 1888, New York City. This daughter of Michael Marks assisted Rebecca Gratz in forming the first Hebrew Sunday School in Philadelphia in 1838. One of the founders and the first president of the Jewish Foster Home and Orphan Asylum in Philadelphia, she was also director of the Female Hebrew Benevolent Society of Philadelphia. In 1875 she went to New York City. On December 10, 1823, she was married to Lewis Allen. (*Morais*, 49, *et passim*; *UJE*, I, 187; VII, 362)

MARKS, Mrs. Anne. Died November 27, 1738. Wife of Hugh Marks, she was in Georgia in 1735. (*Coulter*, 87)

MARKS, David. In 1799 he was a Mason in Harwinton, Connecticut. It is doubtful that he was Jewish. (*PAJHS*, XIX, 27)

MARKS, Dr. Elias. December 2, 1790, Charleston—June 22, 1886, Washington, D.C. This son of Humphrey Marks was a physician, educator, writer, and poet. About 1820 he founded the Columbia Female School; he also conducted the Barhamville School. Marks' first wife was Jane Barham in New York City on April 3, 1816; his second wife was Julia Pierpont Warne. (*EJSC*, 195; *MSGC*)

MARKS, Elizabeth.[1] Daughter of Mordecai Marks,[1] she died young. (*MSGC*)

MARKS, Elizabeth.² Born April 3, 1742. Daughter of Mordecai Marks,¹ she was married to Ebenezer Prindle. She may have been a convert to Christianity. (*JRMP*)

MARKS, Fanny. In Philadelphia in 1748. Cf. Miss Marks. (*PAJHS*, XXVII, 460)

MARKS, Mrs. Frances. 1763—March 20, 1850. Wife of Humphrey Marks. (*MSGC*)

MARKS, Frederick. Son of Humphrey Marks, he lived in Charleston and Columbia, South Carolina, before 1800. (*MSGC*)

MARKS, French. In Philadelphia in 1786. (*MIPR*)

MARKS, Hayman. November 20, 1772—November 5, 1825, Philadelphia. This son of Henry Marks was a merchant and a prominent Mason in Philadelphia, where he became president of Congregation Mikveh Israel. His wife was Grace Judah. (*ELJR*, 80, *et passim*; *PAJHS*, VI, 110; XIX, 53, *et passim*)

MARKS, Henry. About 1726, England—March 10, 1809, Richmond. Merchant son of Mayer Marks, he lived in Philadelphia and Richmond. His wife was Mrs. Sarah Cohen. (*Byars*, 74; *MIPR*; *Morais*, 242; *Rosenbach*, 28; *Wills*, 27)

MARKS, Hezekieh. Son of Mordecai Marks,² he was in Connecticut about 1795. (*WAJA*)

MARKS, Hugh. In Georgia in 1733. His wife was Anne. (*Coulter*, 87)

MARKS, Humphrey. About 1760, London—September 15, 1838, Columbia, South Carolina. In 1786 he was in Charleston. His wife was Frances. (*EJSC*, 137, *et passim*; *MSGC*)

MARKS, Hyam. In Charleston in 1800. (*EJSC*, 137)

MARKS, Isaac.¹ On October 5, 1738, he arrived in Savannah. (*Coulter*, 88; *SRB*)

MARKS, Isaac.² From about 1740 till his death he remained in New York City. On November 25, 1758, he was buried there. (*PAJHS*, XXI, 45; *Pool*, 501)

MARK(S), Isaac.³ A learned Jew, in 1775 he was in Newport. Cf. Isaac Marcus. (*Kohut*, 136; *PAJHS*, X, 32)

MARKS, Isaac.⁴ On March 15, 1797, he was married to Esther (Betty) Hart³ in Philadelphia. (*MIPR*)

MARKS, Isaac.⁵ About 1796—March 12, 1810. Son of Humphrey Marks. (*SCHGM*, XXXIV, 111)

MARKS, Isaac.⁶ Identical with Isaac Marques.

MARKS, Mrs. Isaac. Wife of Isaac Marks,¹ she was with him when he arrived in Savannah. (*SRB*)

MARKS, Isaiah. In 1784 he was a pioneer in Kentucky. It is highly doubtful that he was Jewish. (*PAJHS*, I, 99)

MARKS, Joseph. A merchant and ship-owner, he was a member of the City Dancing Assembly of Philadelphia in 1748. It is doubtful that he was Jewish. (*PAJHS*, I, 54; *UJE*, VII, 361; VIII, 476)

MARKS, Mrs. Joseph. Wife of Joseph Marks, she was in Philadelphia in 1757. It is doubtful that she was Jewish. (*PAJHS*, I, 54)

MARKS, Leah. September 10, 1753—July 4/August 22, 1786, Easton. Daughter of Henry Marks, she was the first wife of Michael Hart.¹ (*MSGC*; *PAJHS*, VIII, 133)

MARKS, Levy.¹ Son of Isaac Marks,¹ he arrived in Savannah in 1738 and was still there in 1760. (*PAJHS*, X, 88; *SRB*)

MARKS, Levy.² In New York City in 1750. In 1770 he depended on charity from Congregation Shearith Israel in New York City. (*MEAJB*, 45)

MARKS, Levy.³ 1737—June 13, 1781, Philadelphia. This son of Mayer Marks received a legacy from Michael Gratz. In 1760 he was a tailor in Philadelphia, where he was active in Congregation Mikveh Israel. About 1780 he was a shopkeeper in Lancaster. About 1764 he was married to Rachel. (*MEAJB*, 44f; *MSGC*; *PAJHS*, IX, 30; *Rosenbach*, 28; *WW*, 39, *et passim*)

MARKS, Levy.⁴ A peddler of a seemingly disreputable nature, he was in Philadelphia in 1771. (*MEAJB*, 44f)

MARKS, Levy.⁵ Born February 6, 1797, Mt. Pleasant, New York. Son of Michael Marks. (*MSGC*)

MARKS, Mary. Born September 5, 1732. Daughter of Mordecai Marks,[1] she was married to Mr. Patterson. She may have been converted to Christianity. (*JRMP*)

MARKS, Mayer (Myer). In 1792 he was in Philadelphia. In 1794 he was a hatter. (*MIPR; WW*, 184)

MARKS, Michael. November 11, 1761, Tower Hill, London—February 11, 1829, Philadelphia. This son of Henry Marks was a merchant and saddler who was in business in Philadelphia, Easton, and Oxford, New Jersey. On October 11, 1786, he was married to Joheveth Isaacs in Newport. (*Morais*, 49, 242, 331; *PAJHS*, XXII, 182; *Trachtenberg*, 53; *Wills*, 28)

MARKS, Miriam.[1] October 8, 1764, Philadelphia—May 25, 1822, Philadelphia. On May 2, 1782, this daughter of Levy Marks[3] was married to Benjamin Nones. (*MIPR; MSGC*)

MARKS, Miriam.[2] November 12, 1769—April 11, 1784, Philadelphia. Daughter of Henry Marks. (*MIPR; MSGC; PAJHS*, VI, 108)

MARKS, Miriam (Maria). May 25, 1798, Sing Sing, New York—March 1, 1877, Philadelphia. Daughter of Michael Marks, she was married to Jonas Barnett on March 20, 1816; and then to Andrew A. Jones on October 21, 1821. (*MSGC*)

MARKS, Mordecai.[1] 1706, London—January 8, 1771, Derby, Connecticut. In 1726 he came to America. On April 20, 1729, he was baptized at Stratford, Connecticut. He was married first to Elizabeth Yorieu, and then to Elizabeth Hawkins. (*JRMP; MSGC*)

MARKS, Mordecai.[2] May 30, 1739—October 30, 1797. Son of Mordecai Marks,[1] he lived in Connecticut and was probably reared as a Christian. His wife was Sarah. (*JRMP; MSGC*)

MARKS, Moses. Born June 12, 1790, Tarrytown. Son of Michael Marks. (*MSGC*)

MARKS, Myer E. In Philadelphia in 1785. (*MIPR*)

MARKS, Nehemiah.[1] In Newport in 1731. It is doubtful that he was Jewish. (*JRMP*)

MARKS, Nehemiah.[2] Born October 9, 1746. Son of Mordecai Marks,[1] he was probably reared as a Christian. He was a Tory. (*JRMP; MSGC*)

MARKS, Rachel. Daughter of Henry Marks. (*Essays*, 116)

MARKS, Mrs. Rachel. About 1747—March 29, 1797. About 1764 she was married to Levy Marks.[3] In 1795 she was in New York City. (*MSGC; SIR*)

MARKS, Sally. Daughter of Mordecai Marks,[1] she was probably reared as a Christian. About 1795 she was in Connecticut. (*WAJA*)

MARKS, Samson. Born March 11, 1794, Mt. Pleasant, New York. Son of Michael Marks. (*MSGC*)

MARKS, Samuel Mendes (Mandel). About 1762—1804. Son of Isaac Marks,[6] he was married to Sarah Harris in 1797. In 1800 he was in Charleston. (*EJSC*, 137; *Wills*, 56)

MARKS, Sarah. December 19, 1788, Easton—May 7, 1857, Philadelphia. Daughter of Michael Marks, she was married to Samuel Lyons on March 14, 1821. (*MSGC*)

MARKS, Mrs. Sarah. Wife of Mordecai Marks,[2] it is doubtful that she was Jewish. (*JRMP*)

MARKS, Sarah Ann. Daughter of Mordecai Marks,[1] she was in Connecticut about 1795. She was probably reared as a Christian. (*WAJA*)

MARKS, Solomon.[1] July 16, 1766, England—September 28, 1824, Richmond. A merchant and hatter, this son of Henry Marks came to Richmond about 1794. (*ELJR*, 77, *et passim; Wills*, 28)

MARKS, Solomon.[2] In Philadelphia in 1784. (*MIPR*)

MARKS, Solomon, Jr. Born Lancaster Pennsylvania. Son of Solomon Marks,[1] he was active in the Democratic Society of Philadelphia. In 1794 he left Philadelphia and moved to Richmond. He later returned to Philadelphia, where he died. (*WW*, 206, 441)

MARKS, Zachariah (Zepheniah). June 28, 1734—about 1802, Milford, Connecticut. Son of Mordecai Marks,[1] he was probably reared as a Christian. (*JRMP; MSGC*)

MARQUE, Abraham. In Lancaster in 1778. (*JRMP*)

MARQUES (MARKAZE), Esther. About 1689—May 21, 1718, New York City. Daughter of Isaac R. Marques, she was married to Lewis Moses Gomez. (*MSGC; PAJHS*, XXIII, 149; XVII, 197)

MARQUES, Isaac Rodriguez. Died about 1706, New York City. He came to America from Denmark. A merchant, importer, and shipowner, on September 17, 1697, he became a freeman of New York City. His wife was Rachel. (*PAJHS*, XXIII, 148f; *Pool*, 460f)

MARQUES, Isaac. Born about 1735, New York City. A private in the New York City militia, he settled finally in Charlestown, where he changed his name to Marks. His wife was Miriam Simpson. (*MSGC; Pool*, 462)

MARQUES, Jacob. March 15, 1699, New York City—1725, St. Michaels, Barbados. Son of Isaac Rodriguez Marques, he was married to Esther. (*MSGC; Pool*, 460f)

MARQUES (MARQUISE), Joseph. During the Revolution he was a member of the Sixth regiment of the South Carolina line. Cf. Joseph Markess. (*EJSC*, 94)

MARQUES, Mrs. Rachel.[1] Died May 19, 1733, New York City. Mother of Isaac Rodriguez Marques. (*Pool*, 460)

MARQUES, Mrs. Rachel.[2] Wife of Isaac Rodriguez Marques, she lived in New York City until about 1707. She went then to Barbados, where she was married to Moses Peixotto. (*Pool*, 460f)

MARQUES, Rebecca. Died December 17, 1797, New York City. Daughter of Isaac R. Marques. (*MSGC*)

MARSHALK, Mrs. In New York City in 1797. It is doubtful that she was Jewish. (*SIR*)

MARX, Mrs. Mother of Joseph Marx, she may have been in Richmond before 1800. (*ELJR*, 47)

MARX, Adelaide. Sister of Joseph Marx, she may have been in Richmond before 1800. (*ELJR*, 47)

MARX, Asher. In Richmond in 1790. (*ELJR*, 85, 240; *PAJHS*, XX, 104)

MARX, Caroline. 1800—December 4, 1883. Daughter of Joseph Marx, she was married to Richard Barton on April 30, 1833. (*MSGC*)

MARX, Emma. Died March 30, 1859, Richmond. Sister of Joseph Marx, she may have been in Richmond before 1800. (*ELJR*, 47, *et passim*)

MARX, Henrietta. Sister of Joseph Marx, she may have been in Richmond before 1800. (*ELJR*, 47)

MARX, Henry. In New York City in 1776. (*Schappes*, 52)

MARX, Joseph. 1772, Hanover, Germany —July 12, 1840, Richmond. A prominent and wealthy merchant who engaged in large real estate enterprises, he was an acquaintance of Thomas Jefferson. He participated actively in the civic and Jewish functions of Richmond. His wife was Ritzel (Richea) Myers. (*ELJR*, 36, *et passim*; *UJE*, VI, 51; IX, 159)

MARX, Judith. January 2, 1799, Richmond —August 4, 1880. Daughter of Joseph Marx, she was married to Myer Myers[3] in September, 1826. (*MSGC; Wills*, 29)

MARX, Louisa. January 28, 1795, Richmond—January 16, 1849. Daughter of Joseph Marx, she was married to Samuel Myers[4] in May, 1816. (*MSGC*)

MARX, Samuel. March 4, 1796, Richmond —December 7, 1860, Richmond. This son of Joseph Marx was graduated from the University of Pennsylvania and became the business partner of his father. Later he was president of the Bank of Virginia. (*ELJR*, 47, *et passim*)

MARX, Solomon. In 1795 he was a member of the Masons in Richmond. It is doubtful that he was Jewish. (*PAJHS*, XIX, 62)

MARX, Wilhelmina. 1788—July 6, 1836, Richmond. She may have been a sister of

Joseph Marx, and may have been in Richmond before 1800. (*ELJR*, 303)

MASSIAS, Mr. Father of Abraham A. Massias, he was in New York City in 1772. (*EJSC*, 195)

MASSIAS, Mrs. Mother of Abraham A. Massias, she was in New York City in 1772. (*EJSC*, 195)

MASSIAS, Abraham A. 1772, Charlestown—June 28, 1848, Charleston. From 1802 till 1809 he served in the New York militia. From paymaster he was promoted to captain in the U.S. Army, where he remained for many years following his service in the War of 1812. When he retired in 1820, he was ranked as major. (*EJSC*, 195; *Reznikoff*, 104, 153, 286)

MATTOS, Abraham de. In 1747 he was given funds in New York City to enable him to go with his family to Barbados. (*PAJHS*, XXI, 57f)

MATTOS, Benjamin. In New York City about 1740. (*PAJHS*, XXI, 45)

MATTOS, Moses de. In 1739 he was a merchant in Charlestown. (*EJSC*, 27)

MAURERA, Jacob de. During the French and Indian War he was in the British forces. In 1768 he was a trader in Montreal. On September 10, 1769, he was married to a gentile, Josette Coyteaux, in a church. (*Malchelosse*, 170; *PAJHS*, I, 117; *UJE*, II, 651)

MAURISCO, Mr. In New York City in 1798. (*SIR*)

MAY, David. In Richmond in 1788. It is doubtful that he was Jewish. (*PAJHS*, XIX, 63)

MAYER, Jacob. In 1777 he was a shopkeeper in Philadelphia. (*PAJHS*, I, 61; *Rosenbach*, 12)

MAYERS, Benjamin. In Philadelphia in 1777. (*Rosenbach*, 12)

MAYERS, Judah. In New Jersey in 1745. (*PAJHS*, XXXIII, 254)

MAYSOR, Rebecca. 1781—December 14, 1852. Daughter of David Maysor, she was probably reared a Jewess although her father was a gentile. She was married to David Hyams. (*MSGC*)

MEARS, Abraham. In New York City in 1730. (*PAJHS*, XXI, 23)

MEARS, Asher Myers. Probably born in America in 1779. He may have been a son of Judah Mears. (*JRMP*)

MEARS, Caty. Born March 10, 1735/6. Daughter of Judah Mears, she was married to Asher Myers. (*MSGC*; *PAJHS*, XXXIII, 203)

MEARS, Grace.[1] 1694, Jamaica, B.W.I.—October 14, 1740, New York City. Daughter of Sampson Mears, she was married to Moses Levy[1] in London in 1718, and to David Hays[1] in New York City on April 28, 1735. (*MSGC*; *PAJHS*, XXXIII, 200)

MEARS, Grace.[2] 1742—March 4, 1817. Daughter of Judah Mears, she was married to Haim Levy on July 26, 1768. (*MSGC*; *PAJHS*, IV, 213; XXXIII, 203)

MEARS, Hannah. Died about 1745. Wife of Abraham Isaacs.[2] (*PAJHS*, XXXIII, 210; *Pool*, 232)

MEARS, Joyce. July 15, 1737—July 19, 1824, Richmond. Daughter of Judah Mears, she was married to Myer Myers[1] in New York City on March 18, 1767. (*MSGC*; *PAJHS*, VI, 111; XI, 155; XXXIII, 205; *SIR*)

MEARS, Judah. Born London, died June 7, 1762, Cape François. Son of Sampson Mears, he was a merchant in New York City by 1728, where he was president of Congregation Shearith Israel. His wife was Jehovit Michaels. (*PAJHS*, VIII, 138f; XXI, 6, *et passim*; XXXIII, 200f; *SIR*)

MEARS, Myer. In 1779 he was in America. He may have been a brother of Sampson Mears. (*JRMP*)

MEARS, Rachel. April 20, 1747, New York City—June 6, 1819, New York City. Daughter of Judah Mears, she was married to Moses Isaacs[1] in Philadelphia on August 30, 1764. (*MSGC*; *PAJHS*, XXVII, 373; XXXIII, 202f)

MEARS, Rebecca. Daughter of Judah Mears, she was married to Jacob Isaacs[2] in

New York City on October 8, 1760. (*PAJHS*, XXXIII, 202f; *SIR*)

MEARS, Sampson.[1] About 1670—before 1711, London. May have been in America. He was married to Tabitha (Joy) Franks. (*MSGC; Morais*, 269; *PAJHS*, XXXIII, 200, *et passim*)

MEARS, Sampson.[2] Died about 1787. This son of Judah Mears was a merchant in New York City, and Hartford and Norwalk, Connecticut, and was an agent for Aaron Lopez.[1] In 1762 he opened his own goldsmith shop. He lived later in St. Eustatia, where he may have died. He was married to Mrs. Robles. (*Arts & Crafts*, 52; *MEAJA*, 103, *et passim; NYHSW*, XIV, 348; *PAJHS*, XXXIII, 199, *et passim*)

MEARS, Sarah. Daughter of Judah Mears, she was married to Solomon Simson on October 26, 1768. (*PAJHS*, XXXIII, 202; *SIR*)

MEARS, Solomon. In Hartford in 1785. It is doubtful that he was Jewish. (*JRMP*)

MEARS, Tabitha (Rebecca). Daughter of Sampson Mears.[1] she was married to Matthias Bush and lived in Philadelphia. (*Morais*, 22; *MSGC; PAJHS*, XXXIII, 209)

MEDINA, Isaac de. About 1722 he was a merchant in New York City and in Hartford and Boston. (*FEAJ*, 155; *JNEA*, 18; *JRMP; PAJHS*, IV, 194, 196; VI, 127)

MEIER, John H. In 1795 he was graduated from Columbia University. (*PAJHS*, XXVII, 389)

MELHADO. Brother of Jacob Melhado of Jamaica, he was living in Philadelphia in 1770. (*AJAM*, VI, 54)

MELHADO, Benjamin. In Charleston in 1798. (*PAJHS*, XIX, 87)

MENCKS, Samuel. In Carolina in 1695. (*AJAM*, III, 9)

MENDES(Z), Aaron. Born Charleston, died August 3, 1818, Savannah. He was slain in a duel. (*EJSC*, 137; *MSP*)

MENDES, Abraham Pereira.[1] On August 31, 1748, he was naturalized in Jamaica, B.W.I. By 1752 he was a merchant in New York City. (*PAJHS*, II, 82; V, 115)

MENDES, Abraham Pereira.[2] Son-in-law of Aaron Lopez, he was married to Sarah Lopez, and lived in Newport and in Portsmouth, Rhode Island, in 1776. (*PAJHS*, XXVII, 348f)

MENDES, Abraham de Sosa. In New York City in 1683. (*POFNW*, 469)

MENDES, fils Cadet. In 1781 he was involved in privateering in Portsmouth, New Hampshire. It is doubtful that he was Jewish. (*Freund*, 66; *PAJHS*, XXIII, 175)

MENDES, David Pereira. In New York City in 1746. (*PAJHS*, XXI, 51)

MENDES, Isaac.[1] In Albany in 1756. (*PAJHS*, XXVII, 248)

MENDES, Isaac.[2] January 8, 1784—January, 1784, Newport. Son of Abraham Pereira Mendes.[2] (*PAJHS*, XXVII, 349)

MENDES, Isaac.[3] Born August 11, 1785, Newport. Son of Abraham Pereira Mendes.[2] (*PAJHS*, XXVII, 349)

MENDES, Isaac Pereira. In New York City in 1752. (*PAJHS*, XXI, 68; XXVII, 248)

MENDES, Mrs. Rachel. Wife of Simon, she arrived in Newport about 1684. (*Gutstein*, 42, 341)

MENDES, Samuel. Born February 3, 1776, Portsmouth, Rhode Island. Son of Abraham Pereira Mendes.[2] (*PAJHS*, XXVII, 348)

MENDES, Simon. Died by April, 1685. He came to Newport from Barbados. (*Gutstein*, 30, 41, 341)

MENDEZ, Joshua. In New York City in 1752. (*PAJHS*, XXVII, 6)

MENDIS, Jacob. A merchant, he was naturalized in Carolina in 1697. (*AJAM*, III, 9)

MENDOZA, David. In Georgia about 1733. (*Coulter*, 88)

MERCADO, David de. Died 1731, New York City. (*PAJHS*, XXIII, 150)

MERCADO, Moses de. In 1728 he was a partner in a snuff mill with Isaac Solomon[1] and Michael Asher in Boston. In 1731 he was probably in New York City. Cf. Moses Mircado. (*JNEA*, 20f; *PAJHS*, XXIII, 150)

MEREDA, Judiq de. In New Amsterdam in 1654. (AJAM, III, 6)

MESA, Issac. In New Amsterdam in 1657. (AJAM, III, 9)

MESQUITA, Abraham Bueno de.[1] Died by 1715, New York City. (NYHSW, II, 154)

MESQUITA, Abraham Bueno de.[2] In New York City in 1738. (NYHSW, V, 115)

MESQUITA, Benjamin Bueno de. Lived in Brazil, Jamaica, and Barbados. In 1683 he was buried in New York City. (MSGC; PAJHS, I, 92)

MESQUITA, Esther Bueno de. Cf. Esther Bueno.

MESQUITA, Joseph Bueno de. Cf. Joseph Bueno.

MESQUITA, Sarah Bueno de. Died October 24, 1708, New York City. (PAJHS, XVIII, 120)

MESQITTO, Jacob F. In 1746 he was a merchant in New York City. Cf. Jacob Ferro, Jr. (MSP)

MEYER, Captain Elias. In the British militia in America in 1761. It is doubtful that he was Jewish. (PAJHS, XXXV, 7f)

MEYER, Joseph. In Philadelphia in 1779. (Morais, 23)

MEYER, Philip. During the Revolution he was captured by the British. In 1781 he was in Charlestown. It is doubtful that he was Jewish. (PAJHS, XII, 56)

MEYERS, Abraham. A member of the Revolutionary army, he was in Charlestown in 1780. It is doubtful that he was Jewish. (EJSC, 106)

MEZA (MESA), Abraham de. In New York City in 1792. (PAJHS, XXVII, 51; SIR)

MEZA, David de. Died August 25, 1796, New York City. Son of Abraham de Meza. (PAJHS, XVIII, 101; Pool, 265f)

MEZA, Jacob de. In 1734 he was in New York City, preparing to leave for Surinam. (PAJHS, XXI, 32)

MIAL, Moses. In 1771 he was a poor boy in New York City who was given fare to St. Croix. (PAJHS, XXI, 109)

MICHAEL, Calman. About 1715 he was a merchant in New York City. (JRMP)

MICHAELS, Asher. Died before 1701. Known also as Asher Michaels de Paul. By 1682 he was in New York City. His wife was Rebecca Falk. (MSGC)

MICHAELS, Blume. Daughter of Moses Michaels, she was married to Aaron Louzada before 1741. (NYHSW, III, 295; PAJHS, XXXIII, 201)

MICHAELS, Elkaley. Daughter of Moses Michaels. (FEAJ, 71)

MICHAELS, Fayle. Born April 7, 1762, New York City. Daughter of Levy Michaels. (SIR)

MICHAELS, Mrs. Hayah Hannah. In New York City about 1728. (PAJHS, VI, 127)

MICHAELS, Isaac. In New York City in 1787. (PAJHS, XXVII, 42, et passim)

MICHAELS, Jochebed. Daughter of Moses Michaels, she was married to Judah Mears. (PAJHS, XXXIII, 200f)

MICHAELS, Joseph. In New York City in 1788. (SIR)

MICHAELS, Levi. 1723—September 13, 1815, Montreal. In 1760 he was in New York City, but later moved to Montreal. In 1759 he was married to Rachel Hays. (Coldoc, 12, et passim; MSGC; PAJHS, XXVII, 26, 151; SIR)

MICHAELS, Michael. Died 1736, New York City. Son of Moses Michaels, he was a merchant. (Emanuel, 261; PAJHS, XXIII, 151)

MICHAELS, Moses. About 1685, Harzfeld, Germany—January 25, 1740, Curaçao. In 1707 he was a merchant in New York City. In 1720 he went into business with Michael Asher of Boston; by 1730 he was the largest importer among the Curaçaon Jews. He maintained official residence in New York City, where his family lived. In August, 1707, he was married to Catherine Hachar. (Emanuel, 260-265; FEAJ, 71; MSGC; NYHSW, III, 223, 294; PAJHS,

XXIII, 151; XXXIII, 201; SCMCNYC, 199f)

MICHAELS, Myer.[1] In Virginia in 1787. It is doubtful that he was Jewish. (PAJHS, XX, 96)

MICHAELS, Myer.[2] July 1, 1760, South Haven, Long Island—August 30, 1815, Montreal. Son of Levi Michaels, he was a merchant in Montreal by 1778. He was married to Frances David. (Coldoc, 106, et passim; HSIM, 15; PAJHS, XXVII, 151; SIR)

MICHAELS, Rachel. 1707—August 21, 1749. Daughter of Moses Michaels, she was married to Samuel Myers Cohen[1] in 1729. (MSGC; PAJHS, XXXIII, 201)

MICHAELS, Rebecca.[1] Died April 9, 1801, Boston. Daughter of Moses Michaels, she was married to Judah Hays[1] about 1734. (MSGC; PAJHS, XXXIII, 200f)

MICHAELS, Rebecca.[2] Born February 27, 1766. Daughter of Levi Michaels. (SIR)

MICHEL, Hannah. In 1745 she was probably in New York City. She may have been the wife of Nathan Levy.[1] (ILI)

MICO, Joseph. In Georgia in 1739. It is doubtful that he was Jewish. (CRG, II, 313)

MIERS, Hannah. In Boston in 1732. It is doubtful that she was Jewish. (PAJHS, XI, 81)

MILHADO, Benjamin. He came to Charleston from Kingston, Jamaica, B.W.I. In April, 1796, he was married to Hannah de Pass in Charleston. Cf. Benjamin Melhado. (EJMC, 6; EJSC, 280; MSP)

MINDIS, Jacob. From Jamaica, B.W.I. In 1766 he was a merchant in Boston. (PAJHS, XXIII, 85)

MINIS (MINAS), Miss. Born July 10, 1733. Daughter of Simon Minis. (Coulter, 89)

MINIS, Abigail. April 8, 1775, Savannah— February 25, 1835, Georgetown, South Carolina. Daughter of Philip Minis. (MSGC; SRB)

MINIS, Mrs. Abigail. August, 1701—October 11, 1794, Savannah. Wife of Abraham Minis,[1] she was in Savannah in 1733. She operated her husband's business after his death. (Coldoc, 265, et passim; Coulter, 89; MEAJB, 291, et passim; MSP; SRB)

MINIS, Abraham.[1] About 1695—January 13/16, 1757, Savannah. By 1733 he was one of the first Georgia merchants in Savannah, and was also engaged as farmer, tavernkeeper, and supplier to the British troops. He was an agent of the Franks of New York. His wife was Abigail. (Coulter, 88; MEAJB, 291, et passim; MSGC; PAJHS, I, 10; X, 73, et passim; SRB)

MINIS, Abraham.[2] February 23/25, 1778, Savannah—August 29, 1801, Newport. Child of Philip Minis, he died as a result of falling out of a chair. (Gutstein, 314; MSGC; PAJHS, XXVII, 197; SRB)

MINIS, David. In 1757 he was a Mason in Georgia. (PAJHS, X, 94)

MINIS, Edward. Born July 14, 1734, Georgia. Son of Abraham Minis.[1] (Coulter, 89)

MINIS, Elizabeth. Daughter of Jacob Minis, she lived in St. George Parish, South Carolina, about 1792. (WAJA)

MINIS, Esther (Hester). About 1731— July 4, 1793, Savannah. Daughter of Abraham Minis,[1] she was in Georgia in 1733. (Coulter, 89; MEAJB, 356f; PAJHS, 73; SRB)

MINIS, Esther. November 21, 1782/4, Savannah—December 2, 1864. Daughter of Philip Minis. (MSGC; SRB)

MINIS, Frances. May 17, 1776, Savannah —September 22, 1827. Daughter of Philip Minis, she was married to Dr. Levi Meyers on February 13, 1794, in Savannah. (EJMC, 6; MSGC; SRB)

MINIS, Hannah. Born June 13, 1744. Daughter of Abraham Minis,[1] she was married to David Leion on April 17, 1798, and was divorced on August 22, 1799, in the first recorded Jewish divorce. In 1779 she was in Savannah. (MEAJB, 356f; SRB)

MINIS, Isaac.[1] Son of Jacob Minis, he lived in St. George Parish about 1792. (WAJA)

MINIS, Isaac.[2] July 30, 1780, Charlestown—November 15, 1856, Philadelphia. Son of Philip Minis, he was married to Divinah Cohen on December 14, 1803, in Georgetown, South Carolina. (*MSGC; SRB*)

MINIS, Jacob. Died about 1792. He lived in St. George Parish, South Carolina. His wife was Mary. (*WAJA*)

MINIS, James. In the Georgia line of the Revolutionary army. It is doubtful that he was Jewish. (*PAJHS, XVII, 99*)

MINIS, Joseph. September 14, 1738, Savannah—September 24, 1757/1760, Savannah. Son of Abraham Minis,[1] he lived in Georgia. (*SRB; Wills, 76*)

MINIS, Judith. June 24, 1742, Savannah—January 30, 1826. Daughter of Abraham Minis,[1] she was in Savannah in 1779. (*MEAJB, 356f; MSGC; SRB*)

MINIS, Leah. 1726—May 26, 1802, Savannah. Daughter of Abraham Minis.[1] (*Coulter, 89; MEAJB, 356f; Wills, 76*)

MINIS, Mrs. Mary. Wife of Jacob Minis, she was in St. George Parish, South Carolina, about 1792. (*WAJA*)

MINIS, Miss Mary. Daughter of Jacob Minis, she was in St. George Parish, South Carolina, about 1792. (*WAJA*)

MINIS, Minis. August 31, 1736, Savannah—November 5, 1771, Beaufort, South Carolina. Son of Abraham Minis,[1] he lived in Savannah and was buried in Savannah. (*SRB; Wills, 76*)

MINIS, Philip. July 11/12, 1733, Savannah—March 6, 1789. Also known as Uri. This son of Abraham Minis[1] may have been the first white male child born who survived in Georgia. A patriot in the Revolutionary cause, he served as acting paymaster and commissary general in the Revolution. He was the first president of Congregation Mikveh Israel in Savannah. On July 20, 1774, he was married to Judith Polock in Newport. (*Coldoc, 232, et passim; Coulter, 89; MEAJB, 237, et passim; MSGC; PAJHS, I, 67; X, 83; XII, 53, 55, 164; XVII, 100, et passim; SRB*)

MINIS, Phillipa. May 30, 1789, Savannah—August 23, 1865. Daughter of Philip Minis. (*MSGC; SRB*)

MINIS, Samuel. Born October 14, 1740, Savannah, died young. Son of Abraham Minis.[1] (*SRB*)

MINIS, Sarah (Sally). Born August 7, 1748, Savannah. Daughter of Abraham Minis,[1] she was in Savannah in 1779. (*MEAJB, 356f; SRB*)

MINIS, Simon. Younger brother of Abraham Minis,[1] he was in Georgia in 1733. (*Coulter, 89; MEAJB, 291*)

MINIS (MINAS), Mrs. Simon. In Hampstead, Georgia, in 1733. (*Coulter, 89*)

MINIS, Stephen. Son of Jacob Minis, he was in St. George Parish, South Carolina, about 1792. (*WAJA*)

MINIS, William. Fought in the Revolution in the Georgia line. It is doubtful that he was Jewish. (*PAJHS, XVII, 99*)

MIRANDA, Abraham. In New York City about 1740. (*PAJHS, XXI, 45*)

MIRANDA, David de. Died December, 1733, Georgia. In July, 1733, he arrived in Georgia. (*Coulter, 71*)

MIRANDA, Elias. His home was in Curaçao. Before 1765 he was in Lancaster, Pennsylvania. In 1765 he was a merchant who was in partnership with Barnard Gratz in New York City. (*Byars, 73f*)

MIRANDA, George. Son of Isaac Miranda,[1] he was probably a convert. In the 1730s he carried on his father's business trading with Indians and others in western Pennsylvania. (*MEAJB, 5*)

MIRANDA, Isaac.[1] Died 1732, Lancaster. He is said to have come from Italy to Philadelphia sometime between 1710 and 1715. In the Lancaster area he became a wealthy Indian trader, and also owned a large amount of property in Philadelphia. In 1727 he was a deputy vice admiralty judge, the first Jew to hold office in the province of Pennsylvania. A convert to Christianity, he asked in his will "to be buried in a Christianlike and decent manner." (*MEAJB, 4f; UJE, VI, 520; VII, 579; VIII, 426, 476; WAJA; WW, 18-20*)

MIRANDA(O), Isaac.[2] During the French and Indian War he fought for the English.

In 1770 he was in Montreal. (*HSIM*, 11; *UJE*, II, 651)

MIRANDA, Jacob de. In Hampstead, Georgia, in 1733. (*Coulter*, 71)

MIRANDA, Jacob. In Georgia about 1733. (*Coulter*, 89)

MIRANDA, Joseph. In 1759 he was a Mason in Pennsylvania. It is doubtful that he was Jewish. (*PAJHS*, XIX, 47)

MIRANDA, Mary. In Lancaster. Daughter of Isaac Miranda,[1] she probably was reared as a Christian. (*MEAJB*, 5)

MIRANDA, Samuel. Son of Isaac Miranda,[1] he was probably reared as a Christian. In 1732 he was in Lancaster. (*WAJA*)

MIRCADO, Moses. In New York City in 1732. Cf. Moses de Mercado. (*PAJHS*, XXI, 29)

MIRRANDA, Bristol. In Boston in 1790. (*PAJHS*, XXIII, 87)

MITCHEL, Abraham. In 1765 he was a merchant in Philadelphia. It is doubtful that he was Jewish. (*Schappes*, 40)

MITCHELL, Joseph. In Philadelphia in 1765. It is highly doubtful that he was Jewish. (*MSP*)

MITCHELL, Robert. In Savannah in 1796. It is highly doubtful that he was Jewish. (*JRMP*)

MITCHELS, Sara. On March 25, 1761, she was married to Samuel Pacifico in New York City. (*SIR*)

MODINA, Moses. About 1702 he was a merchant in Charlestown. (*ELHS*; *UJE*, III, 114)

MOISE, Aaron. June 14, 1783, St. Domingo—December 7, 1852, Charleston. From 1839 through 1851 this son of Abraham Moïse[1] was a physician and a clerk in the Bank of South Carolina. In April, 1805, he was married to Phila Cohen; in December, 1807, he was married to Sarah Cohen.[4] (*EJSC*, 205; *MSGC*; *MSP*)

MOISE, Abraham.[1] Born Alsace, died 1809, Charleston. In 1791 he came to Charleston from St. Domingo and became a merchant. His wife was Sarah. (*EJSC*, 181; *JE*, VIII, 648; *MSGC*)

MOISE, Abraham.[2] June 12, 1799, Charleston—June 11, 1869, Sumterville, South Carolina. This son of Abraham Moïse[1] was prominent in the Jewish and secular Charleston community. An outstanding attorney, he was admitted to the bar in 1822. From 1827 until 1840 he was justice of the peace; from 1842 until 1859 he was magistrate of the city of Charleston. His wife was Caroline Agnes Moses. (*EJSC*, 137, et passim; *MSGC*; *UJE*, VII, 611)

MOISE, Benjamin. 1790, St. Domingo—June 29, 1824. Son of Abraham Moïse,[1] he was in Charleston in 1791. In December, 1817, he was married to Rebecca Levy. (*JE*, VIII, 648; *MSGC*)

MOISE, Cherry. About 1781, St. Domingo—October 5, 1823, New York City. Son of Abraham Moïse,[1] on October 14, 1801, he was married to Esther Moses. (*EJSC*, 137, 145, 280; *MSGC*; *MSP*)

MOISE, Hyam. March 18, 1785, St. Domingo—October 18, 1811, Edisto Island. Son of Abraham Moïse,[1] he was married to Cecilia Wolfe in December, 1807. (*EJSC*, 137, 280; *JE*, VIII, 650; *MSGC*)

MOISE, Isaac. November 23, 1800, Charleston—November 24, 1857. Son of Abraham Moïse,[1] he was married to Hetty Lopez on March 4, 1827. (*EJSC*, 137, et passim; *MSGC*)

MOISE, Jacob. 1798, Charleston—December 28, 1837, Sand Hills, Georgia. Son of Abraham Moïse,[1] he was one of the first Jewish settlers of Augusta, Georgia. In 1836 he was a director of the Georgia Insurance Company. His wife was Rebecca Cohen.[4] (*EJSC*, 137, 170, 196; *MSGC*)

MOÏSE, Penina. April 23, 1797, Charleston—September 13, 1880, Charleston. This daughter of Abraham Moïse[1] was a poet whose first poems, published as early as 1830, were regularly published in the *Charleston Courier*. She also wrote hymns and prose. As a child after the death of her father, she helped support the family by embroidering and making lace. After the Civil War she opened a school with her sister. About 1864 she lost her eyesight. (*EJSC*, 181f; *JE*, VIII, 650; *Reznikoff*, 80, et passim; *UJE*, VII, 612f)

MOISE, Rachel. 1796—March 11, 1872. Daughter of Abraham Moïse,[1] she was married to Mr. Levy. (*MSGC*)

MOISE, Mrs. Sarah. 1762—April 13, 1842, Charleston. Wife of Abraham Moïse.[1] (*JE*, VIII, 648; *MSGC*; *MSP*)

MOLINA, Abraham. In Savannah in 1733. (*Coulter*, 89)

MOLINA, Hester. Daughter of Abraham Molina, in 1733 she was in Savannah. (*Coulter*, 89)

MOLINA, Isaac. In Savannah in 1733. (*Coulter*, 89)

MOLINA, Moses. Died December, 1785, Charleston. In New York City in 1730. (*PAJHS*, XXI, 25; *Wills*, 49)

MOLINA, Mrs. Rachel. Wife of Isaac Molina, in 1733 she was in Savannah. (*Coulter*, 89)

MOLINA, Mrs. Sarah. Wife of Abraham Molina, she was in Savannah in 1733. (*Coulter*, 89)

MOLINE(O), Solomon. From Cape François. In 1792 he fled from Philadelphia with his family and with slaves whom he had freed. (*MIPR*; *WW*, 191)

MOLL, Abraham. About 1703 he was in New York City with his family; he had been there as early as 1675. It is doubtful that he was Jewish. (*AJAM*, III, 9; *CPG*, 172)

MONIS, Judah. February 4, 1683, Algiers (or Italy)—April 25, 1764. He lived in Jamaica, B.W.I., Boston, and New York City. About 1715 he became a freeman. The first Jew to receive a degree from Harvard College, he received his M.A. in 1720. From 1722 to 1760 he was the first teacher at Harvard to bear the title of instructor. Author of the first Hebrew grammar book published in America, he was a Hebrew scholar, a theologian, and an educator. He may also have been a rabbi. While he was teaching he kept a shop as a merchant. He was also a governmental Spanish interpreter. Although he was publicly baptized in Cambridge on March 27, 1722, he continued to observe the seventh day as Sabbath, and consequently there is some question as to the sincerity of his conversion. About 1723 he was married to Abigail Marrett. (*DAB*, XIII, 86f; *PAJHS*, III, 112f; X, 32; XI, 80f; XII, 102f)

MONSANTO, Benjamin. Died about 1795, Natchez. He was a slave trader and planter. His wife was Clara. (*Coldoc*, 456; *UJE*, VII, 586)

MONSANTO, Mrs. Clara. Wife of Benjamin Monsanto, she was in Natchez in 1787. (*Coldoc*, 456; *UJE*, VII, 586)

MONSANTO, Jacob. In Natchez in 1783. (*JRMP*)

MONSANTO, Manuel Jacob. Brother of Benjamin Monsanto, he was in Natchez in 1783. Cf. above. (*Coldoc*, 456f)

MONTAGNIE, Jacob de la. In New York City about 1790. It is doubtful that he was Jewish. (*JRMP*)

MONTE, Abigail del. Daughter of David Cohen del Monte, in 1733 she was in Savannah. On May 2, 1736, she was married to Hyman Abendanone in Savannah. (*Coulter*, 68; *MSGC*)

MONTE, David Cohen del. In Savannah in 1733. (*Coulter*, 68)

MONTE, Grace del. Daughter of David Cohen del Monte, on July 5, 1736, she was married to Simon Abendanone in Savannah. (*Coulter*, 68; *MSGC*)

MONTE, Hannah del. Daughter of David Cohen del Monte, in 1733 she was in Savannah. (*PAJHS*, X, 73)

MONTE, Isaac del. Son of David Cohen del Monte, he was in Savannah in 1733. (*Coulter*, 68)

MONTE, Mrs. Rachel del. Died March 29, 1734, Georgia. Wife of David Cohen del Monte. (*Coulter*, 68)

MONTES, Abraham.[1] In Philadelphia in 1740. (*PAJHS*, I, 24)

MONTES, Abraham.[2] From Cape François. In Philadelphia in 1792. (MIPR)

MONTEYRO, Joseph. In 1706 he was a merchant in Philadelphia. (WW, 14)

MONTSONTE, Abraham. In Savannah in 1733. (Coulter, 89)

MONTSONTE, Melino. In Savannah in 1733. (Coulter, 90)

MONTSONTE, Bernal Rafael. In Savannah in 1733. Cf. Rafael Bernal. (Coulter, 89)

MONTSONTE, Mrs. Rachel. Wife of Bernal Rafael Montsonte, in 1733 she was in Savannah. Cf. Rachel Bernal. (Coulter, 89)

MORALES. A member of the family of Jacob Morales, she was in Charleston in 1800. (Census B, South Carolina)

MORALES, Jacob. In Charleston in 1800. (EJSC, 137)

MORANDA, David. In Georgia about 1733. (PAJHS, X, 73)

MORANDA, Jacob. In Georgia about 1733. (PAJHS, X, 73)

MORAVIA, Joseph. In New York City in 1787. (PAJHS, XXVII, 42)

MORAVIA, Mrs. Martha. Died July 12, 1787, New York City. Also known as Martha Lazarus. She lived also in Newport. (PAJHS, VI, 76; XXVII, 201, 350; Pool, 503)

MORDECAI. Died July, 1780, Charleston, a child. (MEAJB, 362)

MORDECAI, Abram. October 24, 1755, Philadelphia—1847. After service in the Revolutionary army, he traded with Indians in Georgia and was a government Indian agent. One of the first settlers of Montgomery, Alabama, in 1804 he built one of the first cotton gins there. After the Indians destroyed his gin, he served in the War of 1812 in Georgia. He lived the rest of his life in Alabama. (PAJHS, XIII, 71, et passim; UJE, VII, 643)

MORDECAI, Caroline. August 27, 1794—1862. Daughter of Jacob Mordecai, she was married to Achille Plunkett, a gentile. In 1796 she was in Warrentown, North Carolina. (MSGC; PAJHS, VI, 48)

MORDECAI, Ellen. November 10, 1790—1884. Daughter of Jacob Mordecai. (MSGC; PAJHS, VI, 48)

MORDECAI, Esther. About 1758—July 28, 1846, Philadelphia. Daughter of Mordecai M. Mordecai, on November 2, 1776, she was married to Philip Moses Russell. (GBMIP; Morais, 29; MSP)

MORDECAI, Henry. About 1760 he was a merchant partner of Philip Samuel(s) in the Catskills. In 1760 he absconded to Holland. (Beekmans, 393; PAJHS, XLIV, 200; White, 649f)

MORDECAI, Mrs. Hetty. About 1767, Philadelphia—January 17, 1820, Charleston. For thirteen years she lived in Charleston. (MSP)

MORDECAI, Isaac. Son of Moses Mordecai[1] and the stepson of Jacob I. Cohen, he was a merchant in Philadelphia, Richmond, and Baltimore from 1785 through 1797. (ELJR, 72; MEAJB, 208f, 216; MIPR; PAJHS, XIX, 57, 62)

MORDECAI, Jacob. April 11, 1762, Philadelphia—September 4, 1838, Richmond. During the Revolution this son of Moses Mordecai[1] joined a military association for youths. By 1782 he was a merchant in Richmond, and was president of Congregation Beth Shalome there. A cultured and widely read person, he wrote Jewish and Christian theology. In 1809 he founded a seminary for young women in Warrentown, North Carolina. With Haym Solomon, a clerk of David Franks, he formed a business partnership. Mordecai's first wife was Judith Myers[3] on June 16, 1784; his second wife was Rebecca Myers,[2] about 1798. (AJA; ELJR, 14, et passim; MEAJB, 190f; PAJHS, I, 15; III, 10; IV, 21, 23; VI, 39f; WW, 50, et passim)

MORDECAI, Joseph. November 18, 1766—July 10, 1839. By 1784 this son of Moses Mordecai[1] was listed in Richmond as a clerk when he was eighteen years old. A stepson of Jacob I. Cohen, on October 25, 1786, he was married to Esther Marache in Philadelphia. (*ELJR*, 24; *MEAJB*, 208f; *MIPR*; *MSGC*)

MORDECAI, Judith. About 1763—about 1847. Wife of Emanuel Abrahams whom she married in 1779, she lived in South Carolina. (*EJSC*, 92; *EOJCC*, 40; *MSGC*; *PAJHS*, XII, 57)

MORDECAI, Julia. May 17, 1799, Warrentown, North Carolina—March 13, 1852, Richmond. Daughter of Jacob Mordecai. (*ELJR*, 305; *PAJHS*, VI, 48)

MORDECAI, Mordecai M. Came to America from Lithuania. A distiller and merchant in New York City, Philadelphia, Easton, Richmond, and Baltimore, he was in Easton by 1760. He performed religious functions, including a wedding and a funeral. His wife was Zipporah de Lyon. (*EJRF*, 1; *ELJR*, 240; *MEAJB*, 68, 549; *Morais*, 29; *PAJHS*, I, 16, 18; II, 175; IV, 21; XIX, 62, 67f; *Trachtenberg*, 37f)

MORDECAI, Moses.[1] 1707, Bonn, Germany—May 28, 1781, Philadelphia. About 1750 he came to America and became a merchant in Philadelphia. His wife was Elizabeth Whitlock, a gentile who was converted and became an observant Jewess. (*JE*, IX, 10; *MEAJB*, 190f; *Morais*, 22; *PAJHS*, VI, 40f)

MORDECAI, Moses.[2] April 4, 1785, New York City—September 1, 1824, Raleigh. Son of Jacob Mordecai, he became a prominent attorney in North Carolina. His first wife was Margaret Lane, December 9, 1817; his second wife was Anne Willis Lane, January 6, 1824. (*MSGC*; *PAJHS*, VI, 46f)

MORDECAI, Phineas. In Philadelphia in 1783. (*MIPR*)

MORDECAI, Rachel.[1] August, 1782—April 2, 1827, Charleston. Daughter of Samuel Mordecai,[1] she was married to Isaac Harby in December, 1810. (*EJSC*, 176; *MSGC*)

MORDECAI, Rachel.[2] July 1, 1789—June 23, 1838, Petersburg, Virginia. Eldest daughter of Jacob Mordecai, she had an important influence on her father's school for girls. In 1796 she was in Warrentown, North Carolina. On March 21, 1821, she was married to Aaron Lazarus. (*MSGC*; *PAJHS*, VI, 47f)

MORDECAI, Rebecca. 1791/3—May 15, 1833. Daughter of Joseph Mordecai, she was married to Jacob Hertz. (*MSGC*)

MORDECAI, S. In 1797 he was a Mason in Baltimore. (*PAJHS*, XIX, 57)

MORDECAI, Sampson. 1783, Charleston—September 19, 1826, Savannah. Son of Samuel Mordecai.[1] (*MSGC*)

MORDECAI, Samuel.[1] About 1751—February 20, 1819, Savannah. By 1780 he was a merchant in Charlestown. In 1791 he was in Savannah. On December 24, 1778, he was married to Catherine Andrews. (*EJMC*, 5; *EJSC*, 91; *MISR*; *MSGC*)

MORDECAI, Samuel.[2] July 24, 1786, New York City—April 9, 1865, Raleigh. This son of Jacob Mordecai was a merchant in Richmond, and was prominent in Jewish and general communal activities. He was the author of *Richmond in Bygone Days*. (*ELJR*, 19, *et passim*; *MSGC*; *PAJHS*, VI, 47; XIX, 63, *et passim*)

MORDECAI, Solomon.[1] March 20, 1790, Virginia—1843/50. Son of Joseph Mordecai, he was married to Isabella Jane Kincaid on April 20, 1817, in Franklin, Missouri. (*ELJR*, 33; *MSGC*)

MORDECAI, Solomon.[2] October 10, 1792—1869. This son of Jacob Mordecai became a physician in Mobile. On April 22, 1824, he was married to Caroline Waller. (*ELJR*, 33; *MSGC*; *PAJHS*, VI, 42f, 47)

MORDECAI, Mrs. Zipporah. Died April 6, 1806, Maryland. Wife of Mordecai M. Mordecai. (*GBMIP*; *Trachtenberg*, 37)

MORENT, J. Died December 1, 1738, Georgia. A servant. (*Coulter*, 90)

MORESCO, Uriel. In Montreal about 1770. (*HSIM*, 11)

MORIS, Janet. On August 24, 1786, she was married to Abram Levy in Philadelphia. (*MIPR*)

MORRIS, Judah. A merchant, he became a freeman of New York City about 1715. Cf. Judah Monis. (*PAJHS*, VI, 101)

MORRIS, Mark. In Charlestown in 1780. It is doubtful that he was Jewish. (*PAJHS*, XII, 53)

MOS, Moses da Costa la. In New York City in 1769. (*PAJHS*, XXI, 105)

MOSES. Died about 1753, New York City. Daughter of Jacob Moses. (*Pool*, 501)

MOSES. January 21, 1764, Jamaica, Long Island—April, 1764. Daughter of Levy Moses. (*SIR*)

MOSES, Mrs. Died about 1786, Charleston. (*MSP*)

MOSES, Aaron. In North Carolina in 1740. It is doubtful that he was Jewish. (*PAJHS*, XXIX, 141)

MOSES, Abraham.[1] In 1656 he was a Mason in Rhode Island. (*AJAM*, III, 9)

MOSES, Abraham.[2] Died July, 1796, Charleston. As early as 1769 he was a merchant in Charlestown. (*EJSC*, 91, *et passim*; *Wills*, 49)

MOSES, Abraham.[3] In 1785 he was a trader in Philadelphia. (*Feldman*, 3; *MIPR*; *PAJHS*, IX, 124f)

MOSES, Mrs. Abraham. Wife of Abraham Moses,[2] she was in Charlestown in 1769, and in Savannah in 1795. (*MISR*; *Wills*, 49)

MOSES, Andrew. During the Revolution he was a soldier in Virginia. It is doubtful that he was Jewish. (*PAJHS*, XX, 99)

MOSES, Attival (Akival). A member of the Revolutionary army, in 1779 he lived in Charlestown. (*PAJHS*, XIX, 152, 154)

MOSES, Barnard. In Charlestown sometime between 1750 and 1783. On September 23, 1777, he was married to Esther de Lyon in Savannah. (*EJSC*, 278; *SRB*)

MOSES, Barnard, Jr. In 1779 he lived in Charlestown. He fought in the Revolution. (*EJSC*, 91, 278; *PAJHS*, XII, 53; XIX, 152, 154)

MOSES, Barnett. In New York City about 1740. (*PAJHS*, XXI, 45)

MOSES, Bella. Before 1787—1862. Daughter of Myer Moses,[1] she was married to Solomon Cohen. (*MSGC*; *Wills*, 58)

MOSES, Benjamin. During the Revolution he served on General Pulaski's staff. In 1782 he was in Portsmouth, New Hampshire. It is doubtful that he was Jewish. (*JRMP*; *PAJHS*, XXIII, 175)

MOSES, Colman. In 1785 he came from London, and was recommended to the Gratzes by Meyer Josephson. (*AJA*)

MOSES, Daniel. Born January 14, 1765, Jamaica, Long Island. Son of Levy Moses, he was born in prison. (*PAJHS*, XXVII, 152; *SIR*)

MOSES, David.[1] Born November 28, 1755, South Carolina. Son of William Moses, he was buried two days after his birth. It is doubtful that he was Jewish. (*SCHGM*, XXIII, 136)

MOSES, David.[2] June 29, 1776, Philadelphia—March 21, 1858, New York City. Son of Isaac Moses.[1] (*MSGC*; *SIR*)

MOSES, David M. Before 1797—March 20, 1858, St. Joseph, Florida. Son of Philip Moses,[2] he was married to Miriam Seixas on February 1, 1832. (*MSGC*; *PAJHS*, IV, 211)

MOSES, Mrs. Deborah. 1776—August 29, 1848, St. Joseph, Florida. She may have been in America before 1800. On December 5, 1810, she was married to Israel Moses. (*MSGC*)

MOSES, Eleanor. August 1, 1778—May 15, 1857. Daughter of Myer Moses,[1] she was married to Philip Cohen in June, 1799. (*MSGC*)

MOSES, Mrs. Elizabeth. 1745—January 19, 1819. Wife of Henry Moses. (*MSP*)

MOSES, Esther. 1784—April 18, 1860, Charleston. Daughter of Myer Moses, she was also known as Hetty and Henrietta. On October 14, 1801, she was married to Cherry Moïse; in 1827 she was married to Hyam Cohen. (*MSGC*; *Wills*, 58)

MOSES, Ezekiel. Fought in Virginia in the Revolution. It is doubtful that he was Jewish. (*PAJHS*, XX, 99)

MOSES, Fishel. Son of Philip Moses,[2] he was in Savannah in 1787. In 1824 he was married to Rachel de Pass in Charleston. (*MSGC*; *SRB*)

MOSES, Gitlah. On January 11, 1784, she was married to Moses Nunez Cardozo[1] in Philadelphia. (*MIPR*)

MOSES, Hannah. Died 1800. The second wife of Joseph Cohen. (*MSGC*)

MOSES, Mrs. Hannah.[1] In 1755 she was a shopkeeper in Philadelphia. Barnard Gratz boarded in her home for a time. (*MEAJB*, 13f, 401)

MOSES, Mrs. Hannah.[2] 1768—November 9, 1846. Wife of Reuben Moses. (*MSGC*)

MOSES, Hayman Levy. June 2, 1792—June 11, 1846, New York City. Son of Isaac Moses.[1] (*MSGC*)

MOSES, Henry. 1747, Prussia—February 11, 1814, Charleston. In 1780 he came to America, possibly as a Hessian soldier. Until 1782 he was in New York City. He then became a merchant in Charleston. His wife was Elizabeth. (*EJSC*, 98; *EOJCC*, 110; *MSP*)

MOSES, Isaac.[1] 1742—April 16, 1818, New York City. This son of Moses Moses was a prominent and wealthy merchant shipper and privateer who not only served in the Revolutionary army, but also provided the Revolutionary forces with money and materials. On October 22, 1766, he became a freeman in New York City. He was among those who established the Bank of New York. In 1775 he was president of Congregation Shearith Israel in New York City, and was one of the chief organizers and the first president of Congregation Mikveh Israel in Philadelphia. He was also an outstanding Mason. On August 8, 1770, he was married to Reyna Levy in New York City. (*Coldoc*, 99, *et passim*; *MEAJA*, 99f; *MEAJB*, 60, *et passim*; *PAJHS*, I, 13f; II, 86f; III, 84; IV, 210; VI, 102, 130f; XI, 83f; XIX, 29; XXIII, 171f; XXVII, 331f; *Pool*, 39, *et passim*; *SIR*)

MOSES, Isaac.[2] In 1777 he was a captain the Revolutionary forces. (*PAJHS*, XXVII, 390)

MOSES, Isaac.[3] In 1798 he was a Mason in Detroit. (*PAJHS*, XIII, 56)

MOSES, Isaac.[4] 1769, Charlestown—August 26, 1831, New York City. Merchant son of Abraham Moses,[2] he was a Mason in Charleston and New York City. In 1800 he was married to Esther Isaacs.[2] (*EJSC*, 117, *et passim*; *MSGC*; *Wills*, 49)

MOSES, Isaac.[5] March 26, 1789, Savannah —April 20, 1789, Savannah. Son of Philip Moses.[2] (*MSGC*; *SRB*)

MOSES, Isaac, Jr.[1] In New York City in 1798. (*SIR*)

MOSES, Isaac, Jr.[2] In Charleston in 1800. (*EJSC*, 137)

MOSES, Isaac, Sr. Died May, 1803, New York City. He was called "Ribi" and may have been a Hebrew teacher. In 1788 he was a cobbler in Philadelphia. In 1797 he was listed as a shoemaker in New York City. (*MIPR*; *Pool*, 388; *WW*, 151)

MOSES, Isaac Clifton. 1781—September 3, 1835, Connecticut. Son of Myer Moses,[1] in 1819 he was a justice of the peace in Charleston. On November 3, 1802, he was married to Hannah Lazarus. (*EJSC*, 137, *et passim*; *MSGC*; *Wills*, 58)

MOSES, Isaac L. 1795, Charleston—April 27, 1807, Charleston. Son of Lyon Moses. (*EOJCC*, 78)

MOSES, Isaiah. In 1800 he was a planter living in Charleston. He was married to Rebecca Phillips. (*EJSC*, 138, 143, 170; *PAJHS*, XXXII, 126)

MOSES, Israel.[1] 1780, Charlestown—1803, near Kingston, Jamaica, B.W.I. Son of Myer Moses.[1] (*MSP*)

MOSES, Israel.[2] Before 1787, Charleston—January 22, 1849, Apalachicola, Florida. Merchant son of Philip Moses,[2] he was married to Deborah Cohen on December 5, 1810. (*EJSC*, 199; *MSGC*; *PAJHS*, II, 49)

MOSES, Israel (Ariel). March 20, 1785, New York City—July 20, 1801, New York City. Son of Isaac Moses.[1] (*MSGC*; *PAJHS*, XVIII, 105; XXVII, 55; *SIR*)

MOSES, Issachar. Born July 3, 1762, New York City. Son of Levy Moses. (*MSGC*)

MOSES, Jacob.[1] In 1770 he was a merchant in New York City. (*PAJHS*, IV, 89)

MOSES, Jacob.[2] In Charlestown in 1780. (*EJSC*, 91)

MOSES, Jacob.[3] Born March 3, 1770, Jamaica, Long Island. Son of Levy Moses. (*SIR*)

MOSES, Jacob.[4] In 1780 he served with the Continental troops in Maryland and was later lost in action. It is highly doubtful that he was Jewish. (*MTAR*, 142, 284)

MOSES, Jacob.[5] In 1781 he served with the Continental troops in Maryland. It is highly doubtful that he was Jewish. (*MTAR*, 548)

MOSES, Jesse. In 1788 he was a barber, briefly in Savannah. (*SRB*)

MOSES, Joseph.[1] Grandson of Isaac Levy,[1] in 1745 he was in New York City. (*NYHSW*, IV, 57)

MOSES, Joseph.[2] In 1780 he was engaged in privateering in Pennsylvania. It is doubtful that he was Jewish. (*PAJHS*, XXIII, 175)

MOSES, Joseph.[3] 1772—July 5, 1814. He was married to Rachel, a niece of Mordecai Lyons. (*MSGC*)

MOSES, Joseph, Jr. In Charleston sometime between 1783 and 1800. (*EJSC*, 280)

MOSES, Joshua. June 16, 1780—December 6, 1837, New York City. Son of Isaac Moses,[1] he was in New York City in 1793. On March 19, 1817, he was married to Sarah Rodriguez Brandon in London. (*MSGC*; *PAJHS*, XXVII, 55)

MOSES, Judah. In Philadelphia in 1785. (*MIPR*)

MOSES, Judith. Stepdaughter of Philip Moses, she was married to Joseph Solomon. (*WAJA*)

MOSES, Lavinia. April 22, 1786—April 10, 1828, New York City. Daughter of Isaac Moses,[1] she was married to Isaac L. Brandon on March 24, 1824. (*MSGC*; *PAJHS*, XVIII, 122)

MOSES, Leah. Born March 3, 1760, Jamaica, Long Island. Daughter of Levy Moses. (*SIR*)

MOSES, Levy. In Jamaica, Long Island, before 1760. In 1769 and 1770 while he was in prison with his family, he received relief from Congregation Shearith Israel of New York City. During the Revolution he served in the Philadelphia militia. (*PAJHS*, XXI, 105, 108; *SIR*; *WW*, 96)

MOSES, Mrs. Levy. In New York City in 1760. (*MSGC*)

MOSES, Lyon. About 1750, Amsterdam—April 19, 1821, Charleston. During the Revolution he served in the Philadelphia militia. In 1783 he was in business in Philadelphia, but later lived in Charleston for about forty years. (*EJSC*, 117, *et passim*; *EOJCC*, 78; *MEAJB*, 141; *MSP*; *WW*, 96, 171)

MOSES, Mrs. Mary. About 1754, Holland—September 23, 1810, Charleston. Also known as Rachel Miriam Moses. Wife of Solomon Moses, she lived in Charleston for sixteen years. (*EOJCC*, 44; *MSGC*; *SCHGM*, XXXV, 167; *Wills*, 51)

MOSES, Michael. Died about 1769, Philadelphia. (*MSP*)

MOSES, Miriam. Born February 15, 1767, Jamaica, Long Island. Daughter of Levy Moses. (*SIR*)

MOSES, Moses.[1] Born September 18, 1768, Jamaica, Long Island. Son of Levy Moses. (*SIR*)

MOSES, Moses.[2] December 4, 1773, New York City—July 14, 1843, New York City. Son of Isaac Moses,[1] he won a prize at Columbia Grammar School. In 1782 he was in Philadelphia. (*MIPR*; *MSGC*; *PAJHS*, XIX, 119f; *SIR*)

MOSES, Moses L. In business in New York City in 1800. (*ALDINE*, 68)

MOSES, Myer.[1] 1735, England—February 15, 1787, Charleston. In Charlestown before 1771. A merchant, he served in the Revolutionary cause especially through his care for the wounded. Moses' first wife was Frangipini; his second wife was Rachel Andrews about 1772. (*EJSC*, 45, *et passim*; *MSGC*; *UJE*, VIII, 14; *Wills*, 58)

MOSES, Myer.[2] February 12, 1779, Charlestown—March 20, 1833, New York City.

In 1809 this son of Myer Moses[1] was a member of the South Carolina Society for the Promotion of Domestic Arts and Manufactories. Shortly after he was a major in the South Carolina Volunteers. In 1810 he was a member of the South Carolina legislature, and in 1811 was commissioner of Free Schools and director of the Planters and Mechanics' Bank. About 1825 he moved to New York City and wrote the *Full Annals of the Revolution of France*. On November 2, 1803, he was married to Esther Phillips in Philadelphia. (*EJSC*, 138, *et passim*; *MSGC*; *PAJHS*, II, 61; *Reznikoff*, 104, *et passim*; *UJE*, VIII, 12, 14)

MOSES, Paijero. On November 7, 1759, she was married to Judah Barred in New York City. (*SIR*)

MOSES, Pier (Polly). Daughter of Solomon Moses.[1] (*MSGC*)

MOSES, Philip.[1] Before 1800 he came to Charleston from St. Eustatia. Later he was in Newport and Savannah. (*MEAJB*, 326; *Wills*, 51)

MOSES, Philip.[2] From Newport he went south, where he had business contacts with Aaron Lopez.[1] In 1771 he was a merchant and fur trader in Savannah. In 1780 he was in Charlestown. His wife was Sarah Machado. (*EJSC*, 91, *et passim*; *MEAJB*, 326f; *MIPR*; *Wills*, 51)

MOSES, Priscilla. November 19, 1775, Charleston—September 19, 1866, Charleston. On September 20, 1793, this daughter of Myer Moses[1] was married to David Lopez[4] in Charleston. (*EOJCC*, 75; *MSGC*)

MOSES, Rachel.[1] 1777—April 1, 1848, Savannah. Daughter of Abraham Moses,[2] in June, 1791, she was married to Moses Cohen.[5] (*MSGC*)

MOSES, Rachel.[2] Youngest daughter of Myer Moses,[1] in 1780 she was killed by a cannonball during the seige of Charlestown. (*MEAJB*, 362; *PAJHS*, XII, 49)

MOSES, Mrs. Rachel.[1] On November 29, 1764, she was married to Tobias Moses in New York City. (*MSP*)

MOSES, Mrs. Rachel.[2] 1781—May 20, 1860. Niece of Mordecai Lyon, she was married to Joseph Moses.[3] (*MSGC*)

MOSES, Rebecca.[1] October 2, 1768—December 31, 1854, Charleston. Daughter of Myer Moses,[1] in 1787 she was married to Solomon Harby in Charleston. (*EOJCC*, 110; *MSGC*; *PAJHS*, XXXII, 36)

MOSES, Rebecca.[2] April 3, 1778, Easton, Pennsylvania—June 22, 1864, New York City. Daughter of Isaac Moses.[1] (*MSGC*)

MOSES, Reuben. 1765, London—May 26, 1850, Charleston. Son of Solomon Moses,[1] he was married to Hannah. (*MSGC*)

MOSES, Richea. July 30, 1771, New York City—May 7, 1848. Daughter of Isaac Moses,[1] she was married to Aaron Levy[3] in New York City on February 12, 1800. (*MSGC*; *PAJHS*, IV, 209; *Pool*, 384; *SIR*)

MOSES, Sally. December 4, 1787—April 28, 1859, New York City. Daughter of Isaac Moses.[1] (*MSGC*)

MOSES, Samuel.[1] In New York City in 1759. His wife was Teltz. (*PAJHS*, XXI, 79; *SIR*)

MOSES, Samuel.[2] In Newport with his family in 1774. (*Census*, 1774)

MOSES, Samuel.[3] In Salem, Massachusetts, with his family in 1790. It is doubtful that he was Jewish. (*Census A, Massachusetts*)

MOSES, Samuel.[4] In Warwick, Massachusetts, with his family in 1790. It is doubtful that he was Jewish. (*Census A, Massachusetts*)

MOSES, Sarah. March, 1792—December 18, 1869. Daughter of Solomon Moses,[1] she was married to Isaac Woolf on May 31, 1809. (*MSGC*)

MOSES, Simon. In New York City about 1715. (*MSP*)

MOSES, Solomon.[1] About 1734, Amsterdam—June 23, 1828, Charleston. About 1794 he arrived in Charleston and became a shopkeeper. His wife was Mary. (*EOJCC*, 44; *MSGC*; *Wills*, 51)

MOSES, Solomon.[2] September 7, 1774, New York City—September 22, 1857. Merchant son of Isaac Moses,[1] he was married to Rachel Gratz[2] on June 24, 1806. (*MSGC*; *PAJHS*, VI, 110, 154; *SIR*)

MOSES, Solomon, Jr. February 22, 1783, London—September 20, 1857, Charleston. Son of Solomon Moses,[1] he was married to Isabella Myers in November, 1815. (MSGC)

MOSES, Mrs. Teltz. Died November 28, 1767, New York City. Wife of Samuel Moses.[1] (SIR)

MOSES, Tobias. On November 29, 1764, he was married to Rachel Solomon, a widow, in New York City. (SIR)

MOSES, William.[1] From Wales. On May 3, 1750, he was married to Elizabeth Bland in South Carolina. It is doubtful that he was Jewish. (SCHGM, XXIII, 134)

MOSES, William.[2] Born November 5, 1753, South Carolina. This son of William Moses[1] was buried on October 26, 1758. It is doubtful that he was Jewish. (SCHGM, XXIII, 135)

MOSHE, Rabbi ("Ribbi"). In 1770 he is mentioned in Philadelphia as the leader of newcomers who attempted to organize a separate Ashkenazic congregation. A scribe, he wrote Torah Scrolls. (EJRF, 1)

MOSLEY, Lewis. In New York City in 1785. It is doubtful that he was Jewish. (SIR)

MOSS, Jacob. 1793—November 2, 1830, Philadelphia. In 1800 he was in Philadelphia. On August 19, 1812, he was married there to Catherine Lyons. (MSGC)

MOSS. An infant child of John Moss, he died in the yellow fever epidemic of 1798 in Philadelphia. (WW, 347)

MOSS, John. About 1771, London—April 5, 1847, Philadelphia. In 1796 he came to America, and began as a glass engraver and merchant shipper. A pioneer in the use of coal as fuel, he was active in promoting inland navigation and turnpike systems, and in banking and insurance ventures. A member of the boards of many corporations, he served as steward of the St. George Society, as chairman of the Philadelphia Committee of Correspondence in the Damascus Affair, and as a member of the Philadelphia City Council. During the War of 1812 he was in the militia. In the Philadelphia community he was a prominent Mason as well as an outstanding Jew. (GBMIP; MIPR; Morais, 51, et passim; PAJHS, I, 89; II, 171f; XVIII, 210; UJE, VIII, 18; WW, 184, et passim)

MOSS, Merriam (Miriam/Mary). April 12, 1800, Philadelphia—January 14, 1879, Paris. Daughter of John Moss, she was married to Henry Lazarus in Philadelphia on October 7, 1835. (MSGC; WW, 347)

MOSS, Sarah. December 9, 1797, Philadelphia—January 17, 1848, Philadelphia. Daughter of John Moss, on January 16, 1822, she was married to Isaac Phillips in Philadelphia. (MSGC; PAJHS, XVI, 195)

MOTTA, Emanuel de la. January 5/November 2, 1760, Spanish West Indies—May 15, 1821, Charleston. This merchant son of Isaac de la Motta, Jr., lived in Savannah and in South Carolina. He served with Pulaski in the Revolution. Later he became the head of the Supreme Masonic Council for Northern Jurisdiction and organized its Southern equivalent. In 1786 he was hazzan for Congregation Mikveh Israel in Savannah. On December 27, 1787, he was married to Judith Cantor, his niece, in Charleston. (JE, IX, 100; JRMP; MISR; PAJHS, XVII, 102f; XIX, 37, et passim; Reznikoff, 95, et passim; UJE, VIII, 23)

MOTTA. There are three additional members (not listed below) of Emanuel de la Motta's family, who were in Charleston in 1800. (Census B, South Carolina)

MOTTA, Isaac de la.[1] September 8, 1750—June 16, 1802, Charleston. On June 7, 1797, he was married to Sarah Cantor in Savannah. (EJSC, 138; EOJCC, 56; MSGC)

MOTTA, family of Isaac de la.[1] In Charleston in 1800. (Census B, South Carolina)

MOTTA, Isaac de la.[2] January 16, 1791, Savannah—1793, Savannah. Son of Emanuel de la Motta. (SRB)

MOTTA, Isaac de la, Jr. 1726—December 12, 1794, Charleston. On July 9, 1785, he arrived in Savannah from Jamaica but left soon for Charleston. His wife was Sarah. (MSGC; SRB)

MOTTA, J. A. About 1784, Curaçao—February 25, 1839, Charleston. He came to Charleston in 1800. (*MSP*)

MOTTA, Jacob de la.[1] Fought under de Kalb and Pulaski in the Revolution. About 1780 he was in Georgia and South Carolina. (*EJSC*, 84, *et passim*; *PAJHS*, XII, 56; XVII, 103; *UJE*, VIII, 23)

MOTTA, Jacob de la.[2] February 24, 1789, Savannah—February 13, 1845, Charleston. This son of Emanuel de la Motta graduated in Philadelphia as a physician and served in the War of 1812 as a surgeon in the regular army. In 1824 he was elected secretary of the Medical Society of Charleston, and was a corresponding member of the Royal Academy of Medicine in Paris. A highly cultured man, he was interested in philosophy, political science, and natural history, and published many articles of a scientific nature. Prominent in Jewish community activities, he served as minister to the Congregations in Savannah and Charleston. In addition he participated in politics and in general community activities. He owned an apothecary shop. On April 29, 1835, he was married to Charlotte Lazarus. (*EJSC*, 141, *et passim*; *EOJCC*, 56; *PAJHS*, III, 133f; IV, 97, 209; *Reznikoff*, 69, *et passim*; *UJE*, VIII, 23; *Wills*, 39)

MOTTA, Leonora de la. Probably born before 1800. Daughter of Isaac de la Motta,[1] she was married to Levi S. de Lyon in 1818. (*MSGC*)

MOTTA, Moses de la. 1755—December 19, 1800, Charleston. Son of Isaac de la Motta, Jr. (*MSGC*)

MOTTA, Rachel de la. Born about 1768, St. Croix. Daughter of Isaac de la Motta, Jr., in 1784 she was married to Abraham de Pass in Charleston. (*EJMC*, 5)

MOTTA, Rebecca de la. 1798—February 16, 1829. Daughter of Isaac de la Motta.[1] (*MSGC*)

MOTTA, Sarah de la.[1] 1753, St. Croix—December, 1811, Savannah. Daughter of Isaac de la Motta, Jr., she was married to Levi Sheftall[2] on May 24, 1768, in St. Croix (*SRB*; *Wills*, 78)

MOTTA, Sarah de la.[2] Born November 1, 1792, Savannah. Daughter of Emanuel de la Motta, she was married to Abraham Sheftall in 1817. (*SRB*)

MOTTA, Mrs. Sarah de la. 1728—August 18, 1790, Savannah. Wife of Isaac de la Motta, Jr. (*MSGC*)

MUDAHY, Haim. From Constantinople. In 1761 he was an itinerant money collector in New York City. There is noted, however, a Mudhay who came from London. (*POFNW*, 397; *WW*, 55)

MUNEZ, Joseph. Died about 1704, New York City. It is doubtful that he was Jewish. (*NYHSW*, XVI, 43)

MUNEZ, Samuel. In New York City about 1704. It is doubtful that he was Jewish. (*NYHSW*, XVI, 43)

MUSQUETO, Jacob. In 1768 he came from St. Eustatia to New York; he then left for Philadelphia, where he sought passage to Barbados. (*WW*, 55)

MUSQUITA, Abraham Pereira. In 1743 he was a merchant and part owner of a privateer in Newport. Cf. Abraham Bueno de Mesquita.[2] (*JNEB*, 12)

MUSQUITTO, Jacob. In Philadelphia in 1792. (*PAJHS*, XX, 99; *MIPR*)

MUSSIUS, Abraham. In Charlestown in 1732. It is doubtful that he was Jewish. (*ELHS*)

MYER, Jacob. In 1754 he served in the French and Indian War as a private under Washington. It is highly doubtful that he was Jewish. (*JPP*, 16; *PAJHS*, II, 181; XX, 90)

MYER, Soloman. An Indian trader. (*Johnson*, 998)

MYERS. Born December, 1767, Quebec. Stillborn child of Hyam Myers. (*MEAJA*, 223)

MYERS, Mr.[1] In 1775 he was called "Jew butcher" in Newport. His wife was Rachel. (*Coldoc*, 273; *HAB*, 133)

MYERS, Mr.[2] Died November, 1785, Charleston. (*MSP*)

MYERS, A. Son of Myer Benjamin. (*MSGC*)

MYERS, Aaron. December 27, 1774, New York City—August 23, 1775, New York City. Son of Myer Myers.[1] (PAJHS, XXXIII, 210; Pool, 503; SIR)

MYERS, Abraham. In Georgetown, South Carolina, in 1796 he was admitted to the bar. Although he is noted also in Richmond, New York City, and Charleston before 1800, these references may not pertain to the same individual. (ELJR, 78, 83; EJSC, 128, et passim; SIR)

MYERS, Abram.[1] Born November 8, 1788, died an infant. Son of Moses Myers.[1] (MSGC)

MYERS, Abram.[2] Son of Mordecai Myers,[1] he was married to Belle Nathans. (MSGC)

MYERS, Abram.[3] January 31, 1800—November 18, 1821. Son of Moses Myers.[1] (MSGC)

MYERS, Adelaine. June 28, 1791—January 16, 1832. Daughter of Moses Myers. (MSGC)

MYERS, Andrew. In 1779 he was an ensign in the Pennsylvania militia. It is doubtful that he was Jewish. (JRMP)

MYERS, Asher. Before 1725—May 7, 1789. By 1746 this son of Solomon Myers was in New York City, where he became a freeman and, on September 30, 1755, was elected constable. He was a coppersmith, a brazier, and a merchant. His wife was Caty Mears. (MEAJA, 166, 172; MEAJB, 157, 397; MCCCNY, VI, 33; PAJHS, VI, 102; XXI, 51, et passim; XXVII, 151, et passim; XXXIII, 210; SIR)

MYERS, Augusta. December 28, 1797, Norfolk—April 26, 1876, New York City. Daughter of Moses Myers,[1] she was married to Philip I. Cohen on January 25, 1826. (MHM, XVIII, 370)

MYERS, Belle. 1771—December 26, 1855, Charleston. Daughter of Mordecai Myers,[1] she was married to Moses Sarzedas. (MSGC)

MYERS, Benjamin.[1] 1755—December 11, 1851, Pleasantville, New York. Son of Myer Benjamin, he lived in New York City, Richmond, and Baltimore. By 1795 he was the first known Jew in Nashville. His first wife was Hannah Hays; his second wife was Rachel Hays on March 24, 1804. (Coldoc, 273f; MSGC)

MYERS, Benjamin.[2] May 2, 1778—September 1, 1835, New York City. Son of Myer Myers.[1] (MSGC)

MYERS, Benjamin M. From about 1776 until 1786 he was shohet and bodek for Congregation Shearith Israel in New York City. Cf. above. (PAJHS, XXI, 213f)

MYERS, Bilah (Belle). Born February 28, 1764, New York City. Daughter of Hyam Myers, she was married to Asher Samuel Levy on October 3, 1804, in New York City. (MSGC; SIR)

MYERS, Catherine. February 12, 1798—June 1, 1874. Daughter of Moses M. Myers,[3] she operated a coeducational school in Richmond. (ELJR, 57, et passim; MSGC)

MYERS, Mrs. Catherine. Wife of Tobias Myers, she lived in Berkeley County, South Carolina, about 1797. It is highly doubtful that she was Jewish. (WAJA)

MYERS, Christian. In Newport in 1755 he was a Mason who may have been converted to Christianity. (PAJHS, XIX, 19; XXVII, 416)

MYERS, Cohen. Son of Mordecai Myers.[1] (MSGC)

MYERS, Faybes. February 9, 1760, New York City—December 15, 1760, New York City. Son of Naphtali Hart Myers. (Pool, 501; SIR)

MYERS, Frederick, March 11, 1796—June 16, 1832. Son of Moses Myers,[1] he was in business in Norfolk. (MSGC; Wills, 23f)

MYERS, Gabriel. April 3, 1768, New York City—probably September 11, 1770, New York City. Son of Asher Myers. (PAJHS, XXVII, 154; Pool, 502; SIR)

MYERS, Harriet. October 23, 1800, Richmond—March 15, 1882, Richmond. Daughter of Moses Myers,[3] she operated a coeducational school. (ELJR, 57, et passim; MSGC)

MYERS, Hessie. Died February, 1876. Daughter of Mordecai Myers.[1] (MSGC)

MYERS, Henry. Sometime between 1740 and 1760 he was a merchant in Newport. It is doubtful that he was Jewish. (*JNEB*, 8)

MYERS, Hyam. Died about 1801. In 1750 he was a shohet and butcher in New York City, and was naturalized there on January 16, 1759. He then became a merchant and traded exclusively with merchants in Canada. In 1763 he settled in Montreal, but returned to New York City after the Revolution. His wife was Rachel Louzada. (*Hugsoc*, XXIV, 36; *MEAJA*, 211, *et passim*; *MEAJB*, 193, 204; *MSGC*; SIR)

MYERS, Isaac.[1] Fought in the French and Indian War. It is doubtful that he was Jewish. (*UJE*, IX, 622)

MYERS, Isaac.[2] Son of Mordecai Myers.[1] (*MSGC*)

MYERS, Israel. In 1782 he was in Philadelphia. In 1802 he was an import inspector in Charleston. (*EJSC*, 138, 143; *MIPR*; *WW*, 419)

MYERS, Jacob.[1] Born June 24, 1762, New York City. Son of Hyam Myers, he was married to Esther. (*MSGC*; *PAJHS*, XXVII, 152; SIR)

MYERS, Jacob.[2] Died about 1783, Philadelphia. Son of Myer Myers.[1] (*MIPR*; *MSGC*)

MYERS, Jacob.[3] In 1770 he was a merchant in New York City. Cf. above. (*PAJHS*, IV, 89)

MYERS, Jacob.[4] An inkeeper in Baltimore in 1756. It is doubtful that he was Jewish. (*Blum*, 3; *PAJHS*, XXII, 191f)

MYERS, Jacob.[5] In 1793 he was a leather worker in Philadelphia. (*WW*, 184)

MYERS, Jacob.[6] In October, 1793, he inaugurated passenger service between Cincinnati and Pittsburgh. It is doubtful that he was Jewish. (*Byars*, 245f)

MYERS, Jacob.[7] Born Georgetown, South Carolina—died July 14, 1826, Sand Hills, Georgia. Son of Mordecai Myers,[1] he was a postmaster in Georgetown. On July 31, 1806, he was married to Miriam Etting. (*EJSC*, 138, 242f; *MSGC*)

MYERS, Jacob.[8] In Tyringham, Massachusetts, with his family in 1790. It is doubtful that he was Jewish. (*Census A, Massachusetts*)

MYERS, Jacob.[9] In Newport with his family in 1790. It is doubtful that he was Jewish. (*Census A, Rhode Island*)

MYERS, Jacob.[10] Son of Tobias Myers, he was in Berkeley County, South Carolina, about 1797. It is highly doubtful that he was Jewish. (WAJA)

MYERS, James J. In New York City in 1797. It is highly doubtful that he was Jewish. (*NYHSW*, XV, 94)

MYERS, Jochebed. Born June 21, 1775, New York City. Daughter of Asher Myers. (*PAJHS*, XXXIII, 204; SIR)

MYERS, John.[1] September 15, 1787—November 27, 1830. In 1809 this son of Moses Myers[1] entered his father's business in Norfolk. About 1828 he was appointed deputy collector of customs in Norfolk. He fought in the War of 1812. (*MSGC*; *PAJHS*, XII, 164; *Wills*, 24f)

MYERS, John.[2] Son of Tobias Myers, he was in Berkeley County, South Carolina, about 1797. It is highly doubtful that he was Jewish. (WAJA)

MYERS, Joseph.[1] September 12, 1758—September 10, 1817. Son of Myer Myers.[1] (*MSGC*)

MYERS, Joseph.[2] October 11, 1758, New York City—before 1764. Son of Asher Myers. (*PAJHS*, XXVII, 151)

MYERS, Joseph.[3] Born May 24, 1764, New York City. Son of Asher Myers. (*PAJHS*, XXXIII, 203; SIR)

MYERS, Joseph, Sr.[4] In Philadelphia in 1782. (*MIPR*)

MYERS, Joseph.[5] In Charlestown in 1780. (*EJSC*, 90, *et passim*)

MYERS, Joseph.[6] In New York City in 1750. (*PAJHS*, XXI, 63)

MYERS, Joseph.[7] Son of Solomon Myers.[1] (*MSGC*)

MYERS, Joseph A. Died September 29, 1827, Richmond. In 1783 he was in New York City. From 1787 on he was active in the Masons in Richmond. (*PAJHS*, XIX, 62, 69; XXI, 142)

MYERS, Joseph M. In 1781 he was active in the Masons in Philadelphia. He lived also in Charleston, Norfolk, Richmond, Baltimore, and New York City. During the Revolution he was loyal to the English. About 1795 he left for Europe. (*PAJHS*, XIX, 41, *et passim*; XXVII, 253)

MYERS, Judah.[1] January 3, 1761, New York City—June 12, 1831, Richmond. Son of Asher Myers, he was married to Sarah Lopez Isaacs on October 21, 1821, in Richmond. (*MSGC*; *PAJHS*, XXXIII, 203, 206; *SIR*)

MYERS, Judah.[2] February 2, 1768, New York City—June 15, 1768, New York City. Son of Myer Myers.[1] (*PAJHS*, XXVII, 153; *SIR*)

MYERS, Judith. May 8, 1762, New York City—January 9, 1796, Richmond. Daughter of Myer Myers,[1] she was married to Jacob Mordecai on June 16, 1784, and lived most of her married life in Warrenton, North Carolina. (*MEAJB*, 192f; *MSGC*; *PAJHS*, VI, 41f, 110; *SIR*)

MYERS, Mrs. Judith. Died February 19, 1773, New York City. Wife of Solomon Myers,[1] she was in New York City in 1740. (*PAJHS*, XXI, 46, *et passim*; *SIR*)

MYERS, Levi. In Richmond in 1791. (*ELJR*, 281)

MYERS, Levy.[1] Born March 5, 1772, New York City. Son of Asher Myers. (*PAJHS*, XXVII, 51, 84; XXXIII, 204)

MYERS, Levy.[2] Died September 22, 1827, Charleston. This son of Mordecai Myers[1] was a physician who was a member of the legislature of South Carolina in 1796. Prior to 1800 he was appointed apothecary-general of South Carolina and held that position until his death. He operated an apothecary's shop in Georgetown, South Carolina. On February 12, 1794, he was married to Frances Minis. (*EJMC*, 6; *EJSC*, 128, *et passim*; *MSGC*; *MSP*; *UJE*, IX, 664f)

MYERS, Manuel. Died May 21, 1799, New York City. This son of Myer Myers came to America from Germany about 1750. On July 3, 1759, he became a freeman of New York City, where he lived all his life as a shopkeeper, except for the time he spent in Stamford, Connecticut, during the British occupation of New York City. Myers' first wife was Miriam Pinto on May 31, 1759; his second wife was Judith Jacobs. (*Coldoc*, 163, *et passim*; *MSGC*; *PAJHS*, VI, 102; *Pool*, 45, *et passim*; *SIR*)

MYERS, (Marie?). Born before 1800. Daughter of Hyam Myers, she was probably the wife of Jacob Henry. (*MSGC*; *MSP*)

MYERS, Michael. Born October 25, 1763, Sussex, England. This son of Solomon Myers came to America before 1800 and lived in Charleston and Richmond. On October 10, 1810, he was married to Rachel Phillips. (*Census B*, *South Carolina*; *EJSC*, 138; *MSP*; *PAJHS*, XIX, 62)

MYERS, Miriam. December 27, 1774, New York City—August 16, 1775, New York City. Daughter of Myer Myers.[1] (*PAJHS*, XXXIII, 210; *Pool*, 503; *SIR*)

MYERS, Mordecai.[1] Born 1727—December 16, 1788, Georgetown, South Carolina. During the Revolution he was purveyor for General Francis Marion. He became the first postmaster in Georgetown. His wife was Esther Cohen.[2] (*EJSC*, 45, *et passim*; *EVJC*; *MEAJB*, 267f, 422; *MSGC*)

MYERS, Mordecai.[2] May 31, 1776, Newport—1871. This son of Myer Benjamin grew up in New York City, where he was very active in the Democratic party. In 1828, and again from 1831 through 1834, he was a member of the assembly of New York City, and was also a member of the New York state legislature. In 1851 and 1854 he was mayor of Schenectady. During the War of 1812 he attained the rank of major. A prominent Mason, in 1830 he declined the office of grand master. He apparently had little to do with the Jewish community after his intermarriage to Charlotte Bailey on January 24, 1814. (*MEAJB*, 327; *Memoirs* I, 50-75; *MSGC*; *PAJHS*, XII, 164; XIX, 32, *et passim*)

MYERS, Mordecai.[3] November 9, 1794—February 21, 1865. Son of Levy Myers.[2] he was married to (Sarah) Henrietta Cohen about 1820. (*MSGC*)

MYERS, Mordecai.[4] Fought in the Revolution. 1791 he lived in Richmond. Beginning about 1825 he served in the Georgia legislature for five years. (PAJHS, IV, 22; XII, 163f)

MYERS, Moses.[1] About 1752, New York City—July 8, 1835, Norfolk. An active major in the Virginia militia, this son of Hyam Myers was a wealthy merchant who was elected to the presidency of the common council of Norfolk. With his business partners, Isaac Moses and Samuel Myers, he had a large trading company in New York City and Amsterdam. The economic upheavals after the Revolution led to his bankruptcy in 1785, and the partnership was dissolved in January, 1786. In 1787 he settled in Norfolk, where he was superintendent of the Norfolk Bank of Richmond. He served as consular agent for France, the Batavian Republic, and the Scandinavian countries. On March 22, 1787, he was married to Eliza Judd. (MEAJB, 192, et passim; MSGC; PAJHS, XI, 72; XII, 164; XVII, 82, et passim; XX, 17, 103; Wills, 24f)

MYERS, Moses.[2] Born August 23, 1762, New York City. Son of Asher Myers. (PAJHS, XXVII, 152; SIR)

MYERS, Moses.[3] January 18, 1771, New York City—September 9, 1860, Richmond. Son of Myer Myers,[1] he was married to Sally Hays on September 21, 1796. About 1798 he settled in Richmond, where he was a vendue master. (ELJR, 22, et passim; PAJHS, XI, 155; SIR)

MYERS, Moses.[4] February 19, 1772, Georgetown, South Carolina—June 6, 1821, Charleston. In 1793 this son of Mordecai Myers[1] was admitted to the bar. From 1800 until 1817 he was clerk of the Court of General Sessions and Common Pleas in South Carolina. In 1806 he was prothonotary of Georgetown. His wife was Hannah Polock.[2] (EJSC, 128, et passim; MSGC; SCHGM, XLVIII, 200; UJE, IX, 664)

MYERS, Moses.[5] Born December 20, 1794, died an infant. Son of Moses Myers.[1] (MSGC)

MYERS, Moses A. In 1782 he was in New York City. In 1806 he was a merchant in Richmond. (ELJR, 82; PAJHS, VI, 131; XXVII, 42, 462)

MYERS, Moses H. In Philadelphia in 1782. (Morais, 15)

MYERS, Myer.[1] 1723, New York City—1795. This son of Solomon Myers was of Dutch descent. One of the most distinguished silversmiths of colonial New York, his work appeared in many well known museums, churches, and synagogues. A prominent merchant as well, he was involved in land speculation. On April 29, 1746, he became a freeman in New York City. During the Revolution he fled to Norwalk, Connecticut, while the British occupied New York City; he lived also in Philadelphia. He was a Mason. Myers' first wife was Elkaleh Cohen;[1] his second wife was Joyce Mears on March 18, 1767. (MEAJA, 99, et passim; MEAJB, 193, 397; MSGC; PAJHS, I, 19; IV, 195; VI, 130f; XI, 92, 154f; XVIII, 105; XIX, 29f; Rosenbaum; SIR)

MYERS, Myer.[2] Died April 5, 1791, Aux Cayes, Haiti. Merchant son of Hyam Myers. (MSGC; NYHSW, XIV, 356)

MYERS, Myer.[3] June 18, 1793—November 8, 1877. Son of Moses Myers,[1] he was a merchant in Norfolk. In September, 1826, he was married to Judith Marx. (MSGC; Wills, 25, 29)

MYERS, Naphtali Hart. About 1711—October 18, 1788, London. From about 1746 on he was a merchant in New York City, Newport, Philadelphia, and Easton. In 1756 he was president of Congregation Shearith Israel in New York City. In 1771 he returned to London, where he was prominent in the Jewish community and served as head of the Great Synagogue there. He initiated action to expel Jewish criminals from England. His wife was Hester Moses. (Arts & Crafts, 266f; JNEB, 8; MEAJB, 49; PAJHS, II, 82; XII, 167; XXI, 49, et passim; Roth, 129, et passim; Trachtenberg, 29)

MYERS, Nathan. Born February 18, 1774, New York City. Son of Asher Myers, he may have been the Colonel Nathan Myers who served in the War of 1812. (PAJHS, IV, 90; XXXIII, 210; SIR)

MYERS, Rachel.[1] 1738—September 29, 1810, Boston. Daughter of Solomon Myers,[1] she was married to Moses Michael Hays on August 13, 1766, in New York City. (*MSGC; PAJHS*, XXVII, 195; *SIR*)

MYERS, Rachel.[2] Daughter of Mordecai Myers.[1] (*MSGC*)

MYERS, Mrs. Rachel.[1] Wife of Hyam Myers, she was buried in New York City on February 28, 1790. (*Pool*, 503; *SIR*)

MYERS, Mrs. Rachel.[2] October 5, 1786, Newport—October 5, 1870, Charleston. (*EOJCC*, 67)

MYERS, Mrs. Rachel.[3] About 1745—March 30, 1801, New York City. Wife of Mr. Myers, the butcher, she was a loyalist who went to New York City from Newport in 1781. (*Coldoc*, 273f)

MYERS, Rebecca.[1] Daughter of Solomon Myers,[1] she was married to Solomon Marache on August 13, 1766, in New York City. (*MSGC; SIR*)

MYERS, Rebecca.[2] April 26, 1776, Norwalk, Connecticut—October 1, 1863, Richmond. Daughter of Myer Myers,[1] she was married to Jacob Mordecai. She helped her husband operate his school in Warrenton, North Carolina. (*ELJR*, 49, *et passim*; *MSGC; PAJHS*, IV, 23; VI, 42, 45; *SIR*)

MYERS, Ritzel. June 13, 1760, New York City—August 8, 1761, New York City. Daughter of Myer Myers.[1] (*PAJHS*, XXXIII, 210; *SIR*)

MYERS, Ritzel (Richea). June 10, 1769, New York City—March 21, 1837, Richmond. Daughter of Myer Myers,[1] she was married to Joseph Marx. (*ELJR*, 47, 58; *MSGC; PAJHS*, XXXIII, 210; *SIR*)

MYERS, Samson A. 1766, New York City—1798, New York City. Son of Asher Myers, he was a coppersmith. (*PAJHS*, XXV, 123; *SIR*)

MYERS, Samson Mears. December 5, 1772, New York City—August 5, 1805. Son of Myer Myers.[1] (*PAJHS*, XI, 155; *SIR*)

MYERS, Samuel.[1] A shopkeeper in New York City, he became a freeman on October 6, 1730. (*PAJHS*, VI, 102; XXI, 16, *et passim*)

MYERS, Samuel.[2] Son of Asher Myers, he was in Philadelphia in 1786. (*MIPR*)

MYERS, Samuel.[3] April 16, 1755, New York City—August 22, 1836, Richmond. This son of Myer Myers[1] served in the Virginia line during the Revolution. During the war he was also a partner in the firm of Isaac Moses & Company, which acquired great wealth by running the English blockade. In 1789 he was in business in Petersburg, Virginia; he lived also in Norfolk, Petersburg, and settled finally in Richmond, where he became a prominent merchant and alderman by 1800. He was one of the founders of the Richmond Amicable Society. Myers' first wife was Sarah Judah[3] on October 22, 1794; his second wife was Judith Hays on September 27, 1796. (*Coldoc*, 51, *et passim*; *ELJR*, 36, *et passim*; Ginsberg, 7f; *MEAJB*, 147, *et passim*; *MSGC; PAJHS*, XI, 72; XIX, 41, *et passim*; XX, 99, 102; *UJE*, IX, 159; X, 427)

MYERS, Samuel.[4] February 24, 1790, Norfolk—February 21, 1829, Richmond. Son of Moses Myers,[1] he was a merchant who was married to Louisa Marx in May, 1816. (*Coldoc*, 51, *et passim*; *ELJR*, 307; *Wills*, 24f)

MYERS, Samuel Hays. January 1, 1799, Richmond—October 2, 1849, Richmond. This son of Samuel Myers[3] was admitted to the bar of Richmond to practice as an attorney. A prominent Mason, he served also as alderman in Richmond. In 1824 he was made a lieutenant in the Virginia state militia. He aided in the protest in behalf of the persecuted Damascus Jews. On November 21, 1828, he was married to Eliza Mordecai. (*ELJR*, 49, *et passim*; *MSGC; PAJHS*, IV, 24, 27; VI, 48; VIII, 145)

MYERS, Sarah.[1] Born March 29, 1770, New York City. Daughter of Asher Myers. (*PAJHS*, XXXIII, 210; *SIR*)

MYERS, Sarah.[2] December 2, 1795, Nashville—August 13, 1864, New York City. Daughter of Benjamin Myers,[1] on March 23, 1814, she was married to Benjamin Etting Hays in New York City. (*MSGC; PAJHS*, XXVII, 77, 330)

MYERS, Sarah.[3] Daughter of Mordecai Myers.[1] (*MSGC*)

MYERS, Sarah.[4] Born before 1800. Daughter of Solomon Myers.[1] (*MSGC*)

MYERS, Simeon. Born January 4, 1763, New York City. Son of Naphtali Hart Myers, he was married to Deborah Salomon in August, 1804. (*MSGC*; *PAJHS*, XVIII, 108; *SIR*)

MYERS, Sloe. 1728, New York City—April 5, 1811, New York City. Daughter of Solomon Myers,[1] she was married to Hayman Levy on May 15, 1750. (*MSGC*; *PAJHS*, IV, 210f; *Pool*, 324; *SIR*)

MYERS, Solomon.[1] This son of Myer Myers became a freeman of New York City about 1723 and was naturalized in 1723 and 1740. A merchant, he was elected constable there in 1731. He served also in the militia. (*MCCCNY*, IV, 71; *MSGC*; *PAJHS*, II, 92; VI, 101, 105f; XXI, 8, *et passim*)

MYERS, Solomon.[2] Born before 1800. Son of Mordecai Myers.[1] (*MSGC*)

MYERS, Solomon Aaron. A Mason in Newport about 1790. (*PAJHS*, XIX, 18f, 21)

MYERS, Solomon Asher. Son of Asher Myers. (*MSGC*)

MYERS, Solomon Mears. November 30, 1753—November 13, 1791. Son of Myer Myers, in 1784 he was in Philadelphia. (*MSGC*; *PAJHS*, XIX, 41f, 44; XXXIII, 210)

MYERS, Tobias. Died about 1797, Berkeley County, South Carolina. Husband of Catherine. It is highly doubtful that he was Jewish. (*WAJA*)

MYERS, William. Son of Tobias Myers, he was in Berkeley County, South Carolina, about 1797. It is highly doubtful that he was Jewish. (*WAJA*)

N

NAAR, Joshua. 1768—March 10, 1834, New York City. In Philadelphia in 1792. On January 20, 1800, he was married to Sarah Cohen d'Azevedo in St. Thomas. (*MIPR*; *MSGC*)

NAAR, Moses. In Philadelphia in 1740. (*PAJHS*, I, 24)

NABARO, David. In New York City in 1750. (*PAJHS*, XXI, 63)

NALVERDE, Eliahu. (May be a misreading for Valverde.) In Philadelphia about 1780. Cf. Elias Valverde. (*MIPR*)

NAPTALY, Mr. In New York City in 1728. (*PAJHS*, XXVII, 1)

NAPHTALY(I), Abraham. Son of Isaac Naphtaly, he was in Newport in 1695. (*JNEB*, 7)

NAPHTALY, Isaac. Died before 1721. A butcher and merchant, by 1695 he was a shohet in Newport. On December 4, 1705, he was made a freeman of New York City. He left America because of his debts and died abroad. (*AJAM*, III, 9; *FEAJ*, 68; *Gutstein*, 39; *JNEB*, 7; *MEAJA*, 52f; *PAJHS*, VI, 101)

NAPHTALY, Miriam. 1688—September 9, 1733. She was married to Moses Lopez da Fonseca in New York City. (*Emanuel*, 315f; *PAJHS*, XVIII, 97; *Pool*, 205f)

NAPHTALY, Rachel. May have been the wife of Isaac Naphtaly. In 1728 she was in New York City. (*JNEB*, 7; *PAJHS*, XXI, 10, 20)

NAPHTALY, Samuel. In Philadelphia in 1786. (*MIPR*)

NARE, Solomon. Cf. Solomon Bares. (*PAJHS*, XIII, 3)

NASSY, David de Isaac Cohen. Born in Surinam of Portuguese Dutch descent. In 1792 he arrived in Philadelphia and practiced medicine. He disagreed with Benjamin Rush on the nature and treatment of disease. He was the second Jew elected to the American Philosophical Society. In 1796 he returned to Surinam and entered business, but maintained there his leadership of the Jewish community in Holland. He wrote *Lettre Politico-Theologico-Morale Sur Les Juifs* in which he discussed issues relating to Jews and Christians with an implicit plea for the emancipation of the Jews in Holland. (*Coldoc*, 465f; *MIPR*; *PAJHS*, III, 127f; IV, 4f; IX, 132, 134; XVIII, 188; *UJE*, VIII, 103; *WW*, 193f)

NASY, David. In 1679 he sailed from Barbados for Newport. (*Gutstein*, 341)

NATHAN. Two additional daughters of Moses Nathan.[1] (*MSGC*)

NATHAN. Born before 1800. Son of Moses Nathan.[1] He may be one of the sons of Moses Nathan listed below. (*MIPR*)

NATHAN, Mr. On February 1, 1775, he came to Savannah from Polmetalligo, South Carolina, with his wife. (*SRB*)

NATHAN, Mrs. Died February 3, 1775, Savannah. Wife of Mr. Nathan. (*SRB*)

NATHAN, Abraham.[1] A shipowner, he was in Charleston in 1785. He was murdered at sea. (*EJSC*, 280; *Reznikoff*, 51)

NATHAN, Abraham.[2] Son of Isaiah Nathan, he was married to Henrietta Russell. In 1787 he was in New Bern, North Carolina. (*MSP*)

NATHAN, Benjamin. In 1764 he was in Lancaster in business with Joseph Simon. (*Byars*, 55; *Essays*, 104, *et passim*; *JRMP*)

NATHAN, David.[1] In Charleston in 1800. (*EJSC*, 138)

NATHAN, David.[2] In New York City in 1776. (*Schappes*, 52)

NATHAN, David.[3] February 20, 1793—1817. Son of Moses Nathan.[1] Cf. David Levy.[6] (*MSGC*)

NATHAN, David.[4] August 13, 1793—May 20, 1878. Son of Isaiah Nathan,[1] on May 11, 1830, he was married to Sarah M. Russell. (*MSGC*)

NATHAN, Deborah. 1777—January 26, 1850, New York City. Daughter of Joseph Nathan.[1] (*Pool*, 422f; *SIR*)

NATHAN, Donata. For a short time in 1792 he was in Norfolk. About 1800 he was known to have supplied materials to the national government. (*JRMP*; *MSP*)

NATHAN, Esther. Born May 21, 1769, Philadelphia. Daughter of Lyon Nathan, she was married to Dr. Bingley. (*MSGC*)

NATHAN, Isaac. Born about 1794, Philadelphia. Son of Moses Nathan.[1] (*MIPR*)

NATHAN, Isabella. Died March, 1861. Daughter of Moses Nathan.[1] (*MSGC*)

NATHAN, Isaiah.[1] About 1766—December 8, 1843. A moderately successful merchant, he was active in the Democratic party. In 1792 he was in Philadelphia. Nathan's first wife was Sarah Abrahams whom he married in a religious ceremony on February 4, 1802; his second wife was Judith Russell on March 4, 1807. (*MIPR*; *MSGC*; *WW*, 226, *et passim*)

NATHAN, Isaiah.[2] Born March 25, 1795, Philadelphia. Son of Moses Nathan. Cf. Isaiah Levy.[2] (*MSGC*)

NATHAN, Jacob.[1] In Philadelphia in 1784. (*MIPR*)

NATHAN, J(acob).[2] In 1792 he came to America from Haiti and St. Domingo. After a short stay in Virginia, he left America. (*MSP*)

NATHAN, Jacob.[3] August 22, 1790—January 28, 1866. Son of Moses Nathan.[1] Cf. Jacob Levy.[4] (*MSGC*)

NATHAN, Jacob.[4] 1796—February 23, 1866. Son of Isaiah Nathan.[1] (*MSGC*)

NATHAN, Mrs. Jane (Jean). Died April 19, 1823, New York City. A convert to Judaism, she survived her husband, Joseph Nathan,[1] for twenty-five years. (*Pool*, 276, 422f, 500)

NATHAN, Joseph.[1] About 1738—October 1, 1798, New York City. A merchant, he served in the Revolutionary army. His wife was Jane. (*PAJHS*, XXV, 123; *Pool*, 275, *et passim*)

NATHAN, Joseph.[2] He came to America from Germany. By 1786 he was a merchant in New York City, trading with Isaac Moses. (*Pool*, 275)

NATHAN, Joseph.[3] Born about 1795. Son of Moses Nathan.[1] (*MSGC*)

NATHAN, Josiah. In Philadelphia in 1800. Cf. Isaiah Nathan.[1] (*MIPR*)

NATHAN, Leah. June 30, 1760, Philadelphia—February 13, 1854, New York City. Daughter of Lyon Nathan, on November 4, 1778, she was married to Jacob Naphtali Hart. (*MSGC*; *Pool*, 412)

NATHAN, Levi. March 14, 1793, Philadelphia—August 2, 1867. Son of Moses Nathan. (*MIPR*; *MSGC*)

NATHAN, Lyon. In 1750 he was in New York City. By 1773 he was an Indian trader in Pennsylvania and was naturalized in Reading. About 1782 he was a shammas of Congregation Mikveh Israel in Philadelphia. On September 2, 1760, he was married to Caroline Webb, probably a gentile who was converted to Judaism. (*Hugsoc*, XXIV, 88; *JRMP*; *MIPR*; *PA*, II, 216, 627; *PAJHS*, I, 20; XXI, 61, 64)

NATHAN, Maria. Died 1820. Daughter of Moses Nathan.[1] (*MSGC*)

NATHAN, Mordecai. In 1711 he was in New York City. In 1715 he owned land which he may have farmed in South Carolina. (*EJSC*, 22; *PAJHS*, III, 85; XII, 42)

NATHAN, Moses.[1] 1749—February 24, 1815, Philadelphia. By 1771 he was in Philadelphia; he became a shopkeeper and merchant in Easton. On January 11, 1792, he was married to Betty Hart. He petitioned Congregation Mikveh Israel of Philadelphia to have her converted so that he would be permitted to remarry her according to Jewish law. On May 16, 1794, they were remarried in a Jewish rite. Cf. below. (*Coldoc*, 119, *et passim*; *GBMIP*; *MIPR*; *MSGC*; *PAJHS*, XXVII, 462; *Rosenbach*, 24; *Trachtenberg*, 29; *WW*, 127)

NATHAN, Moses.[2] On May 16, 1794, he was married to Sarah Abrahams in Philadelphia. Cf. Moses Nathan Levy, Isaiah Nathan,[1] and above. (*MIPR*; *WW*, 234)

NATHAN, Moses D. By 1785 he was a broker in Philadelphia and New York City. (*MIPR; PAJHS,* XXVII, 253; *SIR; WW,* 412)

NATHAN, Nathan.[1] As early as 1740 he was in New York City. In 1743 he was a merchant in Newport. In 1745 he went bankrupt and later moved to Halifax, Nova Scotia. (*Coldoc,* 325f, 329; *JNEB,* 12; *PAJHS,* XXI, 45, 48, 55)

NATHAN, Nathan.[2] October 14, 1798, Philadelphia—December 21, 1877. Son of Moses Nathan.[1] (*MIPR; MSGC*)

NATHAN, Nathaniel. In 1742 he was a merchant in New City. (*MSP*)

NATHAN, Rachel. June 30, 1760, Philadelphia—November 3, 1802, New York City. Daughter of Lyon Nathan, she was married to Isaac Abrahams[3] on November 4, 1778, in Philadelphia. (*Pool,* 288)

NATHAN, Rebecca. May 12, 1766, Philadelphia—September 5, 1848, New York City. Daughter of Lyon Nathan, she was married to Hart Picard. (*MSP*)

NATHAN, Sally (Sarah). June 24, 1764, Faulkner Swamp, Philadelphia—March 10, 1820, New York City. Daughter of Lyon Nathan. (*Pool,* 288, 401, 403, 412)

NATHAN, Seixas. May 24, 1785, New York City—May 30, 1852, New York City. This son of Simon Nathan[1] was a banker who was one of the first members of the New York Stock Exchange. He was very active in Jewish and communal life. On November 30, 1808, he was married to Sara Seixas.[2] (*MSGC; PAJHS,* IV, 211f; XIX, 31, 33, 40; XXVII, 55, *et passim; UJE,* VIII, 111)

NATHAN, Simon.[1] In 1769 he was a merchant in Montreal. (*Public Archives of Canada*)

NATHAN, Simon.[2] 1746, Frome, England —September 8, 1822, New York City. This son of Judah Nathan traded in Havana before coming to America. During the Revolution he aided the American cause with money and supplies. A Mason, he lived in Philadelphia and New York City and was president of the congregations in both places. He was involved in a commercial dispute with Thomas Jefferson over an exchange of wine for tobacco. In March, 1780, he was married to Grace Seixas.[1] (*Jefferson,* III, 72, *et passim;* V, 87, *et passim;* VI, 197, *et passim; PAJHS,* I, 14; II, 57; III, 8; IV, 211f; XVIII, 119; XIX, 30, *et passim;* XX, 93f; XXI, 147, *et passim;* XXVII, 41, *et passim; UJE,* VIII, 111f; *WW,* 100, *et passim*)

NATHAN, Solomon. About 1776, London —April 3, 1829, Charleston. He lived in Charleston for about thirty years. (*EJSC,* 138; *EOJCC,* 66)

NATHAN, Sophia. Daughter of Moses Nathan.[1] (*MSGC*)

NATHANS, Benjamin. In New York City in 1774. (*PAJHS,* XXI, 129, 132)

NATHANS, David. Died December 5, 1779, New York City. (*Pool,* 503; *SIR*)

NATHANS, Henry. 1800—March 25, 1847. He lived in Charleston. (*EJSC,* 170; *MSP*)

NATHANS, Israel. In Philadelphia in 1783. (*MIPR*)

NATHANS, Sarah. In November, 1790, she was with Jacob Jacobs[5] in Savannah on her way to Charleston. (*SRB*)

NAVARRO, David. In New York City in 1790. (*SIR*)

NAVARRO, Isaac N. Died December 12, 1759, New York City. Also known as Isaac Nabaro. Son of Jacob Navarro, he was in New York City by 1751. A craftsman, he acted as caretaker of Synagogue Shearith Israel, which he painted several times. In 1714 he was married to Rebecca Cardozo in London. (*MSGC; PAJHS,* XXI, 21, *et passim; Pool,* 501; *SIR*)

NAVARRO, Sarah N. July 25, 1722—May 23, 1761. Daughter of Isaac N. Navarro, she was married to Aaron N. Cardozo in London in August, 1739. (*MSGC*)

NEHEMIAH, Moses. The only known Jew in Virginia in the seventeenth century, he was there in 1658. He dealt in tobacco. (*AJAM,* III, 9; *MEAJA,* 165)

NEPHTAL, Mrs. Rachel. Wife of Samuel, she was in New York City in 1721. (*NJP, date unavailable*)

NEPHTAL, Samuel. Died by 1738. In New York City in 1721. (*NJP, date unavailable*)

NETLING, Solomon. Also listed as Nertling, Nutling, and Nurtling. In 1788 he was in New York City. (*PAJHS*, XXVII, 51, *et passim*; SIR)

NEWMAN, Joshua. Fought in the Revolution. It is doubtful that he was Jewish. (*PAJHS*, XXV, 113)

NINIS, Moses Joseph. Died December 2, 1779, Philadelphia. (*MIPR*)

NISSAN, David. In New York City in 1795. (*PAJHS*, XXVII, 60)

NOAH, Elias. 1766—March 21, 1824, New York City. About 1784 he was in New York City and Philadelphia. (*MIPR; MSGC; PAJHS*, XXVII, 42, *et passim*; SIR)

NOAH, Frances. About 1758—June 11, 1843, Montreal. Sister of Manuel Noah, in 1783 she was married to Ephraim Hart in Philadelphia. (*PAJHS*, IV, 215, 217)

NOAH, Henry. In Philadelphia in 1785. (*MIPR*)

NOAH, Judith. March, 1789, New York City—August 2/4, 1868. Daughter of Manuel Noah. (*MSGC; Pool*, 410)

NOAH, Manuel. About 1755, Mannheim, Germany—January 23, 1822, New York City. During the Revolution he served in the Pennsylvania militia. He became a merchant, apparently unsuccessful, and lived in Charleston and New York City. On August 4, 1784, he was married to Zipporah Phillips in Philadelphia. (*EJSC*, 280; *MIPR; PAJHS*, II, 61; VI, 131; XVIII, 118f; XX, 164; *Pool*, 409f)

NOAH, Mordecai. About 1793 he was a child in New York City. Cf. below. (*PAJHS*, XXVII, 55)

NOAH, Mordecai Manuel. July 14/19, 1785, Philadelphia—March 22, 1851. This son of Manuel Noah was a political leader, journalist, and dramatist, and was probably the most distinguished Jewish layman until 1840. He spent his early youth as an orphan in Charleston. After serving a brief apprenticeship to a carver and gilder, he became a clerk in the auditor's office at the U.S. Treasury. His first journalistic experience was as a reporter of sessions of the Pennsylvania legislature. He edited the *City Gazetter* in Charleston and engaged in politics there. In 1823 he was admitted to the bar. In 1826 he established the *New York Enquirer*, and in 1834 the *Evening Star*, which supported the Whig party. As early as 1813 he was consul in Tunis. He was removed from the consulship by James Monroe, but his conduct was later vindicated. In 1822 he was sheriff of New York City. As one of the first pro-Zionist Americans, in 1825 he sought to establish on Grand Island in the Niagara River a Jewish settlement called Ararat. In 1841 he was a judge in the New York Court of Sessions. In 1826 he was married to Rebecca Esther Jackson. (*DAB*, XIII, 534f; *Goldberg; Morais*, 212, *et passim; PAJHS*, XX, *index for partial listing*; *UJE*, VI, 51; VII, 269; VIII, 178, 180, 196, 226f; *WW*, 177, *et passim*)

NOAH, Samuel.[1] July 19, 1779, London—March 10, 1871, Mt. Pulaski, Illinois. This son of Elias Noah came to America in 1799. In 1807 he was graduated from West Point and served in the War of 1812. Until 1820 he taught school in Goshen, New York. After a short visit to England he returned to America, where he taught school in Virginia until 1848. He spent the remainder of his life in Illinois. (*MSGC; PAJHS*, IV, 90f; *UJE*, VIII, 227)

NOAH, Samuel.[2] Born 1783, Virginia. He fought in the War of 1812. (*PAJHS*, XX, 102)

NOAH, Shem. In 1733 he was in Georgia, where he served the Nunes family, probably as an indentured servant. (*Coulter*, 91; *PAJHS*, X, 73; XVII, 168)

NOAH, Uriah. Son of Elias Mordecai, he was a child in New York City about 1793. (*MSGC; PAJHS*, XXVII, 55)

NOHOS, Mr. From France. In 1782 he was in Philadelphia. His name is probably a mistake for Nones. Cf. Benjamin Nones. (*MIPR; PAJHS*, I, 15)

NONES, Aaron. Born October 25, 1798, Philadelphia, or Georgetown, South Carolina. Son of Benjamin Nones, he was married to Caroline Leon on July 27, 1825. (*MIPR; MSGC*)

NONES, Abraham. January 10, 1794, Philadelphia—November 8, 1835, Maracaibo, Colombia. Son of Benjamin Nones, he served as consul general to Maracaibo, Colombia. (*MIPR; Morais*, 401; *MSGC*)

NONES, Benjamin. March 9, 1757, Bordeaux, France—February 9, 1826, Philadelphia. In 1777 he came to America and served in the Revolutionary army. A merchant and broker, he was appointed interpreter of French and Spanish to the United States government. An active Mason, he was also prominent in politics and was a supporter of Jefferson. The Federalist Party attacked him because he was Jewish. From 1791 until 1799, he was president of Congregation Mikveh Israel in Philadelphia. On May 2, 1782, he was married to Miriam Marks. (*Coldoc*, 67, *et passim*; *EJSC*, 84, 95f; *MEAJB*, 141, 212, 226; *MIPR; Morais*, 26, *et passim*; *MSGC*; *PAJHS*, I, 57; XIX, 49; XII, 51f; *UJE*, VIII, 232f; *WW*, 57, *et passim*)

NONES, Clara (Clarissa). October 25, 1798, Georgetown, South Carolina—January 10, 1801, Philadelphia. Daughter of Benjamin Nones. (*MSGC*)

NONES, David. 1783, Philadelphia—August 8, 1837, New York City. Son of Benjamin Nones, on September 6, 1818, he was married to Hannah Abrahams. (*MSGC*)

NONES, Eleazer. Born September 24, 1787, Philadelphia. Son of Benjamin Nones. Cf. Solomon B. Nones. (*MIPR*)

NONES, Esther. July 12, 1790, Philadelphia—1857. Also known as Hetty. Daughter of Benjamin Nones, she was married to Solomon Jacobs in Philadelphia on May 28, 1815. (*ELJR*, 43; *MSGC; Wills*, 26)

NONES, Grace. September 14, 1795, Philadelphia—July 19, 1798, Philadelphia. Daughter of Benjamin Nones. (*MSGC*)

NONES, Isaac. October 29, 1788, Philadelphia—October 28, 1805. Son of Benjamin Nones. Cf. Moses Nones. (*MIPR; MSGC*)

NONES, Isabella. March 12, 1792, Philadelphia—June 24, 1871. Daughter of Benjamin Nones, she was married to Abraham H. de Leon on September 27, 1815, in Philadelphia. (*MSGC*)

NONES, Jonnaton. In 1796 he came to America from Bordeaux. (*SZ*, 121)

NONES, Joseph B. February 15, 1797, Philadelphia—April 13, 1887, New York City. In 1812 this son of Benjamin Nones entered the Navy as a midshipman. He was wounded while on duty, and in 1822 was retired. Thereafter he earned his livelihood as a merchant, an interpreter, and a commissioner of deeds. The report that he was Henry Clay's private secretary seems to have originated from a diary entry Nones made while on a voyage with Clay. On July 23, 1823, he was married to Eveline Leon in New York City. (*Morais*, 401, 447, 470; *MSGC; PAJHS*, XVI, 32; *UJE*, VIII, 233)

NONES, Marianne. Sister of Jonnaton, in 1796 she came to America from Bordeaux. (*SZ*, 121)

NONES, Moses. Died October 28, 1805, Philadelphia. Son of Benjamin Nones. Cf. Isaac Nones. (*MIPR*)

NONES, Rachel. March 2, 1785, Philadelphia—November 7, 1820, Philadelphia. Daughter of Benjamin Nones. (*MIPR; MSGC*)

NONES, Solomon B. September 24, 1787, Philadelphia—August 12, 1819, Norfolk. Son of Benjamin Nones, he was consul general to Portugal. Cf. Eleazer Nones. (*Morais*, 401; *MSGC; UJE*, VIII, 233)

NOONIS, Isaac. Cf. Isaac Nunes Henriques and Hen(riques) Isaac Nunes.

NORDEN, Leon. Died 1798, Savannah. He was a native of Amsterdam. (*Wills*, 77)

NOUNEZ, Benjamin Louis. In 1798 he came to New York City from Bordeaux. (*SZ*, 121)

NUNES, Mrs. Abigail. Wife of Hen. Isaac Nunes, she was in Savannah in 1733. Cf. Mrs. Isaac Nunes Henriques. (*Coulter*, 91)

NUNES, Alexander. Mulatto son of Moses Nunes, he was in Georgia in 1787. (*WAJA*)

NUNES, Daniel.[1] About 1704—September 20, 1789. This son of Samuel Nunes was an early member of the Masons in Savannah in 1733. As early as 1736 he served as government interpreter. In 1765 he was a waiter for the port of Savannah. On January 21, 1767, he was married to Philah Hays in Savannah. (*MEAJB*, 331f; *PAJHS*, III, 150; X, 73; XIX, 88; *SRB*)

NUNES(Z), Daniel.[2] In 1772 he was in Philadelphia. He was married to the daughter of John Avery. (*ALDINE*)

NUNES, David. A Mason in Georgia, in 1765 he served as a waiter for the port of Savannah. Cf. Daniel Nunes.[1] (*PAJHS*, XIX, 88f)

NUNES, Esther. May have been born in Georgia. Daughter of Samuel Nunes, she was married to Abraham de Leon[1] either in Jamaica, B.W.I., or in London. She lived in America. (*MEAJB*, 335; *MSGC*; *Wills*, 77)

NUNES, Frances. Mulatto daughter of Moses Nunes, she was in Georgia about 1787. (*WAJA*)

NUNES, Hen(riques) Isaac. In Savannah in 1733. Cf. Isaac Nunes Henriques. (*Coulter*, 91)

NUNES, Isaac Fernandez. Probably died in New York City in 1732. (*JRMP*)

NUNES, James. In Georgia in 1787. (*JRMP*)

NUNES, Joseph. In New York City in 1728. (*PAJHS*, XXI, 5, *et passim*)

NUNES, Joseph Tores. 1674—October 2, 1704, New York City. A merchant who dealt with Lewis M. Gomez, he came to America from London. (*PAJHS*, XI, 142f; *Pool*, 189, *et passim*)

NUNES, Moses. 1705—September 6, 1787, Savannah. This son of Samuel Nunes came to America, and in 1733 was prominent in Masonry in Georgia. A landowner and merchant, he became a customs officer for the Fort of Savannah, and in the 1760s was a government interpreter to the Indians. Before the Revolution he was loyal to the British, but he seems later to have favored the Whig cause. He was married first to a Jewess named Abrahams, and then to a mulatto. (*Coulter*, 91; *MEAJB*, 331f; *MSGC*; *Wills*, 77)

NUNES, Mrs. Rebecca. The second wife of Samuel Nunes, she lived in Georgia. (*Coulter*, 91)

NUNES, Robert. Mulatto son of Moses Nunes, he was in Georgia about 1787. (*WAJA*)

NUNES, Rycke. In New Amsterdam in 1654. (*AJAM*, III, 9)

NUNES, Samuel. A Marrano who was a court physician in Portugal, he went first to England and then to Georgia, where he arrived with his family in 1733. Apparently he came with wealth, for he purchased land and ministered to the sick of the colony. In 1741 he was in New York City. His first wife was Rachel; his second wife was Rebecca. (*Coulter*, 91; *PAJHS*, I, 8; II, 45f; X, 69f; XVII, 170; XXI, 44; XXII, 158f; *UJE*, VIII, 256f)

NUNES, Zipporah. About 1714, Portugal —November 19, 1799. Daughter of Samuel Nunes, she was born a Catholic. She was a very cultured and charitable woman. Her first husband was David Mendez Machado; her second husband was Israel Jacobs. (*Coulter*, 91; *MEAJB*, 335; *MSP*; *PAJHS*, II, 48f; *Wills*, 77)

NUNES, Mrs. Zipporah. Mother of Samuel Nunes, she was in Georgia in 1733. (*PAJHS*, X, 72f)

O

ODLER, Simon. In New York City in 1788. Cf. Simon Adler and Simon Odler Cohen. (*SIR*)

ODLER, Solomon. In New York City in 1786. (*PAJHS*, XXI, 159)

ODLER, Zekee (Ezekiel). A child in New York City about 1793. (*AJA; PAJHS*, XXVII, 55)

OETTING, Isaac Asher. In Philadelphia in 1784. (*MIPR*)

OFFERMAN, Philip. In Newport in 1746. It is doubtful that he was Jewish. (*PAJHS*, XXXVII, 417)

OLIVE, William. Born about 1710, London. He was educated in Halle, Germany. In 1770 he was in America. He was probably a convert to Christianity. (*Kohut*, 37, 67f)

OLIVERA, David de.[1] Died November 10, 1763. Son of Jacob Lopez de Olivera, he was in Savannah in 1733, and lived also in Charlestown. (*Coulter*, 91; *EJSC*, 30, *et passim*; *MEAJB*, 290f; *MSGC*; *PAJHS*, X, 73, 86; XII, 44)

OLIVERA, David de.[2] Son of David de Olivera,[1] he was in Georgia in 1733. (*PAJHS*, X, 73; XVII, 168)

OLIVERA, Mrs. David de. Wife of David de Olivera.[1] (*PAJHS*, X, 73)

OLIVERA, Isaac. Died November, 1734, Savannah. Son of Jacob Lopez de Olivera, he died as the result of an accidental gunshot wound. (*Coulter*, 91)

OLIVERA, Jacob Lopez de. Died 1751, Charlestown. A merchant, he came to Savannah in 1733, and lived also in Charlestown. His wife was Judith. (*Coulter*, 91; *EJSC*, 30, 38; *MEAJB*, 290f; *PAJHS*, X, 78; XVII, 168, 170)

OLIVERA, Mrs. Judith. Wife of Jacob Lopez de Olivera, she was in Savannah in 1733. (*Coulter*, 91)

OLIVERA, Leah de. January 1, 1715—September 17, 1778. Daughter of Jacob Lopez de Olivera, she was married to Joseph Tobias. She lived in Savannah and Charlestown. (*Coulter*, 91; *Wills*, 57)

OTTOLENGHE, Joseph Solomon. Born Italy, died July, 1775. A trained Hebrew teacher and shohet in Italy, in 1732 he went to England to work for his uncle in the tobacco trade. In 1734 he was converted to Christianity. In 1751 he received a subvention from the trustees of the Georgia colony and went to Georgia, where he served as tax collector, Christian missionary to the Negro slaves, and schoolmaster to the Negroes. He was also Superintendent of Silk Culture in Georgia. Until 1758 or 1759 he continued teaching; in 1769 he was retired from the superintendent's position. By then he was a large landholder. From 1755 until 1775, except for a brief period in 1766, he was elected to the colonial House of Representatives. He held numerous other religious and civic positions, including office as a justice of the peace. (*MEAJB*, 301, *et passim*)

OTTOLENGUI, Abraham. September 6, 1790, Charleston—December 12, 1850, Charleston. This son of Mordecai Ottolengui was a teacher and merchant. From 1843 until 1850 he was a director of the Union Bank. In 1833 he was commissioner of the poorhouse in Charleston. A prominent member of the Jewish community, he was president of Congregation Beth Elohim, and established a congregational fund for "poor Israelites." His wife was Sarah. (*EJSC*, 138, 202; *Reznikoff*, 143, *et passim*; *Wills*, 53)

OTTOLENGUI, Mordecai. Died 1794. He came from Italy, and by 1790 settled as a merchant in Charleston. (*MSGC; Wills*, 53)

OTTOLENGUI, Mrs. Rinah. Born Gibraltar, died 1810. Wife of Mordecai Ottolengui, she was in Charleston by 1790. (*MSGC; Wills*, 53)

P

PACHECO, Benjamin Mendez.¹ November 11, 1711—1749. Uncle of Isaac M. Seixas, he was a merchant who was made a freeman in New York City. The Nuneses were among his correspondents. He donated money for the erection of the first synagogue of Congregation Shearith Israel and for the steeple on Trinity Church, both in New York City. He later returned to London, where he continued as a merchant. In May, 1732, he was married to Judith Seixas, probably in England. Cf. Rodrigo Pacheco. (*Coldoc*, 315f; *MEAJA*, 158f; *MEAJB*, 293; *MSGC*; *PAJHS*, II, 81; III, 85; IV, 192f; VI, 101, 127; XXI, 2, et passim; *POFNW*, 40, et passim)

PACHECO, Benjamin Mendez.² In Philadelphia about 1780. (*MIPR*)

PACHECO, Rodrigo. Same as Benjamin Mendez Pacheco.¹ (*MEAJA*, 158f)

PACIFICO, Samuel Israel. As early as 1740 he was in Philadelphia. On March 25, 1761, he was married to Sara Mitchels in New York City. (*MIPR*; *PAJHS*, I, 24; *SIR*)

PACKEKOE, Moses. May have arrived in 1658. In 1677 he was in Newport. (*AJAM*, III, 9f)

PAIBA, Rowland. A merchant in New York City in 1754. In 1765 he was in Boston with his family. (*AJA*; *Rosenbaum*, 53)

PALACIOS, Joseph de. In 1765 he purchased land in Louisiana. About the same time he was a merchant in Mobile. By 1780 he was in Charlestown. In 1785 he was married to Mrs. Harris. (*EJMC*, 5; *EOJCC*, 103; *EJSC*, 91; *JRMP*; *PAJHS*, XII, 53; *Shpall*, 6; *Wills*, 67)

PALACIOS, Joseph de, Jr. In Charlestown by 1783. (*EJSC*, 278)

PALACIOS, Mrs. Joseph de. Widow of Nathan Harris of St. Eustatia, she was married to Joseph de Palacios in 1785. She is probably identical with Mrs. Sarah de Palacios, who died in Charleston in December, 1785. (*EJMC*, 5; *MSP*)

PALACIOS, Mrs. Sarah de. Died in Charleston in December, 1785. (*MSP*)

PALESKE, C. G. In Philadelphia in 1800. It is doubtful that he was Jewish. (*PAJHS*, I, 114)

PANHA, Moses de la. On July 9, 1785, he arrived in Savannah from Jamaica; he returned to Jamaica on May 10, 1787. (*SRB*)

PARDO. Child of Sarra Lopes Pardo. (*SZ*, 121)

PARDO. A second child of Sarra Lopes Pardo. (*SZ*, 121)

PARDO, Sarra Lopes. In 1796 she came from Bordeaux to Louisiana. (*SZ*, 121)

PARDO, Saul & family. Cf. Brown, et passim.

PARVEH, Abraham. A businessman in New York City in 1676. (*AJAM*, III, 10)

PARVEH, Isaac. A businessman in New York City in 1676. (*AJAM*, III, 10)

PARERA, Moses. In New York City in 1729. (*PAJHS*, XXI, 18)

PAS, David Lopez de. Born Portugal. Arrived in Savannah in 1733. Cf. David Lopez.² (*MSGC*)

PAS, Mrs. Lopez de. Born Portugal. Arrived in Savannah in 1733. Cf. Mrs. David Lopez. (*MSGC*)

PAS, Isaac de. In 1738 he was a merchant and shipowner in Charlestown. (*EJSC*, 27, 277)

PASS. Born 1785, died after eight days. Son of Jacob de Pass. (*SRB*)

PASS, Abraham de & family. He went from Jamaica, B.W.I., to Charleston. In 1800 his family is noted in Charleston. A vendue master, he lived also in Savannah. His first wife was Rachel de la Motta in 1784; his second wife was Rachel Derkeim in August, 1798. (*Census B, South Carolina*; *EJMC*, 5, 7; *MISR*)

PASS, Esther de. On February 28, 1792, she was married to Samuel da Costa in Savannah. She may have been a daughter of Ralph de Pass.[1] (SRB)

PASS, Hannah de. 1778, Kingston, Jamaica —June 4, 1829, Savannah. Daughter of Ralph de Pass,[1] on April 22, 1796, she was married to Benjamin Milhado in Charleston. (EJMC, 6)

PASS, Isaac de. A shipowner in Charlestown in 1744. (MSGC)

PASS, Jacob de.[1] Son of Ralph de Pass,[1] on February 28, 1784, he arrived in Savannah; he returned to Jamaica in 1788. (SRB)

PASS, Jacob de.[2] Born July 10, 1786, Savannah. Son of Jacob de Pass.[1] (SRB)

PASS, Mrs. Jacob de. Wife of Jacob de Pass.[1] (SRB)

PASS, Joseph de.[1] In 1781 he was in business in Woodstock, Connecticut. He lived also in Savannah, New York City, Newport, and Charleston. (EJSC, 134; MEAJA, 179f; MISR; PAJHS, XXVII, 185; XXXV, 142)

PASS, Joseph de.[2] Born July 12, 1786, Savannah. Son of Ralph de Pass,[1] he was married to Hannah Hart in Charleston in 1813. (MSGC; SRB)

PASS, Mrs. Leah de. Died December, 1796, Charleston. Wife of Ralph de Pass.[1] (MSGC)

PASS, Mrs. de. In New York City about 1760. (Pool, 308)

PASS, Ralph de.[1] About 1730—November 24, 1812, Charleston. On February 28, 1784, he arrived in Savannah from Jamaica, and left for Charleston, where he lived for twenty-five years. A vendue master, he may also have been a physician. Pass' first wife was Leah; his second wife was Sarah Judah in 1798. (MSGC; POFNW, 473; SRB)

PASS, Ralph de.[2] Born June 24, 1785, Savannah. Son of Jacob de Pass.[1] (SRB)

PASS, Rebecca de. Daughter of Ralph de Pass,[1] on December 20, 1786, she was married to Joseph da Costa in Charleston. (MSGC)

PASS, Sally. June 24, 1785, Savannah— May 27, 1788. Daughter of Ralph de Pass.[1] (SRB)

PASSO, Isaac. In New York City in 1795. (PAJHS, XXVII, 61)

PAUKORUE, David. In New York City in 1764. It is highly doubtful that he was Jewish. (PAJHS, XXVII, 329)

PAVIAS, Mr. In 1747 he was in New York City, apparently about to leave. Cf. Aaron Depivea. (PAJHS, XXI, 54)

PAX, David Lopez de. Died about 1733, Georgia. Husband of Zipporah. (Coulter, 82)

PAX, Mrs. Zipporah de. Widow of David Lopez de Pax, she was married to Jacob Lopez de Crasto in 1735 in Georgia. Cf. Mrs. Zipporah Crasto. (Coulter, 82f)

PAYSADDON, Hannah. In New York in 1770. (Coldoc, 16)

PAZ, Esther Diaz de. Died 1792, Philadelphia. (MIPR)

PEDRO, John. In Virginia in 1652. It is doubtful that he was Jewish. (AJAM, III, 10)

PEIXOTTO, Daniel Cohen. Died 1769/70, Providence, Rhode Island, on his way from Curaçao. (MSGC)

PEIXOTTO, Moses Cohen. Died May 30, 1721, New York City. From Barbados. In 1711 he was married to Rachel Marques. (MSGC; Pool, 455)

PENEDO, Mr. In New York City in 1751. It is doubtful that he was Jewish. (Pool, 37)

PEORRA, Ephraim. In Philadelphia in 1786. (MIPR)

PERARO, Emanuel. On September 8, 1766, he was naturalized in Massachusetts. It is highly doubtful that he was Jewish. (JRMP)

PEREIRA, Benjamin. By 1715 he was in New York City, engaged as a tallow merchant. From 1748 to 1757 he was hazzan and shohet for Congregation Shearith Israel. He eventually went to Jamaica, B.W.I. (*MSP; PAJHS,* XXI, 45, *et passim;* XXVII, 150, *et passim*)

PEREIRA, Jacob Rodrigues. In Philadelphia in 1792. (*MIPR*)

PEREIRA, Manasseh. In New York City about 1740. (*PAJHS,* XXI, 45)

PERERO, Isaac. In 1676 he was in business in New York City. (*AJAM,* III, 10)

PERES, Samuel. In 1708 he was a merchant in Philadelphia. (*WW,* 14)

PEREYRA, Joseph Rodrigues. In 1792 he came from Bordeaux to Philadelphia. (*SZ,* 121)

PEREYRA, Rebecca Rodrigues. Buried in Philadelphia in 1765. (*Cohen,* 84)

PEREYRA, Rebecca Rodriquez. April 17, 1760, Cadiz—December 5, 1809, Philadelphia. In 1792 she came from Bordeaux to Philadelphia. (*GBMIP; PAJHS,* VI, 108; *SZ,* 121)

PERRERA, Jacob. In Charleston in 1800. (*EJSC,* 138)

PESOA, Abraham. Born February 15, 1799, Philadelphia. Son of Isaac Pesoa, on July 1, 1834, he was buried in Philadelphia. (*MIPR*)

PESOA, Isaac. About 1762—December 3, 1809, Philadelphia. He came to America from Jamaica, B.W.I. On April 13, 1796, he was married to Phila Phillips in Philadelphia. (*MIPR; PAJHS,* VI, 108)

PESOA, Rachel. 1798—November 19, 1856. Daughter of Isaac Pesoa. (*MSGC*)

PESOA. Additional members in the family of Isaac. In Philadelphia in 1800. (*Census B, Pennsylvania*)

PHILADELPHIA, Jacob. Born August 14, 1735, Philadelphia. He may have studied natural science with Dr. Christopher Witt. Early in the 1750s he went to England. He traveled in Europe as a merchant and scientist, but was famed as a traveling magician. An expert mechanic, he was reputed to have been a pioneer in the submarine device. The last half of his life he spent chiefly in Germany, where he tried to promote a German-American trading company. (*MEAJB,* 83, *et passim; PAJHS,* XVI, 73, 94; *UJE,* VIII, 426, 484)

PHILIPS, B. H. In Philadelphia in 1785. (*MSP*)

PHILIPS, G. In New York City in 1796. (*PAJHS,* XXVII, 64)

PHILIPS, Mrs. G. In New York City in 1796. (*PAJHS,* XXVII, 64)

PHILIPS, Harry. In Philadelphia in 1792. (*MIPR*)

PHILIPS, J. In Philadelphia in 1800. (*PAJHS,* I, 114)

PHILIPS, Judah. In New York City in 1789; in Savannah in his own vessel bound for Jamaica, June, 1788. (*SIR; SRB*)

PHILIPS, Levin. Fought in the Virginia line during the Revolution. It is highly doubtful that he was Jewish. (*PAJHS,* XX, 99)

PHILIPS, Susman. In Philadelphia in 1785. (*MIPR*)

PHILIPSE, Phillip. In New York City in 1755. (*PAJHS,* XXVII, 318)

PHILLIPS. Died May, 1795, New York City. Son of Henry Phillips. (*SIR*)

PHILLIPS, Aaron J. July 3, 1792, Philadelphia—1847, New York City. This son of Jonas Phillips was a playwright and actor of comedy. Also a theater manager, in 1829 he conducted the Arch Street Theater. (*MIPR; Morais,* 374f; *MSGC; PAJHS,* II, 61; *UJE,* VIII, 490; *WW,* 319, *et passim*)

PHILLIPS, Aaron N. October 27, 1799, Philadelphia—March 13, 1813. Son of Naphtali Phillips. (*MIPR; MSGC*)

PHILLIPS, Abraham. March 24, 1788, New York City—April 15, 1813, near Norfolk. Son of Jacob Phillips,[1] he served in the Navy during the War of 1812. (*PAJHS,* XXXII, 125f)

PHILLIPS, Benjamin. In Charleston in 1800. (*EJSC,* 138)

PHILLIPS, Benjamin J. 1776, Philadelphia —February 10, 1830. Son of Jonas Phillips, he was a merchant who married Abigail Seixas[5] on January 25, 1804. (*Morais*, 447; *MSGC*; *PAJHS*, II, 60; IV, 211)

PHILLIPS, Daniel. In Newport in 1747 and in 1793. (*PAJHS*, XXVII, 416)

PHILLIPS, David.[1] In New York City in 1787. (*PAJHS*, XXVII, 42)

PHILLIPS, David.[2] In Charleston in 1800. (*EJSC*, 138)

PHILLIPS, David Machado. Born February 10, 1768, died Surinam. Son of Jonas Phillips, he was in Philadelphia in 1796. His wife was Gitlah (Catherine). (*MIPR*; *MSGC*; *PAJHS*, XXVII, 153; *SIR*)

PHILLIPS, Davis. In Philadelphia in 1785. (*MIPR*)

PHILLIPS, Eleanor. In 1735 she was married to Zachariah Cohen in Newport by a Christian minister. It is doubtful that she was Jewish. (*JNEB*, 8)

PHILLIPS, Eleazar. In Philadelphia in 1784. (*MIPR*)

PHILLIPS, Esther. Born December 6, 1794. Daughter of Jacob Phillips, she was married to Isaac Hendricks. (*MSGC*)

PHILLIPS, Esther (Hetty). July 19, 1778, Philadelphia—March 10, 1845, Sumterville, South Carolina. Daughter of Jonas Phillips, she was married to Myer Moses[2] on November 2, 1803. (*EOJCC*, 20; *MSGC*)

PHILLIPS, Ezekiel. In Philadelphia in 1799. (*MIPR*)

PHILLIPS, Fanny. February 5, 1790—May 4, 1848. Daughter of Jacob Phillips,[1] she was married to Isaac Goldsmith. (*MSGC*)

PHILLIPS, Henry. On October 9, 1794, he was married to Godhauer Cohen in Philadelphia. (*MIPR*; *PAJHS*, XXVII, 61)

PHILLIPS, Hindlah. May 28, 1771, New York City—June 17, 1772, New York City. Daughter of Jonas Phillips, she was known also as Hannah. (*PAJHS*, II, 60; *SIR*)

PHILLIPS, Isaac. In Philadelphia in 1782. (*MIPR*)

PHILLIPS, Israel. In Philadelphia about 1772. He was jailed for possessing stolen goods but escaped. (*Exponent*, 13)

PHILLIPS, Jacob.[1] About 1750—November 24, 1822, Philadelphia. He lived in New York City and Charleston. On August 13, 1785, he was married to Hannah Isaacs[2] in Newport. (*MIPR*; *MSGC*; *PAJHS*, XXVII, 43, *et passim*; XXXIII, 203)

PHILLIPS, Jacob.[2] 1800—November 8, 1822, Philadelphia. Son of Henry Phillips. (*GBMIP*)

PHILLIPS, John. 1787, Newport—October 28, 1853, Baton Rouge. Son of Mr. Phillips and Rachel Levy.[6] (*MSGC*)

PHILLIPS, Jonas. 1736, Buseck, Germany—January 29, 1803, Philadelphia. He was buried in New York City. This son of Aaron Uriah Phillips came to Charlestown from London; he later moved to New York City and then to Philadelphia. A fur trader and auctioneer who sold merchandise to soldiers, in 1778 he was in the Philadelphia county militia. By 1759 he was a freeman in Albany. In 1765 he was shohet of Congregation Shearith Israel in New York City, and became a freeman there in 1769. In 1782 he was the first president of the reorganized Congregation Mikveh Israel in Philadelphia. He fought against the Test Oath in Pennsylvania, which prevented Jews from holding office, and tried to get full citizenship rights for Jews. He became a Mason. On November 10, 1762, he was married to Rebecca Machado in Philadelphia. (*MEAJB*, 56, *et passim*; *MIPR*; *Morais*, 27, *et passim*; *MSGC*; *PAJHS*, II, 51, *et passim*; *SIR*; *UJE*, VIII, 492; *WW*, 51, *et passim*)

PHILLIPS, Joseph.[1] In Newport in 1747. (*PAJHS*, XXVII, 451)

PHILLIPS, Joseph.[2] In Savannah in 1754. He was an executor of Abraham Minis' will. (*Wills*, 81)

PHILLIPS, Joseph.[3] In Charlestown in 1780. (*PAJHS*, XII, 53)

PHILLIPS, Joseph.[4] 1780—May 10, 1854. Son of Jonas Phillips, he fought in the War of 1812. On December 10, 1839, he was married to Rachel Phillips in New

York City. (*MIPR*; *MSGC*; *PAJHS*, II, 61; *UJE*, VII, 264)

PHILLIPS, Major Judah. In Georgia in 1788. It is doubtful that he was Jewish. (*JRMP*)

PHILLIPS, Judith. Died September 19, 1770, New York City. Infant daughter of Jonas Phillips. (*Pool*, 293; *SIR*)

PHILLIPS, Levi. Born about 1754. On January 16, 1832, he was buried in Philadelphia. By 1785 he was a merchant in Philadelphia. He was married to Leah Simon in Philadelphia. (*MIPR*; *PAJHS*, V, 35f; IX, 31)

PHILLIPS, Manuel. Died 1826, Vera Cruz. Son of Jonas Phillips, he fought in the War of 1812. He was a physician in Philadelphia. (*Morais*, 416, *et passim*; *MSGC*)

PHILLIPS, Maria. Born New York City, died September 5, 1828, St. George, Canada. Daughter of Mr. Phillips and Rachel Levy.[6] (*MSGC*)

PHILLIPS, Major Moses. In 1775 he was in the British colonial army of Ulster County in New York. It is highly doubtful that he was Jewish. (*PAJHS*, XXVII, 390)

PHILLIPS, Moses Seixas. February 24, 1798, Philadelphia—July 11, 1854, Albany. Son of Naphtali Phillips, he was a prominent actor and theater manager. On November 6, 1822, he was married to Rebecca Hart. (*MIPR*; *Morais*, 374f; *MSGC*; *MSP*; *UJE*, VIII, 490)

PHILLIPS, Naphtali. October 19, 1773, New York City—November 1, 1870, New York City. This son of Jonas Phillips was a journalist who was first employed on Philadelphia's *American Advertiser*; he later became proprietor of the *National Advocate*, which was published in New York City. He served also in the New York Custom House. For almost seventy-five years he was a prominent member of Tammany society. He was president of Congregation Shearith Israel in New York City and was the first American-born president of Congregation Mikveh Israel in Philadelphia. Phillips' first wife was Rachel Hannah Seixas, July 5, 1797, in Newport; his second, Esther Seixas,[1] on October 8, 1823, in New York City. (*Morais*, 27, 45, 292; *MSGC*; *PAJHS*, I, 19; II, 60; IV, 203, *et passim*; XI, 133; XXI, 172f; *UJE*, VIII, 494; *WW*, 228, *et passim*)

PHILLIPS, Nathan. Fought in the Revolution in Charlestown in 1779. (*PAJHS*, XIX, 152)

PHILLIPS, Nathaniel. Son of Daniel Phillips, he was in Newport in 1793. (*PAJHS*, XXVII, 416)

PHILLIPS, Phila. July 15, 1766, New York City—December 23, 1852, Philadelphia. Daughter of Jonas Phillips, she was married to Isaac Pesoa on April 13, 1796, in Philadelphia. (*GBMIP*; *MIPR*; *MSGC*; *SIR*)

PHILLIPS, Phillip. Born November 5, 1796. Son of Jacob Phillips,[1] he was married to a Christian woman. (*MSGC*)

PHILLIPS, Rachel.[1] Died December 23, 1810, Philadelphia. According to tradition she was an indentured servant of Samuel Chew before her marriage to Aaron Levy.[1] (*MIPR*; *PAJHS*, II, 162; *WW*, 186, 435)

PHILLIPS, Rachel.[2] May 23, 1769, New York City—1839, Monticello, Virginia. Daughter of Jonas Phillips, she was married to Michael Levy. (*PAJHS*, II, 60; *SIR*)

PHILLIPS, Rachel.[3] October 5, 1786—October 5, 1870, Charleston. Daughter of Jacob Phillips,[1] she was married to Michael Myers on October 10, 1810. (*MSGC*)

PHILLIPS, Rebecca. March 19, 1792—December 24, 1872, Savannah. Daughter of Jacob Phillips,[1] she was married to Isaiah Moses on November 11, 1807. (*MSGC*; *PAJHS*, XXXII, 125f)

PHILLIPS, Sara. May 23, 1769, New York City—June 28/30, 1770, New York City. Daughter of Jonas Phillips. (*Pool*, 293; *SIR*)

PHILLIPS, Simon. Fought in the Revolution. It is doubtful that he was Jewish. (*PAJHS*, XXV, 113)

PHILLIPS, William. 1783, Newport—April 5, 1829, Quebec. Son of Mr. Phillips and Rachel Levy.[6] (*MSGC*)

PHILLIPS, Uriah. Born July 31, 1763, New York City, died an infant. Son of Jonas Phillips. (*PAJHS*, XXVII, 152; *SIR*)

PHILLIPS. Zalegman. June 28, 1779, Philadelphia—August 21, 1839, Philadelphia. This son of Jonas Phillips was graduated from the University of Pennsylvania in 1795 and was admitted to the bar in 1799. He was an ardent Jacksonian Democrat. He served as president of Congregation Mikveh Israel in Philadelphia. On October 23, 1805, he was married to Arabella Solomons. (*MIPR*; *Morais*, 22, *et passim*; *MSGC*; *PAJHS*, I, 19, 23; XIX, 121f; *WW*, 202, *et passim*)

PHILLIPS, Zipporah. August 31, 1764—November 18, 1792, Charleston. Daughter of Jonas Phillips, she was married to Manuel Noah on August 4, 1784, in Philadelphia. (*MIPR*; *MSGC*; *PAJHS*, II, 61)

PHINEAS, Heineman. A German Jew, he came to America about 1776. (*Malchelosse*, 182)

PHINEAS, Isaac. Born 1764. Son of Heineman Phineas, he was in Three Rivers, Canada, in 1773. He served in the War of 1812. (*Malchelosse*, 182; *PAJHS*, VI, 155)

PICARD, Hart. 1746—January 5, 1821. In New York City in 1800. He was probably married to Rebecca Nathan before 1800. (*MSP*; *SIR*; *Wills*, 8)

PICKENS, Miss. Daughter of a Presbyterian minister, she was in America before 1800. Before being married to Abraham Hyam Cohen on May 28, 1806, in Philadelphia, she was converted to Judaism. She wrote memoirs about her experiences as a Jew. In 1831 she was separated from her husband; she reverted to Christianity. (*ELJR*, 219f; *WW*, 237f)

PIETERSON, Solomon. In 1654 he was a court agent in New Amsterdam. (*AJAM*, III, 10)

PIMENTA, Joel. Daughter of Moses Pimenta, she was married to Isaac Cohen.[1] Sometime after 1750 and before 1783 she lived in Charlestown. (*Wills*, 54)

PIMENTA, Mrs. Leah. Died about 1767, Charlestown. Wife of Moses Pimenta. (*EJSC*, 38; *Wills*, 54)

PIMENTA, Moses. Died May, 1765, Charlestown. A teacher in the Jewish community, he later became a sutler and general merchant. His wife was Leah. (*EJSC*, 32, 40; *ELHS*; *JRMP*)

PIMENTA, Rebecca. Daughter of Moses Pimenta, she was married to Abraham da Costa in Charlestown about 1765. (*EJSC*, 38)

PIMENTA, Sarah. Died October 7, 1793, Charleston. Daughter of Moses Pimenta, she was married to Isaac da Costa.[1] (*Wills*, 38)

PIMENTEL, Aaron. Died March 31, 1789. An auctioneer, he lived in Charleston and New York City. (*EJSC*, 280; *MSP*; *PAJHS*, XXVII, 42; *Pool*, 416)

PIMENTEL, Hannah. Died November 4, 1820, New York City. She lived in Newport until 1816. Her first husband was Sasportas; her second husband was Jacob Rodriguez Rivera.[1] (*Pool*, 402, *et passim*)

PINCUS, Elias. In Philadelphia in 1786. Cf. Mr. Benechus. (*MIPR*)

PINEDO, Gabriel. In New York City in 1753. (*PAJHS*, XXI, 70)

PINEDO, Jacob. In Philadelphia in 1714. (*WW*, 14)

PINES, Hineman. In Montreal in 1778. (*SIMR*)

PINES, Lazarus. About 1767 he was a Philadelphia schoolmaster. It is highly doubtful that he was Jewish. (*JRMP*)

PINES, Joseph. In Montreal in 1779. (*MEAJA*, 235f; *SIMR*)

PINHAS, Isaac. Died 1710, New York City. Identified with Isaac Pinheiro by Pool. (*PAJHS*, XVIII, 120; *Pool*, 453)

PINHEIRO, Abraham. Son of Isaac Pinheiro, he may have been in New York City in 1710. (*NYHSW*, XI, 2)

PINHEIRO, Mrs. Esther (Elizabeth). Wife of Isaac Pinheiro, she was in New

York City in 1707. (*MSGC; NYHSW*, XI, 3; XVII, 367)

PINHEIRO, Isaac. Died February 17, 1710, New York City. A merchant, he came from the island of Nevis, and in 1695 he became a freeman of New York City. His wife was Esther. (*Pool*, 453f)

PINHEIRO, Jacob. Son of Isaac Pinheiro, in 1708 he may have been in New York City. (*PAJHS*, XXIII, 157f; *Pool*, 454)

PINHEIRO, Judith. Daughter of Isaac Pinheiro, in 1708 she may have been in New York City. (*PAJHS*, XXIII, 157)

PINHEIRO, Moses. Son of Isaac Pinheiro, he may have been in New York City in 1708. (*PAJHS*, XXIII, 157)

PINHEIRO, Rebecca. Daughter of Isaac Pinheiro, in 1708 she may have been in New York City. (*PAJHS*, XXIII, 157)

PINIS, Moses Joseph. Died December 2, 1799, Montreal. (*MIPR*)

PINTO, Abigail. Born April 19, 1765, New York City. Daughter of Joseph J. Pinto. (*SIR*)

PINTO, Abraham.[1] About 1697—about March, 1797. About 1740 he was a chandler in New York City, where he became a freeman in 1743. His wife was Sarah. (*PAJHS*, II, 49; VI, 102; XXI, 45, *et passim; Pool*, 248)

PINTO, Abraham.[2] Born March 8, 1757. Son of Jacob Pinto,[1] on December 30, 1779, he was married to Sarah Gault of Boston. (*MSGC*)

PINTO, Abraham.[3] Born February 10, 1764, New York City. Son of Joseph J. Pinto. (*SIR*)

PINTO, Abraham.[4] Born in New Haven. This son of Jacob Pinto[1] entered Yale University but did not graduate. He fought in the Revolution. One of the founders of the Society of Cincinnati, he seems to have had no Jewish associations. (*Kohut*, 109f; *PAJHS*, XI, 93f; XIX, 111f; *UJE*, VIII, 539f; X, 371)

PINTO, Benjamin. About 1787 he came to New York City, seeking funds for passage to Surinam. (*SIR*)

PINTO, David. In New York City in 1788. (*PAJHS*, XXVII, 241)

PINTO, Isaac.[1] June 12, 1720—January 17, 1791, New York City. He came to America probably by way of Jamaica, B.W.I., and was in Norwalk and other parts of Connecticut as early as 1741. In 1760 he was a wholesale wine merchant in Charlestown. Thereafter he seems to have spent most of his time in New York City. He is probably best known as the translator of the first Jewish prayer book printed in America in two parts, the first in 1761, the second in 1766. He was referred to by Ezra Stiles as "a learned Jew of New York," and was generally highly respected for his learning. In the last years of his life he advertised as a Spanish teacher. His wife was Rachel. (*DAB*, XIV, 631f; *EJSC*, 42; *MEAJB*, 471f; *PAJHS*, III, 118f; *Pool*, 248, *et passim; SIR*)

PINTO, Isaac.[2] About 1787 he arrived in New York City, seeking funds for passage to Surinam. (*SIR*)

PINTO, Isaac.[3] December 21, 1777—January 1, 1858, Chillicothe, Ohio. Son of Jacob Pinto,[1] he was probably reared as a gentile. His wife, Maria Marshall, was undoubtedly a gentile. (*MSGC*)

PINTO, Isaac Jeshurun. In Fairfield, Connecticut, before 1800. (*JRMP; MSP*)

PINTO, Jacob.[1] January 26, 1727—about 1806. This son of Abraham Pinto[1] lived in New Haven, Connecticut, and was a prominent patriot during the Revolutionary period. He was married to Thankful, and then to Abigail Peck, a gentile. He seems to have had no Jewish associations. (*Kohut*, 110; *PAJHS*, III, 150; XI, 90, 93f; XIII, 114; *MSGC; MSP*)

PINTO, Jacob.[2] As early as 1736 he was a shohet in New York City. (*PAJHS*, II, 48f; XXI, 53)

PINTO, Jacob.[3] In New York City in 1788. (*PAJHS*, XXVII, 241)

PINTO, Joseph. Died March 5, 1798, New York City. Son of Abraham Pinto,[1] he was a silversmith who was married to Josse Hays on November 6, 1765, in New York City. (*MSGC; Pool*, 39, *et passim*)

PINTO, Joseph Jessurun. Born 1729, Amsterdam. A learned spiritual leader, he became hazzan of Congregation Shearith Israel in New York City in 1758. In 1766 he was naturalized there. He wrote one of the few Jewish publications in the eighteenth century: a thanksgiving prayer. In 1766 he left New York with his family and returned to his former home in England. (MEAJ, 84f; PAJHS, II, 49f; III, 121f; VI, 128f; XI, 152f; POFNW, 128, et passim; UJE, VIII, 540f)

PINTO, Miriam. June 8, 1730—July 1, 1781, New York City. Daughter of Abraham Pinto,[1] she was married to Manuel Myers on May 31, 1759. (MSGC; PAJHS, XVIII, 122; Pool, 248; SIR)

PINTO, Rachel. April 3, 1722, New York City—October 30, 1815, New York City. Daughter of Abraham Pinto,[1] she was one of the chief benefactors of Polonies Talmud Torah at Congregation Shearith Israel. (PAJHS, II, 49; XVIII, 113; Pool, 164, et passim; SIR)

PINTO, Mrs. Rachel. Wife of Isaac Pinto,[1] she was in New York City before 1791. (SIR)

PINTO, Samuel.[1] In New York City in 1744. (AJAM, IX, 77)

PINTO, Samuel.[2] March 2, 1727/8—December 7, 1764, New York City. Son of Abraham Pinto.[1] (Pool, 248, et passim; SIR)

PINTO, Samuel.[3] Born August 18, 1771. Son of Jacob Pinto.[1] (MSGC)

PINTO, Sarah. Born February 3, 1780. Daughter of Jacob Pinto.[1] (MSP)

PINTO, Mrs. Sarah. December 7, 1697—March 8, 1785, New York City. Wife of Abraham Pinto.[1] (PAJHS, XVIII, 122)

PINTO, Solomon.[1] Born February 23, 1725/6. Son of Abraham Pinto,[1] he was married to Anna Green on October 4, 1762. (MSGC)

PINTO, Solomon.[2] In New York City in 1747. (PAJHS, XXI, 53)

PINTO, Solomon.[3] December 29, 1758, New Haven—March 28, 1824. This son of Jacob Pinto[1] was graduated from Yale University in 1777. An officer in the Revolutionary army, he was captured by the British in 1779. One of the founders of the Society of Cincinnati, he seems to have had no Jewish associations. His wife was Clarissa. (Kohut, 110; MSGC; PAJHS, XI, 90, et passim; XIX, 112f; UJE, VIII, 541)

PINTO, Thankful. Born December 22, 1769. Daughter of Jacob Pinto,[1] she was undoubtedly reared as a Christian. (MSGC)

PINTO, William. December 16, 1760—1847, New Orleans. This son of Jacob Pinto[1] was graduated from Yale University and taught school at Groton, Connecticut. A member of the Revolutionary army, he later became a prominent West India merchant. He seems to have had no Jewish affiliations. He had three wives: Fanny Hamilton, Urania Clar, and Lauretta Packard. (MSP; PAJHS, XIX, 111f)

PIZA, David. About 1740 he stopped in New York City on his way to Barbados. (PAJHS, XXI, 43)

POLOCK. Male child born about 1790, Philadelphia. (MIPR)

POLOCK. One additional member of the family of Myer. In Newport in 1774. (Census 1774)

POLOCK, Jr. In 1760 he was in Newport with his family. Cf. Myer Polock. (Kohut, 108)

POLOCK, "old." In Newport with his family in 1760. (Kohut, 108)

POLOCK, Miss. Born about 1755. In Newport in 1770. (Kohut, 44f)

POLOCK, Aaron. Died December 3, 1772, London. He had lived in New York City. (SIR)

POLOCK, Abraham. 1769—September 27, 1790, Savannah. Son of Myer Polock. (SRB)

POLOCK, Bilhah (Beulah). 1753—December 31, 1826, New York City. Daughter of Isaac Polock,[1] she was married to Joseph Jacobs.[1] In 1796 she was in New York City. (MSGC; PAJHS, XXVII, 211, 349)

POLOCK, Catherine. Incorrectly identified as a Louzada. Wife of Isaac A. Abraham. (*MSGC*)

POLOCK, Cushman. Died 1798. During the Revolution he served as an officer in the Colonial army, and he also advanced money to the American cause. He then resumed his position as a merchant in Philadelphia and Savannah. One of the founders of Congregation Mikveh Israel in Philadelphia, he was active in the Savannah congregation of the same name. On October 4, 1786, he was married to Rachel Jacobs.[2] (*GBMIP*; *MEAJB*, 334; *MISR*; *PAJHS*, XVII, 93, *et passim*; XXVII, 461; *SRB*)

POLOCK, David. Born September 21, 1778. Son of Myer Polock, he lived in Savannah in 1793. (*MISR*; *PAJHS*, XXVII, 348)

POLOCK, Hannah.[1] Died November 24, 1779. On June 1, 1763, she was married to Isaac Hart.[1] (*MSGC*)

POLOCK, Hannah (Ann).[2] 1782—1803. Daughter of Myer Polock, she was married to Moses Myers[4] of Georgetown, South Carolina. (*EVJC*; *MSGC*; *Wills*, 78)

POLOCK, Isaac.[1] August 16, 1700—May 23, 1764, Newport. Son of Myer Polock, he was a merchant. In 1742 he was elected constable in New York City, but was ineligible since he was neither a freeman nor a freeholder. (*Gutstein*, 306; *MCCCNY*, V, 62f; *MSGC*; *PAJHS*, XXI, 15, *et passim*; XXVII, 199)

POLOCK, Isaac.[2] November 25, 1766, Rhode Island. Son of Myer Polock. (*PAJHS*, XXVII, 153)

POLOCK, Isaac.[3] In Savannah in 1790. Cf. above. (*MISR*; *Wills*, 81)

POLOCK, Isaac Jacob. Died October 28, 1782, New York City. Son of Isaac Polock, he came from Surinam. (*PAJHS*, XXVII, 193)

POLOCK, Issachar. Died September 26, 1798, probably in Philadelphia. In 1749 he was a merchant in New York City; he lived also in Newport. (*Kohut*, 108; *MEAJA*, 89; *PAJHS*, XXVII, 180)

POLOCK, Issachar, Jr. In New York City in 1747. (*PAJHS*, XXI, 53)

POLOCK, Mrs. Issachar. In 1799 she was a mantilla worker in New York City. (*POFNW*, 471)

POLOCK, Jacob.[1] May 14, 1746, Newport —October 28, 1782, Newport. Son of Isaac Polock.[1] (*MSGC*)

POLOCK, Jacob.[2] November 11, 1777— November 17, 1777. Son of Myer Polock. (*PAJHS*, XXVII, 348)

POLOCK, Joseph. Died December 23, 1794, Savannah. Four months before his death he went from Charleston to Savannah. (*SRB*)

POLOCK, Judith. 1745—June 3, 1819, Georgetown, South Carolina. Daughter of Isaac Polock,[1] she was married to Philip Minis on July 20, 1774, in Newport. She lived later in Savannah. (*MSGC*; *WAJA*)

POLOCK, Levy. Probably in Philadelphia in 1792. (*MIPR*)

POLOCK, Myer. Died February 18, 1779. This son of Isaac Polock[1] lived in Philadelphia, Newport, and New York City. In 1769 he was a shipbuilder and trader in Newport. During the Revolution he was loyal to the British. On January 30, 1765, he was married to Abigail Sarzedas in New York City. (*MEAJA*, 153f; *MIPR*; *MSGC*; *PAJHS*, VI, 73; XXVII, 153, *et passim*; *SIR*)

POLOCK, Rachel. Died 1817, Savannah. Daughter of Myer Polock, she lived in Newport and Savannah. (*MSGC*; *SRB*; *Wills*, 78)

POLOCK, Mrs. Rebecca. August 16, 1698 —March 2, 1764, Newport. Wife of Zachariah Polock. (*PAJHS*, XXVII, 199)

POLOCK, Samuel. In Charlestown sometime between 1770 and 1782. (*EJSCB*, 19)

POLOCK, Sarah. Died 1790, Vainsborough, Georgia. Daughter of Isaac Polock,[1] she was in New York City in 1782. Her husband was Lyon Henry. (*MSGC*; *PAJHS*, XXVII, 349; *SRB*)

POLOCK, Solomon.[1] From Newport. About 1783 he was in Charlestown. (*EJSC*, 280)

POLOCK, Solomon.[2] Born Poland, died August 2, 1805, Charleston. During the Revolution he served in the Charlestown militia. Later he was an express rider. These references may be to more than one Solomon Polock. (*EJSC*, 92, *et passim*; *MSP*)

POLOCK, Tuchar (Tachia). In Newport sometime between 1740 and 1760. (*JNEB*, 8)

POLOCK, Zachariah. A shohet, in 1733 he was elected constable in New York City. His wife was Rebecca. (*MCCCNY*, IV, 195; *PAJHS*, XXI, 21, *et passim*; *Pool*, 23; *RIHM*, VI, 86)

POLONIES, Myer. About 1735—1801, New York City. He was the principal benefactor of the Polonies Talmud Torah, which was attached to Congregation Shearith Israel in New York City. (*PAJHS*, VI, 131; *Pool*, 160; *Wills*, 8)

POOL, Isaac. Born Germany, died August 30, 1813, Charleston. In 1800 he was living in Charleston with his family of six. (*Census B, South Carolina*; *EJSC*, 138; *MSP*)

PORTO. In 1773 he arrived in New York City from Curaçao. (*PAJHS*, XXI, 115)

PORTO, Jacob (Jacob De Porto). In 1695 he was in New York City, and was a merchant there in 1707. (*AJAM*, III, 6; *Pool*, 464; *SCMCNY*, 199f)

PORTSMOUTH, Davis. In Philadelphia in 1784. (*MIPR*)

POSNER (POZNA), Joseph. In 1792 he was a merchant in Savannah. (*MISR*; *SRB*)

POTA—TS, Cauffman. Died 1798, Philadelphia. (*MIPR*)

PRAGER, John. About 1784 he was a businessman in Philadelphia. (*WW*, 436)

PRAGER, Mark, Jr. During the Constitutional Convention in 1787 he dined with George Washington. In 1792 he was in Philadelphia. (*Morais*, 29; *WW*, 189, *et passim*)

PRAGER, Martin. Also noted as Mark. About 1784 he came from England, and was in Philadelphia in 1786. He had no ties to Judaism and probably was converted to Christianity. He may be identical with Mark Prager, Jr. (*PAJHS*, III, 150; *WW*, 224, 446)

PRAGER, Michael. 1740, County Cork, Ireland—1793, Philadelphia. He was active in founding the Insurance Company of North America. In 1792 he was in Philadelphia. (*Morais*, 29; *WW*, 340, 436)

PRAGER, Michael, Jr. Probably from Holland. About 1784 he was in Philadelphia. (*WW*, 436)

PREMENTAL. In New York City in 1757. Cf. Aaron Pimentel. (*PAJHS*, XII, 166)

R

RAFFELD, Solomon. In Philadelphia in 1788. Cf. Solomon Raphael. (*Coldoc*, 143f; *MIPR*)

RAINS, Abraham. About 1792 he arrived in Philadelphia. (*MIPR*)

RAMOS, Jacob. In Charlestown in 1773. (*EJSC*, 45)

RAMOS, Manuel. In Charleston in 1800. (*Census B, South Carolina*)

RAMOS, Moses Lopez. In New York City in 1741. (*PAJHS*, XXI, 44f)

RAPHAEL. Died May, 1793, Philadelphia. Son of Solomon Raphael. (*MIPR*)

RAPHAEL. About 1727—about 1762, New York City. (*PAJHS*, XVIII, 121)

RAPHAEL, Fontaine. In Hartford in 1789. It is doubtful that he was Jewish. (*PAJHS*, XIX, 27)

RAPHAEL, Rubin. In Philadelphia in 1797. (*MIPR*)

RAPHAEL, Solomon. A merchant, auctioneer, and peddler, he was in Philadelphia, Baltimore, and Richmond as early as 1788. In 1795 he was the keeper of a coffeehouse in Philadelphia. Cf. Solomon Raffeld. (*Blum*, 4; *ELJR*, 36, et passim; *MIPR*; *WW*, 184f)

RAPHE, Jacob. In 1798 he came from Bordeaux to New York City. (*SZ*, 121)

REGENSBURG, Myer. In Philadelphia and New York City in 1786. (*MIPR*; *PAJHS*, XXVII, 41, 43, 253)

REHINE, Zalma. 1757, Westphalia—July 2, 1843, Baltimore. This son of Isaac Rehine was a merchant and shopkeeper who was prominent in Jewish and civic affairs. He was the uncle of Isaac Leeser who brought him to America. He served in the Richmond militia. Late in his life he moved to Baltimore and helped establish a congregation there. On January 15, 1800, he was married to Rachel Judah.[4] (*ELJR*, 37, et passim; *MSGC*)

RENNER, Jacob. In Charleston in 1791. (*Coldoc*, 52)

RENNER, Reuben. Son of Jacob Renner, he was in Philadelphia in 1791. (*Coldoc*, 52)

RICARDO, Benjamin. In Charleston in 1800. (*EJSC*, 138)

RICARDO, Benjamin Israel. In Charlestown in 1762. Husband of Sarah. (*PAJHS*, XXIII, 187)

RICARDO, Daniel. In New York City in 1795. (*JRMP*)

RICARDO, Joseph. In 1773 he was in Philadelphia; he was a member of the St. George Society in 1792. (*PAJHS*, VI, 155; *WW*, 265)

RICARDO, Mordecai. In New York City in 1795. (*SIR*)

RICARDO, Samuel. Born New York City. On July 22, 1735, he was married to Ribca Israel in Amsterdam. (*Emanuel*, 298)

RICARDO, Mrs. Sarah. Wife of Benjamin Israel Ricardo, she was in Charlestown in 1762. (*PAJHS*, XXIII, 187)

RICE, Patrick. His name may have been Feibush or Phinehas Reis. In 1776 he was a clerk for David Franks in Pennsylvania. (*Byars*, 210; *MEAJB*, 95)

RIEUS, Isaac. Also listed as Isaac Nunes Ricus. In 1747 he was in Lancaster. Cf. Isaac Nunes Henriques. (*PAJHS*, I, 121; IX, 29, 42f)

RIRNING, Abraham. In New York City in 1737. It is highly doubtful that he was Jewish. (*PAJHS*, XXIII, 151)

RIVERA. Died at birth, August 17, 1727, New York City. Daughter of Abraham Rodrigues Rivera.[1] (*Pool*, 195f)

RIVERA, Aaron. Probably born before 1800. Son of Abraham Rivera, he settled in Wilmington, North Carolina. (*Pool*, 421)

RIVERA, Abraham Rodrigues.[1] Born Spain, died July 7, 1765, New York City/Newport.

He fled persecution in Spain and came to New York City. In 1726 he acquired the rights of a freeman, and in 1740 was naturalized. About 1748 he moved from New York City to Newport, where he became a prominent merchant. After the death of his second wife, he married Lucena. (PAJHS, V, 116; VI, 101; XXVII, 178, et passim; Pool, 15, et passim; UJE, IX, 172)

RIVERA, Abraham Rodrigues.[2] December, 1762, Newport—January 10, 1823, New York City. In 1764 this merchant son of Jacob Rodrigues Rivera[1] opened a school for the Jewish community of Congregation Shearith Israel in New York City. He joined the Newport Artillery Company, and was a member of the Redwood Library and Athenaeum. From 1800 until 1818 he lived in Europe. His wife was Hannah Lopez. (POFNW, 220; Pool, 53, et passim)

RIVERA, Daniel Rodrigues de. In New York City in 1741. (PAJHS, XXI, 44)

RIVERA, Isaac Rodrigues. Died Newport. Son of Abraham R. Rivera,[1] he was in New York City about 1740. His wife was Judith Pardo. (MSGC; PAJHS, XXI, 45, 53, 63)

RIVERA, J. About 1765 he was granted headrights in Georgia. (PAJHS, X, 88)

RIVERA, Jacob Rodrigues.[1] 1717, Spain—February 18, 1789, Newport. This son of Abraham Rodrigues Rivera[1] left New York City early in his career to go to Curaçao. He returned to New York City and was naturalized in 1746. About 1748 he moved to Newport. He became a prominent merchant and manufacturer, who ranked as the second wealthiest Jew after Aaron Lopez.[1] A member of the United Company of Spermaceti Candlers, he introduced the sperm oil industry into the colonies, and is said to have introduced the manufacture of spermaceti candles. When the British occupied Newport he moved to Leicester. A prominent participant in the Jewish community, he was president of the Newport Jewish Congregation, and was one of the founders of what was the first Jewish men's club in America. He was a patron of the Redwood Library. He was married to Hannah Pimentel in Curaçao. (Coldoc, 5, et passim; Gutstein, 308; MEAJA, 120, et passim; MEAJB, 238, et passim; UJE, IX, 172f; X, 348)

RIVERA, Jacob Rodrigues.[2] Born August 28, 1790, Newport. Son of Abraham Rodrigues Rivera.[2] (PAJHS, XXVII, 349)

RIVERA, James Rodrigues. In Newport in 1774. (PAJHS, XXVII, 449)

RIVERA, Manuel. 1795—February 20, 1797. Son of Abraham R. Rivera. (PAJHS, XXVII, 349)

RIVERA, Lopez y. In Philadelphia in 1740. (PAJHS, I, 24)

RIVERA, Rachel Rodrigues. Died October 21, 1731, New York City. Daughter of Abraham R. Rivera.[1] (Pool, 459)

RIVERA, Mrs. Rachel Rodrigues. About 1684—March 14, 1761, Newport. (PAJHS, XXVII, 203)

RIVERA, Rebecca. Died October 17, 1793. Daughter of Abraham R. Rivera,[1] she was married to Moses Lopez.[1] (MSGC; PAJHS, II, 104f)

RIVERA, Rodriguez. In Philadelphia in 1740. (PAJHS, I, 24)

RIVERA, Rodrigo de. In New York City in 1737. Cf. above. (PAJHS, XXIII, 151)

RIVERA, Sarah Rodrigues.[1] 1747, New York City—January 6, 1840, New York City. Daughter of Jacob R. Rivera,[1] she was the second wife of Aaron Lopez.[1] (Pool, 197)

RIVERA, Sarah Rodrigues.[2] About 1789—May 23, 1823, probably in New York City. Daughter of Abraham R. Rivera.[2] (PAJHS, XXVII, 307; Pool, 197, et passim)

RIVERA, Mrs. Sarah Rodrigues. Died August 17, 1727, New York City. Probably the second wife of Abraham R. Rivera.[1] (Pool, 195f)

RIVERA, Solomon. A poor French boy, in 1782 he was seeking assistance from Congregation Mikveh Israel in Philadelphia. (MIPR)

RIZ, David. From Jamaica, B.W.I. In 1709 he was a merchant in Charlestown. (ELHS; Reznikoff, 12)

ROBLES, David. From France. A trader, on May 11, 1687, he became a freeman in New York City. (AJAM, III, 10)

ROBLES, Mrs. David. A widow, about 1703 she lived with her family in New York City. She was probably married to Sampson Mears[2] at a later date. (*CPG*, 179; *PAJHS*, XXXIII, 202; *POFNW*, 468)

ROBLES, Jacob. A French alien, he was in New York City in 1687. (*AJAM*, III, 10)

RODREQUES, Manuel. In Virginia in 1652. It is doubtful that he was Jewish. (*AJAM*, III, 10)

RODREQUES, Silvedo. In Virginia in 1625. It is doubtful that he was Jewish. (*AJAM*, III, 10)

RODRIGUES, Abraham. From St. Domingo. In February, 1797, he was married to Rebecca Sasportas in Charleston. (*EJMC*, 6)

RODRIGUES, Mrs. Esther. 1776, Bordeaux—August 26, 1838. Wife of Moïse Rodrigues, she was in Charleston in 1798. (*MSGC*)

RODRIGUES, Isaac. Died November 7, 1815, Philadelphia. Probably a gentile, in 1783 he was a shopkeeper in Philadelphia. Either he was married to Catherine de Spencer, or she was his common-law wife. (*MIPR*; *PAJHS*, VI, 109; *Wills*, 22)

RODRIGUES, Isaac Raphael. In 1723 he was a shopkeeper who was naturalized in New York City. (*PAJHS*, VI, 105; XXI, 6, 45, 182; *SCMCNY*, 181)

RODRIGUES, Moïse. About 1760, Bordeaux—December 22, 1830, South Carolina. In 1798 he came to Charleston. His wife was Esther. (*MSGC*)

RODRIGUES, Rachel. Died May 19, 1733, New York City. (*PAJHS*, XVIII, 121)

ROGET, Isaac. In Philadelphia and New York City about 1795. (*MIPR*; *PAJHS*, XXVII, 62)

ROPHE, Salomon. Fought in the Revolution. (*PAJHS*, VI, 74)

ROSETTA, Abraham. In New York City in 1750. (*PAJHS*, XXI, 64)

ROSETTA, Elkanah. In New York City in 1746. (*PAJHS*, XXI, 51, 64)

RUBIN, Amsel. In New York City in 1740. (*PAJHS*, XXI, 42)

RUDEN, Jacob (Jaques). January 23, 1770 —October 5, 1806, New York City. In New York City by 1800. (*MSGC*; *PAJHS*, XVIII, 107; *SIR*)

RUSSELL, Henry M. May 23, 1797, Richmond—July 20, 1841, Philadelphia. Son of Philip M. Russell. (*MSGC*)

RUSSELL, Isaac. October 11, 1787, Norfolk—March 25, 1845, Savannah. Son of Philip M. Russell, he was married to Perla Sheftall[2] on July 1, 1808. (*MSGC*; *SRB*)

RUSSELL, Judith. October 4, 1785, Baltimore—April 19, 1868, Philadelphia. Daughter of Philip M. Russell, she was married to Isaiah Nathan.[1] (*MSGC*)

RUSSELL, Moses. Born May 30, 1791, Norfolk. Son of Philip Moses Russell. (*MSGC*)

RUSSELL, Philip Moses. About 1745— August 11, 1830, Philadelphia. A surgeon, he fought at Valley Forge and in Virginia. He was a merchant. On November 2, 1776, he was married to Esther Mordecai. (*Morais*, 29, *et passim*; *PAJHS*, XX, 98; *UJE*, IX, 277f; X, 470)

RUSSELL, Rachel. October 19, 1798, Richmond—June 6, 1887. Daughter of Philip M. Russell, she was married to David de Oliveira Tobias. (*MSGC*)

RUSSELL, Rebecca. December 25, 1794, Richmond—September 13, 1878. Daughter of Philip M. Russell, she was married to David Nathans. (*MSGC*)

RUSSELL, Samuel. June 10, 1783, Baltimore—October 8, 1831, New York City. Son of Philip M. Russell, on March 26, 1806, he was married to Sarah de Lyon in Savannah, where he had settled in 1803. (*MSGC*)

RUSSELL, Sarah. Born before 1800. Daughter of Philip M. Russell, she was buried in Philadelphia on March 3, 1840. (*MIPR*)

RUSSELL, Zipporah. Born July 10, 1781, Baltimore. Daughter of Philip M. Russell. (*MSGC*)

S

SACHES (SEIXAS), Jacob. Imported goods from Jamaica. Cf. Jacob M. Seixas. (*JRMP*)

SALIMEN, Isaac. Cf. Isaac Solomon.[8]

SALOMON, Benjamin. In 1798 he came from Bordeaux to Philadelphia. (*SZ*, 121)

SALOMON, Deborah. January 12, 1783—September 13, 1808, New York City. Daughter of Haym Salomon, she was married to Simon Myers Cohen in New York City on August 14, 1804. (*MSGC*)

SALOMON, Ezekiel. July 20, 1778, Philadelphia—September 27, 1821, New Orleans. This son of Haym Salomon was a banker who became cashier of the New Orleans branch of the U.S. Bank. (*MEAJB*, 138; *MSGC*; *PAJHS*, II, 16; *SIR*)

SALOMON, Haym. 1740, Lissa, Poland—January 6, 1785, Philadelphia. He left Poland and went to Europe and England before coming to America about 1775. First a sutler and then a broker and commission merchant, he dealt in the sale of bills of exchange. During the Revolution he was captured and imprisoned by the British, but escaped to Philadelphia, where he dealt in French and Dutch securities. He was also in the mercantile and import field, and was fiscal agent for the French, Dutch, and Spanish. He aided the Revolutionary cause through his financial activities. A Mason as well as a prominent member of the Jewish community in Philadelphia, he was one of those who protested the discriminatory oath taken from the New Testament, which Pennsylvania required of its office holders. He donated one-sixth of the costs to help finance the synagogue building in Philadelphia. In 1781 he was chief agent for Robert Morris. He lent funds to James Madison and Edmund Randolph. When he died he left four young children. On July 6, 1777, he was married to Rachel Franks.[8] (*DAB*, XVI, 313f; *JRMP*; *MEAJB*, 126, *et passim*; *PAJHS*, II, 5-19; III, 7-11; XXVII, 227f; XXVIII, 225, *et passim*; *UJE*, IX, 322f)

SALOMON, Hyam M. April 23, 1785, Philadelphia—February 15, 1858, New York. This son of Hyam Salomon was a merchant who agitated to recover from the U.S. government large sums of money, presumably expended by his father. In 1809 he was married to Ella Hart. (*MEAJB*, 132; *MSGC*; *PAJHS*, II, 5, *et passim*)

SALOMON, Sallie. October 17, 1779, Philadelphia—July 29, 1845, New York City. Daughter of Hyam Salomon, she was married to Joseph Andrews on August 9, 1794, in New York City. (*MSGC*)

SALOMON, Salomon. In Georgia in 1733. (*Coulter*, 95)

SALOMONS, Collman. In New York City in 1729; in Georgia in 1739. Cf. Solomon Colman. (*JRMP*; *PAJHS*, XXI, 21)

SALOMONS, Moses. In New York City about 1740. (*PAJHS*, XXI, 45)

SALVADOR, Francis. 1747—August 1, 1776, South Carolina. This son of Jacob Salvador came to America in 1773 and settled in Ninety-Six, South Carolina, where he became an important landholder. He probably grew indigo on his plantation. A member of the first Provincial Congress of South Carolina, he was the first Jew to be a representative in a "popular assembly," although he was probably not elected. In a loyalist area he was an ardent patriot for the American cause. He was killed in the Revolution in a battle fought in the village of Essenecca, South Carolina. His wife was Sarah Salvador. (*EJSC*, 45, *et passim*; *MEAJB*, 245, *et passim*; *UJE*, IX, 331)

SALVADOR, Joseph. January 21, 1716, Holland/London—December 29, 1786, Charleston. One of the outstanding financiers and bankers of England in his time, he is said to have financially supported the English crown during the rebellion of 1745 to 1746. A fellow of the Royal Society, he was governor of several hospitals. In England he fought to have Jews given the right of naturalization. He was president of his synagogue in London. The first Jewish member of the Dutch East India Company, after he lost his fortune in England, he came to America, where he was eventually naturalized, and spent his last years. He settled in Charleston and accumulated large landholdings. His wife was Rachel (Lenore) Suasso. (*EJSC*, 33, *et passim*; *MEAJB*, 258, *et passim*; *Wills*, 54)

SAMPSON, Samuel. Fought in the Georgia line in the Revolutionary army. It is highly doubtful that he was Jewish. (*PAJHS*, XVII, 99)

SAMUEL, The Jew. In Boston in 1695. Cf. Samuel Frazon (Frazier). (*AJAM*, III, 10)

SAMUEL, Henry. In Virginia in 1781. It is highly doubtful that he was Jewish. (*PAJHS*, XX, 99)

SAMUEL, Hyman. A silversmith and watchmaker, he lived in Petersburg, Virginia, in 1792; in Richmond by 1796; and also in Baltimore and and Charleston. He was married to Rebecca Alexander. (*Coldoc*, 51, 53f; *PAJHS*, XIX, 57)

SAMUEL, Isaac.[1] Born 1700. Son of Judah Samuel, he was in New York City in 1702. (*PAJHS*, XXIII, 148)

SAMUEL, Isaac.[2] In 1785 he was temporarily the minister of Congregation Shearith Israel in New York City, but was released when the congregation could not afford to pay his salary. (*Pool*, 96)

SAMUEL, Israel. In Philadelphia in 1785. (*MIPR*)

SAMUEL, Joseph. In Norfolk in 1800. (*PAJHS*, XIX, 62)

SAMUEL, Judah.[1] Died 1702, New York City. (*PAJHS*, XXIII, 148; *POFNW*, 228)

SAMUEL, Judah.[2] In New York City in 1740. (*PAJHS*, XXI, 42)

SAMUEL, Judah B. In New York City in 1740. (*PAJHS*, XXI, 42)

SAMUEL, Levy. A merchant, he was naturalized in New York City in 1741. (*PAJHS*, V, 116; XIII, 6)

SAMUEL, Moses. In 1798 he may have been the first peddler in Richmond. (*ELJR*, 78)

SAMUEL(S), Philip. A partner of Henry Mordecai, in 1756 he went from New York City to Boston, apparently absconding. In 1760 he was in Holland. (*Beckmans*, 393; *PAJHS*, XXIII, 83; *UJE*, VII, 403; *White*, 649f)

SAMUEL, Phoebe. 1736, England—1786, Montreal. In 1761 she was married to Lazarus David in Rhode Island. (*JE*, IV, 459)

SAMUEL, Samuel. In New York City in 1776. (*Schappes*, 52)

SAMUELLS, Miss. In South Carolina in 1780. It is doubtful that she was Jewish. (*PAJHS*, XII, 53)

SANGUINETTA, Mr. In New York City in 1796. (*SIR*)

SARPHATINE, Rachel. A niece of Joseph Brown, she may have been in America in 1704. (*PAJHS*, XXIII, 148)

SARZEDAS, Miss. Born December 5, 1764, New York City. Daughter of Abraham Sarzedas. (*SIR*)

SARZEDAS, Abigail. Died November 13, 1811, Savannah. Daughter of Abraham Sarzedas, she lived in New York City and Newport. On January 30, 1765, she was married to Myer Polock. (*Census A, New York*; *MSGC*; *PAJHS*, XXVII, 348; *SIR*)

SARZEDAS, Abraham. Died before 1779. A well known Mason and merchant, he lived in New York, Newport, and in the West Indies. On July 17, 1753, he became a freeman of New York City. In 1764 he farmed in Georgia; in 1767 he was in Savannah. His wife was Caty Hays. (*MEAJB*, 327f; *PAJHS*, VI, 102; X, 94; XIX, 88; XXI, 51, 63, 79; *SRB*)

SARZEDAS, David. About 1760—July 28, 1841. This son of Abraham Sarzedas served in the Revolutionary army in Savannah but went to Charlestown after the fall of Savannah. He became a physician in Charleston and was still practicing there in 1822. He was married to Sarah da Costa. (*EJSC*, 91, *et passim*; *MEAJB*, 330f; *MSGC*; *MSP*; *PAJHS*, X, 94; XVII, 93, *et passim*)

SARZEDAS, David, Jr. 1785—June 15, 1828, Cheraw, South Carolina. Son of

David Sarzedas, he was born in Charleston. (*MSGC*)

SARZEDAS, Judah. Born December 22, 1762, New York City. Son of Abraham Sarzedas. (*SIR*)

SARZEDAS, Moses. October 23, 1767, Savannah—October 7, 1811, Georgetown, South Carolina. Son of Abraham Sarzedas, he was married to Belle Myers, and lived in Camden and Charleston. (*EJSC*, 244, 280; *MSGC*; *SRB*)

SARZEDAS, Rebecca. 1761—December 11, 1840, New York City. Daughter of Abraham Sarzedas, she was married to Gershom Cohen on August 27, 1779. (*EJMC*, 5; *MSGC*; *Wills*, 44)

SASPORTAS, Aaron. Died October, 1798, Charleston. Son of Abraham Sasportas. (*MSGC*)

SASPORTAS, Abraham. About 1756, Bordeaux—November 14, 1825, Bordeaux. A merchant, he lived in Philadelphia, but spent his last years in Bordeaux, where he owned a hotel. His first wife was Rachel da Costa in Charlestown on September 17, 1778; his second wife was Charlotte Cantor in January, 1803. (*EJMC*, 5; *MSGC*; *PAJHS*, I, 24; XIX, 77, 81, 85f; *SCHGM*, XI, 167; *Wills*, 38, 55)

SASPORTAS, Augustus. Son of Abraham Sasportas. (*MSGC*)

SASPORTAS, Isaac. 1791, Charleston—September 2, 1819, Darien. Possibly a son of Abraham Sasportas. (*MSGC*)

SASPORTAS, Jacob. In 1794 he came from Bordeaux to Charleston. (*SZ*, 121)

SASPORTAS, Rebecca. About 1782—February 15, 1800. Daughter of Abraham Sasportas, she was married to Abraham Rodrigues in February, 1797, in Charleston. (*EJMC*, 6; *SCHGM*, XXVI, 58)

SASPORTAS, Sarah. Daughter of Abraham Sasportas. (*MSGC*)

SASPORTAS, Zelmire. Son of Abraham Sasportas. (*MSGC*)

SCHNEIDER, Lipman. Cf. Levy Marks.[3] (*PAJHS*, XXXIV, 96)

SCHWAB, Benjamin Wolf. Identical with Benjamin Jacobs.[1] Son of Jacob Schwab, he was in New York City in 1728. (*PAJHS*, XXXVII, 375; *POFNW*, 460)

SEBY, David. In 1736 he was a shohet in New York City. (*PAJHS*, II, 48)

SECORE, Samuel. In Georgia in 1733. (*Coulter*, 96)

SEGAL, Abraham. May be another name of Abraham Levy. In New York City in 1764. (*PAJHS*, XXXIV, 95)

SEIXAS. Stillborn child of Abraham Mendes Seixas.[2] (*MSGC*)

SEIXAS, Aaron. September 14, 1796—June 28, 1849. Son of Benjamin M. Seixas.[1] (*PAJHS*, IV, 211; XXVII, 163)

SEIXAS, Abigail.[1] November 17, 1742—September 4, 1819, Richmond. Daughter of Isaac M. Seixas,[1] she was married to Hillel Judah in June, 1759. (*MSGC*; *PAJHS*, XXVII, 162)

SEIXAS, Abigail.[2] December 3, 1779—June 6, 1782. Daughter of Benjamin M. Seixas.[1] (*PAJHS*, XXVII, 163)

SEIXAS, Abigail.[3] December 28, 1782, Newport—March 21, 1854, New York City. Daughter of Moses M. Seixas.[1] (*MSGC*; *PAJHS*, IV, 204; XXVII, 347)

SEIXAS, Abigail.[4] Born October 7, 1783, died Savannah. Daughter of Abraham M. Seixas.[2] (*MSGC*)

SEIXAS, Abigail.[5] June 23, 1784—July 30, 1860. Daughter of Benjamin M. Seixas,[1] she was married to Benjamin J. Phillips on January 25, 1804. (*PAJHS*, IV, 211; XXVII, 163)

SEIXAS, Abraham M.[1] November, 1741, New York City—March 31, 1742, New York City. Son of Isaac M. Seixas.[1] (*PAJHS*, XX, 164; XXVII, 161; *Pool*, 466f)

SEIXAS, Abraham M.[2] March 14, 1750/1, New York City—April 9, 1799, Charleston. This son of Isaac M. Seixas[1] was a merchant who spent most of his mature years in Charleston. He served as an officer in the Revolutionary army and fought in Georgia and South Carolina. Later he entered politics but was unsuccessful. On November

18, 1777, he was married to Richea Hart. (*MEAJB*, 255, *et passim*; *MSGC*; *PAJHS*, IV, 202; XXVII, 161, 348)

SEIXAS, Abraham M.[3] January 22, 1786—August 28, 1834. Son of Benjamin M. Seixas,[1] he was married to Rachel Cardozo on April 11, 1821. (*PAJHS*, IV, 211; XXVII, 163)

SEIXAS, Bella. February 24, 1781, New York City—December 17, 1860. Daughter of Moses M. Seixas.[1] Cf. Bilhah L. Seixas. (*MSGC*)

SEIXAS, Benjamin M.[1] January 28, 1748, Newport—August 16, 1817, New York City. This son of Isaac M. Seixas[1] became a freeman of New York City on February 8, 1769. A saddler, he owned his shop. During the Revolution he belonged to the New York militia; during the British occupation of New York he lived in Stratford, Connecticut. With Isaac Moses he engaged in privateering. He was one of the founders of the New York Stock Exchange. A Mason, he was also very prominent in the Jewish affairs of his community. Later in his life he was an auctioneer. On January 27, 1779, he was married to Zipporah Levy. (*Coldoc*, 22, *et passim*; *Gutstein*, 73; *MEAJA*, 159, 161f; *MEAJB*, 121, *et passim*; *PAJHS*, XXVII, 161; *Pool*, 378f)

SEIXAS, Benjamin M.[2] June 6, 1775, Newport—May 19, 1843. Son of Moses M. Seixas,[1] he was a Mason in Richmond in 1804. (*ELJR*, 36, 38; *MSGC*; *PAJHS*, IV, 204; XIX, 62, 71; XXVII, 348)

SEIXAS, Benjamin M.[3] 1783, New York City—February 16, 1847, Baltimore. Son of Gershom Mendes Seixas. (*MSGC*; *Pool*, 250, 350, 371)

SEIXAS, Bilhah Levy. February 3, 1781, Newport—1820/1860, New York City. Daughter of Moses M. Seixas.[1] Cf. Bella Seixas. (*PAJHS*, IV, 204; XXVII, 347)

SEIXAS, Daniel. May 6, 1800—March 19, 1865. Son of Benjamin M. Seixas.[1] (*MSGC*)

SEIXAS, David G. 1788—March 19, 1864, South Bend, Indiana. Son of Gershom Mendes Seixas. During the War of 1812, when English imports were banned, he manufactured crockery, and he has been called the father of this art in America. He was engaged also in the manufacturing of sealing wax, printer's ink, and enamel-surfaced visiting cards; and he virtually introduced daguerreotypes into the United States. Besides many other ventures, such as his establishment of a brewery, he discovered methods of burning anthracite coal which had previously been considered too hard for consumption. A pioneer in methods for training deaf-mute children, he founded a "Deaf and Dumb School" in his own home. The Gratz family was prominent in having this home instituted by the state, but he was later ejected by opponents on his board. He was active in Congregation Mikveh Israel. (*MSGC*; *Pool*, 371f; *UJE*, IX, 462; *WW*, 289, *et passim*)

SEIXAS, Edward. June 21, 1799, New York City—May 17, 1871, Thomasville, Georgia. Son of Jacob M. Seixas. (*MSGC*)

SEIXAS, Elias. In Montreal in 1768. (*PAJHS*, I, 117)

SEIXAS, Elkaleh. Born 1795, New York City. Daughter of Gershom Mendes Seixas, she was married to Benjamin S. Solomons on April 28, 1816. (*Pool*, 372)

SEIXAS, Esther.[1] March 31, 1789, New York City—December 23, 1872. Daughter of Benjamin M. Seixas,[1] she was married to Naphtali Phillips on October 8, 1823. (*MSGC*; *PAJHS*, IV, 211; XXVII, 163)

SEIXAS, Esther.[2] May 2, 1789, Newport—December 4, 1855, New York City. Daughter of Moses M. Seixas.[1] (*PAJHS*, IV, 204)

SEIXAS, Fanny Mendes. May 31, 1787—August 12, 1787. Daughter of Abraham M. Seixas.[2] (*MSGC*)

SEIXAS, Gershom Mendes. January 14/15, 1745/1746, New York City—July 2, 1816, New York City. This son of Isaac M. Seixas[1] was the first native American minister, and was recognized by American society as the chief spokesman of American Jewry. In 1768 he served as the spiritual leader of Congregation Shearith Israel in New York City. During the British occupation of New York City he fled first to Stratford, Connecticut, and then to Philadelphia, where in 1782 he helped establish and served as minister of Congregation Mikveh Israel for two years. He was present at the inauguration of George Washington. From 1784 to 1814 he was regent and trustee of Columbia University. The first rabbi to preach a sermon in English in an American synagogue, he founded the Hebra Hased Va-Amet, one of New York's earliest charitable institutions. His first wife was Elkaleh Cohen[2] on September 6, 1775; his second wife was Hannah Manuel on November 1, 1789. (*DAB*, XVI, 564f; *MEAJA*, 94, et passim; *MEAJB*, 157, et passim; *Pool*, 43, et passim; *UJE*, VIII, 177; IX, 462f)

SEIXAS, Gershom M. September 30, 1784, Newport—October 12, 1784, Newport. Son of Moses M. Seixas.[1] (*PAJHS*, IV, 204)

SEIXAS, Grace.[1] November 24/28, 1752, New York City—November 9, 1831, New York City. Daughter of Isaac M. Seixas,[1] she was very well educated and had literary inclinations. On August 29, 1780, she was married to Simon Nathan.[2] (*MSGC*; *PAJHS*, IV, 202, 211f; XVIII, 122; XXVII, 161; *Pool*, 438f)

SEIXAS, Grace.[2] August 29, 1785—December 17, 1821. Daughter of Abraham M. Seixas.[2] (*MSGC*)

SEIXAS, Grace.[3] December 31, 1786, Newport—November 22, 1865, New York City. Daughter of Moses M. Seixas,[1] she was married to Dr. Benjamin I. Cohen. (*MSGC*; *PAJHS*, IV, 204)

SEIXAS, Grace.[4] December 7, 1789—August 20, 1826, Virginia. Daughter of Gershom Mendes Seixas, she was married to Emanuel Judah on February 1, 1815. (*MSGC*; *PAJHS*, IV, 208)

SEIXAS, Grace.[5] July 15, 1794, New York City—August 21, 1866, New York City. Daughter of Benjamin M. Seixas,[1] she was married to Jacob I. Cohen on April 2/5, 1815. (*MSGC*; *PAJHS*, IV, 211; XXVII, 163)

SEIXAS, Hyman L. December (October) 14, 1792—September 23, 1865. Son of Benjamin M. Seixas,[1] he was married to Abigail Cardozo on September 8, 1824. (*MSGC*; *PAJHS*, IV, 211; XXVII, 163)

SEIXAS, Isaac B. November 22, 1781—August 10, 1839. This son of Benjamin M. Seixas[1] was hazzan for Congregation Shearith Israel in New York City and for Congregation Beth Shalome in Richmond. He served in the militia in Richmond and was a merchant there. On May 31, 1809, he was married to Rebecca Judah. (*ELJR*, 39, et passim; *PAJHS*, IV, 211; VI, 135; XIX, 31, 39f, 63; XXVII, 163)

SEIXAS, Isaac M.[1] September 5, 1709, Lisbon—November 3, 1781/2, Newport. This merchant son of Abraham M. Seixas came to America about 1734. In 1745 he was naturalized and elected constable in New York City, but was not eligible to constable since he was neither a freeman nor a freeholder. He moved to Newport and remained there until the British occupation, when he moved to Connecticut. About 1740 he was married to Rachel Levy.[3] (*Coldoc*, 22f; *MCCCNY*, V, 200, 202; *MEAJA*, 158-163; *MEAJB*, 217, 255; *PAJHS*, IV, 89; XIII, 6; XXVII, 161, 347; *Pool*, 29, et passim)

SEIXAS, Isaac M.[2] Born July 30, 1776, New York City, died an infant. Son of Gershom Mendes Seixas. (*PAJHS*, IV, 208; *SIR*)

SEIXAS, Isaac M.[3] August 18, 1778, Charlestown—October 10, 1826, St. Thomas. Son of Abraham M. Seixas,[2] he was married to Abigail Valencia. (*MSGC*)

SEIXAS, Isaac M.[4] July 28, 1779—February 5, 1786, Newport. Son of Moses M. Seixas.[1] (*PAJHS*, XXVII, 193, 347)

SEIXAS, Jacob B. July 30, 1795—March 15, 1854. Son of Benjamin M. Seixas.[1] (*PAJHS*, XXVII, 163)

SEIXAS, Jacob M. May 22, 1759, France—June 22, 1821, New York City. About 1794 he came to New York City. On December 28, 1807, he was married to Rachel Levy,[6] the widow of an English army officer named Levy. (*MSGC*; *PAJHS*, XXVII, 56; *Pool*, 406f)

SEIXAS, Joseph. Born 1794. Son of Gershom Mendes Seixas. (*Pool*, 372)

SEIXAS, John. 1787, Newport—October 28, 1853, Baton Rouge, Louisiana. Son of Jacob M. Seixas. (*MSGC*)

SEIXAS, Joshua M.[1] August 14, 1781—August 26, 1781. Son of Abraham M. Seixas.[2] (MSGC)

SEIXAS, Joshua M.[2] July 20, 1788—August 7, 1789. Son of Abraham M. Seixas.[2] (MSGC)

SEIXAS, Judith M. 1777, Newport—November 13, 1829, New York City. Daughter of Moses M. Seixas,[1] she was married to Samuel Lopez[2] on March 4, 1806. (MSGC; PAJHS, IV, 204; Pool, 135)

SEIXAS, Mendez. In New York City about 1739. Cf. Isaac M. Seixas.[1] (PAJHS, XXVII, 6)

SEIXAS, Michael Isaac. In Charleston in 1800. (Census B, South Carolina)

SEIXAS, Moïse. Died July 11, 1817, New York City. In 1794 he came to New York City from France. Apparently a convert to Christianity, he was buried in St. Paul's Church Yard in New York City. (MSGC; PAJHS, XXVII, 56; Pool, 407)

SEIXAS, Moses B. October 24, 1780—December 28, 1838/9, New York City. Son of Benjamin M. Seixas,[1] he was married to Judith Levy on November 9, 1808. (PAJHS, IV, 211; XXVII, 163)

SEIXAS, Moses M.[1] March 28, 1744, New York City—November 29, 1809, Newport. This son of Isaac M. Seixas[1] was one of the organizers of the Bank of Rhode Island and was its first cashier. The first grand master of the Masons in Rhode Island, he participated also in the Jewish community, and in 1790 was president of the Newport Jewish congregation. He seems to have had loyalist leanings. His wife was Jochebed Levy. (PAJHS, IV, 201, 203; XIX, 18, et passim; XXVII, 210; Pool, 346; UJE, VIII, 214)

SEIXAS, Moses M.[2] Born March 20, 1793, died a youth. Son of Abraham M. Seixas.[2] (MSGC)

SEIXAS, Mrs. Nancy. In New York City in 1789. (SIR)

SEIXAS, Rachel Hannah. August 9, 1773, Newport—August 5, 1822. Daughter of Moses M. Seixas,[1] she was married to Naphtali Phillips on July 5, 1797. (PAJHS, IV, 204; XXVII, 350)

SEIXAS, Rachel M.[1] June 25, 1782, Philadelphia—May 12, 1797, New York City. Daughter of Abraham M. Seixas.[2] (MSGC; PAJHS, XXVII, 348)

SEIXAS, Rachel M.[2] September 7, 1798—1861. Daughter of Benjamin M. Seixas, she was married to Dr. Daniel L. M. Peixotto on March 19, 1823. (PAJHS, IV, 211; XXVII, 163)

SEIXAS, Raphael. Died 1756, New York City. Infant son of Isaac M. Seixas. (PAJHS, XXVII, 161)

SEIXAS, Rebecca B. November 10, 1782, Philadelphia—October 2, 1868. Daughter of Benjamin M. Seixas,[1] she was married to Bernard Hart on August 13, 1806. (MSGC; PAJHS, IV, 211; XXVII, 163)

SEIXAS, Rebecca M.[1] Born May 8, 1780. Daughter of Abraham M. Seixas.[2] (MSGC)

SEIXAS, Rebecca M.[2] August 20, 1780, Philadelphia—December 2, 1867. Daughter of Gershom Mendes Seixas. (MSGC; PAJHS, IV, 208)

SEIXAS, Samuel. 1792/3—February 13, 1852, New York City. Son of Gershom Mendes Seixas. (MSGC; PAJHS, IV, 208; Pool, 372)

SEIXAS, Sara.[1] February 10, 1778—August 4, 1854. Daughter of Gershom Mendes Seixas, she was married to Israel B. Kursheedt on January 18, 1804. (MSGC; PAJHS, IV, 208)

SEIXAS, Sara.[2] February 27, 1791—August 5, 1834. Daughter of Benjamin M. Seixas,[2] she was married to Seixas Nathan on November 30, 1808. (MSGC; PAJHS, IV, 211f; XXVII, 163)

SEIXAS, Solomon. May 5, 1787—October 7, 1840, New York City. Son of Benjamin M. Seixas,[1] he was married to Esther Gomez on February 1, 1815. (MSGC; PAJHS, IV, 211; XXVII, 163)

SEIXAS, William. 1783, Newport—April 5, 1829, Quebec. Son of Jacob M. Seixas. (MSGC)

SEIXAS, Zipporah. Born August 12, 1793. Daughter of Abraham M. Seixas.[2] (MSGC)

SERRA, Mrs. A widow with family, in 1749 she was about to leave New York City and go to Barbados. (PAJHS, XXI, 60; POFNW, 343)

SEY, Eliezer. In Philadelphia in 1782. (Morais, 15)

SHEFTALL, Miss.[1] and Miss.[2] Born February 26, 1796, Savannah. The twin daughters of Moses Sheftall. (SRB)

SHEFTALL, Abigail Minis. Born February 20, 1796, Savannah. Daughter of Levi Sheftall,[2] she was married to Levy Hart on July 15, 1818. (MSGC; SRB)

SHEFTALL, Abraham. Died December 17, 1831. Son of Levi Sheftall, he had an M.D. degree. In November, 1817, he was married to Sarah de la Motta. (MSGC)

SHEFTALL, Benjamin.[1] 1692—October 3, 1765. In 1733 this son of Mordecai Sheftall came to Savannah and was a farmer. He is reputed to have been one of the founders of the Union Society of Savannah. His first wife was Elizabeth; his second wife was Hannah Solomons on November 20, 1738. (MEAJB, 342f, 348, 355; PAJHS, III, 114f; XVII, 90, et passim; SRB; UJE, IX, 499)

SHEFTALL, Benjamin.[2] October 14, 1767, Savannah—August 5, 1794. Son of Mordecai Sheftall,[1] he fought in the Revolutionary army. He died while at sea on the French privateer Industry. Cf. below. (MEAJB, 351; SRB)

SHEFTALL, Benjamin.[3] Died February 5, 1795, Savannah. (MISR)

SHEFTALL, Benjamin.[4] Born April 6, 1771, Savannah. Son of Levi Sheftall,[2] he was in Savannah in 1788. (SRB; Wills, 82)

SHEFTALL, Elias. February 18, 1765, Savannah—March 2, 1765. Son of Mordecai Sheftall.[1] (SRB)

SHEFTALL, Mrs. Elizabeth. Died 1736. First wife of Benjamin Sheftall,[1] she was in Savannah in 1733. (Coulter, 96; MEAJB, 342)

SHEFTALL, Emanuel. February 16, 1786, Savannah—April 23, 1818, Savannah. Son of Levi Sheftall,[3] he lived in Charleston and Savannah. (MSGC; SRB)

SHEFTALL, Esther. September 16, 1771—September 27, 1828, Savannah. Daughter of Mordecai Sheftall.[1] (MSGC)

SHEFTALL, Frances. 1800—October 28, 1816. Daughter of Moses Sheftall. (MSGC)

SHEFTALL, Hannah. Born April 11, 1773, Savannah. Daughter of Levi Sheftall,[2] she was married to Abraham de Lyon on March 21, 1827. (MSGC; SRB)

SHEFTALL, Isaac. Born October 16, 1779. Son of Levi Sheftall,[2] he was buried on July 20, 1780. (MEAJB, 362; SRB)

SHEFTALL, Judith. Born June 29, 1781, Charleston. Daughter of Levi Sheftall.[2] (SRB)

SHEFTALL, Leah. Sometime between 1750 and 1760 she was granted land in Georgia. (PAJHS, X, 88)

SHEFTALL, Levi., Sr.[1] Died December 6, 1775, Savannah. (SRB)

SHEFTALL, Levi.[2] December 12, 1739, Savannah—January 26, 1809, Savannah. This son of Benjamin Sheftall[1] was a rancher, butcher, and commissary to the American army. He served in the Revolutionary forces against the British, but was unjustly suspected of Tory sympathies. He lived in Charleston for a short time. In 1798 he was president of Congregation Mikveh Israel in Savannah. On May 25, 1768, he was married to Sarah de la Motta in Santa Croix, W.I. (Coldoc, 64, et passim; EJSC, 30, et passim; MEAJB, 338, et passim; MISR; MSGC; PAJHS, X, 83, et passim; XVII, 103, et passim; SRB)

SHEFTALL, Levi.[3] October 27, 1776, Savannah—1796. Son of Levi Sheftall.[2] (MSGC; SRB)

SHEFTALL, Mordecai.[1] December 5/16, 1735, Savannah—July 6, 1797, Savannah. This son of Benjamin Sheftall[1] owned large amounts of land which he ranched. As a merchant he had a warehouse and wharf in Savannah. Later he became a shopkeeper, tanner, shipper, and sawmill proprietor. He owned slaves. Because of his knowledge of leather he was named inspector of tanned leathers serving the Port of Savannah. An active member of the Union Society, he early opposed the rule of the British and was a leader in patriotic activity. In a Georgia brigade he had the titular rank of colonel, and was commissary general for the American forces in Georgia and South Carolina. When the British took Savannah he was captured during an engagement. After his release he settled temporarily in Philadelphia, where he was a merchant engaged in privateering. He returned finally to Savannah and in 1792 was president of Congregation Mikveh Israel there. An observant Jew, he was the driving force in the religious organization of Savannah Jewry. On October 28, 1761, he was married to Frances Hart in Charlestown. Before his death he became a justice of the peace. (*Coldoc,* 39, *et passim; EJSC,* 30, *et passim; MEAJB,* 334, *et passim; MISR; MSGC; SRB*)

SHEFTALL, Mordecai.[2] December 30, 1783, Charleston—June 6, 1856. Son of Levi Sheftall,[2] he was married to Virginia Russell on May 9, 1832. (*MSGC*)

SHEFTALL, Mordecai.[3] Born January 6, 1793, Savannah. Son of Moses Sheftall. (*SRB*)

SHEFTALL, Moses. October 12, 1769, Savannah—January 10, 1835, Savannah. This son of Mordecai Sheftall[1] was a physician and surgeon who studied under Dr. Benjamin Rush from 1790 to 1792; he maintained his friendship with Dr. Rush until Rush died. On two occasions Sheftall was elected to the legislature of Georgia and was judge of the county court. A prominent Mason, he served in many other civic offices. In 1834 he was president of Congregation Mikveh Israel in Savannah. On March 21, 1792, he was married to Elkali Bush in Philadelphia. (*Coldoc,* 57, *et passim; MISR; MSGC; PAJHS,* XII, 163; XVII, 173, 185; XIX, 90f; *UJE,* IX, 500)

SHEFTALL, Perla.[1] November 11, 1763, Savannah—November 3, 1820. Daughter of Mordecai Sheftall.[1] (*MSGC; SRB*)

SHEFTALL, Perla.[2] February 18, 1788, Charleston—June 7, 1850, Savannah. Daughter of Levi Sheftall,[2] she was married to Isaac Russell on July 1, 1808. (*MSGC*)

SHEFTALL, Rachel. Born April 21, 1778, Savannah. Daughter of Levi Sheftall.[2] (*SRB*)

SHEFTALL, Rebecca.[1] February 5, 1775, Savannah—July 12, 1777, Savannah. Daughter of Levi Sheftall.[2] (*SRB*)

SHEFTALL, Rebecca.[2] September 10, 1798, Savannah—April 19, 1881. Daughter of Moses Sheftall, she was married to Isaac Cohen on November 20, 1816. (*MSGC; SRB*)

SHEFTALL, Sarah. Born November 29, 1769, Savannah. Daughter of Levi Sheftall,[2] she was married to Abraham de Lyon[3] on June 1, 1785. (*SRB*)

SHEFTALL, Sheftall.[1] Born August 3, 1734, Savannah. He died an infant after an ignorant nurse gave him acorns to eat. (*SRB*)

SHEFTALL, Sheftall.[2] September 6, 1736, Savannah—August 15, 1817. Son of Benjamin Sheftall.[1] (*Coulter,* 96; *MSGC*)

SHEFTALL, Sheftall.[3] September 8, 1762, Savannah—August 15, 1847, Savannah. Son of Mordecai Sheftall,[1] he fought in the Revolutionary army, supplied materials to the army, and finally was captured by the British. After the Revolution he lived in Charleston. In 1800 he was president of Congregation Mikveh Israel in Savannah. He also practiced law and lived in Philadelphia. (*MEAJB,* 344, *et passim; MISR; MSGC; PAJHS,* XII, 56; XVII, 93, *et passim; SRB; UJE,* IX, 500)

SHEFTALL, Solomon.[1] August 8, 1741, Savannah—1743. Son of Benjamin Sheftall.[1] (*SRB*)

SHEFTALL, Solomon.[2] Born September 9, 1791, Savannah. Son of Levi Sheftall.[2] (*SRB*)

SICCARY (SEQUEIRA), Dr. In Virginia in the early 1700s. (*PAJHS,* XII, 159)

SIEGAL (SEGAL), Hayyim. In Petersburg, Virginia, in 1790. (*ELJR,* 33)

SIEGAL (SEGAL), Mrs. Hayyim. In Petersburg, Virginia, in 1790. (*ELJR,* 33)

SIEGAL (SEGAL), Samuel. Born 1790, Petersburg, Virginia. Son of Hayyim Siegal. (ELJR, 33)

SILVA, Elias. In New Amsterdam in 1656. (AJAM, III, 10)

SILVA, Isaac Cohen da. From 1757 until 1758, and again from 1766 until 1768, he was hazzan of Congregation Shearith Israel in New York City. He had a modest business. (PAJHS, XXVII, 27, 262; POFNW, 164f)

SILVA, Isaac Joao da. A merchant in New York City in 1794. (PAJHS, XXVII, 157)

SILVA, Joseph de. In Montreal early in the 1700s. A Portuguese merchant, he was probably Jewish. (MEAJA, 200)

SILVA, Simha de Torres. Died October 23, 1746, New York City. Daughter of Moses de Silva, she was married to Joseph de Torres. (Pool, 468f)

SILVESTER, Joseph. A freeman in Newport in 1739. It is highly doubtful that he was Jewish. (PAJHS, XXVII, 445)

SIMON. In 1702 he was converted to Christianity in Charlestown; he assumed the name of Barns. (Kohut, 43; PAJHS, XI, 79)

SIMON, Belle. July 16, 1755—January 30, 1833, Philadelphia. Daughter of Joseph Simon,[1] she was married to Solomon M. Cohen. (MIPR; MSGC; PAJHS, XXXIII, 210)

SIMON, Fanny. Daughter of Joseph Simon,[1] she was in Lancaster in 1791. (Coldoc, 62)

SIMON, Mrs. Figlah. Wife of Joseph Simon.[2] (MSGC; SIR)

SIMON, François. In New Orleans in 1766. It is highly doubtful that he was Jewish. (Shpall, 6)

SIMON, Gershom. Born January 29, 1779, probably in Kinderhook, New York. Son of Joseph Simon.[2] (SIR)

SIMON, Hananel. November 22, 1776—June 23, 1778. Son of Joseph Simon.[2] (Pool, 503; SIR)

SIMON, Hester. Daughter of Joseph Simon.[1] (MSGC)

SIMON, Jacob. Son of Joseph Simon.[1] (MSGC)

SIMON, Joseph.[1] About 1712—January 24, 1804, Philadelphia. A prominent fur trader and land speculator in the Lancaster area, he was also involved in the development of the Illinois country. Michael and Barnard Gratz started in business with him; he was also in business and the manufacture of guns with William Henry. During the French and Indian War and during the Revolutionary War, he provided supplies to soldiers. He was married twice: to Figlah Levy on October 15, 1769; and to Rose Bunn. (Byars, 13, et passim; MEAJB, 6; MIPR; Morais, 25, et passim; PAJHS, I, 56, 121f; SIR; UJE, IV, 188; VIII, 426, 545)

SIMON, Joseph.[2] On October 15, 1769, he was married to Figlah in New York City. In 1779 he was in Kinderhook, New York. (MSGC; SIR)

SIMON, Leah. About 1764—August 21, 1842, Philadelphia. Daughter of Joseph Simon,[1] she was married to Levy Phillips on October 19, 1785. (GBMIP; MIPR)

SIMON, Miriam. December 21, 1749—September 12, 1808, Philadelphia. Daughter of Joseph Simon,[1] she was married to Michael Gratz in Lancaster on June 20, 1769. (MSGC; PAJHS, I, 122; IX, 34)

SIMON, Moses.[1] Died February 26, 1816. Son of Joseph Simon.[1] (MSGC)

SIMON, Moses.[2] In Richmond in 1778. (PAJHS, II, 171; XX, 102)

SIMON, Myer. Died December 24, 1785. Son of Joseph Simon.[1] (MSGC)

SIMON, Rachel. October, 1764—January 13, 1790. Daughter of Joseph Simon,[1] she was married to Solomon Etting on September 1, 1783. (JRMP; MSGC)

SIMON, Rebecca. Born August 6, 1774, Kinderhook, New York. Daughter of Joseph Simon.[2] (SIR)

SIMON, Shinah. Born 1762. Daughter of Joseph Simon,[1] she was married to Dr. Nicholas Schuyler on August 13, 1782. Both Jews and Christians were distressed by this union. (*MSGC*; *PAJHS*, XXXI, 241; *WW*, 238f)

SIMON, Simha. Born May 4, 1772, Kinderhook, New York. Daughter of Joseph Simon.[2] (*SIR*)

SIMON, Susanna. Daughter of Joseph Simon,[1] she was married to Levy Andrew Levy. (*MSGC*)

SIMONDS, Samuel. In Long Island in 1741. It is doubtful that he was Jewish. (*PAJHS*, XXVII, 249)

SIMONS. From Virginia. In New York City in 1795. (*PAJHS*, XXVII, 62)

SIMONS, Abraham. Died 1824. In 1773 he was a merchant in Wilkes County, Georgia. He fought in the Revolutionary army. In 1804 he served in the Georgia legislature. He indirectly founded Mercer College. His wife was Nancy Mills. It is doubtful that he was Jewish. (*JRMP*; *PAJHS*, XXXIII, 231, 236)

SIMONS, Barent. In New York City in 1712. (*NYHSW*, II, 121)

SIMONS, David. On August 26, 1795, he was married to Deborah Abrahams in Philadelphia. (*MSP*)

SIMONS, Henry. Son of Montague Simons, he was in England in 1813. (*MSGC*)

SIMONS, Hester. Daughter of Montague Simons, she was married to Simon Moses. (*MSGC*)

SIMONS, Levy. An embroiderer, he came to America from London in 1758. In 1783 he was in New York City. (*PAJHS*, XXI, 142; *Schappes*, 33f)

SIMONS, Montague. 1752, London—September 8, 1812, Charleston. Son of Isaac Simons, he came to America about 1777 and lived in Charleston and Jacksonborough, South Carolina. (*EJSC*, 98, 139; *MSGC*; *Wills*, 55)

SIMONS, Mrs. Montague. She lived in Charleston. (*MSGC*)

SIMONS, Moses.[1] During the Revolution he fled from Long Island to Connecticut. (*PAJHS*, XI, 91)

SIMONS, Moses.[2] 1768—February 5, 1808, Jacksonborough, South Carolina. Son of Isaac Simons, he came to Charlestown in 1782 and was a shopkeeper. (*EJSC*, 99; *MSGC*)

SIMONS, Moses.[3] In Savannah in 1795. (*MISR*)

SIMONS, Mrs. Moses. Wife of Moses Simons.[3] (*MISR*)

SIMONS, Sampson. 1750, Canterbury, England—January 22, 1811, Charleston. Son of Isaac Simons, he was a member of the Charlestown militia in 1780. (*EJSC*, 92; *Wills*, 55)

SIMONS, Samuel.[1] Sometime between 1750 and 1760 he was granted land in Georgia. (*PAJHS*, X, 88)

SIMONS, Samuel.[2] Born London, died February 9, 1824, Charleston. Son of Isaac Simons, he fought in the Revolutionary army. In 1783 he was in Philadelphia. (*EOJCC*, 67; *MIPR*; *MSGC*; *PAJHS*, XIX, 152, 154)

SIMONS, Sarah. Daughter of Montague Simons, she was in England in 1813. (*MSGC*)

SIMONS, Saul.[1] 1757, London—November 22, 1809, Savannah. Son of Isaac Simons, he lived for a short time in Charleston and settled in Savannah. (*EJSC*, 102, 279; *MSGC*; *Wills*, 80)

SIMONS, Saul.[2] Son of Montague Simons, he was in England in 1813. (*MSGC*)

SIMONS, Solomon. In New York City in 1785. (*PAJHS*, XXI, 148f)

SIMPSON, George. In New York City in 1776. It is highly doubtful that he was Jewish. (*Schappes*, 52)

SIMPSON, Michael. In 1768 he studied at the University of Pennsylvania. It is doubtful that he was Jewish. (*PAJHS*, XIX, 121)

SIMPSON, Miriam. Wife of Isaac Marques, she lived in Charlestown about 1760. (*Pool*, 462)

SIMPSON, Samuel. In Newport with his family in 1790. (*Census A, Rhode Island*)

SIMSON, Benjamin. The grandson of Joseph and probably the son of Solomon Simson. (*Wills*, 8)

SIMSON, Mrs. Dyfie. Wife of Nathan Simson, she may have been in New York City in 1704. (*PAJHS*, XXV, 88)

SIMSON, Ella (Helena). May 6, 1773, New York City—September 30, 1819. Daughter of Solomon Simson. (*PAJHS*, XXVII, 371; XXXIII, 202; *SIR*)

SIMSON, Mrs. Frances. Died July 29, 1772, New York City. Wife of Samuel Simson, she came from Holland in 1744. (*MSGC*; *PAJHS*, XXV, 90f; XXVII, 371)

SIMSON, Frumet. July 25, 1774, New York City—September 1, 1774, New York City. Daughter of Solomon Simson. (*PAJHS*, XXVII, 371; *SIR*)

SIMSON, Jochebed. September 14, 1771—October 30, 1814. Daughter of Solomon Simson. (*PAJHS*, XVIII, 112; XXVII, 371)

SIMSON, Joseph.[1] 1686, Germany—November, 1787, New York City. This son of Samson Simson came to New York City from London in 1718. He was naturalized about 1740, and in 1738 served in the New York Volunteers. In 1743 he became a freeman of New York City. In 1747 he served as beadle for Congregation Shearith Israel; he was learned in Hebrew. During the British occupation of New York City he lived and continued his occupation of shopkeeper in Connecticut. In 1722 he was married to Rebecca Isaacs. (*MEAJA*, 163f; *PAJHS*, II, 92; V, 116; X, 109; *POFNW*, 187, et passim; *Pool*, 15, et passim; *UJE*, IX, 551)

SIMSON, Joseph.[2] 1779—October 31, 1842. Son of Solomon Simson, he was married to Frances Mears Isaacs on June 4, 1806. (*MSGC*; *PAJHS*, XXXIII, 202f, 206; *Pool*, 282)

SIMSON, Matthew. In New York City in 1719. It is doubtful that he was Jewish. (*FEAJ*, 67)

SIMSON, Nathan. Born Germany, died 1725, London. In 1704 he came to New York City, where he was elected constable in 1718. He became a prominent shipper and merchant. In the 1720s he returned to England. (*MEAJA*, 64, 163; *PAJHS*, XXV, 84f; *Pool*, 190; *Schappes*, 19)

SIMSON, Rebecca.[1] In 1765 she was married to Abraham Mears. (*PAJHS*, XXXIII, 202, 206)

SIMSON, Rebecca.[2] September 19, 1769, New York City—February 22, 1854, New York City. Daughter of Solomon Simson, she was married to Abraham M. Isaacs on June 18, 1806. (*MSGC*; *PAJHS*, XXVII, 372; XXXIII, 202; *SIR*)

SIMSON, Richa. Daughter of Samuel Simson, she was married first to David Jacob Levy on December 2, 1761, and then to Aaron Hart on November 20, 1774. (*MSGC*; *PAJHS*, XXV, 90; *SIR*)

SIMSON, Sampson.[1] 1725—August 29, 1773, New York City. Son of Joseph Simson,[1] he was a prominent merchant and importer, engaged in the spermaceti industry and in privateering. He was one of the drafters of the constitution of New York City's chamber of commerce. (*MSGC*; *PAJHS*, II, 83; III, 81; X, 109; XXVII, 371; *Pool*, 48, et passim; *SIR*)

SIMSON, Sampson.[2] June 30, 1781, Danbury, Connecticut—January 7, 1857, New York City. In 1800 this son of Solomon Simson was graduated from Columbia College and was admitted to the bar in 1802. In the War of 1812 he was captain of a militia. Prominent in Jewish, civic, and Masonic affairs, he founded Mt. Sinai Hospital in New York. (*MSGC*; *PAJHS*, X, 109, et passim; XIX, 32, et passim)

SIMSON, Samuel. Died July 29, 1772. In 1744 he came from Holland. His wife was Frances. (*MSGC*; *PAJHS*, XXVII, 372)

SIMSON, Sarah. 1727—September 20, 1762, New York City. Daughter of Joseph Simson,[1] she was married to Raphael Jacobs. (*PAJHS*, XXV, 90; *Pool*, 501; *SIR*)

SIMSON, Solomon. September, 1738—January 17, 1801, Yonkers. This son of Joseph Simson was a wealthy merchant engaged in the whaling and spermaceti industry. One of the founders and president of the Democratic Society, he held various public offices, and may have served in the House of Delegates of the State of New York. During the Revolution he served in a militia; while the British occupied New York City he lived in Connecticut. He submitted a proposal for a government mint, which was finally established in 1793. On several occasions he was president of Congregation Shearith Israel in New York City. He was a prominent Mason. On October 26, 1768, he was married to Sarah Mears. (*Coldoc*, 100, *et passim*; *MEAJA*, 163, *et passim*; *MEAJB*, 444, *et passim*; *MSGC*; *Pool*, 39, *et passim*)

SISME, Anne de. In New York City in 1764. (*PAJHS*, XXVII, 329)

SMITH, Sam. In Baltimore in 1792. It is doubtful that he was Jewish. (*JRMP*)

SOLAMAN, Samuel. In 1776 he served with the Continental forces in Maryland. It is highly doubtful that he was Jewish. (*MTAR*, 42)

SOLAS, Aaron Mendez. In New York City in 1733. (*PAJHS*, XXI, 31)

SOLIS, Abraham. From Surinam. In 1790 he was in Boston as an interpreter and physician; in 1800 he was in Philadelphia. (*PAJHS*, XXIII, 86; *WW*, 202)

SOLLOMON ... "the Malata Jew of Bostorni." In 1668 he was charged with profaning the sabbath by traveling. (*AJAM*, III, 10)

SOLOMON. In New York City with his family about 1703. (*CPG*, 180)

SOLOMON. In 1792 he was an actor in Boston. It is doubtful that he was Jewish. (*PAJHS*, VI, 113f)

SOLOMON, Mrs. Wife of Solomon, she was an actress in Boston in 1792. It is doubtful that she was Jewish. (*PAJHS*, VI, 113f)

SOLOMON, Aaron.[1] In Philadelphia in 1785. (*MIPR*)

SOLOMON, Aaron.[2] 1791, Charleston—March 15, 1851, New Orleans. Son of Joseph Solomon.[3] (*MSGC*)

SOLOMON, Abraham. On June 1, 1775, he enlisted in the Colonial army. He eventually settled in Boston as a merchant, but was later expelled. On May 10, 1774, he was married to Elizabeth Love. Cf. Isaac Solomon.[2] (*JNEA*, 26)

SOLOMON, Alexander. March 4, 1793—January 4, 1823, Philadelphia. Son of Myer S. Solomon. (*MIPR*; *MSGC*)

SOLOMON, Arabella. May 26, 1786, Baltimore—December 23, 1836, Philadelphia. Daughter of Myer S. Solomon, she was married to Zalegman Phillips on October 23, 1805. (*GBMIP*; *Morais*, 22; *MSGC*)

SOLOMON, Benjamin. In Richmond in 1790. (*PAJHS*, IV, 21; XX, 104)

SOLOMON, Bernard. A merchant in Philadelphia in 1778, he was caught selling rum and absconded. (*JE*, IX, 671; *PAJHS*, XXXV, 281; *Rosenbach*, 28)

SOLOMON, Chapman. 1769—June 28, 1849, New Orleans. Son of Levy Solomon. (*MSGC*)

SOLOMON, David. In 1779 he served with the Continental forces in Maryland. It is highly doubtful that he was Jewish. (*MTAR*, 247)

SOLOMON, Eleau. Brother of Zadok Solomon, he may have been in Charlestown during the Revolutionary period. (*PAJHS*, XIX, 152)

SOLOMON, Esther. Sister of Ezekiel Solomon, she was married to Moses Hart and lived in Montreal. (*Douville*, 130)

SOLOMON, Exicael. In 1776 he served with the Continental troops in Maryland. It is highly doubtful that he was Jewish. (*MTAR*, 305)

SOLOMON(S), Ezekiel. Born Berlin, died about 1806. He came to America from Berlin and was in Montreal in 1760. A merchant, he supported the English armies with financial aid and supplies. He traded in the Michigan territory (then called Michilimackinac), and was the first Jewish settler in that area. In 1763 he was captured by Indians in the Pontiac uprising. On July 23, 1769, he was married to a Christian, Louise Dubois, and though all their children were baptized, he remained a practicing Jew. (*Katz*, 12, *et passim*; *MEAJA*, 224, *et passim*)

SOLOMON, George. Fought in the Virginia line in the Revolution. It is doubtful that he was Jewish. (PAJHS, XX, 99)

SOLOMON, Haim. Died January 18, 1784, Philadelphia. (MIPR)

SOLOMON, Henry. Died June 19, 1833, Philadelphia. Son of Myer S. Solomon. (MSGC)

SOLOMON, Hertz. In New York City in 1800. (SIR)

SOLOMON, Isaac.[1] In partnership with Michael Asher he had a general merchandise and commission business in Boston in 1728. They were prominent dealers in snuff, which they procured from Mordecai Gomez in New York City. Solomon's wife was Elizabeth Todd. (JNEA, 19f; MEAJA, 110-115)

SOLOMON, Isaac.[2] A Dutch Jew, he was in Boston in 1733. He served in the Revolutionary army. He was married to Elizabeth Lowe. Cf. Abraham Solomon. (FEAJ, 8f)

SOLOMON, Isaac.[3] In 1768 he was visiting in Philadelphia; he was from Lancaster. (PAJHS, XIX, 46)

SOLOMON, Isaac.[4] From Charlestown. He fought in the Revolutionary army. (PAJHS, XIX, 152f)

SOLOMON, Isaac.[5] A merchant, about 1782 he traveled from St. Eustatius to Baltimore. (Blum, 4; JRMP)

SOLOMON, Isaac.[6] In North Carolina in 1784. It is doubtful that he was Jewish. (PAJHS, XXIX, 144)

SOLOMON, Isaac.[7] In Boston in 1790. (PAJHS, XXIII, 86)

SOLOMON, Isaac.[8] Died January 17, 1798, probably in Philadelphia. (JRMP)

SOLOMON, Isaac.[9] An indentured servant of Aaron Levy, in 1788 he signed a four-year agreement in Philadelphia. (Coldoc, 343; WW, 186)

SOLOMON, John. In Roxbury, Massachusetts, in 1742. It is doubtful that he was Jewish. (PAJHS, XXIII, 84)

SOLOMON, Jonas. On October 27, 1763, this merchant of Rhode Island and New York City was naturalized. His wife was Hannah Applegate. He was buried in the burial yard of the Dutch Reformed Church in New Brunswick, New Jersey. (Hugsoc, XXIV, 37; MSP; PAJHS, XIII, 4, 6)

SOLOMON, Joseph.[1] Died February, 1779, during the battle at Beaufort. During the early days of the Revolution he served in the Charlestown militia. (EJSC, 87)

SOLOMON, Joseph.[2] 1700/10, London—February 9, 1769, Lancaster. In 1746 he was in New York City and was naturalized in 1749. He lived later in Lancaster. In 1738 he was married to Bilhah Cohen in London. (Byars, 35; MSGC; PAJHS, V, 117; IX, 30; XXI, 48f)

SOLOMON(S), Joseph.[3] Born Amsterdam, died 1808, Charleston. By 1791 he was a merchant in Charleston. He was married to Judith Moses. (EJSC, 139; MSGC; Wills, 63)

SOLOMON, Joseph.[4] Born 1779, Lancaster. Son of Myer S. Solomon. (MSGC)

SOLOMON, Judith. 1766—April 5, 1837, Baltimore. On December 21, 1787, she was married in Bristol, England, to Israel I. Cohen. She lived in Richmond. (ELJR, 29; MHM, XVIII, 362)

SOLOMON, Lazarus. 1765, Washington County, Georgia—April 20, 1833, Twiggs County, Georgia. He fought in the Revolutionary army. His wife was Elizabeth Bedgood. It is doubtful that he was Jewish. (JRMP; PAJHS, XXIX, 145)

SOLOMON, Levi.[1] From St. Eustatius. In 1790 he was in Baltimore. (Blum, 4)

SOLOMON, Levi.[2] December, 1778—March 8, 1827. (MSGC)

SOLOMON, Levy. 1754, Germany—September, 1827. About 1781 he arrived in New York City with the Hessians. By 1783 he was a shopkeeper in Charleston. He lived also in Georgetown. (EJSC, 98f; MSGC)

SOLOMON, Lewis. Fought in the Georgia line in the Revolution. It is doubtful that he was Jewish. (PAJHS, XVII, 99, 106)

SOLOMON, Mattathias. Born October 28, 1790, Philadelphia. (MIPR)

SOLOMON, Mayer. Born April 10, 1799, probably Richmond. (*ELJR*, 33)

SOLOMON, Moses. A merchant in Charlestown in 1740. (*EJSC*, 24, *et passim*)

SOLOMON, Myer. Fought in the Charlestown militia during the Revolution. (*EJSC*, 92)

SOLOMON, Myer S. A shopkeeper, he lived in Philadelphia, Lancaster, and Baltimore. On December 23, 1778, he was married to Catherine Bush. (*Blum*, 4; *Morais*, 22, 49, 457; *PAJHS*, IX, 30; XIX, 48f)

SOLOMON, Mrs. Myer. In Philadelphia in 1793. (*MIPR*)

SOLOMON, Nathan. In Philadelphia in 1785. (*MIPR*)

SOLOMON, Rachel. Daughter of Joseph Solomon.[3] (*MSGC*)

SOLOMON, Sally. 1796—May 30, 1844, Philadelphia. Daughter of Myer S. Solomon. (*MSGC*)

SOLOMON, Samuel.[1] In 1777 he deserted from the Continental troops in Maryland. It is highly doubtful that he was Jewish. (*MTAR*, 290)

SOLOMON, Samuel.[2] 1783, Lancaster—November 16, 1864, Philadelphia. Son of Myer S. Solomon. (*MSGC*)

SOLOMON, Shinah. December 24, 1744, Lancaster—November 30, 1822, Baltimore. Daughter of Joseph Solomon,[2] she was married to Elijah Etting on January 5, 1759. (*MIPR*; *MSGC*; *UJE*, IV, 188)

SOLOMON, Simon.[1] In Newport in 1748. Probably a servant. (*AJA*)

SOLOMON, Simon.[2] A shopkeeper in Lancaster in 1780. (*PAJHS*, IX, 30)

SOLOMON, Solomon. 1784—December 13, 1836. Son of Joseph Solomon,[3] he was married to Alice Abrahams in Charleston in 1805. (*MSGC*)

SOLOMON, Stephen. In 1760 he was expelled from Boston. It is doubtful that he was Jewish. (*JNEA*, 25)

SOLOMON, William. From North Carolina. He fought in the Revolutionary army. It is doubtful that he was Jewish. (*PAJHS*, XXIX, 144f)

SOLOMON, Zadok. During the Revolution he fought in the Charlestown militia. (*EJSC*, 91; *PAJHS*, XIX, 152, 154)

SOLOMONS. Died 1779, New York City. Son of Ezekiel Solomons. (*SIR*)

SOLOMONS, Alexander.[1] In 1765 he was a merchant in Mobile. (*JRMP*)

SOLOMONS, Alexander.[2] 1756, Poland—July 7, 1835, Charleston. By 1795 he was in Charleston. His wife was Cecilia. (*EJSC*, 139; *MSGC*)

SOLOMONS, Backky. November 25, 1783—February 17, 1789. Daughter of Levi Solomons.[1] (*MSGC*)

SOLOMONS, Benjamin.[1] May 16, 1777—July 25, 1777. Son of Levi Solomons.[1] (*MSGC*)

SOLOMONS, Benjamin.[2] October 25, 1786—May 13, 1831, Montreal. Son of Levi Solomons,[1] he was married to Elkaleh Seixas on April 28, 1816. (*HSIM*, 28; *MSGC*; *PAJHS*, XXVII, 376)

SOLOMONS, Mrs. Catey. Wife of Hyam Solomons, she lived in Charleston. (*WAJA*)

SOLOMONS, Catherine. September 25, 1782, Montreal—March 28, 1851. Daughter of Levi Solomons,[1] she was married to Mr. Aird, a gentile. (*MSGC*; *PAJHS*, XXVII, 376)

SOLOMONS, Mrs. Cecilia. 1765, Germany—August 25, 1839, Charleston. Wife of Alexander Solomons. (*MSGC*; *MSP*)

SOLOMONS, Elias.[1] From 1753 till his death he was shammas of Congregation Shearith Israel of New York City. By 1750 he was in New York City; on April 21, 1759, he was buried there. (*PAJHS*, XXI, 63, 213; *POFNW*, 286; *Pool*, 501)

SOLOMONS, Elias.[2] In 1778 he was in Montreal with at least two daughters. He was probably a merchant. (*JRMP*; *MEAJA*, 267f)

SOLOMONS, Elizabeth. Born December 22, 1779, Montreal. Daughter of Levi Solomons.[1] (*MSGC*; *PAJHS*, XXVII, 376)

SOLOMONS, Esther. April 19, 1784—May 4, 1784. Daughter of Levi Solomons.[1] (*MSGC*)

SOLOMONS, Mrs. Esther. 1769—February 4, 1816, New York City. Wife of Mark Solomons. (*Pool*, 343)

SOLOMONS, Fanny. Born January 29, 1789. Daughter of Levi Solomons.[1] (*MSGC*)

SOLOMONS, Francis. In Charleston between 1783 and 1800. (*EJSC*, 280)

SOLOMONS, Gedaliah. October 26, 1758, New York City—December 1, 1773, New York City. Son of Isaac Solomons.[1] (*PAJHS*, XXVII, 151; *Pool*, 90; *SIR*)

SOLOMONS, Hannah. About 1700—February 21, 1772, Savannah. Second wife of Benjamin Sheftall,[1] she arrived in Savannah on October 5, 1738, and was married on November 20, 1738. (*MEAJB*, 342; *SRB*)

SOLOMONS, Hyam.[1] Died about 1801, Charleston. From England. A merchant in west Florida and Georgia, he went to Charleston about 1783. (*EJSC*, 98)

SOLOMONS, Hyam.[2] During the Colonial period he deserted from the British army. (*Records of the Pennsylvania Historical Commission Collection*)

SOLOMONS, Hyam I. In New York City in 1785. (*PAJHS*, XXVII, 43; *SIR*)

SOLOMONS, Isaac.[1] In 1758 he was a merchant in New York City. (*Beekmans*, 393; *PAJHS*, XXVII, 151)

SOLOMONS, Isaac.[2] Born September, 1779, New York City. Son of Solomon Solomons.[3] (*PAJHS*, XXVII, 156)

SOLOMONS, Mrs. Isaac. Wife of Isaac Solomons,[1] she was in New York City in 1758. (*SIR*)

SOLOMONS, Israel. 1770, Amsterdam—August 10, 1830, Georgetown, South Carolina. Son of Alexander Solomons, he was in Charleston in 1800. His first wife was Esther Sarah Ottolengui; his second wife was Eleanor Joseph. (*EJSC*, 139; *MSGC*)

SOLOMONS, Jacob. In New York City about 1701. (*NYHSW*, II, 66)

SOLOMONS, Jessica. September 15, 1785—October 23, 1853. Daughter of Levi Solomons.[1] (*MSGC*; *PAJHS*, XXVII, 376)

SOLOMONS, Levi.[1] About 1730, England—May 18, 1792, Montreal. Also known as Lucius Levy. About 1760 he came to America and was a merchant who traded in Albany, Montreal, and other areas, including the Michigan country. He was perhaps the largest dealer in furs in Montreal. During the Revolution he served as a supplier to the invading American forces. He was prosecuted for aiding these forces. A leader in the Jewish community, he was president of Congregation Shearith Israel in Montreal in 1778. On May 31, 1775, he was married to Rebecca Franks.[1] (*Coldoc*, 106, *et passim*; *MEAJA*, 225, *et passim*; *MEAJB*, 409, *et passim*; *MSGC*; *PAJHS*, XXVII, 376)

SOLOMONS, Levi.[2] December 23, 1771, Montreal—June 11, 1823, New York City. Son of Levi Solomons,[1] he was a merchant in Albany. On July 29, 1801, he was married to Catherine Manuel. (*MSGC*; *PAJHS*, XXVII, 172, 376)

SOLOMONS, Mark. 1763, London—November 15, 1830, New York City. From 1796 until 1803 he was a shohet in New York City. He then lived in Charleston, but returned to New York in 1814. His first wife was Esther; his second wife was Sarah Abigail. (*Pool*, 343f)

SOLOMONS, Mary (Molly, Polly). March 6, 1776—1826. Daughter of Levi Solomons,[1] she was married to Jacob Franks.[4] (*HSIM*, 28; *MSGC*; *PAJHS*, XXVII, 376)

SOLOMONS, Myer. On November 7, 1773, he was married to Sarah Comb in a Montreal church. (*Malchelosse*, 171)

SOLOMONS, Nahma. In 1787 he lived briefly in Savannah. (*SRB*)

SOLOMONS, Nellie. Daughter of Ephraim Solomons, she was married first to Israel Abrahams, and then to Abraham Andrews in New York City on July 2, 1761. (*MSGC*; *SIR*)

SOLOMONS, Rachel.[1] Daughter of Isaac Solomons, she was married to Tobias Moses in New York City on November 29, 1764. (*MSGC*; *SIR*)

SOLOMONS, Rachel.[2] December 25, 1780, Montreal—October 9, 1855. Daughter of Levi Solomons,[1] she was married to Henry Joseph on September 28, 1803. (*HSIM*, 28; *MSGC*; *PAJHS*, XXVII, 376)

SOLOMONS, Raymond. In North Carolina in 1784. It is highly doubtful that he was Jewish. (*PAJHS*, XXIX, 144)

SOLOMONS, Rose. A woman of bad reputation, she was married to Moses Lyon in New York City on May 22, 1771. (*PAJHS*, XXI, 135; [section left out of page 135, *PAJHS*]; *SIR*)

SOLOMONS, Sarah (Sally). Probably 1770, Montreal—June 13, 1812. Daughter of Levi Solomons,[1] she was married to John McCord, a gentile. (*MSGC*; *PAJHS*, XXVII, 376)

SOLOMONS, Solomon.[1] A stranger, he was buried in New York City on August 18, 1764. (*Pool*, 502)

SOLOMONS, Solomon.[2] In 1769 he was in Georgia petitioning for land. (*CRG*, X, 724)

SOLOMONS, Solomon.[3] In New York City in 1780. (*PAJHS*, XXVII, 156)

SOLOMONS, Mrs. Solomon. Wife of Solomon Solomons,[3] she was in New York City in 1780. (*PAJHS*, XXVII, 156)

SOLOMONS, William. Son of Ezekiel Solomon(s), he was a trader in the Michigan territory about 1780. (*JRMP*; *PAJHS*, XIII, 49)

SOMMERS, Amelia. 1767, Staten Island—July 16, 1834, Philadelphia. Wife of Lewis Allen, she was probably married in England and then returned to America. (*MSP*)

SOMRAH, Henry. In New York City in 1799. (*SIR*)

SORIA. Child of Aaron Soria who came to New York City from France in 1794. (*Pool*, 407)

SORIA, Aaron. February 22, 1762, Bordeaux—January 5, 1852, New York City. Husband of Rachel Mendez Hega, he was in New York City in 1800. (*SIR*)

SORIA, Joseph. July 12, 1798, New York City—April 12, 1877, New York City. Son of Aaron Soria, he was married to Zipporah Cohen in Charleston on December 11, 1833. (*MSGC*)

SOUSA, Mathias de. In Maryland in 1639. It is doubtful that he was Jewish. (*AJAM*, III, 6)

SOUZA, Abraham Henriques de. In 1753 he was a butcher in New York City. (*PAJHS*, XXV, 44)

SPETZER, Solomon. In New York City in 1800. (*SIR*)

SPIERS, Mr. In Savannah in 1788. It is doubtful that he was Jewish. (*JRMP*)

SPITZER, Bernard M. Died January, 1796, Sullivan's Island. From about 1770 on he lived in Philadelphia, the West Indies, and Charleston. A prominent Mason and friend of Haym Salomon, he was one of the founders of Congregation Mikveh Israel of Philadelphia. (*MEAJB*, 151f; *MSP*; *PAJHS*, XIX, 41, *et passim*)

STEINBERGER, Lewis. Fought in the Virginia line in the Revolution. It is highly doubtful that he was Jewish. (*PAJHS*, XX, 99)

STERN, David. Fought in the Virginia line in the Revolution. It is highly doubtful that he was Jewish. (*PAJHS*, XX, 99)

STERN, Jacob. About 1743 he was naturalized in Maryland. It is highly doubtful that he was Jewish. (*PAJHS*, V, 116)

STERN, Samuel. In Philadelphia in 1779. It is highly doubtful that he was Jewish. (*Morais*, 23)

STORK, Mrs. Bilah. 1730, Amsterdam—November 6, 1815, Philadelphia. Mother of Hannah Stork, she may have been in America before 1800. (*GBMIP*)

STORK, Hannah. 1761—June 26, 1850. Daughter of Aaron Stork, she was married first to Hyam Hart, to Israel de Lieben, and finally to Moses David in 1813. (*MSP*)

SUARES, Mrs. Mother of Abraham Suares, she was in Charleston in 1800. (*MSP*)

SUARES, Abraham. 1800, Charleston—October, 1864. (*MSP*)

SUARES, David. About 1785 he came to Charleston from Curaçao. In 1800 he was in Savannah. (*EJSC*, 280; *MISR*)

SUARES, Jacob. Brother of David Suares, he was in Charleston in 1800. He was married to Judith. (*EJSC*, 139; *MSGC*; *SRB*)

SUARES, Jacob I. In Charleston in 1800. (*EJSC*, 139)

SUMMERS, Andrew, Jr. In Philadelphia in 1795. (*MIPR*)

SURYU (SURYEE). In New York City in 1795. (*PAJHS*, XXVII, 59, 61f)

SUSMAN, Moses. In 1727 he was hanged in New York City for stealing from Moses Levy. He is the only Jew known to have been executed in the eighteenth century for a capital crime. (*MCCCNY*, III, 414; *Schappes*, 20f)

(SU)SMAN, Solomon. In Maine with his family in 1790. (*Census A, Maine*)

SYLVIA, Rebecca. From Barbados. In 1729 she was in New York City. (*PAJHS*, XXI, 21)

SYEFORT, Aaron. In Philadelphia in 1789. (*MSP*)

SYMONS, Henry. In New York City in 1764. (*JRMP*)

T

TABERES, Benjamin. In New York City about 1740. (*PAJHS*, XXI, 45)

TABARRE, Moses. From St. Domingo. On April 5, 1797, he was married to Betsy Joseph in Charleston. (*SCHGM*, XXIV, 32f)

TATUM, Joseph R. In Philadelphia in 1795. (*MIPR*)

TAVARES, Benjamin. In Georgia in 1738. Cf. Benjamin Taberes. (*CRG*, II, 313)

TAVAREZ, David. From England. In 1750 he was in New York City. (*PAJHS*, XXVII, 358)

TERRO, Jacob, Jr. About 1740 he was naturalized in New York City. (*Hugsoc*, XXIV, 30)

TOBIAH, Rabbi. From London. In 1774 he was in New York City on his way to Philadelphia. (*POFNW*, 344)

TINOCO, Jacob. In 1679 he left Barbados for Newport. (*Gutstein*, 341)

TOBIAS, Abraham. July 30, 1793, Charleston—June 26, 1856, Charleston. This son of Joseph Tobias[3] was an accountant who later became a prominent merchant in Charleston, where he was a member of the Board of Health, Commissioner of Pilotage, and director of the Union Bank. On March 5, 1822, he was married to Eleanor Lopez in Charleston. (*EJSC*, 139, *et passim*; *MSGC*; *Wills*, 58)

TOBIAS, Isaac.[1] January 28, 1771—April 29, 1803. Son of Joseph Tobias,[2] he lived in South Carolina. (*MSGC*)

TOBIAS, Isaac.[2] February 10, 1796—January 28, 1860. Son of Joseph Tobias,[3] he was married to Isabella Cowan of Charleston on July 1, 1824. (*EJSC*, 139, 280; *MSGC*)

TOBIAS, Jacob.[1] March, 1749—November 16, 1775. Son of Joseph Tobias,[1] he served in the Charlestown militia. In May, 1775, he was married to Rachel da Costa in Charlestown. (*EJSC*, 40; *EJMC*, 5; *Wills*, 57)

TOBIAS, Jacob.[2] August 5, 1786, Charleston—July 14, 1811, Charleston. Son of Joseph Tobias.[3] (*MSGC*; *SCHGM*, XXXVI, 138)

TOBIAS, John. In 1791 he served in the Richmond militia. He later became a merchant in Richmond and Baltimore. (*ELJR*, 72, 77, 240; *PAJHS*, XIX, 57)

TOBIAS, Joseph.[1] About 1685—January 29, 1761, Charlestown. On November 26, 1741, this prominent merchant and shipowner was naturalized. He became the first president of Congregation Beth Elohim when it was organized in 1750. In 1737 he was married to Leah Olivera in Charlestown. (*EJSC*, 24, *et passim*; *ELHS*)

TOBIAS, Joseph.[2] March 31, 1751—February 27, 1798. Son of Joseph Tobias,[1] he was married to Judith da Costa on November 2, 1785, in Charleston. (*EJSC*, 40, *et passim*; *MSGC*)

TOBIAS, Joseph.[3] September 3, 1764, Charlestown—April 4, 1810. Son of Joseph Tobias,[2] he was married to Rachel Aarons on November 3, 1785. (*MSGC*; *Wills*, 57)

TOBIAS, Joseph.[4] Son of Joseph Tobias.[3] (*MSGC*)

TOBIAS, Judith.[1] Daughter of Joseph Tobias.[1] (*MSGC*)

TOBIAS, Judith.[2] Born April 15, 1798, Charleston. Daughter of Joseph Tobias.[3] (*MSGC*; *Wills*, 57)

TOBIAS, Leah. January 28, 1771—November 25, 1799. Daughter of Joseph Tobias,[2] she was married to Lyon Levy in 1790. (*MSGC*)

TOBIAS, Mesoad. April 1, 1740—February 27, 1798. Son of Joseph Tobias.[1] (*MSGC*)

TOBIAS, Rinah.[1] June 20, 1741, Charlestown. Daughter of Joseph Tobias,[1] she was married to Isaac de Lyon. (*MSGC*; *Wills*, 57)

TOBIAS, Rinah.[2] Born September 18, 1788, Charleston. Daughter of Joseph Tobias.[3] (*MSGC*; *Wills*, 57)

TOBIAS, Sarah. Her will is dated 1775 in Granville County, South Carolina. It is doubtful that she was Jewish. (*WAJA*)

TOBIAS, Solomon. Born January 15, 1791, Charleston. Son of Joseph Tobias,[3] he was married to Margaret McManus. (*MSGC*)

TONGUES, Mark. In Charleston in 1792. (*EJSC*, 117)

TORAS, Leah. Cf. Leah Benjamin.

TORES, Abraham. From Bordeaux. On October 2, 1800, he was married to Sarah d'Aguilar in Charleston. (*MSP*; *Pool*, 308)

TORES, B. In New York City in 1795. (*PAJHS*, XXVII, 62)

TORES, Benjamin. In Charleston in 1798. (*EOJCC*, 109)

TORES, Miss (T). Died 1791, New York City. (*SIR*)

TOROBS, Jacob. In New York City in 1798. (*SIR*)

TORRE, Rebecca de la. Daughter of Moses de la Torre, she was married to Joseph Jessurun Pinto on August 1, 1762, by proxy; she then joined her husband in New York City. (*PAJHS*, VI, 128f; *POFNW*, 165; *SIR*)

TORRES, Daniel. About 1684—May 16, 1770, New York City. (*Pool*, 475; *SIR*)

TORRES, Rachel de.[1] August 22, 1762, New York City—November 6, 1847, Charleston. On December 11, 1776, she was married to Marks Lazarus in Charleston. (*MSP*)

TORRES, Rachel (Ritzel).[2] Daughter of Daniel Torres, she was married to Todros Benjamin on September 24, 1760, in New York City. (*Pool*, 476; *SIR*)

TORRES, Rebecca de. About 1701, Jamaica, B.W.I.—October 14, 1729, New York City. Daughter of Joseph de Torres, she was married to Daniel Gomez on February 10, 1724, in Jamaica, B.W.I. (*Pool*, 204, 468)

TORRES, Mrs. Simha. Wife of Joseph de Torres, she was one of the leading benefactors of New York's Mill Street Synagogue. (*POFNW*, 108)

TOURO, Abraham. About 1777, Newport—October 18, 1822, Boston. This son of Isaac Touro was a wealthy merchant shipper and a prominent citizen of Boston. An outstanding philanthropist, he left his estate to both Jewish and Christian organizations. He left $15,000 to maintain a synagogue and cemetery in the Newport Jewish community; both synagogue and cemetery bear his name. (*FPNL*, 133f; *Gutstein*, 231, et passim; *PAJHS*, XII, 105f; *UJE*, X, 285)

TOURO, Isaac. About 1737—December 8, 1783, Kingston, Jamica. In 1760 he came to America and became a merchant. During the Revolution he was loyal to the British. When the British occupied New York City he served the members of Congregation Shearith Israel who had also remained. At one time he was minister of the Newport Jewish congregation. In 1773 he was married to Reyna Hays in Newport. After the Revolution he went to Kingston, Jamica. (*JRMP*; *MEAJA*, 154f, 193f; *PAJHS*, VI, 78, 138; X, 7, et passim; XXVII, 100, et passim; *UJE*, X, 284)

TOURO, Judah. June 16, 1775, Newport—January 18, 1854, New Orleans. This son of Isaac Touro lived as a youth in the home of his uncle, Moses Michael Hays, who trained him in business. After living briefly in New York City and Boston, he settled in New Orleans in 1802. He became a very wealthy merchant with large investments in shipping and real estate. He fought in the War of 1812 and was seriously wounded. A philanthopist who donated large amounts of money to causes both Jewish and Christian, he contributed to Mt. Sinai Hospital in New York City (then called the Jewish Hospital and later renamed Mt. Sinai Hospital); the Bunker Hill Monument; a synagogue in Newport; the Free Library and a hospital in New Orleans; and two churches for Unitarian groups and a synagogue in New Orleans. He is said to have had anti-slavery sentiments. For forty years he lived with his friend, Rezin Shepherd. On June 6, 1854, he was buried in Newport. (*PAJHS*, XIII,

93-111; XXVII, 121, et passim; UJE, X, 285f)

TOURO, Nathan. Born January 1, 1781, New York City. Son of Isaac Touro. (MSGC; PAJHS, XXVII, 156, 417)

TOURO, Rebecca. About 1779, Newport—December 19, 1833. Daughter of Isaac Touro, she was married to Joshua Lopez on March 18, 1829. (PAJHS, XXVII, 207, et passim)

TRISTE, Abraham. In 1736 he was a shohet in New York City. (PAJHS, II, 48)

TUBIA, Jacob. In Philadelphia in 1784. (MIPR)

TRUBEE, Alexander. Born October 27, 1747, Fairfield. Son of Andris Trubee. (Jacobus, 971)

TRUBEE (TRUBYEE, TRUBY, TROIB), Andris (Asher, Anshil). Died about 1758. A shopkeeper in Fairfield, Connecticut, he was converted to Christianity. His wife was Abigail Crane, a gentile, and all their children were reared as Christians. (Jacobus, 971f; MEAJA, 175f)

TRUBEE, Ansel. May 13, 1747, Fairfield, Connecticut—December 25, 1823, Fairfield. Son of Andris Trubee, he was married to Isabel Beers. (Jacobus, 971f)

TRUBEE, Comfort. November 9, 1754, Fairfield—about 1758. Daughter of Andris Trubee. (Jacobus, 971)

TRUBEE, David. Born December 22, 1750, Fairfield. Son of Andris Trubee. (Jacobus, 971)

TRUBEE, Esther. February 23, 1757, Fairfield—July 12, 1815, Greenfield, Connecticut. Daughter of Andris Trubee, she was married to John Mitchell on May 30, 1775. (Jacobus, 971)

TRUBEE, Eunice. Born July 11, 1740, Fairfield. Daughter of Andris Trubee. (Jacobus, 971)

TRUBEE, Getlo. January 27, 1746, Fairfield—October 18, 1748. Daughter of Andris Trubee. (Jacobus, 971)

TRUBEE, Samuel Cohen. September 22, 1744, Fairfield—about 1758. Son of Andris Trubee. (Jacobus, 971)

U V

URIE, William. In Richmond in 1788. It is highly doubtful that he was Jewish. (*PAJHS*, XIX, 63)

URY, Benjamin. From Canada. In Philadelphia in 1792. (*MIPR*)

VAL, Isaac de. In Savannah about 1735. (*Coulter*, 71; *PAJHS*, X, 78f)

VALENCIA, Moses. In Charleston in 1800 with one other member of his family. (*Census B, South Carolina*)

VALENTINE. In 1713 he was a butcher in New York City, where he was one of the first shammasim of Congregation Shearith Israel. (*MSP*)

VALENTINE, David.[1] In New York City in 1695. (*AJAM*, III, 10; *POFNW*, 469)

VALENTINE, David.[2] 1758, London—April 16, 1837, New York City. Husband of Elizabeth Jewel, he was in New York City with his family in 1800. (*Census B, New York*; *MSGC*)

VALENTINE, Isaac.[1] In West Chester, New York, in 1776. (*PAJHS*, XXVII, 390)

VALENTINE, Isaac.[2] Son of Isaac Valentine,[1] he was in West Chester in 1776. (*PAJHS*, XXVII, 390)

VALENTINE, Isaac.[3] 1787—December 28, 1842, Montreal. Son of David Valentine,[2] he was married to Phoebe Hays on August 30, 1830. He was a hazzan in Montreal. (*MSGC*)

VALENTINE, Mrs. Judith. Wife of Simon Valentine, she was in Charlestown about 1701. (*ELHS*)

VALENTINE, Kitty. 1788—January 16, 1849, Montreal. Daughter of David Valentine.[2] (*MSGC*)

VALENTINE, Matthias. In New York City with his family in 1800. (*Census B, New York*)

VALENTINE, Rebecca. Died February 27, 1821. Daughter of David Valentine,[2] she was married to Jacob Gershom Berlin on May 17, 1809, in New York City. (*MSGC*)

VALENTINE, Simon. His full name was Simon Valentine Vander Wilden. A merchant, he lived in New York City, Jamaica, B.W.I., and Charlestown. In 1684 he was in Albany, New York. In 1699 he held land in Charlestown and was police commissioner; he is noted again in Charlestown in the early 1700s. His wife was Judith. Cf. Simon Valentine Vander Wilden. (*AJAM*, III, 10; *ELHS*; *MEAJB*, 229f; *PAJHS*, III, 68f; VIII, 22)

VALENTINUS, H. In New York City in 1798. (*SIR*)

VALK, Jacob. In South Carolina in 1780. (*PAJHS*, XII, 53)

VALVERDE, Eleazer. A merchant who came from Barbados, he was in Philadelphia in 1706. (*WW*, 14)

VALVERDE, Elias. About 1691—August 30, 1739, New York City. He was a merchant from Barbados. Cf. Eliahu Nalverde. (*PAJHS*, XVIII, 121; *Pool*, 464, 466)

VALVERDE, Rebecca. In New York City about 1740. (*PAJHS*, XXI, 45)

VAN AMRING, Lion. A Philadelphia merchant by 1795, he was one of the early organizers of Congregation Rodeph Shalom. He was married to a gentile, Elizabeth, and their three sons were raised as Christians. (*WW*, 226, *et passim*)

VANLEER, Benjamin. About 1783 he was a physician and surgeon in Philadelphia. (*Morais*, 29)

VAN SHELEMAH, Colonoms. In Philadelphia in 1782. (*Morais*, 16)

VENEREAL. On July 11, 1733, he arrived in Savannah. (*SRB*)

VERSE, Aron. In 1695 he was a trader in Rhode Island. (*AJAM*, III, 10)

VEUSSIS (NEUSSIS), Benjamin. In Philadelphia in 1782. (*MIPR*)

[171]

VIALL, Samuel. From Rhode Island. In 1776 he served in the U.S. Navy. It is highly doubtful that he was Jewish. (*JRMP*)

VIERA, Joseph. In Philadelphia in 1786; in Savannah briefly in 1787. (*MIPR; SRB*)

VILLAROEL (VENE REAL, VILLA-REAL), Isaac. In Hampstead, Georgia, about 1733. (*Coulter*, 100; *PAJHS*, X, 73; XVII, 168)

VINERA, Daniel Rodrigues. A resident of New York City, he was naturalized about 1740. (*Hugsoc*, XXIV, 30; *PAJHS*, XXXVII, 373)

VOWEL, Jacob. In Savannah in 1733. Cf. Jacob Yowel. (*Coulter*, 100)

VRIEST, Nathan de. Cf. Nathan de Freeze.

W

WAGG, Miss. August 30, 1782, New York City—August 31, 1782, New York City. Daughter of Abraham Wagg. (*MSGC; PAJHS*, XXI, 56)

WAGG, Abraham. 1719, probably in London—April 27, 1803. A merchant sympathetic with the American cause at the beginning of the Revolution, he served in a militia. But when the British occupied New York City, he transferred his loyalty to the English. In 1779 he returned to England. He presented to the British Peace Commission a plan for peace between the colonies and England. Wagg's first wife was Rachel Gomez on July 4, 1770; his second wife was Rebecca de Lucena. (*PAJHS*, XXI, 33-75; *UJE*, X, 438)

WAGG, Hart (Naphtali). June 29, 1778, New York City—December 26, 1778, New York City. Son of Abraham Wagg. (*PAJHS*, XXI, 56)

WAGG, Judith. Born May 14, 1786. Daughter of Abraham Wagg. (*MSGC*)

WAGG, Matthias. Born November 8, 1788. Son of Abraham Wagg. (*MSGC*)

WAGG, Margoles. November 8, 1788—January 2, 1789. Son of Abraham Wagg. (*MSGC*)

WAGG, Minky. Born March 25, 1774, New York City. Daughter of Abraham Wagg. (*PAJHS*, XXI, 56)

WAGG, Mordecai. Born February 1, 1776, New York City. Son of Abraham Wagg, he returned to America from England in order to serve in the War of 1812 against England. He settled eventually in Charleston. (*PAJHS*, XXXI, 42, 55f)

WAGG, Myer.[1] February 27, 1773, New York City—June 13, 1773, New York City. Son of Abraham Wagg. (*PAJHS*, XXXI, 56)

WAGG, Myer.[2] Born November 10, 1783. Son of Abraham Wagg. (*MSGC*)

WAGG, Uriah. In New York City in 1747. (*PAJHS*, XXI, 55)

WAGG, Zipporah. Born May 18, 1771, New York City. Daughter of Abraham Wagg. (*PAJHS*, XXXI, 56)

WALLACH, Reuben Haim. In Philadelphia in 1784. He may have been married to a gentile. (*MIPR; PAJHS*, XXII, 34; *WW*, 446)

WALLACH, Moses. He received a gift from Congregation Mikveh Israel's tsedaka fund before 1800. (*WW*, 446)

WALLACK, Moses Abraham. In Boston in 1790. He was married to a gentile; at his death he left a widow and ten children. (*PAJHS*, XXIII, 86)

WARBURG, Levy. In Charleston in 1795. (*Wills*, 63)

WEBB, Caroline. Wife of Lyon Nathan, she was probably converted to Judaism. (*MSP*)

WEISS, John. A German Jew, he came to America as a political refugee. He kept a tavern in Germantown, Pennsylvania. His grandson, John Weiss, was a prominent Boston Unitarian minister and author. (*DAB*, XIX, 615)

WELCOME, Isaac. A poor stranger who came to New York City in 1786. (*Pool*, 302f)

WERMSE, Eliezar. In New York City in 1751. (*Pool*, 37)

WEXLER, Joseph. In the British colonial army in 1760. It is doubtful that he was Jewish. (*PAJHS*, XXXV, 6)

WHITLOCK, Elizabeth. About 1744, England—August 22, 1804, Richmond. Converted to Judaism before her first marriage to Moses Mordecai, she subsequently adopted the name of Esther. Her second husband was Jacob I. Cohen whom she married in Richmond in 1782. (*ELJR*, 18, 23; *MHM*, XVIII, 361; *PAJHS*, VI, 40f)

WILD, Joseph. In Lancaster in 1757. It is highly doubtful that he was Jewish. (*LCHS*, V, 93)

WILDEN, Simon Valentine Vander. Cf. Simon Valentine.

WINN, Isaac Lascalles. A merchant and ship captain, he was in New York City in 1767. It is highly doubtful that he was Jewish. (PAJHS, XXII, 40)

WOLF, Barnet. In Lancaster in 1751. Cf. Barnet Woolf. (Klein, 21)

WOLF, Benjamin.[1] About 1662—October 13, 1739, New York City. Son of Jacob Wolf of Amsterdam, he served Congregation Shearith Israel in New York City as its hazzan for about six years. (PAJHS, II, 50; VI, 126; XVIII, 98)

WOLF, Benjamin.[2] An Indian trader in Pennsylvania in 1772. (WW, 70)

WOLF, Benjamin.[3] On September 27, 1795, he was married to Betsy Hart in Philadelphia. (MIPR)

WOLF, David. In Virginia in 1784. It is doubtful that he was Jewish, (PAJHS, XX, 100)

WOLF, Isaac. In Lancaster in 1772. (AJA; Essays, 114)

WOLF, Jacob. In the British colonial army in 1760. It is doubtful that he was Jewish. (PAJHS, XXXV, 6)

WOLFE, Benjamin. About 1767—January 2, 1818, Richmond. By 1797 he was a merchant in Richmond, where he became one of the founders of Congregation Beth Shalome. In 1804 he was a major in the Richmond militia, the highest rank held by a Jew in Richmond. A prominent participant in Richmond's Jewish and general community affairs, in 1816 he was elected to the Common Hall. His wife was Sophia. (ELJR, 39, et passim)

WOLFE, Joel. Born about 1796, Richmond. Son of Benjamin Wolfe, he was a merchant. He was married to Rachel Marx, and then to Mrs. Van Schconhaven. (ELJR, 88, 133; MSGC)

WOLFE, Mrs. Sophia. Wife of Benjamin Wolfe, she lived in Richmond. (ELJR, 87f)

WOLFF, Rachel. 1768, probably in the Virgin Islands—January 22, 1843. Daughter of Moses Wolff, she was married to Isaac Cohen d'Azevedo. She lived in Newport and Charleston. (Wills, 39)

WOOLF, Barnet. In Lancaster in 1778. Cf. Woolf Barnsley and Barnet Wolf. (LCHS, V, 93)

WOOLF, Cecilia. January 2, 1789, Charleston—February 6, 1871, Charleston. Daughter of Solomon Woolf, she was probably in Charleston by 1800. In December, 1807, she was married to Haym Moïse. (JE, VIII, 650; MSGC; Wills, 58)

WOOLF, Jacob. In Virginia in 1784; in Charleston in 1800. (EJSC, 242; Ginsberg, 11; PAJHS, XX, 100)

WOOLF, Solomon. In Charleston sometime between 1783 and 1800. He was married to Rachel Andrews. (EJSC, 280; MSGC)

WOOLIN, Dr. Elias. In New York City in 1744. He was an army surgeon. (Arts & Crafts, 316; PAJHS, XXI, 45, 47f)

WORDON, Lion. Died September 18, 1798, Savannah. A nonobservant Jew. (SRB)

XYZ

XIMENES, Isaac. In 1789 he gave money to Congregation Mikveh Israel in Philadelphia. (*MSP*)

YATES, Samson. In Philadelphia in 1783. (*MIPR*)

YATES, Samuel. In Philadelphia in 1783. (*MIPR*)

YATES, Simon. In Philadelphia in 1784. (*MIPR*)

YOWEL, Jacob. Cf. Jacob Vowel.

ZANWILL, Samuel. About 1677—May 5, 1719, New York City. A merchant. Cf. Samuel. Levy.[1] (*PAJHS*, XVIII, 96)

ZARINE, Gabriel Cohen. In Philadelphia in 1795. A poor Jew who came from Hamburg, Germany, he probably returned immediately. (*MIPR*)

ZARZEDAS, Anthony. Fought in the Revolutionary army. Cf. David Sarzedas. (*JRMP*)

ZELTMAN. In Savannah in 1778. He may have been a Hessian Jew. (*PAJHS*, IV, 98)

ZUNTZ, Abraham. Died November 22, 1814, New York City. Son of Alexander Zuntz, he was in New York City about 1793. (*PAJHS*, XVIII, 112; XX, 164, XXVII, 55)

ZUNTZ, Alexander. May 15, 1742, Westphalia—October 15, 1819, New York City. In 1779 he came to America as a Hessian. He manufactured starch and hair powder, and later opened a broker's office. For three terms he was president of Congregation Shearith Israel in New York City. On May 4, 1779, he was married to Rachel Abrahams in New York City. (*Pool*, 398f)

ZUNTZ, Ellen. June 3, 1781, New York City—November 29, 1866, New York City. Daughter of Alexander Zuntz. (*MSGC*; *Pool*, 399, 436)

ZUNTZ, Judah. About 1783, New York City—March 4, 1829, New York City. Son of Alexander Zuntz, he was an attorney who was very active in the Jewish community. (*Pool*, 435f)

ZUNTZ, Moses. Died July 22, 1810, New York City. Son of Alexander Zuntz, he was in New York City about 1793. (*PAJHS*, XXVII, 55; *Pool*, 399)

ZUNTZ, Uriah. Son of Alexander Zuntz, he was a cripple in New York City about 1793. (*PAJHS*, XXVII, 55; *Pool*, 399)

ZUPBEILER (probable spelling), Meyer. In Lancaster in 1761. (*Essays*, 111)

JOSEPH R. ROSENBLOOM, lecturer in Hebrew at the University of Kentucky and rabbi of Temple Adath Israel in Lexington, is a native of Rochester, New York. A graduate of the University of Cincinnati, he continued his education at Hebrew Union College in Cincinnati, earning the degree of Doctor of Hebrew Letters in 1957.

A *Biographical Dictionary of Early American Jews* was composed and printed at the University of Kentucky. It is set in Linotype Electra, with the large display type in Klingspor Kumlein. The book is printed on Warren's Olde Style antique wove paper and bound by the C. J. Krehbiel Company in Columbia's Riverside linen cloth.

www.ingramcontent.com/pod-product-compliance
Lightning Source LLC
Chambersburg PA
CBHW020738230426
43665CB00009B/483